CONTEMPORARY CHINA INSTITUTE PUBLICATIONS

MAO TSE-TUNG IN THE SCALES OF HISTORY

Publications in the series are:

Party Leadership and Revolutionary Power in China (1970) *edited by John Wilson Lewis*

Employment and Economic Growth in Urban China, 1949–1957 (1971) *by Christopher Howe*

Authority, Participation and Cultural Change in China (1973) *edited by Stuart R. Schram*

A Bibliography of Chinese Newspapers and Periodicals in European Libraries (1975) *by the Contemporary China Institute*

Democracy and Organisation in the Chinese Industrial Enterprise, 1948–1953 (1976) *by William Brugger*

MAO TSE-TUNG IN THE SCALES OF HISTORY

A PRELIMINARY ASSESSMENT ORGANIZED BY
THE CHINA QUARTERLY
AND
EDITED BY
DICK WILSON

CAMBRIDGE UNIVERSITY PRESS
CAMBRIDGE
LONDON NEW YORK MELBOURNE

Published by the Syndics of the Cambridge University Press
The Pitt Building, Trumpington Street, Cambridge CB2 1RP
Bentley House, 200 Euston Road, London NW1 2DB
32 East 57th Street, New York, NY 10022, USA
296 Beaconsfield Parade, Middle Park, Melbourne 3206, Australia

© Cambridge University Press 1977
First published 1977
Printed in the United States of America
Printed and bound by R. R. Donnelley and Sons Company,
Crawfordsville, Indiana

Library of Congress Cataloguing in Publication Data
Main entry under title:
Mao Tse-tung in the scales of history.
(Contemporary China Institute publications)
Bibliography: p. 331
Includes index.
I. Mao Tse-tung, 1893–1976. I. Wilson, Dick.
II. The China Quarterly. III. Series: London. University.
Contemporary China Institute. Publications.
DS778.M3M2865   951.05'092'4 [B]   76-57100
ISBN 0 521 21583 8 hard covers
ISBN 0 521 29190 9 paperback

CONTENTS

PREFACE

Mao Tse-tung, the communist leader of China who died in September 1976, at the age of 82, was a world figure of more than ordinary proportions. Not only did he preside, during his quarter-century of leadership of the People's Republic, over the international redemption and internal modernization of the 900 million Chinese people, but he also assumed for much of that time the role of the conscience of international Marxism–Leninism as one of its leading practitioners and innovators – the first person to do so from outside the Western tradition.

Men and women, including the contributors to this book, may dispute the degree of greatness to be attributed to this Chinese leader, the extent of his success and the durability of his achievements. Yet none, I believe, would deny that Mao has already influenced more human lives more profoundly than anyone else in our century, and is likely to remain persuasive beyond the grave. This is to speak of Mao from the world point of view, in which he has to contend with figures like Lenin: within the purely Chinese frame there has been no man of such stature for at least two centuries. If there had been, China would not have fallen so low in world esteem and the challenge posed to Mao in our own day would have been lighter. Mao was a titan of our era, and there is no single personality or mind whose secrets and subtleties are everywhere more ardently probed, not least by the young.

Mao Tse-tung was born into a peasant family in the central part of China on 26 December 1893: he thus grew up in the closing decadence of the last of China's imperial dynasties as well as in the heyday of the Victorian imperialism of the West. In his first half-century he lived through two world wars and numerous revolutions and civil wars in his own country without

vii

having the responsibility of national government: instead he devoted himself to the organization of revolutionary social change at grass-roots level. One of the founders of the Chinese Communist Party in 1921, he nevertheless stood outside the mainstream of its leadership for 15 years, disliking its dogmatic importation of ideas and methods from Moscow and its neglect of the Chinese peasantry. Then in 1935 he was thrust into the front seat at a moment when the Party seemed doomed to destruction. A combination of luck and good sense, however, saved the day and Mao never again lost his authenticity as the voice of Chinese Communism. Another stroke of fortune came with the Japanese invasion of 1937, which publicized the failings of the Chinese anti-Communists while allowing Mao to parade in the robes of patriotism.

But only in 1949, when Mao was already 55, could he proclaim the People's Republic of China and turn from revolution to rule. In the event he had 27 years of governing the Chinese state, running the gamut from the uneasy alliance with Stalin to the Nixon visit spectacular, from the agricultural co-operatives to the Communes to the Great Proletarian Cultural Revolution, and falling out with successive colleagues from Liu Shao-ch'i to Lin Piao and even his own wife Chiang Ch'ing. It is a story to which there is no equal in modern times. Few men of action have done so much, over such a long period, so thoroughly and with such originality.

For this very reason it is doubtful if any one person alive today can write Mao's just epitaph. He was too big a man, acting on too many levels over too great a period of time, with too large a vision and too controversial ideas for any one mind satisfactorily to evaluate, at least so soon. The difficulties are enhanced by the quantity of new material by and about Mao, often highly informal and revealing, which was released by the Red Guards during the Cultural Revolution and has gradually become available to the outside world during the past few years. This has had to be considered first for its authenticity and second, if that were accepted, for its impact on earlier judgments on Mao.

Yet an assessment, albeit provisional, is called for. The China Quarterly has frequently opened its columns to debate and argument about Mao and his ideas and policies. When the chairman died, we therefore invited many of the scholars who had participated in those debates to collaborate in a tentative "verdict" which is this book.

The 11 men and women whose essays follow are each distinguished in their own spheres. They represent a wide variety of generation and viewpoint, and are drawn from centres of modern Chinese studies all over the world – in the Far East and Europe as well as the U.S. Each was asked to reflect upon one particular aspect of Mao's achievements.

The 10 themes which they treat cover, with some unavoidable (and fruitful) measure of overlapping, the major areas of Mao's public life. In the first, Professor Benjamin Schwartz of Harvard considers his lifelong interest in philosophy. In the second, Mao's biographer, Stuart Schram, examines his contributions to Marxism–Leninism, qualifying some of the earlier judgments he had offered. Michel Oksenberg of the University of Michigan then provides a highly original analysis of Mao's methods and style of political leadership, in and out of office. In the fourth essay Professor Jacques Guillermaz of Paris describes Mao's military theories and practice, which have become so admired in the Third World. Dr Enrica Collotti Pischel of the University of Milan then sets out Mao's views on education, showing how the basic dilemmas of "Maoism" come back to the teacher–pupil relationship.

The sixth essay, by Christopher Howe and Kenneth R. Walker of the School of Oriental and African Studies in London, is a pioneering study of Mao's economic policies and his interventions in the ups and downs of the Chinese national economy. Frederic Wakeman of Berkeley next places Mao in his context as heir to a century of Chinese nationalism, including its provincial variants in Hunan, after which John Gittings, the Guardian's China commentator, shows how Mao actually behaved as an actor on the world stage in international relations. Wang Gungwu of Canberra then discusses those aspects of Mao's career which may be seen as intrinsically Chinese, while Edward Friedman concludes the book with a consideration of Mao's claims to global universality as an innovator of our century.

This collection is among the best that modern scholarship can offer on the significance of the life of this great Chinese leader. In the pages that follow readers will find aspects of Mao that are positive, others that appear negative or indecisive; claims to eternal fame and suggestions of far shorter durability. What they will also find are views, judgments and arguments all based on sound knowledge and first-hand research into Chinese-language materials. Each one of the contributors has devoted his or her entire life to modern Chinese studies, and each view, however it may differ from the others, deserves a thorough consideration. The authors' common bond lies in the fact that each has already written deeply and penetratingly (though not always before in English) about Mao and Maoism, whether in the pages of *The China Quarterly* or elsewhere.

We believe that this collection, appearing relatively promptly after the chairman's demise, will help all students of international affairs to come to terms in their own minds with Mao Tse-tung's importance, both to China and its future and to the world and its future, and to understand the differing conclusions to which the same evidence can lead honest observers in evaluating this remarkable man.

Many debts must be acknowledged in the task of producing such a book so quickly after the event. Most of them lie with the Executive Committee of the Editorial Board of *The China Quarterly*, especially Michel Oksenberg (the first to suggest and discuss the project), Christopher Howe (who made all the business arrangements) and Stuart Schram (who was unstinting in helping to plan and implement the editorial side of the book). I also thank Roderick MacFarquhar for his sustained encouragement, Gail Eadie for her patient and thorough copy-editing, Alistair Campbell and Dennis Johnson for their help in translating, Ed Friedman for providing the book's title, and Cambridge University Press for helping us keep a very tight timetable.

London, January 1977   Dick Wilson

ABBREVIATIONS

1. PUBLICATIONS

CB

Current Background. Collections of articles or documents grouped according to subject, issued several times a month. (Translation: U.S. Consulate-General, Hong Kong).

CQ

The China Quarterly, London.

JPRS, Miscellany

Miscellany of Mao Tse-tung Thought (1949–1968). Parts I and II. (Arlington Virginia: Joint Publications Research Service (JPRS), 1974, Nos. 61269–1 and 61269–2.

MTC

Takeuchi Minoru (ed.), Mao Tse-tung chi (Collected Writings of Mao Tse-tung), Vols I to X (Tokyo: Hokubosha, 1970–72).

Schram, Ma

Stuart R. Schram, Mao Tse-tung (Harmondsworth: Penguin Books, 1967).

Schram, Thought

Stuart R. Schram, The Political Thought of Mao Tse-tung (Harmondsworth: Penguin Books. Revised and enlarged edition. 1969).

Schram, Unrehearsed

Stuart R. Schram (ed.), Mao Tse-tung Unrehearsed (Harmondsworth: Penguin Books, 1974); also published in U.S. under the title: Chairman Mao Talks to the People (New York: Pantheon).

SCMP

Survey of China Mainland Press (Hong Kong: U.S. Consulate General).

SR

Selected Readings from the Works of Mao Tse-tung (Peking: Foreign Languages Press, 1967).

ABBREVIATIONS

SW   Mao Tse-tung, *Selected Works,* Vols I to IV (Peking: Foreign Languages Press, 1961–65).

SWL   *Selected Works of Mao Tse-tung,* Vols I to IV (London: Lawrence and Wishart, 1954).

Wan-sui   *Mao Tse-tung ssu-hsiang wan-sui (Long Live Mao Tse-tung's Thought),* (1967) or (1969). No publisher (Chinese Red Guard publications). Taiwan reprints.

Wan-sui (April 1967)   *Mao Tse-tung ssu-hsiang wan-sui (Long Live Mao Tse-tung's Thought),* (April 1967). No publisher (Xerox copies of Chinese Red Guard publications).

2. ORGANIZATIONS

CCP   Chinese Communist Party

KMT   Kuomintang

PLA   People's Liberation Army

INTRODUCTION

Dick Wilson

Any leader who ruled a quarter of mankind for a quarter of a century would be assured of a place in history. Mao Tse-tung's place rests on far more than that, however, and to take only his most obvious source of fame he is renowned throughout the world as the writer of the famous *Quotations*, which in the form of millions of little red books seemed in the 1960s set to rival the circulation figures of the New Testament. "To rebel is justified," "Political power grows out of the barrel of a gun," "The atom bomb is a paper tiger," "Doing is itself learning," "No investigation, no right to speak," "Imbalance is normal, balance is temporary" – these phrases have joined the world vocabulary and made Mao almost the sloganeer for an entire generation.

Yet the coiner of these 20th century aphorisms is not the founder of a new world religion nor the man with all the answers to our modern ills. His universalism must be seen against his Chinese context, remembering the extraordinary fact that during his entire lifetime he visited only one foreign country (Russia). Mao's Chineseness is illuminatingly discussed by Wang Gungwu below, but for the present context it is enough to show how his narrow patriotism has offended internationalists. Mao was quite open about the issue. "The Chinese Communists," he told Agnes Smedley in 1937, "are internationalists ... But at the same time they are patriots who defend their native land." And in the 1960s and 1970s that meant befriending every enemy of the Soviet Union, from Richard Nixon to Franz-Josef Strauss, from Augusto Pinochet to Holden Roberto – at the expense, some would say, of other people's revolutions.

The Nixon visit to Peking in 1972 was, as John Gittings adjudges below, "a magnificent victory for the Chinese nation," but it was also "hard to describe it as a socialist foreign policy."

1

Gittings concedes, of course, the basic foreign policy dilemma of a country like China: how far should it encourage revolutionaries and class struggle abroad, how far should it rather protect itself by all possible means against the one country that threatens it? Mao was not, after all, a computer: he was a human being with human emotions and failings, and one of these was probably the sense of personal embitterment he nursed against the Soviet Union for its betrayal of his cause. When he came back from his first meeting with Stalin, in Moscow in 1949–50, seeking help in China's reconstruction, he described the experience as like "getting a piece of meat from the mouth of a tiger."

Another aspect of Mao's fallibility was the fact that his power was limited and discontinuous, even within China. His constituents were one hundred times more numerous than Castro's, more than forty times more than Tito's. He was never a mere dictator, as Michel Oksenberg shows, and had to fight hard and long to have his policies accepted by his lieutenants in the Chinese Communist Party. Oksenberg describes him as a monarch among barons, like King Arthur, or Sung Chiang in *Water Margin* (who in turn is often likened to Robin Hood), who had to go to extraordinary lengths and prepare intricate schemes to prevent others from side-stepping, ignoring or thwarting him. In 1959 he threatened to tear up his Party card and go it alone if his policy on the People's Communes were not followed, and similar threats came close to fulfilment during the Cultural Revolution. Only in what Oksenberg calls Mao's "halcyon years" between 1955 and 1959 was he fully effective: for the rest of his career in government he was often cold-shouldered, surviving only because of his high personal prestige and his adroitness in occasional intervention in the affairs of the administrative and Party machine. This meant, for example, manoeuvring key military units loyal to Lin Piao out of Peking during the 1960s, and other classically praetorian devices.

Yet for a man so determined to cling to power Mao often exhibited a refreshing personal humility. Enrica Collotti Pischel quotes a passage where he says that "The masses are truly heroic, and we ourselves often are immature and ridiculous." In 1959, amid the chaos of the Great Leap Forward, he blandly

2

confessed: "I am a complete outsider when it comes to economic construction and understand nothing about industrial planning," and again: "In economic construction we were as children, lacking experience; unfamiliar with tactics or strategy we made war on the earth." Small wonder that one of his critics saw him as "a blind man riding a blind horse."

Mao was also sometimes inconsistent and erratic in his arguments. In the 1950s he outlined his theory of economic advance by waves or wave-like movements rather than by logical stages, but, as Howe and Walker show, we heard no more of this in the 1960s and 1970s. Similarly in the 1950s Mao spoke of endless cycles of oscillation between disequilibrium and equilibrium, each one of which irreversibly raised the level of development. Yet Stuart Schram finds that in the last two decades of his life Mao appeared to abandon the Marxist notion of history's inexorable forward march in favour of a certain indeterminacy. Benjamin Schwartz in the first essay asks whether the epic march of the Chinese Revolution leads to a fixed destination of peace and harmony, "or is the destination ever-receding?" Mao would presumably have answered that there is always a next goal, but not perhaps with the same conviction and verve in 1975 as in 1955.

In the end, even the Chinese peasants disappointed him. After observing their selfish behaviour in the new Communes during the extraordinary Leap Forward winter of 1958–59, he spoke scathingly of the contrast with their good revolutionary behaviour of the previous summer: "These, then, are the two sides of the peasantry: peasants are still peasants" (see Howe and Walker's essay below). And during the Cultural Revolution it was clear that he felt let down by the masses. But he never allowed scepticism about human capabilities to become institutionalized in his mind.

So Mao was human, and being human he erred. What then does he have to say to us? Can we not say that he was the first Chinese to speak to the rest of the world in plain, blunt language about issues that concern all of us, to speak without chauvinism or national self-consciousness and to speak common-sense — taking for granted the universal desire for justice and for the rehumanization of our industrialized, individualized, im-

3

perialized network of lives? Indeed, Mao was surely the first non-white, non-Western person to speak thus in modern times. He thereby simultaneously subverted the myths of China's spiritual isolation, of the West's monopoly on moral and intellectual leadership, and of the supremacy of the industrial nation-state as the ultimate frame for our activities.

What is the specific content of Mao's message? The item to head the inventory must surely be the unlocking of Marxism–Leninism from its prison of old dogmas. To the extent that Mao wins back would-be revolutionaries to the central project of social change, reminding us that Marxism means a personal commitment to such change rather than a sterile debate about the contradictions of 19th century capitalism, he gains the support of Ed Friedman in his conclusion to this book. Gittings credits him with the reassurance that socialism is not constructed merely by building steelmills and nationalizing property. Pischel even suggests that Mao has smuggled a bit of Kant back into the revolutionary portmanteau, while Schram argues that Mao has introduced a moral element into Marxism which derives from the Chinese instinct that you cannot really separate "the inner mental world of the individual from his outward behaviour." A good man can become a revolutionary even if he had the wrong parents, by a process, if you like, of what Wakeman calls "social trans-valuation." (One is reminded of the preference of the Chinese authorities under Mao to re-educate opponents rather than execute them.)

This leads to Mao's second major contribution, which is about the de-bureaucratization of the Party. The Russians had shown that capitalist injustices could be remedied by the intervention of a vast new bureaucracy, but that this in turn created its own injustices. Mao was the only major leader seriously to tackle this problem. Schram shows how Mao's mass line is supposed to work, by leaders taking the masses' inchoate ideas, systematizing them through study, explaining them back again to the masses in their new form so that the masses embrace them as their own, and then implementing them. It is an excellent consultative-participatory method of leadership of the kind which has excited Western intellectuals, for example in the dramatization of *Fanshen* by David Hare, the British playwright.

4

But by its very nature it is hard to institutionalize, and in the end all depends on the sensitivity of the individual leaders concerned.

The great show-down for de-bureaucratization was, of course, the Cultural Revolution of the late 1960s, which Mao opened by drawing his own Big-Character Poster where the masses were urged to "Bombard the [Party] Headquarters," but which he ended by calling in the soldiers of the People's Liberation Army to control the ensuing chaos. It is important here, as Schram insists, to see that even during this experiment, the most exciting of our generation, Mao did not downgrade authority or question its legitimacy. Instead he stoutly disputed the premises of Chang Ch'un-ch'iao's Shanghai Commune in 1967, thus remaining a Leninist at heart, for all the populist drive of the Cultural Revolution. Pischel is strikingly illuminating on what she calls "the most momentous political question in Maoism" – how can the CCP both lead the masses with confidence and at the same time learn from them with humility? One man such as Mao can accommodate both activities in his own persona, but for a party of 30 million members it is more damagingly schizophrenic. So Mao's contribution is not a ready-made overall solution but rather an unblinkered look at the problem and several specific preventative policies – including the regulations about cadres taking turn at manual work in the Tachai model agricultural brigade.

The third major strand of Mao's significance is the assurance that the glittering prizes of socialism are not won only by the white or Western world, but can be enjoyed by others even *before* capitalism. He spurned Marx's notion of "redemption through technology," and in 1955 forced upon his then protesting colleagues the collectivization of Chinese agriculture in advance of electricity or tractors. As a result thousands of pilgrims from Africa, Asia and Latin America now go every year to visit the modified multi-purpose People's Commune, which is arguably the most generally successful model of agricultural development in the Third World. This does not mean, of course, that it is imitated, even in Tanzania, or that its admirers are unmindful of elements in Chinese sociology, psychology, terrain and climate which render it less than automatically copi-

5

able. When President Julius Nyerere made his joke about wanting to send every Tanzanian on a study course in China it was not to learn the secrets of organization but the secret of hard work, for which Mao would be the last to claim the credit.

Mao would have been disappointed by Nyerere's joke, since to grow more grain, while important, is not the ultimate aim of human existence. The Commune is intended as a way of life as well as a way of work, an aspect of Mao's legacy savoured more by the younger generation in the industrialized West than in the Third World. Friedman, though, argues that there may be forces of divisiveness at work in human society which in the future may get out of control, and that history may credit Mao with having prepared his own country most successfully against this threat – so that Maoism may acquire a more compelling attraction in the years to come.

These, then, are the great things for which the world will remember Mao Tse-tung, bearing in mind that much of what he did was predicated on the particular conditions of China. Guillermaz, for instance, doubts if his military doctrine and his famous injunctions about guerrilla war are relevant any longer for most parts of the world. But by the same token Mao has redressed a balance in international prescriptions which had previously been monopolized by the West. Where Marx and his European followers took for granted the superiority of the urban-industrialized society of the West, Mao has decisively lowered its place in history and opened up new alternatives. And yet he had no preconceived notions about the West and was shrewd enough to admire it for its intrinsically admirable qualities – not its military power, which he saw as transient, but its talent, most developed in the U.S., for organization and innovation. There is much discussion below about how Mao hoped to go to the U.S. several years before his first reluctant call on Stalin in Moscow.

Mao was a great all-rounder. His first published essay was on the unlikely topic of physical education, and he made almost a fetish of keeping fit. He was tough and immensely practical. When Lin Piao attacked his dictatorial methods, Mao calmly circulated the criticism to the Central Committee to exhibit Lin's ignorant innocence of the true demands of leadership. But he was also an intellectual. Schwartz opines that we would not be paying any more attention to Mao's thought had he not had the political power to implement it: if he had remained a Hunanese schoolmaster no essays would be written about his philosophy. The truth is, I suppose, that thought and action are so interwoven in Mao's life that one cannot be considered apart from the other. Schram concludes that Marx would have rebuffed him as a disciple, but then goes on to list the three riders which Mao added to Leninism, namely that socialism, unlike the industrial revolution, is about changing human nature; that leaders must listen to the led if they are to lead effectively; and that peasants can participate as well as factory workers in building the new society. These are substantial intellectual contributions, however much grounded in the particularities of the Chinese experience.

But China in the end preferred to head for the millennium in lower gear than the chairman recommended. Wang Gungwu believes that after so many decades of strife and disorder (luan), China in 1949 was yearning for a new era of order (chih), and that once Mao had achieved this his subjects were no longer responsive to his restless idealism. Having supplied China with a new orthodoxy, with a new sense of international self-respect and with the minimum degree of social change necessary, Mao was in the end rebuffed. His power, in Oksenberg's phrase, became "curtailed through the emergence of a stable society." The Cultural Revolution was an attempt to revive the heady dreams of egalitarian youth, and in that aim it failed. Hence the conclusion of Schwartz that Mao's enduring legacy is the People's Republic itself. China has in the past three decades been transformed from a demoralized and stagnant society into a nation with self-respect.

The test will be whether that system now continues to develop along Maoist lines or not. The social energy lying beneath the surface is immense, and the world waits with fascination to see whether that potential will be used to further socialist modes of life or whether it will gradually assume more individualistic and entrepreneurial realizations. One of the compulsions of Mao as a phenomenon of our time is that he crosses the great divide between Marxists and non-Marxists, just as he casually broke through the line between whites and non-whites, the West and the Third World. What Mao has done for China goes beyond the mere application of Marxism, it stands for a four-square reappraisal of what life is all about, and what matters in it. Nixon and Kissinger and Galbraith are just as interested in the result as Brezhnev and Berlinguer. In the end, despite his impressive-looking *Selected Works*, Mao's strength was as a methodologist of social change – and we are all in the business of social change, Marxist or not. His genius was in sensing so often the right mix of policies for the time, and how far the population could be pushed into desired changes without provoking a reactionary backlash. Where he went wrong, as in 1959 over the Great Leap Forward or in 1967 over the Cultural Revolution, was because of technical miscalculations and insufficiently informed (or insufficiently loyal or insufficiently sophisticated) lieutenants. Where he proved brilliantly correct, as in the 1955 collectivization, he stood almost alone among his colleagues.

What he endearingly strove all his life to do was to set down in simple principles how others could acquire this sense of judgment: he wanted to be remembered, above all, as a teacher. A good teacher, of course, is also a good learner, and the final expression of Mao's political dilemma could be, in domestic terms, how at one and the same time to both lead and learn, and in international terms, how to both love and live at one and the same time – how to love and encourage the world's oppressed while at the same time safeguarding the Chinese homeland in a fundamentally hostile world. Yet in spite of being unable to resolve these contradictions, Mao remains one of those rare men who could see both far and near, in both time and space, more alertly perceptive of the full dimension of the human predicament than any contemporary. On the one hand, as Oksenberg notes, he was ready to lecture his colleagues about the eventual cooling of the sun and its impact on our planet. On the other, he wrote in one of his most brilliant and moving poems:

> Millennia are too long,
> Let us dispute about mornings and evenings.

1

THE PHILOSOPHER

Benjamin I. Schwartz

With the death of Mao Tse-tung, we may soon witness a gradual – or even precipitous – retreat from the tendency to seek in Mao himself the key to all of recent Chinese history. As the world becomes aware of a variety of actors in China, as it becomes more and more obvious that Chinese society has a life of its own apart from the "thoughts of Chairman Mao," we may even witness a swing to the opposite pole – a trend to dismiss his impact on his times and to attribute everything to "objective forces" and "processes of development." Yet if we leave aside for a moment the question of the durability of his legacy, the fact remains that there is much in the recent history of China that is simply unthinkable without him. I, for instance, would be willing to defend the proposition: no Mao, no Cultural Revolution. This does not mean that he anticipated the Cultural Revolution or created all the circumstances which led up to it or that he foresaw its outcome. It simply means that his actions and modes of thinking were an indispensable component in this whole mesh of events. The same holds true for the entire history of the People's Republic until this point.

I have been asked to make some reflections on Mao the philosopher. I shall interpret the word "philosophy" in the broadest possible sense to refer to some of the central and dominant themes and ideas which may have shaped his mental world over the course of his stormy career. Whether the most important themes are all "philosophical" in the most precise academic sense of that term may well be doubted. To be sure, one can find philosophy even in the more precise sense in Mao's writings and conversations. "On Contradiction" and "On Practice" are certainly philosophic treatises. Furthermore, Mao's philosophic writings and reflections are significant. They throw

9

light on some of his basic tendencies. Whether they are the "heart of the matter" is, however, another question. Nothing in them negates the plausibility of Gramsci's observation[1] that "a man of politics writes about philosophy. It could be that his true philosophy should be looked for rather in his writings on politics." I take this to mean that there may indeed be philosophic implications of a sort in the writings on politics. We all know that in addition to being a philosopher Mao was also a poet of some accomplishment and I shall suggest below that if there is indeed a heart of the matter it may be more readily found in some of the images of his poetry than in his reflections on dialectics and epistemology.

Even if we interpret the word philosophy in this extremely loose sense, how significant is Mao's thought? Does not his real significance lie in the fact that he was one of the most successful and brilliant political leaders of our time? Would any of us be concerned with his thought if he had remained an obscure Chinese intellectual? Obviously we would not. Nor does his thought in itself fully explain his success – a success which cannot be understood without referring to various traits of his remarkable personality, to his combination of shrewdness, patience, boldness and ruthlessness, and to the remarkable political intuition which he often displayed. I would also maintain that it is extremely unwise to treat the "thought of Mao Tse-tung" as an abstract whole divorced from his political biography. After he embarks on his political career his world of ideas becomes an emergent world which can be safely understood only within the context of concrete historical situations. The ideas may or may not transcend the situation. The depth of his commitment to various ideas cannot be deduced from a group of abstract axioms. Thus one might have thought that his stress on the universal and eternal nature of "contradictions" in his pamphlet of 1937 would immediately have led to his concept of a "permanent revolution" and to a rejection of any notion of a static utopia. In fact, the idea of the "permanent revolution" only emerges within the particular atmosphere of the Great Leap Forward of 1958. The idea of "non-antagonistic contradictions"

[1] See *Prison Notebooks* (New York: International Publishers, 1973), p. 403.

plays a meaningful role in the "Hundred Flowers" Campaign. What has been its significance since then?

In brief, it is quite true that the significance of Mao's thought cannot be considered in isolation from his role as a political leader. At the same time, his role as a revolutionary leader has made his thought significant. It has in many ways touched the lives of hundreds of millions of people. Whether the effect has always been the effect anticipated, whether it has been deep and whether it will all be durable will be decided by the course of history. As of the present, it is there. It might be added that the questions to which Mao has addressed himself are themselves of abiding intrinsic interest.

The attack on the excessive preoccupation with the content of Mao's ideas comes from yet another quarter. Professor Lucian Pye in his *Mao Tse-tung: The Man in the Leader*[2] suggests a psycho-historic approach to Mao. Those who are preoccupied with the sources and content of Mao's ideas, he contends, have failed to explain why he thinks that way. They concern themselves with effects rather than causes. They dwell on the end-products of his psychic processes rather than on the roots. Pye has many very vivid and interesting observations to make concerning certain abiding traits of Mao's personality and we would all concede that his personality is of utmost importance. The description of Mao's personality is not, however, Pye's goal. The personality, like the thought, is after all, an end product. What Pye aspires to do is *explain* Mao's personality as well as his thought. While acknowledging the presence of non-psychological factors, in the end he finds that there is little that he cannot explain in terms of his own causal account, which like so many explanations of Freudian origin leads us back to the primary family relations of early childhood. Refreshingly, he abandons the by now exhausted explanations in terms of father hatred and in fact offers some effective refutations of that notion. Many, however, will be equally dissatisfied with his own explanation in terms of Mao's ambivalent attitude towards his mother, who had at first enveloped him with her nurturing love and had then partially withdrawn this love, dividing her affection with his siblings.

[2] New York: Basic Books, 1976.

11

However, the question goes deeper than the adequacy of this particular psychological account. The question of the relationship of the world of thought to the world of psychic mechanisms is a question of enormous philosophic complexity. In our own lives, we tacitly tend to assume that our thought is a response to "something out there" as well as an expression of something "in here." We go on believing that there are reasons for our thought as well as causes of it. The European phenomenological philosophers have wrestled bravely with the question of whether the contents of our thought can or cannot be dealt with in terms of psychological reductionism, and have emerged with a negative. Psychological factors influence and limit our thought, but to what extent and how is a question which remains unresolved. Nor can we assume that we have any adequate psychology available to us. Can one possibly believe that the extraordinary and unprecedented life experience of Mao after early childhood did not fundamentally affect both thought and personality? Quite apart from the question of presumed causes, whether psychological or sociological, the ideas are worth examination in their own right because in the end it is the ideas (as well as the socio-political strategies) of Mao which work their influence in the world "out there" whatever their genesis. Furthermore in examining Mao's ideas and their sources, we soon discover that Mao is not operating in a vacuum but participating in an intellectual and cultural milieu shared by others. Anyone who studies the intellectual world of Mao's generation, as well as the generation which preceded his, soon realizes the extent to which he draws on a common world of ideas.

One can nevertheless share Professor Pye's conviction that a concern with Mao's childhood and, one should add, his youth is essential to an understanding of his subsequent development. This concern however, need by no means be focused entirely on the question of his immediate family relations. Those concerned with the development of his ideas will be immediately struck by the fact that Mao's earliest years were spent almost entirely in "traditional" China. In the early 1890s the village of Shaoshan had certainly not been affected in any directly perceptible way by the "impact of the West." Yet "traditional China" is not entirely synonymous with "peasant China." Mao's father was an upwardly mobile prosperous peasant-businessman prepared to give his son a respectable elementary education. He may have wanted his son to follow him in business but there is really little evidence that he stubbornly resisted the son's efforts to pursue his education further. Mao himself informs us that at a very early age he began to think of himself as a student. This means that at a very early point in his life he was in touch not only with the popular culture of the villagers but with the traditional high culture as well. In fact it may have been the latter which exercised the more profound influence. The adoption of the self-image of a scholar in pre-modern China was an act fraught with deep significance. In undertaking it, one took on the perspective of those with a responsibility for leading society. Mao's youthful fondness for "popular" novels does not diminish the truth of this observation. For one thing many other students including those of gentry background shared this taste. His favourite novel, *The Romance of the Three Kingdoms*, concerns itself not with popular uprisings but with heroic deeds and cunning strategies of the great generals and statesmen of the Three Kingdoms who are definitely establishment figures. The warriors on the Liang Shan Moor in *Shui-hu chuan* (*Water Margin*) were to be sure a "counter-elite" who fought against injustice (and for plain revenge) but they were also leaders rather than led. His extreme fondness for these works may suggest that he may have already been much more attracted to the traditional image of the virile hero leader than to the Confucian image of the sage-statesman, but both images are leader images.

To be sure, he was a villager and in immediate touch with the rhythms of peasant life. We can believe him when he tells us of his indignation at the injustices and iniquities which he observed in his rural environment. There was in fact nothing either in the classics or the romances which would necessarily have run counter to this sense of indignation. He was also quite able in later years to employ the earthy peasant idiom whenever it suited his purposes just as he was able to use quite obscure allusions from classical literature. No doubt, his early contacts with the turbulent political restlessness of the peasantry of his native Hunan made it difficult for him in later years to inter-

13

BENJAMIN I. SCHWARTZ

nalize Marxist generalizations concerning peasant passivity and rural idiocy. Yet despite all these threads which bound him to his village environment he was already thinking the thoughts and dreaming the dreams of a "student." The young Mao aged 13, having read Cheng Kuan-ying's tract on China's perilous plight, was already able quite easily to identify himself in his own mind with those who were concerning themselves with the plight of the empire.

To be sure, when Mao enrolled in the Tungshan Primary School in Hsiang-hsiang at the age of 16 we are told that his well-heeled fellow students regarded him as a country bumpkin. His burning sense of injured self-esteem may have arisen precisely from his own feeling that he was anything but a country bump-kin. He had in fact read many books and pondered many thoughts. It is probably quite true that experiences such as this and later experiences may have laid the foundation for his later hostility to establishment intellectuals and enhanced his sense of soli-darity with the "people," but in his relationship towards the people he already regarded them from the perspective of a poten-tial leader of the people rather than as a member of their ranks.

Traditional Chinese thought has much to say about the people and the obligations of rulers towards the people. The treatment of "the people" as a kind of abstract uniform category is very ancient. In Confucian thought the dominant attitude towards the people is overwhelmingly benevolent. The people are often regarded as good, albeit ignorant. Chinese Confucian literature down through the centuries is full of eloquent denunciations of injustice towards the people. Equality within the ranks of the people is often set forth as an ideal and there is an unfailing recognition of the need for satisfying the elemental economic needs of the masses. Popular rebellions are most often treated as a symptom and result of the corruption, greed and malfeasance of rulers. All of this the young Mao could have found not only in his novels but in classical Confucian literature even before his contact with populist ideas brought in from abroad. Thus if it is indeed true that the adolescent Mao was already sensitive to the mistreatment of the "people" which he observed in his en-vironment, this was by no means incompatible with what he read in his books or with his "scholar's" perspective.

14

It should also be remarked that Mao's early life in "traditional" China left an indelible imprint on his entire personal culture. His aesthetic and literary sensibility (not populist) remained wholly Chinese. His personal "style of life" remained Chinese. He continued to the end to find categories of thought derived from the tradition quite as compelling as Western categories even though he subsumed them under the higher truths of Marxism–Leninism. One has the feeling that the Western urban style of life as he might later have observed it in Shanghai's foreign concessions held no charms for him. One might contrast this with Lenin who in spite of his hatred of the Western bourgeoisie continued to regard modern Western European urban life as the norm and epitome of all that which is *kul'turnyi*.

Yet if Mao was born in traditional China, his readings and school experiences very soon brought him into contact with a new world of ideas. At a very early point he came into contact with the writings of that remarkable group of transitional figures – Liang Ch'i-ch'ao, Yen Fu, K'ang Yu-wei, and others – who were to introduce him to some of the basic notions and orientations which were to define the boundaries of his intellectual world. Their influence was to be enriched by the ideas of the pre-1911 revolutionaries and later by figures such as his beloved teacher at the Provincial Normal School in Changsha, Yang Ch'ang-chi. His contact with these new influences did not signify a total break with his traditional education. Like Mao, most of the members of this pre-May Fourth generation had been born in traditional China, albeit on a different social level. In spite of their involvement with new ideas from the West, they did not yet think in terms of a sharp dichotomy between "Traditional China" and "Modern West." They had lived sufficiently deeply within the traditional culture to see in it not a monolith but a complex of differing and contending tendencies. Rightly or wrongly, they thought that they could discern affinities and comparabilities as well as contrasts between Chinese ideas and the new ideas from the West. Even though most of them were of gentry origins their preoccupations were very much shared by the young scholar from Shaoshan.

The more we study their writings, the more impressed we

15

become with the role which they may have played in defining some of the basic motifs and boundaries of Mao's thought. Stuart Schram in his life of Mao Tse-tung[3] observes that Mao may well have come to modern nationalism before he developed any clear ideas on social problems. If this was so then one must strongly credit the transitional figures mentioned above. I am well aware of the perils involved in any attempt to define the word nationalism. The distinction made by China scholars between traditional Chinese "culturalism" and modern nationalism has been challenged by some. The Chinese ruling class, it is maintained, was always intent on preserving the interests of the Chinese state (as indeed were the rulers of the Roman empire). The Chinese in the past were often anti-foreign and often displayed a strong "we feeling" as Chinese. The validity of the distinction remains. In the writings of the transitional figures there is an overwhelming preoccupation with the preservation and enhancement of China as a political-societal entity in a world of other societal entities known as nation-states, and a decline of identification of "Chineseness" with universal cultural, ethical and social values. Values and ideas to a degree come to be judged in terms of their contribution to the survival of the societal entity rather than vice-versa. There can be no doubt that the young Mao who as a student already identifies himself with public affairs is immediately responsive to this shift in preoccupation and that his concern with the wealth, power and dignity of China as a nation will remain a constant preoccupation to the end without in any way precluding more universalistic goals.

The transitional thinkers of the late 19th century and early 20th century also found it possible to combine their nationalism with universalistic goals. One strand of traditional Chinese thought very much present in their writings is the tendency to think in terms of universal impersonal patterns of world history. The patterns, while applied essentially to Chinese history, were universalistic to the extent that Chinese civilization was regarded as civilization *tout court*. To be sure, in China where the Cartesian split between man and cosmos had not occurred, the historical patterns were often thought to correspond to cer-

[3] Schram, *Mao*, p. 23.

ain cosmic cycles and rhythms. These modes of thinking even made possible a kind of historical relativism – a notion that ideas which may have applied to one region of time did not apply to another. These habits of thought undoubtedly provided a bridge to many aspects of Western 19th century evolutionism and historicism. What was dazzlingly new, however, was the notion of progress – of irreversible innovation and infinite possibility of growth. Progress was a kind of infinite energy which would break through all the constraints and structures of the past carrying mankind to the realization of all its highest potentialities. This was in striking contrast to the cyclical views of the past based on conceptions of finite possibilities. It was thus possible for these thinkers to place their nationalism within a world historic framework. It was even possible to dream of an ultimately trans-national world without in any way diminishing the sense of urgency of the immediate nationalist task. Long before the arrival of Marxism–Leninism, these men were thinking in terms of historical stages.

The historical thought of the past had also concerned itself at great length with the question of whether great sages and heroes could or could not influence the larger impersonal patterns. One could find a gamut of views running from an almost complete determinism (e.g. Wang Ch'ung, Shao Yung) to the view that the intellectual and political vanguards could significantly affect the course of history. Thus Chinese discussion lent a certain air of familiarity to Western debates about whether intellectuals and politicians could affect the course of history or evolution.

The transitional thinkers were also the bearers of striking new views concerning the individual. Both Yen Fu and Liang Ch'i-ch'ao had tended, as a result of their Western readings, to see a close link between the nation's debility and the failure of Chinese culture to nourish the intellectual, physical and emotional energies of the individual. Confucianism had, to be sure, concerned itself with the moral cultivation of the individual (particularly of the ethical vanguard) but had thought of this task negatively in terms of crushing the sinister aggressive, self-assertive energies of the individual. The modern West had demonstrated that the release of individual energies could only redound to the welfare of nation and society. There is every evidence that the young Mao responded most eagerly to this variety of individualism. To be sure, in Yen Fu and Liang Ch'i-ch'ao this view of the individual was still somewhat influenced by Adam Smith's insistence that the motivation of the individual's enterprising spirit would be found in his own enlightened self-interest. It is quite likely that the young Mao found the version of individualism preached by his later cherished teacher Yang Ch'ang-chi more in tune with his own proclivities. Yang Ch'ang-chi, who had been influenced by Kant and the British idealists such as T. H. Green (who had reacted strongly against British utilitarianism), stressed the compatibility between the new promethean view of the individual and a theory of motivation based on a deep sense or moral obligation to the larger societal whole. This promethean heroic and "idealistic" view of the individual is quite vividly illustrated in Mao's first published article, "A Study of Physical Culture."[4] It is to be noted here that this modality of "individualism" is quite particular. It does not necessarily involve any belief in the infinite worth of individuals as such or any belief that individuals may not be sacrificed for what are deemed to be collective goals. If we think of the intellectual energies of individuals mainly in technical terms, it does not offer any deep support for freedom of thought or expression. When one reads the story of Mao's love life one does indeed feel that he may have been somewhat influenced by the notion of the individual's right to emotional "fulfilment" but it is not a doctrine he readily extended to others.

From these same sources, Mao could have derived a particular new attitude towards authority. The holders of authority in the past – whether familial, political, or religious – had represented the powers of darkness because of the negative, repressive nature of their authority. They had crushed and repressed the vital energies of the people. This view of authority did not necessarily preclude the belief in new vital forms of authority. On the contrary, in the immediate future what China required was the creation of a new positive authority which would nourish and channel the energies of the people. While the young Mao may have had moments of interest in an anarchism which simply called for the removal of all authority on the presump-

[4] *Hsin ch'ing-nien*, April 1917.

18

tion that the released energies of the masses supported by the movement of history would find their own proper channels, in the end he would lean towards the need for enlightened authority.

From the theme of Social Darwinism which played such an important role in the thought of some of the transitional thinkers, Mao may well have derived the exciting idea of the role of conflict and struggle as a positive propellant force in the onward march of evolution. To some extent the novels he read as a youth had already affirmed the positive values of conflict, but Buddhism, Taoism and Confucianism had been as one in their devotion to peace and harmony and their aversion to conflict as an unmitigated source of evil. Social Darwinism as presented by Yen Fu and Liang Ch'i-ch'ao tended to operate at two levels. On the level of individuals it tended to support the competitive struggle for survival among individuals and on this level it could be fused with orthodox classical economy. On another level it was applied to groups as in the contention for supremacy among nation-states. One suspects that it is on the second level – as a metaphor for group conflict – that the idea made its appeal to the young Mao who probably remained quite allergic to the appeals of economic liberalism.

Yet if the transitional thinkers did not convert Mao to economic liberalism they must have certainly given him some appreciation of the role of what we now call economic development as a vital ingredient in the achievement of state power and human welfare. If we shall raise questions about the depth of Mao's later commitment to the Marxist conception of the forces of production as the driving force of history, this has nothing to do with the question of whether he regarded "economic modernization" as one of the essential tasks of the future. The question was not whether economic development was essential. It was whether the driving forces of history were to be sought in the inertial forces operative within the economic realm. Mao did not have to wait for Marxism to teach him that economic progress was a vital necessity if China were to achieve wealth and power however uninterested he may have remained in questions of pure economics.

One vital element which the pre-communist Mao may have

19

derived not from the transitional thinkers but rather from the literature of the pre-1911 revolutionaries (some of whom were extremely active in Hunan) was the concept of the people as a dynamic historic force in its own right. We have already touched on some of the ideas about the "people" which Mao may have derived from his readings in traditional literature. What was lacking was the notion of the "people" as a primary force in its own right. While popular resentments were traditionally regarded as a symptom of a disordered society, they were not regarded as a primal force engendering change. The transitional thinkers espoused Western evolutionary doctrines which also did not encourage views of "the people" as the dynamic bearer of evolutionary progress. On the contrary, it was evolutionary progress itself or rather evolutionary progress implemented by an enlightened elite which would bring an ignorant and undeveloped people into the stream of historic progress. Given the resentments of the young Mao, one may well imagine that he responded eagerly to the new populist ideas of the revolutionaries and one may doubt whether he was very much troubled by the objections of Yen Fu, Liang Ch'i-ch'ao and others to the notion that an unenlightened people could act as an instrument of progress. So long as one thinks of the people not as an aggregate of individuals and groups but as a collective body united by a Rousseauian General Will, the people becomes more than the sum of its parts. What is more, if in speaking of the nation one eliminates the holders of wealth, power and privilege who embody the repressive authority of the past, one can envision a fusion of people and nation, of populism and nationalism.

The notion of a popular General Will immediately suggests all sorts of ambiguities. It may, on the one hand, suggest a kind of anarchism in which the people itself as a kind of self-constituting force rushes forward like a torrent breaking down all barriers in its way and creating the free and good society of the future. As late as 1919, Mao's article "The Great Union of the People"[5] suggests a vision of this sort. While the Chinese people is described as a conglomerate of many parts including such strange categories as students and primary school teachers,

[5] Stuart Schram, "From 'The Great Union of the Popular Masses' to the 'Great Alliance'," *CQ*, No. 49 (January–March 1972), pp. 88–105.

these parts are rapidly becoming fused into one great whole embodying the higher vision of history. It will be noted that students are a significant part of this alliance but the article does not suggest the need of a vanguard. This emphasis on spontaneity may well reflect the apocalyptic mood of the May Fourth period. Yet the concept of General Will may also lend itself to a much more Jacobinist–Leninist view that the popular masses must be led by a conscious vanguard which "concentrates" the General Will and guides the masses on the way to the future.

Closely related to this populism is the idea of revolution itself as a kind of total qualitative break with the past. If one conceives of the people-nation as a kind of total organism, this makes the notion of the total break all the more plausible. While Yen Fu, Liang Ch'i-ch'ao and others had drawn non-revolutionary conclusions from their evolutionary outlook, the notion of a progressive history was not, of course, incompatible with the idea of revolution. Mao Tse-tung's mentor at Peking University, Li Ta-chao, had developed a kind of Hegelian view of a historical process which might lead to new dialectical breaks in the agonizing processes of history.

It should also be noted that vague notions of "socialism" as a name for the good society of the future were certainly available to Mao before 1919 although we have no evidence of any deep commitment to it on his own part. On the other hand, we already note the tendency to include "capitalists" in his categorization of the holders of power, privilege and wealth. Whether at the time he simply meant the very rich, whatever the source of their wealth, or capitalists in the more precise sense is not clear. Yet these notions were certainly available to him in the literature of the times.

All of these strands and themes drawing on both the Chinese past and the modern West were very much available to Mao and his young contemporaries before the arrival of the October Revolution. Not all those who were influenced by them were impelled to adopt Marxism–Leninism as their faith. Yet one can readily observe how many of these general notions prepared the way for the more specific doctrines of Marxism–Leninism. In the case of Mao, not only did these more general notions prepare the ground for the acceptance of Marxism–Leninism, but I

21

would suggest that they continued ever after to condition and blur his perception of many of the more specific doctrines of Marxism–Leninism.

In his conversation with Edgar Snow in 1936 Mao stated "Once I had accepted it (Marxism) as the correct interpretation of history I did not afterwards waver." This is no doubt a statement he would have reiterated to his dying day. In considering once more some of the factors which may have led Mao to this irreversible self-identification as a Marxist–Leninist, the following factors among others come to mind. There was the fact of the October Revolution itself. Mao's own statement of 1949 that the "salvoes of the October Revolution brought Marxism to China" is certainly inaccurate as far as China is concerned but it may be most accurate as it applies to Mao himself. The progress of World History in the West had not led to any major revolution since the second half of the 19th century. Historical progress had moved forward in an incremental, evolutionary way which held no promise of a total breakthrough in a China bogged down in misery and chaos. China's own revolution of 1911 had certainly not produced the breakthrough. It had instead aggravated China's weakness. To Mao's mentor Li Ta-chao, the Russian revolution was the signal that World History was again on the move. "The Russian revolution has shaken off the last dismal autumn leaves from the tree of the world."[6] The Russian revolution was part of World History and China was part of the world. This perception may have become as important for Mao as it was for his mentors Li Ta-chao and Ch'en Tu-hsiu who were soon led to form the Chinese Communist Party. Many of us have stressed the degree to which Mao has, in the course of his political life, emphasized the power of the human will and de-emphasized the "objective forces" of history. None of this has been incompatible with a kind of deeper general faith that history (as a kind of general cosmic force) has been supportive of his efforts, or with the faith that history (as a series of events) will inevitably lead to Communism. It was the October Revolution which kindled this faith. The sage-king can shape history but History will also support the sage-king. Finally, the October Revolution

---

[6] "The victory of Bolshevism," Hsin ch'ing-nien, Vol. V, No. 5 (1918).

having proved that World History was on the move also force-fully called the attention of Mao and his two influential mentors to the doctrinal foundations of that Revolution.

The behaviour of the Great Powers at the Paris Peace Confer-ence (resulting in the Treaty of Versailles) and the Soviet renun-ciation of Russian privileges in China also turned the attention of Mao and others to the Leninist theory of imperialism in its rougher outlines. The theory both provided a coherent explana-tion of the behaviour of the capitalist powers and envisioned an active role for non-Western "national liberation" movements in the world historical drama. What may not have come through so clearly to Mao may have been Lenin's views concerning the provisional and transient nature of nationalism in a world in which the proletarian revolution was imminent. Mao's nationalism was never to become a merely "bourgeois democra-tic" strategy. It was not instrumental.

Lenin's conception of the vanguard party basically cured Mao of his anarcho-populist tendencies. His arguments for the need of a vanguard of professional revolutionaries were to finally confirm Mao's more deeply-laid feeling that the masses required leaders. It also committed him more specifically to the concep-tion of the Communist Party as the ideal organization of the vanguard. Yet the experiences of later years were to reveal an ongoing tendency to discern a possible distinction between the true leaders of the masses and the organization as such.

A much more problematic contribution of Marxism–Leninism was the Marxist doctrine of class struggle. Since Mao read the Chinese translations of the *Communist Manifesto* and of Kaut-sky's "Class Struggle" in 1920 one assumes that some of the specificities of Marx's concept of class must have come through to him. We have already seen that Social Darwinism had already created the disposition to regard group conflict as a positive propellant of progress. In his pre-communist populism there was already implicit a kind of loose notion of class struggle in the early French revolutionary sense – the struggle of those without power, wealth and privilege against the possessors of power, wealth and privilege. Marx, of course, specifically pointed out that he had not discovered the concept of class conflict in this sense. His innovation lay in the fact that he had

23

defined social divisions in terms of the relations of production and had seen the relations of production in terms of their organic relationship to the ongoing march of the forces of production. It was on the basis of this analysis that he was able to determine which classes in fact represented the cutting edge of historical progress. I shall not dwell here on Lenin's transformations of Marx's class doctrine which have been amply discussed elsewhere, except to point out that in a much modified form, the idea of the primacy of the industrial proletariat as the mass basis of the Communist Party and as the leading World Historical class had survived in Lenin. The fact that immediately after the formation of the Chinese Communist Party Mao's attention was first drawn to the area of labour organization would indicate that the notion of the industrial proletariat as the Party's class basis had come through to him. To what extent had it, however, truly become central to his whole image of the world?

During the period of the first Kuomintang–Communist alliance, the idea was somewhat blurred by the concept of the Kuomintang as the party of the people-nation (the four-class alliance). This was a concept he readily accepted and he seemed quite prepared to work within its framework when he turned his attention to work in the peasant movement. During the "Soviet" period he devoted all his attention to Hunan-Kiangsi rural strategy but acknowledged in orthodox fashion that this was auxiliary to the proletarian movement in the cities. By the time he had established his spiritual leadership of the movement in the north-west, the term "proletarian" had already acquired new connotations. It had already come to refer to a cluster of proletarian moral qualities which could be set before both Party and masses as a norm of true collectivist behaviour. To a considerable extent, it had already been disengaged from its concrete class reference.

The Marxist concept of class was of course, organically tied to the Marxist view that the dynamic principles of history are immanent in the economic order. To what extent had Mao internalized this idea? While he may have read Kautsky, basically it came to him with all its Leninist modifications. One could, of course, easily apply it to past history and Mao eventually would provide his own simple abstract Marxist account of Chinese history basing himself on Soviet models. However, whenever he discussed Chinese history in concreto he continued to the end to refer most often to ideas and phenomena (e.g. Confucianism versus Legalism) which were largely "superstructural." As for the present and future, as stated above, he had no doubt already been converted to the need for "economic development" in China even before coming to Marxism–Leninism. Yet this in itself did not involve any commitment to the idea that the dynamic secrets of China's future were to be sought in tendencies inherent in the economic order itself. No doubt, one of the reasons for his seemingly uncritical acceptance of the entire Stalinist development in the Soviet Union (however exasperated he may have been with Stalin's policies on China) is to be sought in Stalin's own sweeping modifications of Marx's conception of the mode of production. In the Soviet Union, Stalin insisted, the building of the industrial mode of production would be undertaken by the "superstructure" itself. The "proletarian dictatorship" would itself build industry and would do so with "socialist" methods. It would also successfully build socialism in one country. There is every reason to believe that Mao found all of these ideas extremely congenial to all his previously held predispositions.

There are, no doubt, other factors in the specific appeal of Marxism–Leninism to the Mao of the May Fourth period. At this point, however, we might briefly consider how his precommunist and communist ideas may have shaped his life as a political actor and leader. It is, of course, at this point that the various dimensions of his personality, his capacities as a political leader and above all, the concrete circumstances within which he operated, interacted with and shaped his outlook. One can readily agree with Mao's emphasis in "On Practice" on "concrete history"[7] even if one does not necessarily accept his analysis of that history. I do not propose to recapitulate the long history of the Maoist revolutionary strategy (a strategy in whose development others played no small part) but something should be said about the particular Yenan image of reality which emerged out of that long and arduous experience. It was an image which was in varied and complex ways to affect the whole

[7] SW, Vol. 1, p. 296.

subsequent history of Mao's role as the leader of the People's Republic.

In considering some of the elements of this image I would like to look again both at its specifically Maoist core and at its more "Marxist–Leninist" dimensions. The fact that the mass basis of the movement was now overwhelmingly peasant, the fact that the leadership of the Party was now drawn from a variety of strata – intellectuals, semi-intellectuals and peasants – provided, as it were, the objective conditions for the use of the concept of "proletarian spirit" as the designation of a cluster of moral qualities. On the other hand, the enormous stress by Mao on the internalization of these qualities as a *sine qua non* for the success of the movement may have in part reflected the deep impression left by the Long March experience. It also linked up with the younger Mao's deep concern with the moral cultivation of the individual – a concern which he had shared with all his early mentors from Liang Ch'i-ch'ao to Yang Ch'ang-chi and – some would say – a concern which he shared with the whole cultural heritage of the past. Yet the content of this panoply of "proletarian" virtues was, of course, by no means entirely traditional. The virtues of self-abnegation, limitless sacrifice to the needs of the collectivity, guerrilla-like self-reliance, unflagging energy, implacable hostility to the enemy, iron discipline, etc., were in the first instance, to be instilled in the leading cadres and then imparted to the masses as a whole, for in spite of all the insistence on the masses as the fountainhead of all wisdom and virtue, the notion of proletarian virtue as an ideal made it possible to admit that the masses in the flesh remained unredeemed.

The realities of the Yenan period also facilitated the stress on the "mass line." Party personnel in the border areas did indeed operate in close quarters with the masses. They did indeed "travel" rather than remain confined in offices. They did indeed pay close attention to mass organization and mass indoctrination. Given the loose organization and scattered nature of the "liberated" area of the north, no doubt a great deal of attention had to be paid to local conditions and particular needs of time and place. The extent to which the masses participated in policy-making is, of course, a moot point even as applied to the

Yenan period. While there may be considerable truth to this picture of moral solidarity between cadres and masses, this does not mean, however, that at the time Mao perceived any con- tradiction between this and the need for highly articulated organization on the Leninist model.

In addition to proletarian spirit and mass line, the Yenan experience also led Mao to formulate many particular maxims. There is thus the maxim that the proletarian spirit when in- stilled in cadres and masses is more important than material resources whether military or economic; that Party cadres endowed with the proper spirit should be able to put their hand to any task – military, economic, educational or political. Given the proper spirit (te), the specific skills (ts'ai) could be easily mastered. Again, within the conditions of north-west China at this time this maxim was by no means implausible. Finally, in Mao's discussions of the sinification of Marxism, it became quite clear that the spirit of nationalism was back in place. This nationalism whatever its relation to the world communist movement was neither provisional nor strategic. Mao's own esoteric version of the united front strategy saw the CCP and Yenan base as the vanguard of all the "healthy" forces of the Chinese nation.

If this is the Maoist core what shall we make of Mao's assertion that Marxism–Leninism was the arrow being used to strike at the target of the Chinese revolution? We know, first of all, that even while Mao was establishing his own claim and his own physiognomy as spiritual leader of the movement, he was also intensively studying Soviet ideological literature. He still seems to have drawn enormous comfort from the belief that his move- ment (whose success was far from certain) was part of a World Historical movement led by the world's first socialist state. This led him, on the whole, to accept without much reflection the picture of the outside world projected from Moscow. In spite of all his ambivalence towards Stalin, in spite of his assertion of his own authority as the theorist of the Chinese revolution, there is no evidence that he in any way doubted the socialist nature of the Soviet Union. We have already reflected on why he may have found some of Stalin's doctrines most congenial. Not only does he seem to have been attracted to the notion that one can use

27

socialism to build industry, but he also seems to have found the Stalinist model of socialism as described in the literature quite acceptable. As a potential builder of socialism within one country, he was probably not shocked by Stalin's lop-sided emphasis on heavy industry. In fact, he may have sympathized with the nationalist motives which underlay it. While he may have regarded Stalin's purges as excessive, while his own style of leadership was quite different, his moral sensibilities were probably not outraged

To be sure, China was still far from socialism. The doctrine of "New Democracy" postulated that China was so backward that a mixed economy would be required for some time to come. In retrospect, however, it would appear that Mao's interest in embracing the "national bourgeoisie" in his people's alliance was more political than economic. The speed and eagerness with which Mao passed over to the period of "transition to socialism" after the consolidation of the People's Republic was based on a full acceptance of Stalin's doctrine that "socialist" methods could be used to build industry in an under-developed society.

This deference to Soviet views on the nature of the world and the shape of the future may also have served to inhibit his own perception of the deeper implications of his own Yenan ideas. It was the Soviet Union after all which had built socialism. He and his colleagues were still dealing with the humbler tasks of the new democratic stage and all his maxims were perhaps only applicable to the task of winning the new democratic revolution. It was only in retrospect after the disillusionment with Soviet models that Yenan itself began to take on the aspects of a quasi-communist idyll. "Until the early stage of liberation," states Mao in 1967, "all party members by and large lived on an equal footing carrying on their daily pursuits energetically and fighting quite bravely. All this had nothing to do with so-called material incentives. What really counts is inspiration drawn from the revolutionary spirit."[8]

Another powerful "Marxist–Leninist" influence was the Stalinist model of the Leninist philosopher-king and theoretical

[8] SCMP, No. 4088 (December 1967), cited in Rice, Edward, Mao's Way (Berkeley, Los Angeles and London: University of California Press, 1972), p. 426.

helmsman. In projecting himself both as the theorist of the Chinese revolution and as a leader interested (as he no doubt genuinely was) in the most philosophical questions of Marxist dialectic and epistemology, he was very much basing himself on the Leninist–Stalinist model, although some may also see here echoes of the Chinese sage-king.

When we turn to the content of Mao's Marxist–Leninist theory of the Chinese revolution as provided in "On New Democracy" and elsewhere, I continue to feel now as in the past that it is the strategy which guides the theory rather than vice-versa. It represents an effort to provide a Marxist–Leninist categorical framework for strategies based on a long political experience (and experience which, to be sure, includes the entire gamut of ideas discussed above) and excellent political insights.

What then of Mao's philosophic works such as "On Contradiction" and "On Practice"? There are many who feel that in these writings one can find the algebraic key to Mao's Marxist methodology. No doubt, these writings are significant. "On Contradiction" illustrates Mao's ongoing obsession with conflict not only as a propulsive force of history but almost as a good in itself. The treatise illustrates his continuing fascination with the "twoness" of things and an ongoing tendency to place almost every dyadic relationship in the universe under the category of contradictions. "On Practice" illustrates his Baconian inductionist view of natural science (which he may have acquired very early),[9] as well as his aversion to the authority of mere book-learning and abstract intellection. At the same time, he combined this inductionism and pragmatism with firm views about the absolute and eternal validity of certain abstractions of his own choosing. Do these works provide a key to Mao's life as a political actor? One might simply point out that Mao himself seemed to believe that this entire dialectical and epistemological apparatus could be applied correctly only by men of superior insight. The ability to distinguish between the principal contradiction and secondary contradictions in any given historic situation hardly derived automatically from the method itself. Similarly, the "summing up" and synthesizing of the "scat-

[9] Benjamin I. Schwartz, "Thoughts on Mao Tse-tung," The New York Review of Books, 8 February, 1973.

tered and unsystematic ideas" of the masses could be done correctly or incorrectly. Once more we are faced with a situation which requires the presence of a higher intuition and superior insight.

If one must seek for the "heart of the matter" I would suggest that we might rather look to certain themes in the corpus of Mao's poetry (both pre- and post-Liberation). If we combine certain recurring images of this poetry we can construct a kind of overriding poetic vision. To a degree this vision corresponds to what Stuart Schram has called Mao's "military romanticism" and yet it is even more than that. Given the overwhelmingly military cast of the Chinese Communist revolutionary experience, the prevalence of military imagery is no surprise. Again and again we see the surging ranks marching onward and fighting constant battles against foes on all sides "holding light the ten thousand crags and torrents." One must assume that these are not only armies marching across the impossible terrains and against overwhelming odds, but the popular masses – the people-nation marching into the future over the terrain of time and prevailing against all hostile forces both human and natural. Interwoven with this image is the image of the heroic leader who like the "victorious hero" Kung Kung of old butts against Mount Pu Chou "breaking the pillars of heaven and snapping the ties of earth." We also have the evocation of vast and grandiose landscapes of mountain, sea and plain viewed as it were from above. One assumes that the eye which beholds these vast vistas is again the eye of the hero leader who like Chuang Tzu's roc bird with "the blue sky on his back looks down to survey Man's world with its towns and cities." One might say that it is the hero leader who surveys the entire scene from the larger historic perspective who alone is able to guide the masses and "sum up" their experiences. Leader and led are bound together by the epic drama in which both are involved. They share all the toils and austerities of the march as well as all its triumphs and sorrows. It is the leader himself who sees to it that the masses are never diverted from the historic task. It is the leader who strives mightily to preserve the heroic virtues of his troops.

We are dealing here with a poetic vision and as such it allows for many fruitful ambiguities when translated into the language of prose. Does the epic march lead to a fixed destination of peace and harmony or is the destination ever-receding, and does the real significance of life lie in the march itself even though there may be many specific goals along the way? Does the image of the hero leader represent only the transcendent leader himself or does it embrace the army's "general staff" as well? Must the army and its leaders rely heavily on efficiency of organization and technical competence or is the main thing the high morale and collective virtue of the troops? (The two of course are not mutually exclusive.) Are the troops themselves all equal to the historic project or will individuals and entire groups fall by the wayside? Indeed may not the army as a whole, as well as its officer corps, flag in its devotion and fall back unless constantly inspired by the proletarian virtues inculcated by the leader? Finally, while the overwhelming image is that of surging advance, may there not at times be need for strategic retreats and periods of quietude even though such quietude always holds the danger of diversion and desertions from the line of march?

To a degree one can think of the whole role of Mao since 1944 in terms of this poetic vision without in any way derogating from our image of him as a hard-headed, canny politician. The speedy consolidation of the People's Republic after 1949 was, of course, still based on the universalization of Yenan methods. The quick achievement of law and order, and of a new sense of national efficacy in these first years is certainly one of the major triumphs of the People's Republic. Yet when we turn to the "transition of socialism" we sense a new modesty and diffidence on the part of the hero leader. He does not clearly envision the terrain lying ahead. He (like his colleagues) suspects that in building socialism one must defer to the technical wisdom of the Soviet friends who have already achieved socialism. The Yenan ideas are, to be sure, not completely thrust aside and Mao continues to cling to some Chinese differences. Yet the main thrust is in the direction of Soviet models. By 1955–56, there is, to be sure, a revival of the leader's exuberant self-confidence. The Chinese people had displayed their ability to achieve socialist goals and had in a sense "done it better" than the Soviets themselves. At the same time Mao, like his colleagues, was by 1956

31

becoming more aware of the limitations of the Stalinist model of socialism. For a moment, the confidence that socialism had been "basically achieved," combined with a realization that many problems remained unsolved led to the relaxation which came to be known as the "Hundred Flowers" period. The intellectuals were for a moment again taken back into the ranks of the masses.

However the true resurgence of Mao's poetic vision in its pure Yenan form coincides with the "Great Leap Forward" of 1958. It was this experience which provided the revelation in China that the maxims of Yenan were, after all, applicable not only to the new democratic revolution of the past but to the present tasks of modernization as well. The unreliable intellectuals had fallen out of the ranks but the "poor and blank" masses would march on into the future. They remained a source of infinite moral energy. If this energy could be tapped, mobilized and directed by dedicated leading cadres, the masses would surge forward to scale the formidable heights of agricultural and industrial production. If socialism merely meant the nationalization of the means of production it was now obviously clear that socialism in the purely structural sense was not the end of the road in China as is seems to have become in the Soviet Union. The masses inspired by the proletarian ethic of Yenan were again marching into the future.

While Mao may have grudgingly accepted the retreat from the Great Leap Forward, he did not renounce the vision which underlay it. Instead, he seems to have come to the conclusion during the 1960–66 period that his own general staff was now abandoning the epic march. Conflicts between the leader and other Party leaders had occurred before but now it became increasingly clear that these others held views of the future which clearly diverged from his own. Their views of the requirements for building a "wealthy and powerful China" (a goal which he shared with them) had clearly come to diverge from his own. They did not accept his perception that these goals would be achieved by relying on the "proletarian" Yenan spirit. It was this failure of vision on their part as well as his meditations on Soviet corruption which really led him to the view that bureaucratic power as such was laden with "bourgeois" potentialities (bourgeois vices were defined as the opposite of proletarian virtues). The leader was now alone with the masses. Yet this was also not to be the end; the masses in the form of the Red Guards and "revolutionary mass organizations" also failed him. Instead of maintaining proletarian solidarity and discipline they fell into complete disorganization and thus made it necessary for him once more to call on the forces of organization to preserve the nation and carry on the business of the state. He would, however, continue to foster and carry on the cultural revolutionary spirit within the vital cultural and educational spheres. It was at this somewhat uncertain moment in the leader's 10,000 mile march that death overtook him.

One is tempted at this point to speculate as to which parts of Mao's legacy will endure. I would suggest that the poetic vision as a whole will retreat from the centre of the stage. The great mass of mankind may at times be wholly caught up in epic marches but the masses (including the Chinese masses) are also people and as people they are inevitably concerned with other things. Even people who live on modest material levels tend to have a lively concern with their own personal destinies (which does not simply mean material incentives), and with their personal relations with others. They may crave peace and harmony as much as the excitement of battle. Like the much criticized intellectuals, they are aware that life has many vital dimensions which can not be squeezed into Mao's historic drama. The hero leader can derive endless gratification from his roc-like position on the mountain peak but the foot soldiers involved in the grimier routines of the campaign may require other things as well.

Mao's really enduring legacy may perhaps be found in some of the more specific achievements along the way. The attainment of social peace and order after 1949 and the restoration of China's national dignity, the success in maintaining a general equity of distribution while carrying on an arduous effort to achieve economic development, the ultimate realization (no doubt shared with the other leaders) that the Stalinist model of development did not apply to China's needs, the realization that in China agriculture required primary attention, the final realization that there was no readily available formula of "modernization" and that China would have to find its own way to modernization – these seem to me some of the more solid legacies of the Maoist period. Another curious legacy is a legacy of awkward questions raised by Mao for his own reasons during recent years. May bureaucratic and political power be as real a source of exploitation, oppression and corruption as power based on property? Are there any political institutions – including the Communist Party – immune to corruption and error? As new leaderships attempt to create stable institutional bases in China these questions will remain to haunt them.

2

THE MARXIST

Stuart R. Schram

There is a double ambiguity about the title of this chapter. Is Mao's Marxism merely one facet of his thought, or does it, as some believe, define the very essence of his contribution to the theory and practice of revolution? And what "Marxism," or whose "Marxism," are we talking about?

For some of Mao's admirers in the West, as for the Soviets from their quite different position, Marxism (as they conceive it) is synonymous with both truth and virtue; it therefore becomes an article of faith either that Mao was a Marxist first, last and always, or that there was nothing Marxist about him at all. Others, who see Mao's thought as the confluence of many disparate influences, ancient and modern, Chinese and Western, may question whether there is any reason to give one of these strands primacy over all the rest. To argue that the structure and content of Mao's thought were essentially determined by Marxism, and bore no relation to the cultural environment in which they developed, is to ignore the evidence, including Mao's own repeated calls not only for the adaptation of Marxism to Chinese conditions, but for the fusion of Chinese and Western elements in a new synthesis. To treat Mao's Marxism as merely one component of his thought among many others is to make light of the fact that for half a century Mao Tse-tung strove to guide himself by the lessons he had learned from Marx, Lenin and Stalin, and to explain and justify his policies in Marxist terms.

As for the standard against which Mao's originality (which some may call "heresy," and others "creativity") should be measured, many students of his thought, myself among them, have in the past referred to "Marxist orthodoxy," meaning by that the basic axioms which, in their view, were common to Marx and Lenin, and often to Stalin and Trotsky as well. There are, however, three disadvantages to this usage. First of all, it suggests that there is a Pope, Patriarch, or other layer-down of correct doctrine, whereas since the death of Stalin quite clearly there has not been. Secondly, there is the implication that if Mao's stance on a given question at a given time is characterized as incompatible with Marxist orthodoxy, this amounts to saying that his thinking was wrong and his policy misguided. As a general proposition, this has never been my view, but since the term "orthodoxy" appears to have created on occasion the impression that it was, the term had best be abandoned. Finally, the loose and interchangeable use of "Marxism," "Marxism–Leninism," "orthodoxy," "the Marxist tradition" and other such locutions leads to confusion, for it blurs the differences between Marxism at various stages in its development, and above all, between the Marxism of Marx and that of Lenin.

The writings of Marx himself embrace almost every conceivable domain, from philosophy to sociology and economics. Lenin, though he wrote one outrageously utopian book (*The State and Revolution*), and expended considerable energy on now largely-forgotten controversies about the philosophy of science, is commonly considered to have narrowed the scope of Marxism to concentrate essentially on the tactics of the struggle for power. A decade or two ago, almost everyone would have said the same of Mao, whose image was primarily that of the guerrilla fighter who had devised a new pattern for revolution in the non-European countries based on encircling the cities from the countryside. Today, in the light of recently-published materials, it is abundantly clear that the mature Mao was very much a philosopher as well as a strategist.

Mao not only fought (as neither Marx nor Lenin did), and reflected on the ultimate destiny of humanity (as Marx was more inclined to do than Lenin); he also assumed the responsibilities of power, and strove (as had Lenin during the few years before his career was cut short by illness) to build a revolutionary state, and to transform society and the economy. There were significant differences between him and Lenin, both in the circumstances they faced and in the solutions they adopted, but in one respect their attitude was very much the same. Both before and after the conquest of power, politics remained for Mao, as it had been for Lenin, the leading factor – the dimension of human activity which ultimately shaped all others.

Was this emphasis in conflict with the implications, if not with the letter, of Marx's own thinking? While arguing that the evolution of human society was governed by objective laws, Marx had also stressed the capacity of men to understand these laws and, having understood and grasped them, to use them in order to change their own fate. The principal instrument by which men could shape their history was, in Marx's view, class struggle, and politics, as one of the theatres in which class interests fought for the control of society, constituted a semi-independent realm. And yet, in the last analysis, Marx held that political changes must follow and grow out of developments in technology and in the economic system. Lenin's idea of a revolution in a country where capitalism is as yet not fully developed, which goes through a "bourgeois-democratic" phase under the "hegemony of the proletariat," has no counterpart in Marx's writings. When Mao ultimately came to assert the primacy of politics in these terms, he was therefore following Lenin and not Marx.

In any case, however important politics was for Marx, it was not, as it is perhaps in the thought of Mao Tse-tung, the key to progress, and the most important single dimension of human freedom. Mao's views of political power not only as the midwife of revolutionary change, but as the locus of the imagination which generates new values, and of the authority which decides what is morally right, brings him in some ways closer to traditional Chinese thought than to either Marx or Lenin.

Mao was in fact slower and more reluctant than most members of China's May Fourth generation, to which he belonged, to move towards a Westernizing stance. His first published article, written during the winter of 1916–17, when he was 23, displays the imprint of a wide range of traditional and traditionalist influences, from the Confucian and Taoist classics to the great conservative statesman (and fellow – Hunanese) Tseng Kuo-fan. Two years later, he was as eager as anyone to "overthrow the Confucius family shop," and to seek inspiration in the "new thought" from the West. And yet, not only for Mao but for all Chinese, there were psychological as well as intellectual obstacles to the assimilation of Western ideas. Mao himself evoked the problem with characteristic verve in 1958:

> Ever since Ch'in Shih-huang [we Chinese] have looked down on foreigners, calling them savages and barbarians. When, at the end of the Ch'ing dynasty, the foreigners attacked us and forced their way into our country, they frightened us [to such an extent] that we became slaves, [constantly] feeling that we were inadequate. Formerly we were arrogant, but now we have become too humble. Let there be a negation of the negation.[1]

To learn from the foreigners who had held China in semi-colonial subjection since the mid-19th century was indeed galling to a people who had long regarded themselves as the centre of the civilized world. There was also the intellectual difficulty of understanding concepts and ideas elaborated in a totally different cultural and historical setting, though this was in some ways smaller in China than in other Asian countries. In the encounter between Marxism and traditional culture, one aspect of Western thought which appears strange and alien in many non-European countries is the emphasis on the historical dimension of human experience. All the major and significant Western interpretations of history, including even such aggressively secular philosophies as Marxism, are ultimately outgrowths of a Judaeo-Christian theology of history, and reflect in some guise the eschatological perspectives of the latter. Though the main schools of thought in pre-revolutionary China shared neither these apocalyptic visions, nor the idea of progress (which is a relatively recent development in the West), they did tend for the most part to take history seriously.

To take history seriously meant to take politics seriously also. However wide the gap which separated them in other respects from Confucianism, even the classic Taoist authors saw government as an essential function in the process of adaptation by humanity to a universe ultimately beyond its control.[2]

---

[1] JPRS, Miscellany, Part I, p. 123; Wan-sui (1969), p. 225. (In this and other instances where a reference is given both to a translation and to the Chinese text of a quotation, I have checked the English version against the original and modified it wherever appropriate in the interests of accuracy and readability.)
[2] As a leading Western authority has put it: "... the Tao-te-ching ... advises Doing Nothing as a means of ruling, not as an abdication of ruling." See Angus Graham, The Book of Lieh-tzu (London: John Murray, 1960), p. 10.

If China thus presented a relatively favourable terrain for a modernizing dictatorship of a Leninist type because of the role long attributed to the state, there were sharp contradictions as well between the aims of those who undertook to make revolution in China half a century ago, and existing attitudes and patterns of organization. The most acute lay in the domain of the relations between those who worked with their brains and those who worked with their hands, and between government and society.

In an article published in July–August 1919, when he had already begun his apprenticeship in revolution, but knew as yet little of Marxism, Mao put the basic dilemma in forceful and prophetic terms:

> In reality, for thousands of years the Chinese people of several hundred millions all led a life of slaves. Only one person, the "emperor," was not a slave (or rather one could say that even he was a slave of "heaven"). When the emperor was in control of everything, we were not allowed to exercise our capacities. Whether in politics, study, society, etc. we were not allowed to have either thought, organization or practice.
>
> Today, things are different, and in every domain we demand liberation . . .[3]

Within a year, Mao had been converted to Marxism, within a decade he had acquired a basic understanding of Leninist strategy and tactics, and within two decades, in Yenan, he had mastered the subject sufficiently to begin producing works of major theoretical significance. The problems he had to face, both in organizing his forces for the conquest of power and then in undertaking to lead China towards socialism, remained, however, those he had formulated in 1919, when he still preferred Kropotkin to Marx. What was to be the relation between the "thought" and the "practice," both of which the Chinese people required for their renewal? How was one to conciliate the overriding need for organization, if the great undertakings of which Mao dreamed were to succeed, and the universal demand for "liberation" which he shared, and which, he predicted, would burst forth like a torrent in the wake of the oppression and

---

[3] Mao Tse-tung, "The Great Union of the Popular Masses," translated in CQ, No. 49 (January–March 1972), pp. 86–7.

stagnation from which the Chinese people had suffered for centuries?

Prior to the foundation of the Chinese Communist Party in July 1921, Mao had acquired considerable experience in organizing urban intellectuals, both for political action and for the study of radical ideas. Thereafter, he spent two years as a trade union organizer, and then a further year or two as a bureaucrat in the Kuomintang apparatus, in Shanghai and Canton, in the context of the "First United Front." It is, however, to the lessons he learned in leading the peasant movement during the years 1925–27 that the inspiration for a large part of his original contribution to revolutionary theory can be traced.

In a crucial article published in September 1926, entitled "The National Revolution and the Peasant Movement," Mao began with the statement: "The peasant question is the central question in the national revolution." This in itself was not at all remarkable, for the upsurge of revolutionary activity in the countryside, since the middle of 1925, had forced itself on the attention of even the most urban-oriented, to such an extent that a bow in the direction of the peasant movement had become a cliché automatically included in almost every speech by a Communist and/or Kuomintang spokesman. Mao's argument demonstrating the importance of the peasantry in terms of the structure of Chinese society was, on the other, very remarkable indeed.

In essence, it can be summed up in two propositions. First of all, "the greatest adversary of revolution in an economically-backward semi-colony is the feudal-patriarchal class (the landlord class) in the villages," which constitutes the foundation of the whole reactionary order; because of this, it is in the villages that the decisive blows must be struck.". . . [I]f the peasants do not arise and fight to overthrow the privileges of the feudal landlord class the power of the warlords and of imperialism can never be hurled down root and branch." Secondly, despite a passing reference to the leadership of the "progressive working class," the peasants are depicted as more consistent and thoroughgoing revolutionaries than the workers. The latter are seeking, at the moment, merely limited objectives such as freedom of association, not the immediate overthrow of the bourgeoisie. In contrast, "the peasants in the countryside, . . . as soon as they arise . . . run into the political power of those village bullies, bad gentry, and landlords who have been crushing the peasants for several thousand years . . . , and if they do not overthrow this political power which is crushing them, there can be no status for the peasants."[4] In other words, the workers ("at present," but for how long?) are merely reformists; they are animated by "trade union consciousness." The peasants, on the other hand, are aware of their central position in society, and are deliberately waging a broad struggle, political as well as economic.

Although Mao remained convinced, from this time forward, that the centre of gravity of the Chinese revolution lay in the countryside, he was never again to go so far in exalting the role of the peasants in theoretical terms. On the contrary, he constantly reiterated the Marxist axiom that the peasantry must accept the leadership of the working class. Indeed, the whole record of Mao Tse-tung's intellectual itinerary during the ensuing decades can be read as a persistent search for ways to combine the principle of proletarian hegemony with the vision of Chinese society which had gripped him in 1926.

Mao's efforts to integrate Marxism with Chinese reality continued for half a century, both before and after the establishment of the Chinese People's Republic. The circumstances during the struggle for power were, of course, very different from those encountered in building socialism, but the continuity of themes across the great divide of 1949 is sufficient to justify a unified treatment of the whole period from 1926 to 1976.

If we are to endeavour to understand what the encounter between China and a revolutionary theory of Western origin meant to Mao himself, instead of merely evaluating the result from the outside, it is appropriate to begin with Mao's view of the relation between these two entities. In 1938, in the context of the impending showdown with the "internationalist" (i.e. pro-Soviet) faction in the Chinese Communist Party, Mao discussed

[4] For the text of this article, see MTC, Vol. 1, pp. 175–9; I have given a more extended analysis of it in "Mao Zedong and the role of the various classes in the Chinese revolution, 1923–1927," in The Polity and Economy of China (The Late Professor Yuji Muramatsu Commemoration Volume) (Tokyo: Toyo Keizai Shinposha, 1975), pp. 227–39.

this issue in terms of the concept of the "Sinification of Marxism." Two decades later, bent once again on throwing off Soviet tutelage and devising a distinctive "Chinese road to socialism," Mao returned to this question again and again, though he no longer used the term "Sinification," no doubt because it appeared to suggest that his thought was relevant only to China, and was in fact used as a term of abuse by Thorez and other European Communists. Mao's many statements on this theme, from the 1930s to the 1960s, are by no means identical, and some of them are downright contradictory. It is possible, however, to define certain of his unvarying convictions, and to note some unresolved contradictions.

Mao's classic statement of October 1938 calling for the "Sinification of Marxism" defined the term as "making certain that in all of its manifestations it is imbued with Chinese characteristics, using it according to Chinese peculiarities." To imbue Marxism with Chinese characteristics meant for Mao to clothe it in "a new and vital Chinese style and manner, pleasing to the eye and to the ear of the Chinese common people." But such Sinification of the form of Marxism was only the outward manifestation of a more fundamental enterprise, which aimed to transform the very substance of Marxism to adapt it to Chinese conditions.

In what should this transformation, in Mao's view, consist? On the one hand, it should consist in re-shaping the ideas and methods of Marx and Lenin to fit the conditions in an economically backward, semi-colonial and largely agrarian country. This was, however, only part of what he had in mind. "Today's China," he said, "is an outgrowth of historic China. We are Marxist historicists; we must not mutilate history. From Confucius to Sun Yat-sen we must sum it up critically, and we must constitute ourselves the heirs to this precious legacy. Conversely, the assimilation of this legacy itself becomes a method that aids considerably in guiding the present great movement."[5] Similarly, in February 1942, Mao urged his comrades to "take the standpoint, viewpoint and method of Marxism–Leninism, apply them to China, and create a theory from the conscientious

[5] Schram, Thought, pp. 172–3. (Translation slightly revised.)

study of the realities of the Chinese revolution and Chinese history."[6]

The "national form" which, in Mao's view, Marxism must assume, thus involved drawing not merely rhetoric, but substance, from the Chinese past. What was the nature of the method Mao proposed to distil from the experience of "historic China," and which elements in the past were to contribute to it? There are hints in his writings of the Yenan period that he was thinking about a domain which could be loosely defined as that of statecraft, and this was fully borne out when he returned to the problem in the 1950s. "There are some things," Mao remarked in March 1959, "which need not have any national style, such as trains, airplanes and big guns. Politics and art should have a national style."[7]

Although by the mid-1950s Mao was beginning to have doubts about the value of the Soviet example, he continued to revere the heritage of Marx, Lenin and Stalin, but the emphasis gradually shifted from the "fundamental character" of their contribution to the need to modify and develop it. Thus, in 1956 Mao wrote: "Marxism is a general truth which has universal application. We must accept it. But this general truth must be combined with the concrete practice of each nation's revolution."[8] In January 1961, on the other hand, replying to the criticism of the Chinese at the 1960 Moscow meeting for having "Sinified Marxism–Leninism," Mao declared:

Marxism–Leninism is basically the same, but the leaves and branches are different, just as [trees which are all] trees, but have different leaves and branches. Conditions are different in each country. In the past we suffered from paying attention only to the universal truth [of Marxism–Leninism], without paying attention to investigation and research . . .[9]

This is an intriguing statement, and it reflects the basic ambiguity of Mao's position. The metaphor "leaves and branches" normally refers in Chinese to inessentials, but Mao's

---

[6] Ibid., pp. 179–80.
[7] Wan-sui (1967), p. 48.
[8] Schram, Unrehearsed, p. 86.
[9] JPRS, Miscellany, Part II, p. 241; Wan-sui (1967), p. 262. My translation here differs from that of the JPRS in crucial respects which affect the whole sense of the passage quoted.

STUART R. SCHRAM

formulation none the less appears to leave open the possibility that the Marxist–Leninist tree, transplanted to China, has undergone a significant transmutation. In endeavouring to determine whether or not this has been the case, I shall look at three crucial dimensions of Mao's thought and practice: patterns of leadership; the role of the workers and the peasants; and the dialectics of development and of the historical process.

Mao Tse-tung's conception of the role of political leadership in social change, as it took shape during the Yenan period, combined two seemingly contradictory, but in fact complementary dimensions. On the one hand, he reaffirmed in rigorous terms the principles of centralized guidance by a revolutionary elite which constituted one of Lenin's main contributions to Marxism. "Some comrades," he complained in his speech of 1 February, 1942 launching the Rectification Campaign, "... do not understand the Party's system of democratic centralism; they do not know that the Communist Party not only needs democracy, but needs centralization even more. They forget the system of democratic centralism, in which the minority is subordinate to the majority, the lower level to the higher level, the part to the whole, and the entire membership to the Central Committee."[10] At the same time, he called for the implementation of the "mass line," which he defined as follows in a celebrated passage of the directive dated 1 June, 1943:

... all correct leadership is necessarily from the masses, to the masses. This means: take the ideas of the masses (scattered and unsystematic ideas) and concentrate them (through study turn them into concentrated and systematic ideas), then go to the masses and propagate and explain these ideas until the masses embrace them as their own, hold fast to them and translate them into action, and test the correctness of these ideas in such action. Then once again concentrate ideas from the masses and once again take them to the masses so that the ideas are persevered in and carried through. And so on, over and over again in an endless spiral, with the ideas becoming more correct, more vital and richer each time. Such is the Marxist–Leninist theory of knowledge, or methodology ...[11]

To suggest that ordinary people may be a source of the ideas from which correct policies are elaborated, and that they can in

[10] Schram, Thought, p. 313.
[11] Ibid., pp. 316–17 (Emphasis added).

44

turn understand these policies rather than blindly applying them, marks a very great rupture with one of the central themes of traditional Chinese thought. Confucius said, according to the *Analects*, "The people may be made to follow a path of action, but they may not be made to understand it."[12] This is one of the aspects of Confucianism that Mao has sought to eradicate from the minds of his compatriots ever since the May Fourth Movement, even as he called for preserving what was still progressive and useful in the Chinese heritage. He did not, however, cast doubt in so doing on the Leninist axiom that class consciousness can only be imported into the working class from outside, and more broadly that the Communist Party, as the vanguard of the proletariat, must provide ideological guidance to society as a whole. As the words I have italicized in the above quotation from Mao's mass-line directive make plain, the masses, although taken into the confidence of the leaders of the revolutionary movement, were in the end to be made to embrace ideas which, left to themselves, they were quite incapable of elaborating in systematic form.

The ideas put forward by Mao in Yenan, both regarding patterns of leadership and regarding the epistemological aspect of the leadership process, continued to constitute the core of his thinking on these problems down to the end of his life. As for the structure of power, Mao declared in April 1956, summing up a lengthy discussion of the relations between the central authorities and the various lower levels:

> There must be proper enthusiasm and proper independence. Provinces, municipalities, regions, counties, districts and townships should all possess both . . . Naturally, we must at the same time tell the comrades at the lower levels that they should not act wildly, that they must exercise caution. Where they can conform, they ought to conform . . . Where they cannot conform . . . then conformity should not be sought at all costs. Two enthusiasms are much better than just one . . . In short, the regions should have an appropriate degree of power. This would be beneficial to the building of a strong socialist state.[13]

The building of a "strong state" remained to the end of his life

[12] *Confucian Analects*, Book VIII (T'ai-po), Ch. IX, translated in James Legge, *The Chinese Classics*, Vol. I (Hong Kong: Hong Kong University Press, 1960), p. 211.

[13] "On the Ten Great Relationships," in Schram, *Unrehearsed*, p. 73.

one of Mao's central concerns. In January 1958, in a directive which constituted in effect the blueprint for the Great Leap Forward, Mao quoted with approval an eight-line rhyme coined in 1953 (for the purpose, he said, of opposing "the dispersionism which existed at that time"), presenting it as a summary of the principles which should guide the proper functioning of the political and economic system:

> Great power is monopolized,
> Small power is dispersed.
> The Party committee takes decisions,
> All quarters carry them out.
> Implementation also involves decisions
> But they must not depart from principles.
> Checking on the work
> Is the responsibility of the Party committee.

Expounding the meaning of this jingle, Mao declared:

The reference in these sentences to the responsibility of the Party committee means that in major matters, a decision must first be taken by the Party committee, which must also check on things while its decision is in the course of implementation. "Great power is monopolized" [ta-ch'üan tu-lan] is a cliché which is customarily used to refer to the arbitrary decisions of an individual [ko-jen tu-tuan]. We borrow this phrase to indicate that the main powers should be concentrated in collective bodies such as the Central Committee and local Party committees, we use it to oppose dispersionism. Can it possibly be argued that great power should be scattered? . . .[14]

What was left to the lower levels was thus innovation in the course of implementing the basic policy decisions taken by the "great power" at the Centre. But although the various bodies at the grass roots had only a limited parcel of authority, they had a crucial role to play in the leadership process in the context of Mao's definition of the mass line as the "Marxist–Leninist theory of knowledge." Thus, in January 1962, after asserting once again that centralism and democracy must be combined "both within the Party and outside," and repeating that centralism was even more indispensable than democracy, Mao went on to say:

[14] "Sixty Articles on Work Methods," translated in CB, No. 892, p. 9; Wan-sui (April 1967), Supplement, pp. 34–5.

Without democracy, there cannot be any correct centralism because people's ideas differ, and if their understanding of things lacks unity then centralism cannot be established. What is centralism? First of all, it is a centralization of correct ideas, on the basis of which unity of understanding, policy, planning, command and action are achieved. This is called centralized unification . . . If there is no democracy we cannot possibly summarize experience correctly. If there is no democracy, if ideas are not coming from the masses, it is impossible to establish a good line, good general and specific policies and methods. Our leading organs merely play the role of a processing plant in the establishment of a good line . . . Everyone knows that if a factory has no raw material, it cannot do any processing . . . Without democracy, you have no understanding of what is happening down below; the general situation will be unclear; you will be unable to collect sufficient opinions from all sides; there can be no communication between top and bottom; top level organs of leadership will depend on one-sided and incorrect material to decide issues, and thus you will find it difficult to avoid being subjectivist; it will be impossible to achieve unity of understanding and unity of action, and impossible to achieve true centralism.[15]

This passage stresses very heavily that the leadership must listen to the masses if it wishes to lead correctly and effectively. But at the same time Mao makes it abundantly clear that the "processing plant" which ultimately elaborates correct decisions is to be found in the Centre. In any case, for better or for worse, Mao's approach to politics remained to the end of his life far more thoroughly impregnated with Leninism than many people (myself included) were prepared to admit a decade ago, during the high tide of the Cultural Revolution. At that time, Mao's position seemed to involve not only an onslaught on the Party, but a downgrading or even a denial of the importance or legitimacy of authority as such. It was widely believed that Chairman Mao had endorsed something like the view advocated by some ultra-leftists in the West, according to which power not only ultimately resides in, but should be effectively exercised by, the masses and their spontaneously-formed organizations at various levels.

In fact, however drastically Mao called into question during the Cultural Revolution every authority but his own, we now

[15] "7,000 Cadres Speech," 30 January, 1962, in Schram, Unrehearsed, pp. 163–4.

know that when he was confronted explicitly, at the beginning of 1967, with a sharp choice between Leninism and anarchy, he had no doubts at all as to which of these positions was correct. In February 1967, talking to the Shanghai leftists Chang Ch'un-ch'iao and Yao Wen-yüan, he noted that the Shanghai People's Committee had demanded the abolition of "heads," and commented: "This is extreme anarchism, it is most reactionary. If instead of calling someone the 'head' of something, we call him 'orderly' or 'assistant,' this would really be only a formal change. In reality, there will still always be 'heads'."[16] He then proceeded to discuss the various objections to establishing Communes, like that which Chang and Yao had just set up in Shanghai, throughout the rest of the country, and ultimately changing the name of the state to "People's Commune of China," saying:

> If all [of these organizations] are changed into communes, what will we do with the Party? Where will we put the Party? In the committees set up under a commune, there will be members who belong to the Party, and others who don't. Where will we put the Party committee? . . . There has to be a nucleus. It doesn't matter what it's called, it is all right to call it a Communist Party, it is all right to call it a social-democratic party, it is all right to call it a social-democratic workers' party, it is all right to call it a Kuomintang, it is all right to call it the I-kuan-tao, but in any case there has to be a party. In a commune there has to be a party; can the commune replace the Party?[17]

The history of the ensuing nine years made it abundantly clear that in the chairman's view it could not.

In terms of the structure of power in society, Mao thus remained very much in the Leninist tradition. There were, however, important differences between his approach to problems of leadership and that of Lenin, not to mention Stalin. On the one hand, the emphasis on listening to and learning from the masses was generally greater than it had been in the Soviet Union. Secondly, the "masses" whose active participation Mao sought,

---

[16] Schram, Unrehearsed, p. 277.
[17] JPRS, Miscellany, Part II, pp. 453–4; Wan-sui (1969), pp. 670–1. This passage is taken from a version of Mao's February 1967 conversations with Chang and Yao different from that translated in Schram, Unrehearsed. The I-kuan-tao was a secret society put down by the new regime in the early 1950s.

and from whom he proposed to learn, were in the first instance China's rural masses.

When Mao was first characterized, many decades ago, as a "peasant revolutionary," the reference was, of course, to the pattern of the struggle for power, centring on guerrilla warfare from bases in the countryside. The problem of working-class leadership arose in this context, but in a different and less intractable form than it was to assume after 1949.

During the period of the Chingkangshan base and Kiangsi Soviet Republic, the Comintern frequently complained about the unorthodox character of the communist movement in China. Thus, a resolution of 26 August, 1931 declared: "The hegemony of the proletariat and the victorious development of the revolution can be guaranteed only on condition that the Chinese Communist Party becomes a proletarian party not only in its political line but in its composition and the role played by the workers in all of its leading organs."[18] As the Sino-Soviet dispute became acute, Kuusinen recalled these directives of the 1930s and asserted that the Comintern's criticism had been absolutely justified.[19]

To this it could fairly be replied that the Chinese Communist Party had first developed among the workers of the coastal cities, that there remained some workers (though not many) among the cadres of the Chinese Communist Party and the Red Army, and that these two organizations were thus in a position to exercise proletarian leadership. And if the army was for the time being a far larger and more powerful body than the Party, this could be explained by the circumstances of the struggle. In any case, Mao had clearly laid down the principle that the Party must always command the gun.

To build socialism in an overwhelmingly agrarian country, and above all to build it in the villages at the same time as in the cities, was another matter altogether. In March 1949, with victory in sight, Mao turned his thoughts to the problems which would arise after the conquest of power, and announced his intention of doing things henceforth in the orthodox way.

[18] H. Carrère d'Encausse and S. Schram, Marxism and Asia (London: Allen Lane, The Penguin Press, 1969), p. 246.
[19] O. V. Kuusinen, speech of February 1964, in Marxism and Asia, p. 333.

"From 1927 to the present," he declared, "the centre of gravity of our work has been in the villages – gathering strength in the villages, using the villages in order to surround the cities, and then taking the cities. The period for this method of work has now ended. The period of 'from the city to the village' and of the city leading the village, has now begun. The centre of gravity of the Party's work has shifted from the village to the city."[20]

The policy of "copying from the Soviets" (as Mao put it in 1962) was, however, partly repudiated as early as mid-1955, when, in his speech of 31 July on co-operativization, Mao explicitly overturned the position of both Lenin and Stalin, according to whom mechanization was a necessary precondition for modernization and collectivization in the countryside,[21] and declared that, because of the conditions prevailing in China, "the technological transformation [would] take longer than the social," though the two would proceed step by step and side by side.[22]

There were solid grounds for the shift in emphasis towards a more even balance between cities and countryside which began in 1955, both in the economic and demographic problems faced by the Chinese Government, and in the social and political consequences of allowing the transformation of the countryside to lag behind that of the cities. I cannot go into this dimension of the problem here; what is important for our purposes is that, from the moment this change in policy got under way, the whole issue of the relation between the workers and the peasants in the further development of the Chinese revolution was posed in a different context.

In December 1955, during the "High Tide" of co-operativization which followed Mao's July speech, he compared the Chinese revolution to the Russian revolution in the following terms:

---

[20] SW, Vol. IV, p. 363.
[21] For Lenin's conception of how one should transform the peasant's mentality by giving him a tractor, see his report of 15 March, 1921 to the Russian Communist Party, in V. I. Lenin, Selected Works, Vol. III (Moscow: Progress Publishers, 1967), pp. 564–5. For Stalin's view that tractors constituted a precondition, see his speech of 27 December, 1929, in J. V. Stalin, Works (Moscow: International Publishers, 1953), Vol. 12, p. 171.
[22] SR, p. 335.

If you compare our country with the Soviet Union: (1) we had twenty years' experience in the base areas, and were trained in three revolutionary wars; our experience [on coming to power] was exceedingly rich ... Therefore, we were able to set up a state very quickly, and complete the tasks of the revolution. (The Soviet Union was a newly-established state; at the time of the October Revolution, they had neither army nor government apparatus, and there were very few Party members.) (2) We enjoy the assistance of the Soviet Union and other democratic countries. (3) Our population is very numerous, and our position is excellent. [Our people] work industriously and bear much hardship, and there is no way out for the peasants without co-operativization. Chinese peasants are even better than English and American workers. Consequently, we can reach socialism more, better, and faster. We should not always be comparing ourselves with the Soviet Union.[23]

Thus, even at the end of 1955, when he was only just beginning to think about the possibility of an independent road for China, Mao saw the problem first of all in political terms. On the one hand, he suggests, because they came to power after 20 years' struggle in the countryside, instead of by suddenly seizing the reins of government in the capital city, the Chinese Communists knew more in 1949 than Lenin and his comrades had known in 1917 about exercising authority over the population at the grass roots and securing their support. Thus they were able to establish their new state on a solid foundation. On the other hand, the Chinese peasantry, in his view, provides remarkable human material for building a socialist society, and the peasants must be given their full role in the process.

To give them their full role did not, however, mean for Mao to place them on the same level as the workers. "The peasants," he said at the First Chengchow Conference of November 1958, in the aftermath of the Great Leap Forward, "after all remain peasants, throughout the whole period when the system of ownership by the whole people has not yet been implemented in the countryside, they after all retain a certain dual nature on the road to socialism."[24] At the Second Chengchow Conference of February–March 1959, he reiterated this statement several times, adding that at the present stage the workers, not the peasants,

[23] JPRS, *Miscellany*, Part I, p. 29: *Wan-sui* (1969), p. 27.
[24] JPRS, *Miscellany*, Part I, p. 128; *Wan-sui* (1969), p. 247.

still played the role of "elder brother" in the relationship between the two.[25]

If the workers were, in Mao's view, the "elder brothers" of the peasants, this was not so much because, in the manner of Marx and Lenin, he believed them to be endowed with qualities of organizing capacity and discipline which the peasants could not match. It was rather because, in the realm of economic development and the technology which underlies it, they were the bearers of the modern knowledge required to solve what he had called in 1949 the "serious problem" of educating the peasants.[26] On the other hand, to adopt the classical Marxist stance calling for the political and economic primacy of the urban working class meant, in a country such as China, to confer a privileged status on a group far removed from the centre of gravity of Chinese society, and on ideas in many respects alien to the national tradition.

Mao's solution was not to be, as is sometimes suggested, to stand Leninism on its head, and to hand over the leadership of the revolution to the peasantry, in the name of some populist myth of the moral superiority of the countryside. Instead, he moved increasingly towards a synthesis of Leninism and Chinese realities. Whether or not, in the process, he arrived at an adequate theoretical solution to the dilemma of a peasantry which was simultaneously the salt of the earth, and the younger brother of the workers in building socialism, is a moot point. In any case, Mao's ideas about the relation between the workers and the peasants can be adequately understood only in the broader context of his vision of the social changes characterizing the various stages in the Chinese revolution, the methods by which he sought to bring them about, and the philosophical outlook underlying his approach to revolution, and to development.

If we compare Mao's vision of history with that of Marx, two points above all merit attention, both of them directly linked with the fact that Marx was a European of the mid-19th century. Firstly, Marx lived through, or immediately after and in the shadow of, the climactic phase in the industrial revolution,

[25] *Wan-sui* (1967), pp. 12, 17, 49, etc.
[26] *SW*, Vol. IV, p. 419.

which saw the most dramatic increase in man's mastery over nature in the whole of recorded history. As a result, he conceived, and freely expressed, profound admiration for the achievements of the European bourgeoisie in carrying out this gigantic enterprise. The time had come, in his view, when the capitalist class was no longer capable of leading society forward, and bourgeois dictatorship must therefore be replaced by the dictatorship of the proletariat. This step was possible, however, only on the basis of the expansion of production already effected by the bourgeoisie, without which the very idea of socialism would have remained a chimera. In other words, the idea of redemption through technology was not the invention of Khrushchev or his disciples, or even of Lenin and Stalin, who also shared it, but lay at the very heart of Marx's intellectual world.

Secondly, though Marx had seen, in 1848 particularly, the mopping up of some of the "feudal remnants" which had survived the great French revolution and the Napoleonic era, he lived the whole of his life in essentially capitalist societies. He wrote, to be sure, about the transition from feudalism to capitalism in Western Europe, and he also followed contemporary events in "Oriental Despotisms" such as Russia, India and China. But he had no personal experience of what it meant to move from one "mode of production" to another, and completely different one, still less to live through two or three such changes, as fell to the lot of Mao and his generation in China.

It was in this context that Marx elaborated his vision of redemption in history. In his view, the material basis for the individual and collective freedom which constituted the highest form of experience attainable by humanity had already been laid. As soon as the dictatorship of the proletariat had been established, and the necessary changes in social and economic organization carried out, these ideals could be realized. The realm of freedom was within man's grasp, and there was no doubt as to the direction in which it lay. The single act of the socialist revolution would open the way, even if it would not bring about utopia overnight. Thus, however great the scope Marx allowed for human initiative in shaping the course of history as a whole, the next step forward for those living in a capitalist society seemed so self-evident as to be virtually pre-determined.

In all these respects, the contrast between Mao's experience and that of Marx could hardly be more marked. The material basis for creating a new realm of freedom did not exist in China. The working class, which was supposed to lead the struggle for socialism, was as yet, in the 1920s, and even in 1949, a marginal, though not an insignificant, phenomenon. The society into which Mao was born, whether we choose to call it "feudal," "semi-feudal and semi-colonial," "Asiatic," or whatever, had been barely touched by the influence of foreign and domestic capital, and the landlords long continued to wield more power than the bourgeoisie. Lenin had been faced with similar, though not quite such acute problems, and had forged the instrument to deal with them in the shape of the "vanguard party": the organization calling itself the "party of the proletariat" which seized power in 1917 and proceeded to carry out the industrial revolution in the place of the bourgeoisie, thereby greatly expanding the urban working class and creating its own class basis.

When Mao said in 1949 that the direction of the Chinese Communist Party's work would henceforth be "from the cities to the countryside," he was indicating very precisely that he proposed to follow Lenin's example in this respect. But the social basis on which he would rely for such an operation was infinitely smaller, the process infinitely more complex, and the outcome more uncertain. Under the circumstances it is not surprising that he began to reflect in his approach to development, and even in his formulations of the principles of dialectics, some of the indeterminacy which he saw as implicit in a complex society formed by many layers of cultural and institutional accretions.

On several occasions, Mao used the metaphor of peeling away "skins" to evoke the successive stages in the Chinese revolution:

I say that China had five layers of skin; the three old ones were imperialist property, bureaucratic capitalist property, and feudal property. In the past, the intellectuals relied on these three skins for their sustenance. Apart from this, they relied on national capitalist property, and the property of the small producers. The democratic revolution which has already taken place merely removed these three skins;

in all, it lasted a hundred years, beginning with Lin Tse-hsü. The socialist revolution removes two skins: the property of the national bourgeoisie, and that of the small producers (petty bourgeois property). At present, all five of these skins have ceased to exist; the three old ones have long ceased to exist, and the two new ones no longer exist either. What skins are left now? The skin of socialist public property. Of course, this is also divided into two parts, one being the property of the whole people, and the other being collective property . . .[27]

Thus, in Mao's thinking, the succession of stages, from the "bourgeois-democratic" revolution to the socialist revolution, and from socialism to communism, the definition of the nature of the state during the latter two phases as the dictatorship of the proletariat, and the axiom that progress towards communism would involve a transition from collective property (which had already replaced individual property) to the property of the whole people, remained fixed as they had long been in the Leninist tradition. The forces which would bring about these developments, and the way in which they should be mobilized and combined, were not however perceived by Mao exactly as they had been by Lenin.

It was in his speech of April 1956 "On the Ten Great Relationships" that Mao first developed systematically the ideas regarding the dialectics of Chinese society, seen as the prototype of a non-European society involved in a process of economic development and cultural change, which constitute perhaps his single most important contribution to Marxism. Underlying this analysis was his intuition that the situation, when pushed to one extreme, will move towards its opposite. He argued, therefore, that if you really want to develop one aspect of the economy, such as heavy industry, you must stress its complements, light industry and agriculture.[28]

By thus sketching out a pattern of economic work in which exclusive emphasis was no longer placed, as it had been in the Soviet Union, on heavy industry as the sole key sector, Mao had laid the foundations for a "road to socialism" adapted to Chinese realities, and in particular to the weight of the

[27] Speech to the Supreme State Council, 13 October, 1957, Wan-sui (1969), pp. 139–40.
[28] Schram, Unrehearsed, pp. 61–83 passim, especially pp. 62–7. For a comparison between this text and the official version published on 26 December, 1976, see my research note in CQ, No. 69 (March 1977), pp. 126–35.

peasantry and the countryside. Mao's speech of April 1956, though it did not present a static image of the Chinese society, stressed rather the relations between sectors than the dynamics of the development process as a whole. Two years later, on the eve of the Great Leap Forward, Mao evoked this discussion, in his theory of the "permanent revolution" [pu-tuan ko-ming lun].[29]

The adjective "permanent" in the title of Mao's theory has, in fact, two rather different connotations, corresponding to the two main dimensions of a very complex intellectual structure. On the one hand, it refers to the ceaseless changes and upheavals which inevitably occur in Mao's view in a society riven with contradictions and undergoing very rapid transformation. On the other hand, it constitutes an injunction to the leadership never to let people rest on their laurels, but constantly to rouse their enthusiasm by setting new tasks. The second of these aspects raises fewer problems, and I will therefore deal with it first.

The rapid development of the economy, and in particular of industrial production, was consistently seen by Mao as a necessary, but in itself wholly insufficient condition for building socialism. Discussing this question in May 1958, he summoned up Lenin to criticize Stalin's fetishism of technology and of managerial expertise:

> Stalin's two slogans are insufficiently dialectical. [If you say] "Technology decides everything," what about politics? [If you say] "Cadres decide everything," what about the masses? Lenin put it well: "Communism equals the Soviets plus electrification." The Soviets mean politics, and electrification means technology. The union of politics and professional work leads to communism.[30]

Mao did not dispute the need for a technically-trained elite; indeed, he repeatedly paid tribute to its role. But he also laid persistent stress on the importance of human and moral factors, and of mobilizing the political zeal of the masses. One of the most terse and forceful of his statements to this effect is to be

[29] For the reasons for translating "permanent" rather than "uninterrupted," "continuous," or "continued" revolution, as Peking Review and other official Chinese publications have done at various times, see S. Schram, "Mao Tse-tung and the theory of the permanent revolution, 1958–1969," CQ, No. 46 (April–June 1971), pp. 221–44, especially p. 222.

[30] JPRS, Miscellany, Part I, p. 115; Wan-sui (1969), p. 216.

found in his criticism of Stalin's *Economic Problems of Socialism in the U.S.S.R.*:

From the beginning to the end of this book Stalin does not say a word about the superstructure. He gives no thought to man, he sees things but not people . . .

. . . [The Soviets] are concerned only with the relations of production, they do not pay attention to the superstructure, they do not pay attention to politics, they do not pay attention to the role of the people. Without a communist movement, it is impossible to reach communism.[31]

If a movement was necessary in Mao's view, how was it to be generated? Dealing with this issue in the passage of the directive of January 1958, entitled "Sixty Articles on Work Methods," devoted to the theory of the permanent revolution, Mao wrote:

After winning one battle, we must immediately put forward new tasks. In this way, we can maintain the revolutionary enthusiasm of the cadres and the masses, and diminish their self-satisfaction, since they have no time to be satisfied with themselves even if they wanted to . . .[32]

"Permanent revolution" did not, of course, mean maintaining tension always at the same extreme pitch. As Mao declared in March 1958 at Chengtu, using once again the metaphor of warfare, it was necessary to alternate "hard fighting" and "rest and consolidation," "haste" and "deliberation" in a "wave-like form of progress."[33] But in the last analysis the theory of the permanent revolution remained, as a Chinese author wrote during the Great Leap Forward, "an ideology which continuously stimulates the enthusiasm of the cadres and the masses."[34]

The wave-like pattern of advance which Mao advocated was, of course, paralleled in his view by the movement of reality. Thus, in his directive of January 1958, he wrote:

[31] Notes made in late 1958 or early 1959, JPRS, *Miscellany*, Part I, pp. 191–2; *Wan-sui* (1967), pp. 156–7.
[32] I quote here from the version of paragraphs 21 and 22 given in my article already cited, CQ, No. 46, pp. 226–9. Mao did not draft the whole of this directive, but he revised it and put his name to it on 31 January, 1958. For a complete translation see CB, No. 892, pp. 1–14.
[33] Talk of 20 March, 1958, Schram, *Unrehearsed*, pp. 106–7.
[34] Kao Yang-chih, article in *Cheng-chih hsüeh-hsi*, No. 18 (1959), p. 19; translated in S. Schram, *Documents sur la théorie de la "révolution permanente" en Chine* (Paris: Mouton, 1963), pp. 57–8.

The advanced and the backward are the two extremities of a contradiction, and "comparison" is the unity of opposites . . . Disequilibrium is a universal objective law. Things forever proceed from disequilibrium to equilibrium, and from equilibrium to disequilibrium, in endless cycles . . . , but each cycle reaches a higher level. Disequilibrium is constant and absolute; equilibrium is temporary and relative.[35]

At first glance, there is considerable similarity between this view and that of Trotsky, who wrote:

During a period of indefinite duration, all social relationships are transformed in the course of continual internal struggles. Society is constantly changing its skin . . . The upheavals in the economy, in technology, in science, in habits and customs form, as they take place, combinations and reciprocal relationships so complex that society cannot reach a state of equilibrium. It is in this that the permanent character of the socialist revolution itself is revealed.[36]

The Soviets have, of course, been denouncing Mao for nearly a decade as a "Trotskyite," but despite the striking coincidence in the use of the metaphor of a society shedding its skin, there are notable differences between Mao's theory of the permanent revolution, and that of Trotsky. One of the most obvious lies in the attitude of the two men towards the peasantry. Trotsky took an even dimmer view than Lenin of the political capacities of peasants, whether European or Asian, and therefore insisted even more implacably than Lenin on working class hegemony throughout the socialist stage of the revolution. Mao, on the other hand, attached more importance to the primacy of politics than to the absolute predominance of the workers. Discussing the relation between politics and professional work, in terms of the "unity of the two opposites," redness and expertise, he wrote:

Ideological work and political work are the guarantee that economic and technical work will be carried through, they serve the economic basis. Ideology and politics are the supreme commander; they are the soul. Whenever we are even slightly lax in our ideological and political work, our economic and technical work will certainly take a false direction.[37]

[35] "Sixty Articles on Work Methods," in S. Schram, article cited, CQ, No. 46, p. 229.

[36] L. Trotsky, La révolution permanente (Paris: Rieder, 1932), p. 36. For a comparison of aspects of Mao's and Trotsky's theories not dealt with here, see S. Schram, Documents sue la théorie de la "révolution permanente," pp. xix–xxix.

[37] "Sixty Articles on Work Methods," paragraph 22, in S. Schram, CQ, No. 46, 228–9.

To be sure, political leaders who understood too little of specialized work, and therefore had no grasp of reality, were merely "pseudo-red"; it was necessary to "integrate politics with technology." But the whole burden of the discussion was that everyone, not only among the leading cadres, but throughout Chinese society, must ultimately become as far as possible both red and expert, with politics firmly in command of the whole process, Peasants, as well as workers, must undergo this transformation, and the dissemination of rudimentary technical knowledge in the countryside therefore became an increasingly important concern.

Mao's view of the peasants as almost, though not quite, the equals of the workers found expression in the way he divided up the social categories existing in China in the spring of 1958. Enumerating all those groups making up the "three big classes" in China at the present moment in his speech of 20 March, 1958 at Chengtu, he said, after mentioning the "enemy classes" and the "national bourgeoisie": "The third is the left, that is to say the labouring people, the workers, the peasants. (In reality there are four classes – the peasants are a separate class.)"[38]

A fortnight later in Hankow, the existence of two separate "labouring classes" was no longer an afterthought. Both of them were said to be working and cultivating the land "under the leadership of our Party," and they were contraposed to the "two exploiting classes," of which the second (the national bourgeoisie) had been extended to include even the "well-to-do middle peasants."[39] In other words, the whole of society had been divided into two opposing blocs, and it was this duality which appeared to Mao to be fundamental.

Mao's formulation reflects, among other things, a difference between him and Lenin regarding the respective contributions of the peasantry and of the bourgeoisie in a modernizing country of which Mao was well aware. He summed it up in a few pithy sentences, in his notes of the early 1960s on the Soviet manual of political economy, when he said:

[38] Schram, Unrehearsed, pp. 112–13.
[39] Speech of 6 April, 1958, JPRS, Miscellany, Part I, pp. 85–6; Wan-sui (1969), pp. 180–2.

STUART R. SCHRAM

In carrying out socialist transformation, we united with the peasants to deal with the capitalists, whereas Lenin said at one time that he would rather establish links with the capitalists, with the intention of turning capitalism into state capitalism, in order to cope with the spontaneous tendencies of the petty bourgeoisie. These different policies were determined by different historical conditions.[40]

Mao's polarization of Chinese society into two opposing forces which were not well-defined entities, but shifting alignments of disparate classes and strata, likewise reflected the indeterminacy which was increasingly to permeate both his vision of reality and the structure of his dialectics. It has often been suggested that the key to Mao's thought lies in his essay of 1937 "On Contradiction," to such an extent that his whole theory of revolution can be deduced from the ideas set forth there. This is, to put it mildly, somewhat exaggerated. The importance Mao attached to contradictions, in which he saw not only the motor of all change and development, but the very stuff of reality, is indeed a central feature of his thought. The implications of this for his interpretation of Marxism are to be found, however, most notably in his view that meaningful contradictions persist under socialism, which was hinted at in "On Contradiction"[41] but spelled out only in the 1950s. Moreover, Mao himself has told us that many people in China in the period after 1949 regarded his interpretation of contradictions as derived not so much from Marx as from the yin and the yang[42] and it is certainly true that there are echoes of the old Taoist dialectics in Mao's writings from 1918 to the end of his life.

In May 1958, Mao claimed that his views on dialectics were "more or less in accord" with those of Lenin, but "not very much in accord" with Stalin, who had "negated contradictions" by writing that "the relations of production in a socialist society were completely adapted to the development of the productive forces." But, said Mao, "before his death [Stalin] wrote an article to negate himself . . ."[43]

[40] JPRS, Miscellany, Part II, p. 309; Wan-sui (1967), p. 242.
[41] SW, Vol. I, p. 318.
[42] Speech of 20 March, 1958 at Chengtu, in Schram, Unrehearsed, p. 109.
[43] The reference is to Stalin, Economic Problems of Socialism in the U.S.S.R., originally published in 1952, which did not quite negate what he had written in 1936, but "explained" what he had meant in the sense indicated by Mao.

Mao's insistence on the universality of contradictions, even under socialism, constantly reiterated from 1957 onwards, was indeed more in tune with the thinking of Lenin than with that of Stalin. But he also began to sound, in the 1960s, notes which are scarcely to be found in the Marxist tradition at all. Thus, in his criticism of the Soviet manual, he wrote, commenting on the phrase "Consolidate completely the system of collective farms":

When I read these two words "consolidate completely," I feel ill at ease. The consolidation of anything is relative; how can it be complete? If, since the human race has existed, all men had not died, but had been "completely consolidated," what would this world be like? In the universe and on this earth, all things are constantly emerging, developing and dying; none of them can be completely consolidated.

Socialism will definitely pass over to communism, and at the time of transition to a communist society, some things from the socialist stage will certainly die. In the communist period too, there will also be uninterrupted development. Communism may well go through many different phases, can it be said that after communist society is reached there will be no changes in anything any more? That everything will be "completely consolidated," so that there will be only quantitative change and not uninterrupted partial qualitative change?[44]

Some perspectives of this kind had been opened by Mao in 1958, when he wrote in his directive on the permanent revolution that even when the era of communism had been reached, there would still be many stages linked by mutations amounting to "revolutions," and involving struggle.[45] He had also shown something then of the acceptance of human mortality and of the order of things expressed in the first paragraph of the above quotation.[46] In the mid-1960s, however, this note became more insistent, and was accompanied by explicit references to the Taoist classics. "I approve of Chuang-tzu's approach," he said in 1964. "When his wife died, he banged on a basin and sang. When people die, there should be parties to celebrate the victory of the dialectics, to celebrate the destruction of the old. Socialism, too, will be eliminated, it wouldn't do if it were not

---

[44] JPRS, *Miscellany*, Part II, pp. 262–4; *Wan-sui* (1967), pp. 186–7.
[45] "Sixty Articles on Work Methods," paragraph 22, quoted in S. Schram, *CQ*, No. 46, p. 229.
[46] See, for example, his talk of 20 March, 1958 at Chengtu, in Schram, *Unrehearsed*, pp. 108–10.

eliminated, for then there would be no communism."[47] Mao likewise voiced his increasing philosophic detachment, and his conviction that socialism and communism, however they might be achieved, were not the last word in mankind's experience, which was in any case only a passing phase in the development of the universe. "When the theologians talk about doomsday," Mao said in 1964, "they are pessimistic and terrify people. We say the end of mankind is something which will produce something more advanced than mankind."[48]

While this Olympian detachment is a distinctive trait of Mao the man, especially in his later years, it should not be taken to imply any lessening of his determination to press forward with the revolution, still less as a symptom of resignation or disillusionment. On the contrary, in the very sentences which follow those just quoted Mao characterized the difference between his outlook and classical Marxism in terms of greater emphasis on the need for men to strive actively to make their own history:

> Mankind is still in its infancy. Engels spoke of moving from the realm of necessity to the realm of freedom, and said that freedom is the understanding of necessity. This sentence is not complete, it only says one half and leaves the rest unsaid. Does merely understanding it make you free? Freedom is the understanding of necessity and the transformation of necessity – one has some work to do too . . . When you discover a law, you must be able to apply it, you must create the world anew, you must break the ground and edify buildings, you must dig mines, industrialize. In the future there will be more people, and there won't be enough grain, so men will have to get food from minerals. Thus it is that only by transformation can freedom be obtained. Will it be possible in the future to be all that free? . . .[49]

The notion of "creating the world anew" by industrializing is, of course, wholly in harmony with the Leninist approach to building socialism. Mao's query as to whether man will be "all that free" even under communism reflects, however, an unusual scepticism, and in some texts of the early 1960s, he expressed even deeper doubts as to whether the forward march of the

[47] "Talk on Questions of Philosophy," in Schram, Unrehearsed, p. 227.
[48] Ibid., p. 228.
[49] Loc. cit.

revolution would be continued, and whether communism would ever be reached.

The immediate cause of this anxiety lay in Mao's conviction that leadership in the Soviet Union had been "usurped by the revisionists," and in his discovery that "new bourgeois elements" might still be produced in China itself.[50] In response to this threat, Mao called for the strengthening of the proletarian dictatorship, and for diminishing the scope of "bourgeois right,"[51] but he also turned increasingly to China's own culture and historical experience to seek remedies for the gaps and shortcomings of the Soviet model.

One curious consequence of Mao's rediscovery of Taoism (and also of Buddhism) in 1964 was his abandonment of two of the "three categories" of Marxist dialectics, including the negation of the negation. In 1958, he had explicitly reaffirmed these, saying: 'The law of the unity of opposites, the law of quantitative and qualitative change, the law of affirmation and negation, exist forever and universally."[52] Now he declared that he "did not believe" in the second two, at least as basic laws; he regarded the transformation of quality and quantity into one another merely as a special case of the unity of opposites, and denied the existence of the negation of the negation altogether.[53]

By arguing that "every link in the chain of events is both affirmation and negation," Mao could be held to have seriously undermined the whole Marxist and Hegelian justification, in philosophical terms, for the idea that history moves irreversibly forward. His vision of a random succession of opposites, or in any case the absence in his thought of a continuing progression in a definite direction built into the structure of the dialectical

[50] Speech of 30 January, 1962, in Schram, *Unrehearsed*, pp. 180–1 and 168. For Mao's statement, at a forum of 20 December, 1964 on Central Committee work, that these new bourgeois should be referred to as "elements" or "cliques" rather than "strata," see JPRS, *Miscellany*, Part II, p. 413.

[51] Mao had already stressed in November 1958 the need to destroy "bourgeois right" as the revolution progressed, JPRS, *Miscellany*, Part I, pp. 130–1; he returned to the point in his opinions of *c.* 1960 on the free supply system (*ibid.*, p. 233).

[52] "Sixty Articles on Work Methods," paragraph 22, in S. Schram, *CQ*, No. 46, p. 228.

[53] "Talk on Questions of Philosophy" with K'ang Sheng and Ch'en Po-ta, 18 August, 1964, in Schram, *Unrehearsed*, p. 226. For a reference to "Buddhist and Taoist materialism," see *ibid.*, p. 230.

process, may have certain advantages over the original Marxist view of an inexorable trend leading to a communist stage in which the dialectic breaks down or evaporates. (As we have seen, in Stalin's interpretation of Marxism the dialectic already broke down to a large extent in the socialist phase.) Mao's ideas on this theme none the less raise serious problems about the conformity of his thinking as a whole to the basic logic of Marxism, and of Leninism.

The indeterminacy which is increasingly to be found in Mao's view of the historical process during the last two decades of his life should, no doubt, be seen rather as the reflection of the circumstances in China as he perceived them than as the consequence of the dialectical axioms he employed. At the same time, the changes which took place in the structure of his thought may well have contributed to his increasing uncertainty about the future of socialism in China – and in the world at large.

One answer to the problem – since Mao by no means proposed to abandon the goal of socialism – was to re-emphasize the subjective dimension of the political struggle, and the influence of men's attitudes on their objective roles, to which Mao had devoted so much attention from the 1920s onwards. In 1928 on the Chingkangshan, confronted by the fact that a majority of the soldiers in his army were not workers, or even proper peasants, but rural vagabonds or *éléments déclassés*, Mao had concluded that the only remedy was "to intensify political training, so as to effect a qualitative change in these elements."[54] On the basis of this and similar passages, I have in the past argued that Mao saw a person's class nature as very largely determined by his subjective attitudes. There still seems to me to be an important element of truth in this conclusion, but at the same time I think this line of analysis has been carried much too far in recent years.

It has repeatedly been suggested since the Cultural Revolution that Mao defined a "proletarian" as someone who had a correct understanding of his thought. This is not only an extreme formulation, which ignores the fact that the real flesh-and-blood working class played a significant role even during the very exceptional era of the Cultural Revolution – for example, in July 1968.

[54] Report of 25 November, 1928, in Schram, *Thought*, p. 269.

It also perhaps puts the question the wrong way round. Instead of (or in addition to) saying that Mao saw class attributes as partially determined by ideological or other subjective attitudes, should we not say that he regarded moral criteria as complementary to political criteria? Consider the definition which he put forward in the 1950s for the so-called "five bad elements," still used today: landlords, rich peasants, counter-revolutionaries, bad elements and rightists. Two of these categories are sociological, two political and one moral. Mao did not appear to see any contradiction or problem in lumping them all together. Did he not perhaps see the revolution as the work of proletarians, peasants *and* good men? Does not all the available evidence suggest that Mao in fact shared with Liu Shao-ch'i the very Chinese and indeed Confucian notion that it is impossible to separate the inner moral world of the individual from his outward behaviour, and from the political realm as a whole?

How, then, shall we define the essential traits of the tree, representing his own brand of Marxism, which Mao planted in China? And what is likely to be the future imprint on China of Mao the Marxist, to the extent that it can be distinguished from his legacy as a whole? In a word, Mao's Marxism was of the Leninist school, but it was modified by contact with Chinese realities, and enriched by a philosophical dimension which to some extent paralleled the thought of Marx, and to some extent diverged from it.

Mao placed himself squarely in the mainstream of Leninism by his insistence on the need for centralized leadership, and for leadership vested in the Party. The implications of Mao's onslaught on the Party during the early phases of the Cultural Revolution were exaggerated at the time by Western observers (including myself); the history of the period 1949–76 as a whole shows conclusively that Mao regarded the Party as not only a useful instrument, but the only appropriate instrument, for leading the revolution. Mao was likewise wholly Leninist in his view that a "proletarian" dictatorship, led by the Party, could guide and control the evolution of a largely pre-capitalist society, through a series of transitional stages, to lay the foundations for socialism and then proceed to build socialism and communism.

Mao parted company with Lenin in substantially attenuating the primacy accorded by the Soviet model to the urban working class, to the technical and managerial elite, and to technology. To the extent that Marx had not set vanguard or elite elements apart from, or above, the ordinary members of society to the same extent as Lenin and his disciples, this could be seen as a movement back towards Marx. The unique role of the working class in the passage of humanity from pre-history to the history of the collective mastery of man over his environment is, on the other hand, as much at the core of Marx's thinking as it is at that of Lenin. Mao's subtle re-interpretation of the axiom of proletarian hegemony reflected on the one hand the heterogeneous character of Chinese society, and on the other a downgrading not only of the workers, but of the bourgeoisie, and of the place of Western urban and industrial society in world history.

Like Marx, but unlike Lenin, who was essentially preoccupied with the techniques of the political struggle, Mao constantly raised questions, especially during the last two decades of his life, about the scope and significance of human endeavours. He wanted to know not merely how to build socialism, but also why. Some of his concerns were identical with those of Marx: for example, to eradicate selfishness and replace private interest with the public good. In other cases, such as the elimination of the difference between the cities and the countryside, his stated aim was the same, but the route by which he pursued it was different. Marx wanted to lift the villages from their state of "rural idiocy" to the level of the cities; Mao saw virtue as well as backwardness in the countryside, and endeavoured to work from both sides at once. In one crucial respect, finally, Mao largely parted company with Marx, for whom freedom, though it could flourish only on the foundation of a collective economy, was in essence the self-expression of Renaissance man. Mao, as the heir to a culture in which the ends of individual self-cultivation were more strictly subordinated to the political and public good than ever they had been in modern Europe, and a member of a generation of Chinese who had felt themselves enslaved in the first instance by the domination of their country by the imperialists, could not but see these things differently.

Marx had made a place for "wars of liberation" in Asia in his global vision of revolution, but he had not explicitly connected them with a social revolution even remotely comparable to that which was to be carried out by the European proletariat. To the extent that he and Engels talked about a "non-capitalist path" in Russia and other "Asiatic" countries, this hypothesis was firmly predicated on the assumption that such a development would be initiated and guided by proletarian revolutionaries in Western Europe.[55] Lenin did conceive of a "bourgeois-democratic" phase in the revolution in Asian countries taking the form of a struggle for national liberation, but for him, and even more for his successor, national liberation was a force to be exploited on the world scene in order to promote revolution and defend the Soviet Union. The struggle of the Asian peoples to preserve their own national heritage had for Lenin no value in itself.

Mao's perspective was totally different. For him, the struggle of the Chinese people to seize control of their own destinies, first by throwing off imperialist domination, then by building China into a "rich and powerful" socialist nation, and finally (and no less importantly) by rejecting Soviet tutelage, was an integral part of what he understood by making Marxist revolution.

That Mao Tse-tung made an important contribution to the theory and practice of revolution there can be no doubt. That he was a kind of Marxist is also certain, for he drew extensively on both Marx and Lenin, whatever the other elements that went into the making of his thought. But did he make a contribution to Marxism? That depends on the answer each of us may give to another question: "Does a system of thought as important and as influential as Marxism belong to its author, or to history?" If the former, Mao cannot be regarded as having contributed to the development of Marxism, for there is little doubt that Marx would have rejected him as a disciple. (There are, of course, those who totally disagree with this judgment, but I believe the weight of evidence is against them.) If, on the other hand, Marxism is what those who seek to follow Marx make of it in every era, then Mao must be counted among the major Marxist theoreticians of our own day.

To the Leninist tradition (which is, by any reasonable stan-

[55] See *Marxism and Asia*, pp. 7–15 and 115–25 *passim*.

STUART R. SCHRAM

dards, one of the theoretical currents deriving from Marx, though not the only one), he contributed three crucial insights: (1) that the socialist revolution is not the same thing as the industrial revolution, but also involves changing man; (2) that although leaders, endowed with consciousness and broad historical vision, are indispensable, the leadership will become ineffectual and corrupt if it does not listen to those below; and (3) that peasants as well as workers are worth listening to, and capable of participating in the creation of a new society. Mao's achievement would no doubt have been greater, and in consequence his reputation as a Marxist theoretician would have stood higher, if he had been able to leave well enough alone, temporarily at least, in 1973, instead of launching yet another offensive against the newly-renascent bureaucracy, which in fact led only to replacing one set of bureaucrats by another. Perhaps, indeed, despite the fragmentary directives which are all he has left us for the last five years of his life, he did not launch these campaigns but, old and sick, was simply unable to prevent the ultra-leftist clique, seemingly well qualified to speak in his name, from doing so on his behalf. If so, is it not ironic that our judgment of his contributions as a theorist should be affected by historical accidents of this kind? But history is not always just.

And what, finally, was the nature of Mao's Marxist legacy to his countrymen? Was it a complete system of revolutionary thought, a method (which his successors would have to apply, if at all, in their own way), or something between the two? Despite the element of indeterminacy which Mao injected both into the laws of dialectics, and into the analysis of the reality of a very complex society, he left behind him, in my opinion, by no means simply a method, but something which, though open and undogmatic, was already more like a system. Perhaps its exact nature can best be evoked by one of Mao's own metaphors. Expounding, in January 1958, his conception of the theory of the "permanent revolution," Mao recalled a Hunanese folk saying: "Straw sandals have no pattern – they shape themselves in the making."[56] In other words, the revolution is a process of con-

[56] Speech of 28 January, 1958 to the Supreme State Conference, in Schram, Unrehearsed, p. 94.

tinual improvisation. And yet, as he goes about his task, the weaver has always in mind a clear vision of the sandal he is striving to make. Mao has left the sandal of the Chinese revolution unfinished, but it has already begun to take shape, and for a long time to come it can scarcely fail to bear his stamp.

3

THE POLITICAL LEADER

Michel Oksenberg

How did Mao Tse-tung organize and employ power? How did he seek to dominate and draw upon his colleagues? How did he rule his nation? What was the pattern of interaction between Mao and those he sought to influence? These are the fascinating questions to be addressed in this essay. Before turning to them, however, a few caveats about Mao as a politician are in order.

Mao was both a philosopher and a politician. Possessed of both a sense of what China could become and a will and capacity to lead his people in new directions, he combined qualities that rarely coexist in one being with such intensity. He was an inquisitive thinker who savoured power; a visionary who remained an activist; simultaneously a revolutionary who revelled in disorder, and a dictator who sought to impose a new order. In temperament, he was mercurial yet disciplined, benevolent yet ruthless, solicitous yet tyrannical.

Portraying such a man in understandable terms is no easy assignment. One difficulty in sketching Mao arises from deciding which portion of his complex intellect and personality deserves emphasis. Another problem is that philosophical and political analysis involves a search for pattern and coherence. Yet there is a real possibility that both Mao's thought and his rule were sufficiently disjointed and unintegrated that the intellectual's effort to impose system upon him is misguided. Perhaps Lucian Pye was correct in arguing Mao is best explicated in emotional rather than rational terms.[1] However, the available information is insufficient to permit a totally satisfying, comprehensive psychological interpretation of Mao. The evidence only allows a portrait that dwells in the realms of ideas

[1] Lucian W. Pye, *Mao Tse-tung: The Man in the Leader* (New York: Basic Books, 1976).

and power. Even in these areas Mao remains elusive, for he had an impish quality which caused him to reject any effort to characterize him. He scorned attempts by others to place labels on him – in part because of his petulant personality and in part to preserve his future options.[2] This deliberate cultivation of an enigmatic image compounds the difficulties of description. In sum, our effort to cast Mao as politician in bronze and to locate him in intellectual and leadership traditions runs counter to the man. As suggested by the water, nuclear physics and scatological metaphors which pervade his writings and speeches – imagery which evokes motion and transformation – Mao was the antithesis of being localizable: his essence was as much fluid, spirit and change as it was lodestone, substance and durability.

This essay begins with a brief summary of Mao's quest and of his concept of power, considerations which largely determined Mao's approach to rule. I then examine Mao's specific techniques of rule: the precise challenge which he faced, the system he created to meet the challenge, and the mechanisms he employed to obtain information and to bring his rule to bear. A discussion follows of Mao's own office and its relationship with the four types of arenas which exist in the political landscape: (1) the policy-specifying bodies; (2) the vast government, CCP and army bureaucracies; (3) the campaign mechanism; and (4) local communities. I then trace Mao's effort to control the allocation or distribution of issues among these different types of institutions, noting the limits which constrained his capacity to set the agenda of decision confronting various policy-makers, which leads to an exploration of the variation in Mao's power over time, place, institution and issue area. I end by addressing the old question: was Mao in command of the policy process

[2] For example, one brief transcript from a Party meeting is available in which Mao, seeking to distinguish himself somewhat from the harsh first unifying emperor Ch'in Shih-huang, noted that he did not like to quote the sayings of Ch'in Shih-huang. Lin Piao, always eager to ingratiate himself, chimed in listing the evils of Ch'in Shih-huang. The chairman then swiftly turned the tables on Lin, saying that he was more violent and oppressive than the emperor of ancient times. The swift exchange suggests it would have been unwise either to compare or contrast Mao with the nefarious emperor; the chairman would have rebuffed either effort. See Mao, "Speeches at the Second Session of the Eighth Party Congress," May 1958, in JPRS, *Miscellany*, Part I, p. 98.

during his tenure as chairman of the CCP and leader of his country? My conclusion is that he retained command over some issues but not others, and that the degree of his control waxed and waned. He retained a decisive capacity to intervene selectively throughout his reign, but the effort he had to exert for successful intervention varied over time.

MAO'S QUEST

In oversimplified terms, Mao's hope was to create a wealthy, powerful, socialist China – a vision derived partly from late 19th century Chinese reformers and partly from Marxism. Mao eloquently summarized his goals on several occasions, including this one in 1954:

> Our general task is to unite the people of the whole country, win the support of all international friends, fight for building a great socialist country, and fight for defending international peace and developing the progressive undertakings of mankind . . . We should be prepared to build within the period of a number of five year plans our country, which presently is economically and culturally backward, into a great industrialized nation with a high degree of modern culture.[3]

And in an oft-quoted passage from his July 1957 address to a high level Party meeting. Mao described his ideal political system as follows:

> We must bring about a political climate which is both centralized and democratic, both disciplined and free, both with a unified will and yet in which the individual temperament would be at ease.[4]

In the social realm, he sought a society with minimum status differences among occupations, with minimum income differences, and with professionals capable of rising above their occupational norms to attain a broad view of societal needs.

Mao's dreams for China were tension-ridden. The acquisition of independent military power diverted resources from economic development projects. Striving for wealth jeopar-

---

[3] Mao Tse-tung, "Opening Address to the First Session of the First National People's Congress," 15 September, 1954, translated in CB, No. 891 (8 October, 1969), p. 17.
[4] Mao Tse-tung, "The Situation in the Summer of 1957," Wan-sui (April 1967), p. 16.

dized the creation of a socialist society. Maximizing economic growth required organizational patterns and incentive systems that over the short run detracted from efforts to achieve cultural change. More profoundly, given the current level of productivity and the current level of man's consciousness, centralization and decentralization, freedom and discipline, collectivism and individualism, can coexist only in tension. Mao's quest was for the ultimate reconciliation of attributes which, at this stage in human development, appear irreconcilable.

The exact route to be traversed in the pursuit of a Chinese modernity, however, remained unclear to Mao. In January 1962, for example, Mao recalled his 1960 conversation with Edgar Snow:

> Snow wanted me to say something about China's long term construction plan. I said, "I don't know." He said, "You are being too prudent." I said, "It's not a question of being prudent. It's just that I really don't know. We just haven't any experience, that's all."[5]

Mao then went on to observe, "In our work of socialist construction, we are still to a very large extent acting blindly. For us, socialist economy is still in many respects a realm of necessity not yet understood."[6] Given the vagueness of the ultimate goal – interestingly, except briefly in 1958, no utopian literature emerged in China during Mao's era describing life during the communist millennium – it seems appropriate to conclude that Mao's major emphases were with societal and political processes, and that his major objective was to commit his people and succeeding generations to continue the quest for a wealthy, powerful, socialist China.

MAO'S CONCEPTS OF POWER AND LEADERSHIP

As revolutionary, then, Mao's concern was to preserve the ideals for which so much had been sacrificed. Since the French Thermidor, this problem has been endemic to revolution. Mao's distinctiveness was his high degree of awareness of the problem and his resoluteness in attacking it.

---

[5] Mao Tse-tung, "On Democratic Centralism," 30 January, 1962, translated in Schram, Unrehearsed, pp. 173–4.   [6] Ibid., p. 175.

As politician, Mao's effort was to reconcile conflicting goals. This too is not unique; all statesmen have to balance contradictory objectives. Mao's distinctiveness was in his conviction that the divergent ends could be pursued simultaneously, or at least in close proximity. He acted upon a dialectical view of historical development. To understand how and why he did so, we must turn to his concept of power and leadership.

A World in Flux. Mao certainly viewed power in dynamic rather than static terms. He saw a world in eternal flux and ceaseless change. Nothing was constant:

> One class is eradicated and another emerges; one society is eradicated and another rises ... Eradication and development apply to everything. If someone else does not do the eliminating, you do it yourself ... Dialectical life is a continual progression toward its opposite. Ultimately mankind will also arrive at an end.[7]
> There is hardly a matter which is not transformable. The urgent becomes relaxed and the relaxed becomes urgent. Labor becomes leisure and leisure becomes labor ...
> What we have failed to do well will be transformed in the end. If we had developed our industry to become the world's most advanced, it would fall to the world's last as our thinking becomes inflexible ...
> There is nothing in the world which does not go through the process of development and extinction. The monkey developed into the human form, and the human race came into existence. Yet, the human race will eventually become extinct or change into something else, and by that time, the earth will disappear ... and the sun will cool ...
> Matter always has a beginning and an end. Only two things are limitless: time and space ... Everything develops gradually and changes gradually.[8]

It is a rare political figure, to put it mildly, who lectures his colleagues on the eventual cooling of the sun. These passages betray a different sense of time and history than that possessed by typical Western leaders. Mao was attracted to the fluidity of any situation, and as a result he was less concerned with immediate power balances than with trends. He tended to classify individuals, classes and nations not so much in terms of the

[7] Mao Tse-tung, "Conversation with Ch'en Po-ta and K'ang Sheng," 1965, translated in JPRS, No. 49826 (12 February, 1970), p. 28.
[8] Mao Tse-tung, "On Dialectics," 1959, translated in JPRS, No. 5079 (23 June, 1970), pp. 30 and 32.

strong and the weak as in terms of those becoming stronger and those becoming weaker. Hence, he dared challenge the overwhelmingly superior forces of the KMT in 1945–46 because he sensed that the trend was against them. In 1955, he sought to nip in the bud through collectivization the emergence of a new middle class in the countryside, for he felt that it could rapidly grow in strength. In the mid-1960s he supported the younger, articulate, radical ideologues, such as Yao Wen-yüan, Kuan Feng and Ch'i Pen-yü. Though they were in a minority, he perceived their capacity to become a major social force through which he could articulate the policies of the Cultural Revolution. And with the 1968 Russian invasion of Czechoslovakia and the clear peaking and initial withdrawals of U.S. forces in Vietnam in 1968–69, Mao saw a change in the *trend* of the relative assertiveness of the two super powers: the U.S. beginning to wane, but the U.S.S.R. ascendant. In short, Mao acted upon not only what he perceived his adversaries, allies, and oneself *were* but what they were *becoming*.

Since he saw everything in constant motion, he did not see power as a definite attribute of any individual, group or nation. Its maintenance could hardly be taken for granted; its absence could be remedied. Perhaps reflecting Taoist influences, Mao often expressed the view that in weakness there is strength and in strength, weakness. One quality of the weak was the capacity to become strong, while power contained the seeds of its own destruction. It was a view which his own career and the history of the CCP confirmed.

The Task of Leadership. While change was inevitable, the outcome was not. Man could affect both the pace of change and, within constraints, its direction. Through his more complex perceptual lenses, Mao saw a world populated by such actors as the weak-but-potentially-becoming-rapidly-strong, the strong-but-certainly-becoming-weak (the pace of decline a function of leadership), the strong-yet-potentially-becoming-slowly-stronger, and so on. The preliminary tasks of enlightened leaders involved intelligence: to have a clear sense of the interests of one's own camp, to identify clearly one's adversaries and allies, and to know what the major trends were. It probably is no accident that the opening sentences of Mao's *Selected*

Works are, "Who are our enemies, and who are our friends? This question is one of primary importance in the revolution." The populace could not simply be divided into "enemies" and "friends," however, for a large portion of it was in the middle. These "wavering elements" could either be alienated or won over to the cause, depending on their treatment.

In keeping with both the Leninist and dominant Chinese traditions of Legalism and Confucianism, then, Mao placed a premium upon informed leadership and organizational capacity as determinants of political outcomes. And the task of leadership in a world of flux was to manipulate the forces of change to one's advantage: to accelerate the beneficial changes and to retard the harmful ones, to ally with those whose interest and movement coincided with one's own, and to isolate and vanquish those forces which inhibited favourable trends.

Omnipresent tensions or contradictions – the struggle between opposites – are what cause continual change. According to Mao, "Without contradiction and struggle, there would be no world, no development, no life, or anything."[9] Leadership requires the effective exploitation of the opportunities offered by the existing tensions in society. Indeed, Mao's approach to leadership was based on tension management. He repeatedly surveyed the existing cleavages in society, and sought to select the one – then labelled the "major contradiction" (chu-yao mao-tun) – which could be best played upon. He would seek to enmesh in a network of organization those who stood on the same side of the fault line as he. He then sought to harness the energy of his allies by deliberately exacerbating the tension, by arousing their emotions, and by directing their hostility towards the "enemies" (those on the other side of the fault line). Maximum participation in the struggle yielded maximum commitment to the goals.

Mao's career can be written in terms of the successive cleavages he used in pursuit of his quest: (1) from 1935 to 1945, between the entire Chinese people and the Japanese invaders; (2) from 1945 to 1953, between the dispossessed and deprived within China (the rural and the urban poor) and the privileged; (3) from 1954 to 1965, between the Chinese eager to build a new

[9] Ibid., p. 33.

society and the vestige groups who had enjoyed privilege in pre-1949 China; and (4) from 1965 to his death, between the less privileged sectors under the new system and the emerging new ruling bureaucratic class in China. To be sure, other cleavages were also exploited. And Mao's success in manipulating these tensions fluctuated over time, with a long-term decline in his efficacy. But the underlying commitment to the leadership technique remained for a lifetime, from the arousal of Hunan peasants against the landlords and local warlords in preparation for the Northern Expedition in 1926, to the call for national resistance to the Japanese invasion, through his pursuit of land reform in the late 1940s and early 1950s, to his campaign against remnant "capitalists" and "rightists" in 1957–58 which played a crucial role in establishing the mood for the Great Leap, and ending with the arousal of youth to attack the bureaucracy during the Cultural Revolution.

Maintenance of Initiative, Flexibility and Ruthlessness.[10] Mao's concept of leadership was not particularly complicated. In fact, it was elegantly simple. The complexity was in the execution, for his approach to leadership demanded not only intelligence but great ruthlessness and tactical and strategic flexibility. Tactical agility was required to forge and break alliances with groups whose interests temporarily coincided with and then departed from his own. Mercilessness was needed to turn upon former friends and to eliminate enemies. The list of former allies turned victims is a long one: outside the Party, it comprised the KMT, the Soviets, capitalist entrepreneurs and Western-trained intellectuals, while inside the Party the list stretched from Chang Kuo-t'ao through Kao Kang, P'eng Teh-huai, Liu Shao-ch'i and Ch'en Po-ta to Lin Piao.

Strategic flexibility was also required, however. The strategy suitable for the "weak-and-becoming-gradually-strong," for example, is different from the strategy for the "strong-and-possibly-becoming-rapidly-weak." The strong, to be specific,

[10] This section draws on Mao, "Problems of Strategy in Guerrilla War Against Japan" and "On Protracted War," in *SW*, Vol. II; Mao, *Basic Tactics* (New York: Praeger Press, 1966); and Mao, *Guerrilla Warfare* (translated by Samuel B. Griffith) (New York: Praeger Press, 1961). See also, Sun Tzu, *The Art of War* (New York: Oxford University Press, 1963) and Scott Boorman, *The Protracted Game* (New York: Oxford University Press, 1969).

can attempt to entangle the weak in enduring alliances that keep the subordinates in an inferior position, while the weak must avoid alliance systems that deprive them of their initiative. Protracted struggle, however, accrues to the advantage of the weak, for it allows the weak to sap the resources and will of the strong, while the superior force should seek decisive encounters. What we observe here is that Mao's strategy of guerrilla war in the 1930s and 1940s was an application of his more general approach to the exercise of power and influence. As he said in 1959, "Military affairs are politics under special conditions. They are a continuation of politics. Politics are also a type of war."[11] Put another way, a similar strategic orientation guided Mao in his plotting of warfare, social change, or inner-Party strife.

A vital ingredient in political battle, it followed, was the maintenance of initiative. For Mao, the essence of power was to be able to choose the battlefield and control one's own and one's adversaries' moves. The tactical aims in political manoeuvre were neither to move forward nor to expand but to seize the advantageous position and to manoeuvre one's opponent into a less favourable stance. A comparison between Oriental and Western sports is appropriate here. To be powerful in the West means having the ball, being on the offensive, and moving inexorably down field. The great fears are loss of momentum or of forward movement. The striker in European football and the quarterback who throws the long bomb win plaudits in Western society. But in Oriental sports such as judo or even the sedate wei-ch'i (Go), retreat and entrapment are essential ingredients of the contest. In Graeco-Roman wrestling the goal is to pin the opponent through overwhelming force. In Chinese wrestling, the goal is to cause the opponent to fall from his own weight and from his tactical blunders. Hence, passivity and inaction – wu-wei – may be the proper posture, for the best exercise of power may be to do nothing. The natural flow of events may be sufficiently favourable. This is certainly contrary to the typical Western emphasis upon action and the frustration that develops with inaction.

[11] Mao, "On Dialectics," p. 34. He expressed a similar view in his 1938 essay "On Protracted War" excerpted in Schram, Thought, pp. 286–7.

With this orientation, timing, stage-setting and image-management become crucial. For Mao, key tasks were to move at the propitious moment for purpose of surprise, to stage confrontations in the most favourable environment, and to project an image of one's trend-in-power which counters the strategy of the adversary. That is, retaining initiative required trying to control the selection of the strategy of adversaries, which was done partly by projecting a false image of one's intentions and capabilities to induce the adversary into selecting a strategy most suitable to one's own objective condition. For example, the proper strategy for a "strong-and-getting-weaker" power probably is to vanquish a "weak-and-getting-weaker" adversary, but to co-opt a "weak-but-inevitably-getting-stronger" adversary. The proper counter for the "weak-and-getting-weaker" force is to project the appearance of being "weak-but-getting-stronger."

To summarize, Mao believed that participants in political conflict treated allies and adversaries differently, depending on whether they were perceived as "weak-and-inevitably, rapidly-getting-stronger," as "strong-and-reversibly, slowly-getting-weaker," etc. Manipulation of image became important in order to appear to be the type of power which would receive the treatment most favourable to one's situation. But, since Mao had many potential adversaries and allies and desired different behaviour from each, it frequently became necessary to project different images to different targets. This required deception, bluff and compartmentalization of image.

In this context descriptions of Mao by two adversaries over whom he gained the ascendancy are pertinent. To be sure, both Chang Kuo-t'ao and Lin Piao had become embittered by the time they gave their descriptions, but it is also worth remembering that these two similar descriptions recall a Mao separated by 35 years. Their similarity is striking. Here is how Chang Kuo-t'ao recalled the Mao of 1935–36, when Mao eliminated Chang as a rival for leadership of the CCP:

> Mao Tse-tung is stubborn and proud, has a high regard for power, and achieves his ends regardless of the means . . . [He] acts in a tyrannous manner by using his deceitfulness . . .[12]

[12] Chang Kuo-t'ao, The Rise of the Chinese Communist Party (Lawrence: University of Kansas Press, 1972), pp. 436–7.

Prone to speculation, [Mao] would stop at nothing, even in the way of evil, to attain his end. Yet, he was adept in playing two-faced tricks. While trying to deal blows at me from all sides, he still turned a smiling face towards me when we met . . .[13]

Communism had disappeared [in the CCP]; all that was left was Machiavellianism and struggle, which had become unalterable principles for the maintenance of Mao Tse-tung's power . . . [His] unreasonable savageness did not always work; so he sometimes assumed a smiling face . . .[14]

Under the cloak of Communist thinking, Mao Tse-tung had hidden his guerrilla concepts, his peasant mentality, and his strategy of the rule of might.[15]

It is doubtful that Lin Piao ever read Chang Kuo-t'ao's memoirs, nor did the two ever candidly share their views of the chairman. Yet, here is how Lin Piao purportedly described the Mao and his followers of the late 1960s and early 1970s:

They manufacture contradictions and splits in order to attain their goal of divide and rule, destroying each group in turn to maintain their ruling position. They know that launching an attack on everyone at the same time is suicidal, so each time they use one force to attack another.

Today [Mao] uses this force to attack that force; tomorrow he uses that force to attack this force. Today he uses sweet words and honeyed talk to those whom he entices, and tomorrow he puts them to death for some fabricated crimes. Those who are his guests today will be his prisoners tomorrow. Looking back at the history of the past few decades, is there anyone whom [Mao] had supported initially who had not finally been handed a political death sentence?[16]

Chang and Lin had been subjected to the ruthless side of Mao, and their reactions reveal important facets of his character. But from our perspective, what we see here is the chagrin and outrage of former colleagues who learned the hard way about Mao's strategic and tactical flexibility in the pursuit of his broader objectives. To many outside observers, these qualities reveal unbridled opportunism and a lust for power for its own sake: Mao the tyrant. The chairman's response to Lin Piao's condem-

[13] *Ibid.*, p. 497.   [14] *Ibid.*, p. 511.   [15] *Ibid.*, p. 578.
[16] The quotation is from the document Lin Piao allegedly instructed his son to draft in justification of his plot to seize power. See the "Outline of 'Project 571'," drafted 22–24 March, 1971, reprinted in Michael Y. M. Kau, edited, *The Lin Piao Affair* (White Plains: International Arts and Sciences Press, 1975), p. 89.

nation is interesting in this regard. The Lin statement supposedly was circulated privately among the plotters, but upon its discovery, Mao ordered it distributed for study throughout the Party. He did not deny Lin's portrayal. To the contrary, he said Lin had not gone far enough. But Mao concluded that rather than being an indictment, Lin's words unwittingly but accurately portrayed Mao's revolutionary character, for his ruthlessness and flexibility were necessary in pursuit of broader goals. In fact, Lin's would-be opprobrium demonstrated he was an unworthy successor who did not understand the nature of leadership.

Sources of Power. Inextricably intertwined with all the foregoing considerations were Mao's views on the sources of power. Sociologists state that several types of political power exist to alter another's behaviour: wealth, the force of arms, emotional appeal (charisma), ideology (including the appeals of morality and the automatic response to calls deemed politically legitimate or authoritative), knowledge, or the force of personal relations (drawing upon social ties and obligations in the political realm). Strategy and psychological manipulation can be considered additional dimensions of power, for they deal with the way a political figure sequentially draws upon his resources for maximum gain. Obviously, political figures may weigh the various sources of power differently; some may consider material resources particularly important, while others may attach primacy, say, to controlling the means of coercion. What a political figure considers the most important source of power, the attribute that can be used to acquire the other sources, becomes important in understanding his whole approach to rule.

Mao's views on this subject, while never explicitly and systematically developed, can be pieced together from many separate statements and from his actions. At no point did Mao stress wealth or material abundance as a major source of power. To the contrary, Mao considered that the use of this resource to elicit desired behaviour – i.e. the use of material incentives – was particularly detrimental to his goals in the long run. (He recognized its efficacy and necessity in the short run, however.) In the early 1960s, he criticized the view that providing material incentives to workers would have a powerful, beneficial motivating force. He wrote that ". . . '[The] concern for personal material interests' courts the danger of developing individualism . . . To consider the distribution of consumer goods as a decisive motivating factor is a revision of Marx's correct viewpoint."[17] To be sure, Mao was not averse to using material incentives, as he did for example during the collectivization campaign of 1955–56 when he guaranteed that sweeping agricultural reforms would lead to a much higher standard of living. Rather, given a choice, Mao preferred to rely on other types of power. Moreover, wealth facilitates corruption. Power begets material abundance, but the abundance becomes one of the reasons the powerful subsequently decay. This does not mean Mao wished China to remain impoverished; on the contrary, he sought a wealthy China. But he recognized the risks that would be created thereby.

Mao's view of military strength was more ambivalent. He certainly realized its efficacy:

> Political power grows out of the barrel of a gun . . . Viewed from the Marxist theory of the state, the army is the chief component of the political power of a state. Whoever wants to seize and hold on to political power must have a strong army . . . Experience of the class struggle of the era of imperialism teaches us that the working class and the toiling masses cannot defeat the armed bourgeois and landlord except by the power of the gun; in this sense, we can even say that the whole world can be remoulded only with the gun.[18]

Similarly, in his classic essay, "On Coalition Government," Mao pointed out that "without a people's army, the people have nothing."[19] In terms of his actual behaviour, moreover, Chang Kuo-t'ao trenchantly observed that "Mao kept a tight grip on the real power – the Army."[20] And Lin Piao described Mao's care in making sure the chairman would not face cohesive opposition from the military: "Because of [Mao's] divide and rule policy, the Army's internal contradictions are fairly complex, which makes it difficult to form a united force which we can control.[21]

[17] Mao Tse-tung, "Reading Notes on the Soviet Union's Political Economics," JPRS, *Miscellany*, Part II, p. 278.
[18] Mao Tse-tung, "Problems of War and Strategy" (November 1938), in SW, Vol. II, pp. 224–5.
[19] In SW, Vol. III, pp. 296–7.
[20] Chang, *Chinese Communist Party*, p. 577.   [21] In Kau, (ed.), *Lin Piao*, p. 85.

On the other hand, Mao also noted that "Our principle is that the Party commands the gun, and the gun must never be allowed to command the Party."[22] The key to Mao's estimate of the limits of weapons is this oft-cited passage from his 1938 essay, "On Protracted War":

> Weapons are an important factor in war, but not the decisive factor; it is people, not things, that are decisive. The contest of strength is not only a contest of military and economic power, but also a contest of human power and morale. Military and economic power is necessarily wielded by people.[23]

A similar philosophy pervaded his attitude towards the use of coercion internally. Certainly willing to crush his opponents he none the less sought to avoid physical excesses. He was not attracted to the Stalinist use of terror and murder, except as an act of last resort. His desire was to "cure the disease to save the patient." As he noted in March 1951, even while unleashing a harsh campaign against hidden "enemies":

> The suppression of counter-revolutionaries always must be carried out precisely, cautiously, and in a planned and methodical way. Besides, it must be controlled from above. Whether this work is done well or poorly should be measured by the way the masses react to it.[24]

Mao perceived two interrelated limits to power based on coercion: its use risked alienating the population and its maintenance required popular support. In sum, Mao appears to have adopted a position akin to the Hsün Tzu interpretation of Confucius: force was a necessary but not sufficient ingredient of power; it had to be accompanied by morality and propriety if rule were to be effective.

We can begin to sense, then, that Mao's estimate of the sources of power departs somewhat from dominant, popular Western thinking. While absorbing the lessons of the Vietnam War and the 1973 Yom Kippur War, for example, Americans still tend to perceive their country as the most powerful on earth because it is the richest and strongest militarily. Also pertinent is Stalin's derisive question in dismissing the importance of the Pope.

[22] In SW, Vol. II, p. 224. [23] Ibid., pp. 143–4.
[24] Mao Tse-tung, "Comments on the Work of Suppressing and Liquidating Counter-revolutionaries" (March 1951), in JPRS, Miscellany, Part I, p. 8.

"Ah, the Pope, how many divisions does he have?" Mao would not have uttered such a thought. He did not deride the power that one derived from being able to claim morality. Nor did U.S. military might engender his respect; he considered it a temporary phenomenon. Rather, the organizational and innovative talents of the American people drew his admiration.

For Mao, the keys to power were knowledge and popular support derived from the people's faith in the essential goodness and virtue of their rulers:

> The army must become one with the people so that they see it as their own army. Such an army will be invincible.[25]
> Every comrade must be helped to understand that as long as we rely on the people, believe firmly in the inexhaustible creative power of the masses and hence trust and identify ourselves with them, we can surmount any difficulty, and no enemy can crush us while we can crush any enemy.[26]

"Trust in the masses; rely on the masses." "The people and the people alone are the motive force in the making of world history." "The masses are the real heroes." "The masses have boundless creative power." "To link oneself with the masses, one must act in accordance with the needs and wishes of the masses." Phrases such as these so punctuate Mao's writings that one is led to believe they express his real conviction.

But such a conclusion would be only partially correct, for Mao also supported such dicta as, "To rebel is justified" and "The majority is not always correct." After all, Mao did not seriously believe in the inherent wisdom of popular beliefs, since he dedicated his life to their transformation. The apparent contradiction can be easily reconciled. Power stemmed from making the masses believe in their leaders. The task is not to be moral but to be cloaked in morality. As Mao stated in the Cultural Revolution, "When you make revolution, you must first manage public opinion."[27] Here, then, lay the root of Mao's emphasis upon the superstructure in his analysis of the relationship be-

---

[25] Mao Tse-tung, "On Protracted War" (May 1938), in SW, Vol. II, p. 186.
[26] Mao Tse-tung, "On Coalition Government" (April 1945), in SW, Vol. III, p. 316.
[27] Mao Tse-tung, "Talk to Central Committee Cultural Revolution Group" (9 January, 1967), in JPRS, No. 49826 (12 February, 1970), p. 39.

tween the "superstructure" of a society and its economic base. Men who were properly motivated and organized, according to Mao, could transform their environment and enhance their power. Mao felt that those who controlled the thoughts of the Chinese people thereby determined their destiny.[28]

Still, Mao did not believe the realm of ideas to be undetermined. He saw limits, set by objective conditions, to the range of beliefs he could inculcate among followers. He sensed a need to retain credibility and legitimacy, which in turn required retaining close contact with popular opinion. Power therefore was linked to knowledge, particularly information about social conditions and about policies which public opinion could be cultivated to support. Concomitantly, power flowed from control over the processes of communication.

Finally, Mao recognized the importance of strategy itself as an important ingredient of power. His writings are infused with a sense of sequence and an awareness of the ceaseless quality of political struggle.

We shall not have thoroughly discharged our responsibility as directors of strategy if we are occupied only with the counter-offensive and neglect the measures to be taken subsequently in case we win the counter-offensive or perhaps even lose it. When a director of strategy finds himself in the strategic phase, he should take into consideration many succeeding phases, or, at the very least, the one that immediately follows. Even though future changes are difficult to foresee and the farther away the perspective the more blurred it seems, a general calculation is possible and an appraisal of distant prospects is necessary. The method of directing by which the director watches only the immediate next step is harmful not only in politics but in war as well . . . A generally thought-out, long-term plan covering an entire strategic phase and even a number of strategic phases is certainly indispensable.[29]

---

[28] This stress upon the potential of man grows out of Chinese traditional thought concerning the malleability of man. That is, Mao concluded that the spiritual transformation of man which would unleash new energies was possible because Mao also believed man was not limited by innate moral characteristics. At a more profound level, then, Mao's view of power grows out of his views concerning the basic nature of man. For an elaboration, see Donald J. Munro, "The malleability of man in Chinese Marxism," in CQ, No. 48 (October–December, 1971), pp. 609–40.

[29] Mao Tse-tung, "Problems of Strategy in China's Revolutionary War" (1936), in SW, Vol. I, pp. 232–3.

This cursory survey of Mao's views concerning the sources of power indicates that Mao esteemed the long-run force inherent in ideas and knowledge. He valued the short-term importance of military capability. He felt material abundance was a mixed blessing. And human emotion could yield great energy when channelled through organization. The task of the successful politician was to select the proper strategy for the use and development of these sources of power in combination and sequence.

MAO'S PATTERN OF RULE

Mao's concepts of power and leadership gave basic shape to his pattern of rule. Five qualities particularly marked his reign: (1) the pursuit of a "zig-zag" strategy of development; (2) the fostering of tensions among his subordinates; (3) the retention of certain key decisions in his hands; (4) the careful cultivation of a popular image; and (5) the effort to control not so much political outcomes as the process of policy-making by determining communication channels, personnel appointments and military deployment.

Constraints upon Rule. Before we turn to these qualities, however, the enormity of the leadership challenge confronting Mao bears mention. During the revolutionary era, the overlapping Party and Red Army organization was scattered over a wide area of China. Each base area faced its own distinctive problems, and the communication links between them were tenuous. Mao gradually consolidated his position within the central apparatus in Yenan, but his reach into the various base areas was not total. Then, after 1949, he led a nation which grew in population from about 500 million to nearly 900 million at his death. No less than eight tiers of government separated Mao from the peasants: the central apparatus, the regions, provinces, local or special districts, counties, communes or townships, brigades, and teams. Vast bureaucracies were needed simply to unify and administer the country: a three to four million military apparatus, well over 10 million civil servants, and a Communist Party which, by 1975, numbered over 28 million. Mao's desire was to rule rather than passively preside over this huge apparatus, to infuse the bureaucracies with his objectives and to elicit from them policy choices plus the information necessary to make those choices well. If he truly wished to rule, the imperatives of his office demanded that he avoid becoming the captive of the administrative apparatus.

Mao was constrained in this effort, however, by the poverty of the nation. While the Chinese have not provided state budgetary figures for Mao's last 16 years in office, a fair inference is that the national budget did not mushroom; the sums available to Mao for discretionary expenditures were limited. Mao ruled within strict economic constraints. The competition over scarce resources was intense. Mao had to develop strategies of rule which did not depend on budgetary allocations – on the "pork barrel" – to secure co-operation.

In addition, Mao inherited many of the institutions over which he presided. To be sure, he helped found the CCP, but many of its customs were well developed before Mao became its dominant figure. The rapidity of the CCP victory over the KMT meant that many Nationalist government agencies and officials were absorbed into the new government. And technological considerations to a considerable extent shaped the range of organizational practices which he could employ in a particular situation. All these factors meant that, even as a founding father, Mao could not shape the institutional structure at will. To an extent which Western observers frequently underestimated, therefore, Mao had to use informal means (such as the use of personal ties) or counter-institutions (such as campaigns) in order to make the formal mechanisms which he only partially created responsive to his will.

Finally, although Mao selected his closest colleagues and advisers – Liu Shao-ch'i, P'eng Chen, Chou En-lai, Lin Piao, and so on – he did not lift them from obscurity. Except perhaps for Ch'en Po-ta and for some he helped elevate during the Cultural Revolution, Mao's Politburo associates and immediate subordinates were not his creatures, but had an independent standing in revolutionary history. Mao could not count on their rapid, automatic obedience to all his commands. Although it changed over time, for the bulk of his reign the setting bore some resemblance to King Arthur and the knights of the round table, a monarch among barons; it was not a classic instance of the despot surrounded entirely by sycophants. Mao's pattern of rule can be seen as the product of his seeking to overcome these economic, organizational and personnel factors in ways compatible with his quest and his views about power and leadership.

A Dialectical Process of Development. One of the most striking aspects of Chinese politics during Mao's era was the alternation between a period of social ferment, mass mobilization, unleashed advance and conflict on the one hand, and a period of consolidation, institutionalization, planned advance and reconciliation on the other. The initial mood of harmony and economic rehabilitation ended in late 1950, and the next 18 months witnessed the "Three-Anti, Five-Anti" campaigns in the urban areas and the acceleration and completion of land reform in the rural areas. A period of consolidation and institution-building ensued from mid-1952 through mid-1955, which then was followed by the 1955–56 collectivization drive in agriculture, the nationalization of industrial and commercial enterprises, the harsh rectification campaign (*su-fan yun-tung*) in state organs, and (somewhat earlier) the crackdown on intellectuals (the Hu Feng Campaign). Then, 1956–57 witnessed another major era of reconciliation and institutionalization, only to be followed by the frenetic upsurge of the Great Leap Forward of 1958–60 and the retrenchment of 1960–62. The complicated Socialist Education Campaign era of 1963–65 cannot be neatly characterized, since the period simultaneously contained strong elements of both consolidation and social experimentation, each pursued vigorously in different locales and institutions, but then came the Cultural Revolution of 1966–69, the turmoil and conflict of which brought the nation to the very precipice of civil war. An era of greater calm and planned economic growth followed from 1969 to 1973, whereupon new major campaigns, the "Criticism of Lin, Criticism of Confucius," and the "Criticism of Bourgeois Rights," affected national political life from 1974 to 1976.[30] To be sure, not all

[30] For a comprehensive treatment of each epoch through the Cultural Revolution, see Ezra Vogel, *Canton under Communism* (Cambridge: Harvard University Press, 1969).

developments fit easily into the cyclical pattern of change. For one thing, certain important trends persisted relatively unabated throughout the period from 1949 to 1976, such as increasing industrialization, the spread of primary and secondary schooling, and the expansion of the communication network. In addition, each of the upsurges (such as the Great Leap and the Cultural Revolution) differed greatly from each other. Finally, during each of the periods of mass mobilization, many programmes continued to be implemented through more planned, bureaucratic means, while during the eras of institutionalization, some programmes were the object of campaigns. As a result of these qualifications an exclusive, or perhaps even a heavy focus on the cyclical aspects of China's post-1949 developmental experience is misplaced.[31]

Yet, the pattern did exist. Certainly interviews with former officials who migrated from China indicate that the policy cycle loomed large in the eyes of the participants. They perceived themselves to exist under two types of political system – when there was a movement and when there was not. There are many, not necessarily mutually exclusive explanations for the oscillations.[32] But in addition to their systemic, economic, or sociological roots, one must also look to Mao. Not only did he play a major role in helping to unleash the eras of unbridled social experimentation but at least his acquiescence and endorsement were necessary to usher in an era of consolidation.

It seems fair to conclude that, although other factors helped generate the oscillations, to the extent his power allowed, Mao deliberately piloted China along this fluctuating course. He saw it as the only way to maintain his quest for the irreconcilables, letting the emphasis shift from economic growth to cultural change to economic growth, from freedom to discipline to freedom, from democracy to centralization to democracy, and from

---

[31] For trenchant, conflicting views of this see the exchange between Andrew Nathan and Edwin A. Winckler in CQ, No. 68 (December 1976), pp. 720–50.
[32] See in particular G. William Skinner and Edwin A. Winckler, "Compliance succession in Communist China," in Amitai Etzioni (ed.), Complex Organizations (New York: Holt, Rinehart and Winston, 1969) and Alexander Eckstein, "Economic fluctuations in Communist China's domestic development," in P'ing-ti Ho and Tang Tsou (eds.), China in Crisis (Chicago: University of Chicago Press, 1968), Book 2, pp. 691–729.

struggle to unity to struggle. The development was supposedly dialectical, with each stage representing a closer approximation to the ultimate synthesis.

Mao explicitly acknowledged his approach on many occasions. One European diplomat, who saw Mao towards the end of the Cultural Revolution, for example, claims that in their conversation, the chairman had likened his approach to rule to making broth. Every so often, Mao apparently said, one had to throw more logs on the fire to heat up the cauldron to make the impurities bubble to the surface.[33] He described the same view this way in 1958:

> What is the situation of the class struggle in the transition period [of socialist construction]? There probably won't be more than a few more rounds in the struggle between the two roads. We must have a strategy, cooling off for awhile and then letting loose. Without such cooling off and letting loose, it won't flare up.[34]

He stated this idea most clearly in a letter supposedly drafted to his wife on the eve of the Cultural Revolution, and disseminated nationally in 1972:

> The situation changes from a great upheaval to a great peace once every seven or eight years. Ghosts and monsters jump out by themselves ... Our current task is to sweep out the Rightists in all the Party and throughout the country. We shall launch another movement for sweeping up the ghosts and monsters after seven or eight years, and will launch more of this movement later.[35]

In sum, Mao viewed the process of social change as the object of grand strategy, with the fomenting of high tides of development central to his design. Those eras of ferment, with their induced and controlled spontaneity, revealed to the leaders the underlying grievances of the people. The energies unleashed through the outpouring of hostility could then be channelled in directions which the leaders deemed advisable. Mao also made use of those eras to test the mettle of his associates and to recruit new cadres into the ranks, for he felt that such times revealed the

---

[33] This is based on a private conversation with the diplomat concerned.
[34] Mao Tse-tung, "Speech at the Hankow Conference" (April 1958) in JPRS, *Miscellany*, Part I, p. 85.
[35] Mao Tse-tung, "Private Letter to Chiang Ch'ing" (8 July, 1966), reprinted in Kau (ed.), *Lin Piao*, pp. 118–21.

capacity of the leaders to handle raw social forces no longer mediated by institutions. The clearest instance of Mao's principle in action came during the Cultural Revolution. On the eve of that upheaval, Mao had stated:

Successors to the revolutionary cause of the proletariat come forward in mass struggles and are tempered in the great storms of revolution. It is essential to test and judge cadres and choose and train successors in the long course of mass struggles.[36]

It should be stressed, however, that when Mao called for an era of struggle, he was not sure of the result. Further, he recognized that risks were entailed: excessive violence, disruption of production and so on. But he judged the risks to be necessary.

Fostering Political Tensions among Subordinates. To recapitulate with an obvious but sometimes neglected point, Mao could not and did not rule China alone. He, perforce, relied on his Politburo associates and the vast bureaucracies under their command to transfer his guidelines into action. Mao, therefore, faced the challenge of structuring the political process so that it would yield him the opportunity to pursue his dialectical strategy of development. During a high tide, Mao reckoned the greatest danger would be extreme "leftist" or radical excesses. During consolidation, he feared the excesses of "rightism," "liberalism," or "revisionism." To guard against these excesses and to maintain policy alternatives, Mao simultaneously advocated contradictory policy lines (one dominant, the other in eclipse) and relied on two or more competing subordinates. When he promoted an upsurge, he still purposefully retained some advisers who were opposed to the unleashing of social forces at that moment and encouraged certain organizations and institutions to pursue a more moderate policy line. Liu Shao-ch'i, for example, had reservations about the collectivization of agriculture in 1955–56, while Chou En-lai was not enthusiastic about the Great Leap and repeatedly sought to curb the excesses of the Cultural Revolution. Similarly, Liu Shao-ch'i and P'eng Chen may not have been supporters of some aspects of the 1956–57 moderation, Lin Piao pursued policies in the army that

---

[36] "On Khrushchev's Phoney Communism" (14 July, 1964), quoted in *Quotations from Chairman Mao Tse-tung* (Peking: Foreign Languages Press, 1966), p. 279.

diverged from the 1960–62 consolidation, and Chiang Ch'ing found elements of the 1969–73 policies quite objectionable. Yet each retained a position of prominence.

Mao's power was never so total that he was easily able to dismiss his opponents at will. But he also found the opposition useful, for when he decided to abandon the previous thrust for its antithesis, he had ready support among his erstwhile doubters. He was able to curb the excesses, for frequently he had the alternative institutions and programmes in place which he could then expand to implement his new desires. And he could deflect the discontent directed against him by saying that the previous dominant programmes and their implementors had not maintained the balance he had instructed. His commands were usually sufficiently ambiguous to permit this.

To perhaps oversimplify, then, at any moment in time, Mao relied on a chief minister to implement the main thrust of his policies while retaining a secondary minister who pursued an alternative set of policies. The terms "chief minister" and "secondary minister" are meant in a functional sense; they refer to Mao's primary and secondary administrative officers. The formal positions which these aides held varied from the ranking vice-chairman of the CCP to the prime minister of the government to the vice-chairman of the Military Affairs Commission. He sought to pit the chief and secondary ministers against one another in order to avoid becoming entirely the captive of either.

Time	Chief Minister	Secondary Minister	Chief Organization	Secondary Organization
1955–57	Chou En-lai	Liu Shao-ch'i	Government	CCP
1958–64	Liu Shao-ch'i	Chou En-lai	CCP	Government
1965–66	Liu Shao-ch'i	Lin Piao	CCP	PLA
1966–69	Lin Piao	Chou En-lai	PLA	—
1970–74	Chou En-lai	Chang Ch'un-ch'iao	inapplicable	
1975	Teng Hsiao-p'ing	Chang Ch'un-ch'iao	for post-Cultural Revolution,	
1976	Hua Kuo-feng	Chang Ch'un-ch'iao	post-Lin Piao era	

The table lists the chief and secondary ministers from the time the informal system jelled in the mid-1950s. Each change roughly corresponded with a change in policy emphasis, though Liu Shao-ch'i remained as Mao's chief minister through the three periods of the Great Leap mobilization, the post-Leap consolidation, and the Socialist Education Campaign. As we have already noted, however, the relationship between Mao and his chief and secondary ministers was not one between a superior and subordinates; a measure of reciprocity remained and a certain amount of tacit bargaining occurred. Simply fostering tensions among his associates – what Lin Piao called Mao's strategy of "divide and rule" – was insufficient to guarantee Mao's rule. He had to elicit commitment and compliance from his associates. Otherwise, he risked these dangers: (1) a coup attempt by the chief minister once he sensed Mao was ready to degrade him (as happened with Lin Piao); (2) a temporary, even tacit alliance between his ministers, which would isolate the chairman (as may in part have happened in 1963–64); or (3) unbridled, even violent conflict among his ministers, with Mao unable to obtain the necessary co-operation among the competitors to make the system work (as occurred in 1966–67 and again in 1975–76). The latter danger, of course, came increasingly to the fore as Mao's death neared, for the system demanded a vigorous and cunning chairman at the helm.

Several factors explain Mao's success until his last years in using his "divide and rule" technique. Three are elaborated at greater length below. At the tactical level, Mao's primary and secondary ministers themselves supervised a group of leaders united in their desire for a stronger, socialist China, but divided in terms of skills, responsibilities and policy preferences. Mao as playwright – perhaps unconsciously and by accident rather than design – had cast himself well as the central actor. Each associate mirrored only a portion of Mao's totality; each balanced or contributed an attribute which Mao lacked. Mao needed each member of the team, but each needed Mao more than Mao needed him. Hence, Chou En-lai provided both the foreign and domestic negotiating skills which balanced Mao's capacity to provoke. Chou provided the cosmopolitan sophistication of the Lower Yangtze to supplement the cruder nativism of Mao's hinterland origins. Liu Shao-ch'i, P'eng Chen, Jen Pi-shih, and Teng Hsiao-p'ing provided the organizational capacity which complemented Mao's ability to arouse commitment and passion. Ch'en Yun and Li Hsien-nien recognized organizational and economic necessities and thereby tempered Mao's faith in human will. Ideologues such as Ch'en Po-ta, Ai Szu-ch'i and later Chang Ch'un-ch'iao possessed a sufficient yet culturally rooted understanding of Marx to enable them to develop Mao's Marxism into a persuasive Chinese ideology. P'eng Teh-huai, Lo Jung-huan, Lin Piao and Yeh Chien-ying understood weaponry and battlefield tactics to give meaning to Mao's strategic doctrine. K'ang Sheng had the sinister temperament and the sense for secret internal security to supplement Mao's more tempered inclination to use coercion more sparingly and openly. Ho Lung and Chu Teh represented the native military tradition of the rebel heroes, mirroring a similar strand in Mao. Indeed Mao's team was remarkably similar in its array of talent to the rebel band that gathered around Sung Chiang at Liang shan po in the Chinese novel, *Water Margin*. The team took shape in Yenan, and persisted up to 1966 and the Cultural Revolution. To be sure, some changes occurred through attrition and purge. But from the early 1940s on, the basic pattern at the top was of a group of interdependent leaders, with Mao at the hub and reliant on a chief minister to supervise the sytem on a day-to-day basis.

Then, beginning in the mid-1950s, in preparation for his own succession, Mao began to reduce the level of his own involvement.[37] As he later put it, he retreated to the second line. He expected the interdependent group, working under his first and second lieutenants, to work with only the broadest guidelines from him. He sought to retain his leverage over his associates and particularly his chief and secondary ministers by retaining key issues, by cultivating mass appeal, and frequently by circumventing his immediate associates through direct appeals to their subordinates. (He sometimes made these appeals while on tour in the provinces, and sometimes in specially convened meetings of higher level cadres.)

However, by the mid-1960s, he considered (quite probably inaccurately) that the system was no longer effective; he felt superfluous and disregarded. (It is possible he came to an erroneous conclusion about his own powerlessness through the

37 This process is well discussed in Roderick MacFarquhar, *The Origins of the Cultural Revolution*, (New York: Columbia University Press, 1974), pp. 152–6.

malicious intrigue of his wife.) So in 1965–66, he turned to his then second minister and several other key aides – Lin Piao, Chou En-lai, Ch'en Po-ta, K'ang Sheng, his wife Chiang Ch'ing – to destroy the collaborative system. From 1966 to the end of his life, Mao continued to pit a chief against a secondary minister, but instead of the 1940–66 era of collegial dependence on Mao, Mao witnessed a faction-based system involving conflict between what could be called the "inner" and "outer" court. The "inner" court were those whose influence derived from their personal access and ideological ties to Mao; they seemingly included Chiang Ch'ing, Chang Ch'un-ch'iao, Yao Wen-yüan and Wang Hung-wen (the four who were removed soon after Mao's death). The outer court were the pre-Cultural Revolution leaders of the Party, government and army bureaucracies, such as Chou En-lai, Yeh Chien-ying, Li Hsien-nien and Teng Hsiao-p'ing. From the late 1960s to his death, the ailing, ageing Mao tried to channel the conflict over succession, a struggle as old in human history as the monarchical institution itself.

Retaining Key Decisions. During the peak of his rule, Mao also jealously guarded certain key policy decisions. He clearly sought the ultimate choice over whether the nature of the current situation demanded an emphasis on struggle or on unity, on economic development or on cultural change. He also sought to identify the principal contradiction or tension which was to be exploited at any particular moment. He clearly believed he had special insight into such questions as: Was the moment propitious to launch the drive for total power against the KMT? Had the time come to collectivize agriculture? Was violence necessary to rid China of its remnant capitalist class? Should the tension between state and society be tapped? He did not hesitate to stipulate policy on these questions even in the face of considerable opposition. Because of his demonstrated acumen and political resolve, he usually got his way on these issues as well.

He also sought to keep three issues in his grasp: foreign policy, rural social policy and cultural policy. These three issues concerned areas about which Mao felt passionately but which also vitally involved his power. Mao had attained power in the 1940s first within the CCP and then within China as a whole because he had articulated the aspirations of the bulk of

95

the populace. He came to represent the force of Chinese nationalism during an era of extreme national duress, in a way somewhat analogous to Charles de Gaulle or Winston Churchill in their countries at the same time. He came to equate his personal fate with the national destiny. And as the ultimate arbiter of Chinese nationalism, he could destroy any opponent by saying that he or she represented an alien force. This is precisely what he did against P'eng Teh-huai in 1959. Certainly, this helps explain why Mao personally was so immersed in managing the Sino-Soviet relationship and why he would tolerate no opposition on the matter. Not only did he sincerely believe in his policy, but he also probably realized that if he allowed someone successfully to challenge his policy, he would have lost his stature as the person who defined China's national interest.

Similarly, Mao deemed rural social policy to be his issue. Not only did he believe he had special competence in this area, but he believed he spoke for the rural poor in the councils of the Politburo. The self-identified champion of the vast majority of the peasantry, Mao claimed a popular support which could overwhelm adversaries with the Party. Given the rural origins of the Chinese revolution and the commitment of the communist movement to improving the lives of the rural populace, Mao's assertion was powerful. Not surprisingly, he did not tolerate anyone else trying to encroach on his monopoly preserve. One particularly clear instance of this came in the spring of 1959, when Mao defended his recommendation to curb the "leftist" excesses of the Commune movement of late 1958. The chairman said, "I speak for 10 million cadres at the level of production team head and for 500 million peasants. If you do not join me in firmly and thoroughly carrying out right opportunism [as contrasted to leftist adventurism against which he was arguing] I will carry it out thoroughly alone, even to the point of giving up my Party membership."[38]

From this perspective, one can understand why Mao reacted with such force in purging P'eng Teh-huai during the acrimonious Lushan gatherings in the summer of 1959. Mao perceived the challenge which the minister of defence offered him to be

[38] Mao Tse-tung, "Remarks at the Second Chengchow Meeting," in Wan-sui (1967), p. 41.

particularly serious because P'eng's criticisms of Mao were on the twin grounds of Mao's rural policy during the Great Leap and his conduct of Sino-Soviet relations. If our analysis is correct, Mao had to react as toughly as he did because P'eng, knowingly or not, attacked the chairman on the two issues upon which Mao based his legitimacy.

One qualification does need to be made. Although Mao made foreign and rural policies his own, he did not insist on monopolizing their elaboration or implementation. As long as his underlying authority went unchallenged and he could recast policies in these areas, he was willing to share in the actual formulation of many programmes and even to limit his own involvement from prolonged periods to an interventionist one. Thus, it appears that in the two eras during which Chou En-lai served as Mao's chief minister, the making of Sino-American policy may have been a genuinely shared, co-operative venture. But the relationship only moved forward in 1969–71 with Mao's symbolic blessing of a new opening to the U.S. through his interview with Edgar Snow in late 1970 and the *People's Daily* photograph of Snow and Mao on the T'ien An Men Square, engrossed in friendly conversation.

Mao also sought to be the ultimate arbiter of cultural questions. In the Chinese context, "cultural matters" subsume a wider range of issues than the phrase implies in English. It includes not only policies towards the media, literature and the arts, but also embraces educational affairs, programmes in science and technology, policies towards the intellectuals, and even extends to public health and sports. Mao's focus on these issues flowed naturally from his assessment of their importance in determining China's future. But unlike the foreign policy and rural realms, Mao never established his absolute authority in this realm. For one thing, the issues could not be easily reduced to proportions manageable by one man. In addition, Mao's colleagues did not appear to believe he had special wisdom in this area. In fact, many leaders of the CCP had their own, rather definite views on the changes that needed to be made in China's culture. The notion that China demanded a cultural revolution antedated the founding of the CCP and Mao's rise within it. Whereas the CCP's attention to national resistance against Japan and to mobilizing the peasantry was partly the result of Mao's efforts, the desire for cultural change antedated Mao's rise in the Party and was one of the factors that had led to the CCP's formation. In spite of Mao's recognition of the issue's importance, therefore, he never succeeded in making it his own.

In another sense, however, he did ensure that the interpretation of the ideology remained his prerogative. That is, the basis of the Party's claim to legitimacy, the reasons it asserted for claiming the obedience and loyalty of the populace, was based on Mao's thought: his creative adaptation of Marxism–Leninism to the Chinese context. As a result of his successfully claiming to be the sole Chinese source of the ideas upon which the political system was based (the reality was much more complicated), Mao could destroy any rival by saying the opponent had departed from his thought. As Lin Piao's son noted, "The Chairman commands such high prestige that he need only utter one sentence to remove anybody he chooses."[39] Obviously best exercised as a threat and even then sparingly, none the less Mao employed it with devastating effectiveness, especially against potential successors with whom he had grown disenchanted; Mao proclaimed the former heir apparent deficient in ideological understanding of his beliefs. It was the charge which turned Liu Shao-ch'i into a symbol of evil,[40] a pattern repeated with Lin Piao.

Cultivating Authority.[41] There can be little doubt that Mao carefully manipulated his image in order to elicit maximum support from his policy-making associates, the bureaucracy and the population at large. But, as noted earlier, to establish his authority, he had to project a somewhat different image to each constituency. His colleagues saw the total Mao and were exposed to the full range of his power: his willingness to coerce, his ideas, his capacity to reward, and his ability to manipulate psychologically. The bureaucrats were somewhat removed from

---

[39] See "Outline of 'Project 571'," translated in Kau (ed.), *Lin Piao*, p. 92.
[40] See Lowell Dittmer, *Liu Shao-ch'i and the Chinese Cultural Revolution: The Politics of Mass Criticism* (Berkeley: University of California Press, 1974).
[41] This section owes much in its conceptualization to Edwin Winckler of Columbia University.

his direct lash, and primarily were the objects of his ideas and his material rewards and denials. But to the populace as a whole, Mao remained a remote figure whose presence was felt primarily in its symbolic-ideological dimension. He sought to be held in awe, and drew upon the imperial tradition to foster a sense of reverence. In sociological jargon, those far from the chairman felt only his normative power; remunerative power was added for his bureaucrats; and a coercive dimension was added for his colleagues. To be sure, as with any classification scheme, the types of power are imperfectly drawn, the boundaries between the types of constituencies are not easily delineated, and exceptions to the generalization exist. But still, the images of Mao held by colleagues were vastly different from those seen by the remote populace. Colleagues knew him infinitely better because they were exposed to facets of Mao that the public did not see.

When the Red Guards shouted in emotional frenzy as Mao appeared before them during mass rallies in 1966, or when peasants pasted the chairman's picture on the family altar, they were responding to him as the spiritual symbol of their nation. According to one prisoner who spent considerable time in labour camps, they did not associate Mao with their harsh treatment.[42] Even prisoners revered the chairman and blamed their condition either on their own shortcomings or on Mao's evil, deceitful subordinates. It must be added, however, that in Mao's last years he was less successful in projecting solely a benevolent image. He became inextricably linked with the violence of the Cultural Revolution in the minds of many urban dwellers and, in the "Criticism of Lin, Criticism of Confucius" campaign of 1973–74, he even encouraged mass media comparisons of him with the cruel founder of Ch'in. How much of the awe and reverence of the 1950s and early 1960s had been destroyed by the mid-1970s, particularly in urban areas, remains open to question.

But certainly, until his last years, Mao perceived a wish among the populace to worship their leader. Upon occasion, he

---

[42] Bao Ruo-wang and Rudolph Chelminski, *Prisoner of Mao* (New York: Coward, McCann and Geoghegan, 1973).

explicitly acknowledged his deliberate use of this desire to enhance his power within the Party. In a remarkable passage, he described his situation in a letter to Chiang Ch'ing:

I have never believed that the several booklets I wrote would have so much supernatural power. Now, after [Lin Piao] exaggerated them, the whole nation has exaggerated them. [Referring to Lin's idolatrous praise of Mao – ed.] . . . In the conference held in May in Peking, he spoke in the same manner . . . I guessed that [Lin and his supporters'] very intention was to strike the ghosts by the help of Chung K'uei. [Chung K'uei is a semi-mythical folk hero whose picture was widely pasted on doors on the eve of the New Year to protect houses against evil spirits – ed.] I became the Chung K'uei of the Communist Party as early as in the 1960s. Things always go toward the opposite side. The higher a thing is blown up, the more serious it is hurt at the fall. I am now prepared to be broken to pieces. This does not bother me. For that matter, I can never be destroyed; I may become pieces, that's all.[43]

Mao recognized the risks of allowing the "cult of the personality" and, if the 1966 dating of this letter is accurate, he believed Lin's lavish praise was false flattery which he had to endorse in order to weaken the bureaucratic base of his opponents. As he told Edgar Snow in 1965, "Probably Khrushchev fell because he had had no cult of personality at all.[44] In his subsequent 1970 interview with Snow, the chairman recalled that at the time of their 1965 colloquy, a great deal of power had escaped his control.[45] That was why, he explained to the American journalist, a more extensive personality cult was needed, so as to stimulate the masses to dismantle the anti-Mao Party bureaucracy. It was hard, Mao explained, for people to overcome the habits of 3,000 years of emperor-worshipping tradition. But Mao asserted that the cult had become excessive during the Cultural Revolution and ought to be cooled down. Still, he asked, could any leader, even in the U.S., get along without some people to worship him? Mao concluded that there was always the desire to be worshipped and the desire to worship. Snow's reflection on this conversation is pertinent: obviously the chairman had pondered very much over this phenomenon – the human need for

[43] "Mao's Letter to Chiang Ch'ing," in Kau (ed.), Lin Piao, p. 120.
[44] Edgar Snow, The Long Revolution (New York: Vintage, 1971), p. 205.
[45] Ibid., pp. 169–70.

and to worship, about gods and God.[46] As Mao confessed to Snow, the one image which he hoped the populace would retain about him would be as a simple schoolteacher – purely his normative dimension.

Bureaucrats also had direct contact with Mao's ideas, principally through the enforced study of his works and the dissemination of his directives through inner-organizational channels. But bureaucrats also sensed Mao's capacity to affect their careers. He determined the fates of the high-ranking protectors of lower level bureaucrats. He launched rectification campaigns and opened up opportunities for advancement. He affected pay scales. Unfortunately, the necessary survey data is unavailable to document the point, but it does seem that bureaucrats tended to perceive Mao's power primarily in terms of his ability to bestow rewards or to deprive officials of their security. They frequently attributed policy errors to his advisers or to his ageing. He was not held responsible for the physical punishment meted out to bureaucrats. Hence, during the Cultural Revolution, several stories came out of officials who had been purged and even imprisoned as a result of some campaign which Mao had helped launch. Yet, the aggrieved cadre had turned to Mao as the person to right the felt injustice; petitions or letters were addressed to him in confidence that if only his benevolent attention could be drawn to the degraded official's plight, all would be better. (A similar phenomenon existed in Stalinist Russia.)

His colleagues, with their richer experience, appear to have been somewhat intimidated by him. In fact, Mao deliberately created a sense of fear. Here are extracts from Politburo meetings which capture Mao's capacity to threaten his colleagues:

> We now have some first secretaries who cannot even match Liu Pang of the feudal period, and are somewhat like Hsiang Yu. [Liu and Hsiang were historical personages of the early Han dynasty – ed.] If these comrades don't reform, they will lose their jobs. You all know the play called The Tyrant Bids his Lady Farewell; if these comrades don't reform, the day will surely come when they too will be saying farewell to their ladies (laughter). Why do I say this so bluntly? It is because I intend to be mean and make some comrades feel sore so they think over things properly. It wouldn't be a bad thing if they couldn't sleep for a

[46] Ibid., p. 170.

night or two. If they were able to sleep, then I wouldn't be pleased because it would mean that they have not yet felt sore . . .[47]
Here in my speech I have criticized certain phenomena and criticized certain comrades, but I have not named them. I have not pointed out who Tom, Dick and Harry are. You yourselves must have some ideas in your minds (laughter).[48]

Needless to say, the laughter mentioned in the transcript was a nervous one. But Mao was not always so indirect in his intimidation. The comrades whom Mao chastised in this passage from the Lushan Plenum knew they were the objects of his wrath:

Now I am going to admonish some comrades who have made mistakes. Prepare yourselves to listen to some off-hand remarks . . . As soon as your mistakes are mentioned, you shouldn't be frightened out of your wits, as though people were going to talk about you for years on end. I can't go on all that long. It depends on how you go about correcting your errors . . .

Comrades who have committed mistakes must prepare to listen quite a lot . . . All they have to do is observe these few points, and I think they can definitely reform . . . If they aren't prepared to listen, if they aren't sincere, then it will be very difficult.[49]

But we see Mao at his most acerbic in his written exchange with Politburo member and long-time associate Chang Wen-t'ien who was attacked and then was purged by Mao at the July Lushan meetings. On 2 August Mao wrote to Chang after he had fallen seriously ill following the meetings:

You are getting the consequences of your own doings. Whom can you blame? In my opinion, you have relapsed into your old illness . . . Now you are having spells of cold and fever again. A scholar composed a poem on malaria as follows: "[Mao quotes at length from a poem graphically describing the pain of malaria – ed.]" Comrade, is it not like this? If so, then that is fine. One like you needs to go through a serious illness.[50]

Mao then went on to advise Chang to read a particular essay, Mei

[47] Mao Tse-tung, "Talk at an Enlarged Central Work Conference" (30 January, 1962), in Schram, Unrehearsed, p. 166.   [48] Ibid., p. 186.
[49] Mao Tse-tung, "Speech at the Enlarged Session of the Military Affairs Committee and the External Affairs Conference" (11 September, 1959), translated in Schram, Unrehearsed, pp. 152–3.
[50] Mao Tse-tung's Letter to Chang Wen-t'ien (2 August, 1959), in The Case of P'eng Teh-huai, 1959–1968, (Hong Kong: Union Research Institute, 1968), p. 315.

Cheng's "Chi Fa," calling it indeed a wonderful literary piece. Mao concluded his sharply worded, cruel missive:

What is to be done now? Comrade, I would like to give you a piece of advice: "Thoroughly rectify yourself." Since you [profess to] respect me, have phoned me several times, and have wanted to come to my place for a talk, I am willing to talk to you. But I am busy these days. Please wait for some time. I am writing you this letter to express my sentiments.[51]

Fortuitously, Chang Wen-t'ien's 18 August reply to this barrage is available.

Comrade Tse-tung, I have just undergone a major operation which should be beneficial to my health. I sincerely thank you and other comrades of the Central Committee for your help. I must sever my relations with my reactionary self of yesterday. Today I read your comments on Mei Cheng's essay, "Chi Fa," on machine guns, and other subjects, and was greatly moved . . . I hope to receive more instructions from you.[52]

Mao's reaction to this letter is also pertinent. He warmly welcomed it, and ordered 160 copies distributed to Central Committee members. As if in anticipation of his subsequent treatment, Chang Wen-t'ien had described Mao as "very brilliant and very strong-handed in rectifying people like Stalin in his late years."[53] It seems to have been a widely shared view among his colleagues.

Control of Communications, Personnel and Military Forces. One underlying theme of his essay is that a precondition for Mao's effectiveness as ruler of China was his dominance of the Politburo. But we have not yet identified the real ingredients of his power in the policy process. Since the Chinese system was not highly institutionalized, it cannot be said Mao's power flowed automatically from the positions he held. There was a contingent, almost tenuous quality to his power. In the final analysis, his ability to pursue his strategies, to bring his forceful personality to bear, and to control certain critical issues depended upon his control over the communication process through which policy was formulated, over the appointment

[51] *Ibid.*, p. 316.
[52] "Comment on Chang Wen-t'ien's Letter" (18 August, 1959), translated in JPRS, *Miscellany*, Part I, p. 186.
[53] Quoted in *The Case of P'eng Teh-huai*, p. 36.

103

process to high office, and over the disposition of military forces. Let us therefore provide a few of the rare glimpses of Mao employing these three raw sources of his power. The chairman provided one such moment of illumination when he revealed how he set about to weaken Lin Piao's position in 1970–71:

> I adopted three methods. One was to throw stones [disseminating information – ed.], one was to mix in sand [changing personnel – ed.] and the third was to dig up the cornerstone [changing troop assignments – ed]. I criticized the material Ch'en Po-ta had used to deceive people, and I commented on reports of the 38th Army and of the Tsinan Military District. I also made critical comments on a document of the long forum of the Military Affairs Committee, which didn't criticize Ch'en at all. My method was to get hold of these stones and make critical comments, and then let everyone discuss them – this was throwing stones. When soil is too tightly packed, it can not breathe, but if a little sand is mixed in, then it can breathe. The staff of the Military Affairs Committee was too uniform in composition and needed new people mixed in. This called for mixing in sand. Reorganizing the Peking Military Region is called digging up the cornerstone.[54]

Military Command. On more than one occasion, Mao ordered troop redeployment as a preliminary step in a power struggle.[55] The military contained units with different sets of loyalties, and as Mao sought to weaken one subordinate and strengthen another, he transferred units loyal to his ally to key strategic points, and ordered the troops of his opponent away from crucial locales. In this game, military occupancy of Peking was particularly significant. On several occasions, Mao shuffled the Peking garrison command prior to a major showdown. For example, he began to deprive Lin Piao of his strength by ordering the 38th Division, crack troops highly loyal to Lin, out of Peking at an early stage in the struggle, before Lin was fully aware of Mao's

---

[54] "Summary of Chairman Mao's Talks to Local Comrades During his Inspection Tour" (August–September 1971), in Kau (ed.), *Lin Piao*, p. xxiv.

[55] This is effectively stressed in Michael Pillsbury," Patterns of Chinese power struggles: three models," prepared for University Seminar on Modern China, Columbia University, New York City, 27 March, 1974. For the chain-of-command which enabled Mao to command forces, see Harvey Nelson, "Military forces in the Cultural Revolution," *CQ*, No. 51 (July–September 1972), pp. 444–74. For an assertion that Mao could circumvent the normal chain-of-command and directly order combat units to undertake actions, see a presumably informed article by a CIA analyst: Roger Brown, "Chinese politics and American policy," *Foreign Policy*, No. 23 (Summer 1976), pp. 3–23.

intent against him.[56] Throughout Mao's rule, Chinese elite politics were more praetorian than the external image would lead observers to believe. Mao accrued power from his ability to manipulate and use the tensions within the military.

Control over Words. In the delicate balancing act, he also secured leverage over the military through his command over words.[57] Throughout Chinese history, words and arms – *wen* and *wu* – have been counterposed as approaches to rule. There exists an eternal contest for power, according to Chinese historiography, between men of letters and men of arms. Of necessity, periods of disunity were ended and new dynasties were established by men of arms, who then in the great dynasties were succeeded by bearers of the literate culture. Just as Mao pitted his subordinates against each other, so too he sought to dominate both realms of *wen* and *wu* by retaining and using each to control the other.

Several instances exist not only of Mao's personal attention to the writing of authoritative *People's Daily* editorials, but also his selecting the slogans which pervaded the media and wall space throughout China. These slogans encapsulated complex policies and set the tone for the politics of the entire nation. They provided the cues upon which millions judged how to behave politically, and changes in slogans communicated to the masses that a shift in the political winds had occurred. Mao revealed his attentiveness to slogans in various discussions. For example, in 1958, Mao disclosed the care with which he had penned the major Great Leap slogan "Go all out, aim high, and achieve more, better, faster, and more economical results."[58] He disclosed that he had considered saying "go out" instead of "go all out," but found the latter formulation preferable. He wished to stimulate the masses to the utmost, he admitted. He recognized that the slogan was not easily understood by foreigners, and as a result, he had contemplated altering it. But in retrospect, he was pleased with the untampered slogan.

In December 1958 Mao expressed reservations about another

---

[56] Kau (ed.), *Lin Piao*, p. xxiv.
[57] For one explanation for the importance of words in Chinese politics, see Richard Solomon, *A Revolution is not a Dinner Party* (New York: Doubleday, 1975), Ch. 3.
[58] Mao Tse-tung, "Speeches at the Second Session of the Eighth Party Congress" (23 May, 1958), JPRS, *Miscellany*, Part I, p. 117.

Great Leap slogan: "Basically transform the entire country after three years of hard struggle."[59] Mao recalled that the slogan had been adopted in January, with its primary emphasis on the rural transformation. But by December the chairman was chagrined to find that the qualifying word "basically" had been dropped from the slogan and that it was being applied everywhere with this alteration. He sensed that the slogan should be modified, retaining the optimism of the initial call but introducing a longer time span for achieving a thorough transformation. Mao called for a discussion as to what the appropriate slogan should be.

Clearly Mao did not authorize every slogan, and towards the end of his life, his slogans were sometimes distorted, not well disseminated, or even forged. More broadly, by the 1960s he felt the cultural bureaucracy was unresponsive to him, and one major reason why he launched the Cultural Revolution was to reassert his control over the "word" and its disseminating agencies. He turned to his inner court, particularly his wife, to perform the monitoring task, but it seems likely Chiang Ch'ing abused Mao's trust.

Control over the Communication Process. Mao also specified the process through which many key policies were to be formulated. He scanned the nation continually for places which had solved vexing problems in ways that evidenced Mao's "spirit." He read written reports and heard oral reports by his subordinates. Whenever he came across a description of a unit or a report which he particularly liked, he ordered its distribution. Hence, the torrent of words which flowed from his office was full of injunctions such as these:

Several documents should be printed, including the statements of Wang Ming and K'u Hsi-ming and the letters of a branch secretary in Tientsin and the party committee secretary of Nanking University.[60]

The commerce work of Hsin-hui County, Kwangtung, is well handled. An on-the-spot meeting [bringing people from many places to examine its accomplishments – ed.] should be held there.[61]

I recommend printing and distributing the [attached] article [on the

[59] Mao Tse-tung, "Speech at the Sixth Plenum of the Eighth Central Committee" (19 December, 1958), in *ibid.,* p. 141.
[60] Mao Tse-tung, "Speech at the Conference of Heads of Delegations to the Second Session of the Eighth Party Congress" (18 May, 1958), in *ibid.,* p. 121.
[61] *Ibid.,* p. 123.

situation in the Physics Department at Tsinghua University] to the party committees of all universities, special schools, and scientific research organs for their perusal . . . It should also be distributed to the party committees and general branches of literary and art organizations, newspapers, periodicals, and publishing organs for their study and discussion. Please consider and decide. [62]

The very dissemination of such materials was a way to influence the policy process, for the small study groups in each unit then had to examine whether their approach to problems coincided with the methods described in the document.

Even more exacting, on many occasions Mao spelled out in elaborate detail the process through which a new policy was to be transmitted to the populace. Here is how Mao ordered the news to be handled concerning his resignation as chairman of the People's Republic in 1958:

A formal resolution must be passed . . . Within three days [of its passage] the provinces should hold a telephone conference to notify the regions, counties, and people's communes. The official notice should be published [in the open media] three days later. This way, lower level officials will have already been forewarned.[63]

In addition, he indicated precisely how policy evaluations were to be carried out. The most concrete illustration of Mao's operating style comes from a March 1959 inner-Party bulletin he penned at a time when he and his colleagues were engrossed in modifying the recently formed Communes.[64] Mao's instruction of 9 March went to all provincial first Party secretaries, whom he instructed immediately to convene a conference of cadres from the six administrative levels within the province. He specified the major theme (a discussion of the People's Communes), the length (about 10 days), its format (the first secretary was to give the summing-up speech to explain in depth the various problems confronting the Communes), and some of the documents to be distributed at the provincial gathering (to be provided by the Central Committee and delivered by special aeroplane). Mao

[62] "Speech at the Sixth Plenum," in ibid., p. 149.
[63] Ibid., p. 148.
[64] Mao Tse-tung, "Inner Party Correspondence," (9 March, 1959), in ibid., pp. 164–5. Another such example is Mao Tse-tung, "Letter of Instruction on the Question of Agricultural Mechanization," in ibid., JPRS, Miscellany, Part II, pp. 373–4.

notified the secretaries that he required them to assemble in Shanghai on 25 March for an expanded Politburo meeting. Since only 16 days intervened, Mao told them to plan to adjourn their provincial gatherings by 22 March. Simultaneously with the Shanghai meeting, a series of meetings should be held at the county level, convened by those cadres who attended the 10-day provincial gathering. The chairman instructed that these county meetings should have one to two thousand people in attendance and last from seven to 10 days, and they should be followed by Commune and brigade meetings.

The chairman also supervised the process of drafting many key documents. For example, the origins of several programmatic statements are now known: the National Agricultural Development Programme,"[65] the "Sixty Points on Work Methods" and the "Former Ten Points," to mention only a few. Mao's role was crucial in all of these. Typically he appointed a drafting group to submit a document to him for his editing and approval, or he presided over a meeting which enumerated the points contained in the draft document.[66] Frequently the document would then be submitted to a large conference convened by the Central Committee for discussion and possible revision, with Mao often specifying who should attend the conference. This administrative style gave Mao an important though not necessarily controlling voice in setting the agenda of issues to which the major political figures had to devote their attention. In effect, Mao played a major role in budgeting the time of his associates.

Personnel Appointments. We do not know precisely how or to what extent the chairman controlled personnel assignments. Could he select, for example, division commanders in the PLA or vice-governors in the provinces? If so, how many positions did he keep under his personal purview, and who collected the dossiers on which he based his decisions? Answers to these questions are not known, but the scanty evidence is that he kept close tabs on personnel. He knew about such matters as the

[65] This is well traced in Parris Chang, *Power and Policy in China* (University Park: Pennsylvania State Press, 1975), Ch. 1.
[66] January 1962 talk in Schram, *Unrehearsed*, p. 158. See also Mao Tse-tung, "Introduction to Sixty Points on Work Methods" (31 January, 1958), translated in Jerome Ch'en, *Mao Papers* (London: Oxford Press, 1970), pp. 57–8.

state of his comrades' health and the political inclinations of their children. His Politburo speeches contain frequent, biting remarks about the foibles of his associates, about their work style, and what the chairman believed they thought of him. One senses not only a reliance upon information filtered to him through the CCP Organization Department but possibly upon information derived from secret surveillance and upon confidential disclosures by some comrades about the behaviour of others.

Mao also monitored the cases of purges. He set up special investigation committees to trace the sources of their errors, and he helped determine their subsequent fate.

Yet, one senses the limits to Mao's control over personnel as well. It took him time, effort and strategy to remove rivals. He had to secure support for his nominees to new positions. Ultimately, he had to pick his allies where he could find them, and they may not always have been to his liking.

THE EXTENT OF MAO'S RULE

China specialists have debated widely among themselves precisely how Mao's rule should be characterized. Some have suggested that the political system from 1949 to Mao's death was essentially "pluralistic," with various autonomous, bureaucratic, factional and social groupings competing for influence. Policies were the result of negotiation and compromise; budget allocations involved bargaining among contesting sectors. In this schema, in addition to being the unifying symbol of the regime, Mao's primary role was to reconcile and balance interests. His capacity to strike compromises that coincided with his value preferences fluctuated with his own changing power position. Occasionally, his power and circumstances permitted him to sponsor major new programmes.

Some China specialists, influenced by the descriptions of power struggles emanating from Peking, seem almost to suggest Mao never was in power. That is, until the mid-1950s, power resided in the regions, and from the mid-1950s on, Mao was continually shunted aside and manipulated by ambitious, devious lieutenants. First Liu Shao-ch'i usurped power, then Lin

Piao and Ch'en Po-ta brought on the excesses of the Cultural Revolution, and finally the dying chairman was unable to control his shrewish wife. Poor old Mao was valiantly trying to implement his programmes of social justice and economic development, but he could never fight his way to the top!

Clearly, a portrayal of Chinese politics that places Mao in a weak position or makes bargaining central to a "pluralistic" policy process has a lot to explain away. The available evidence convincingly demonstrates that the collectivization of agriculture in July 1955, the "Hundred Flowers" episode of May 1957, the unleashing of the Red Guards in August 1966, and the invitation to President Nixon in 1970, to name some of the major initiatives, would not have occurred without Mao's power and resolve. More broadly, the commitment to reducing urban-rural inequities, the ceaseless efforts to create a responsive bureaucracy, and the boldly experimental policies in the educational and public health realms can be clearly traced to Mao's persistence and will. And we have already noted the considerable success which Mao encountered in creating a dialectical approach to development and in fostering analytical categories and modes of political discourse that permeated the entire system during his lifetime. A grave danger exists that analysts may give undue weight to his last few years in office, when he was but a shadow of his former self, and neglect the decisive impact he had on his nation's earlier political course.

Other analysts have sketched a policy process which Mao clearly dominated. All power flowed from him; all subordinates sought to obey his fickle and vague desires, competing among themselves to prove their loyalty to him. To these observers, Mao was a dictator. But this view also has its troubles, and not just with Mao's apparent inability to control rampant factional strife in his last years and with his being the alleged target of an assassination attempt by Lin Piao. For, as this essay has shown, Mao had to manoeuvre constantly to enforce his will. His resources were limited. He did have domestic adversaries who had their own power to thwart Mao's designs.

So where does the truth rest? Was Mao one politician in a pack, a monarch among barons, a figure-head, a dictator, or a captive of others? While each caricature contains an element of

110

truth, the best answer seems to be that no static assessment of Mao's power can be accurate, for his roles changed significantly over time, as did the entire system. At a minimum and to over-simplify, one can say the system and Mao's position in it passed through five stages. To trace this evolution, it pays to conceive of the Chinese political order during Mao's era as consisting of several types of policy-making arenas: (1) Mao's arena, which was not highly institutionalized, but consisted of the mech-anisms available to him to communicate and obtain his will – meetings he convened, reports he read and approved, directives he gave through the Military Affairs Commission, directives he gave while on trips, comments he issued to the press, and so on; (2) policy-specifying bodies led by Mao's associates, including the State Council under Chou En-lai, the Military Affairs Commission under Lin Piao, and the Cultural Revolution Group under Ch'en Po-ta; (3) the vast Party, govern-ment and army bureaucratic hierarchies, with their functional subdivisions and their various administrative levels; (4) the *ad hoc* campaign organizations, composed of officials from the bureaucracies who were seconded to the temporary campaign staffs to mobilize the populace for specific objectives (the campaign staffs could be variously commanded directly by Mao, by one of the policy-specifying bodies, or by a bureau-cratic agency itself); and (5) local communities – factories, schools, urban neighbourhoods, commercial enterprises, Communes, hospitals and so on. The evolution of the system can be described in terms of the waxing and waning authority of each arena, of the changing agenda of decisions confronting the leaders in each arena, and the changing relationships between arenas.

Establishing a New Order, 1949–55. The dominant policy-making arenas during this era were Mao and his top policy-specifiers in Peking, the six powerful regional organizations into which the nation's territory had been grouped, and the *ad hoc* campaigns which swept the country during those early years: land reform, the resist-America aid-Korea campaign, "Three-Anti, Five-Anti" campaigns, the patriotic health cam-paign, the local election campaign and the related national census, the campaign for the new marriage law and numerous

111

others. Remarkably little is known about Mao's precise power and interventions during those years, but a great deal of authority resided at the regional levels. Mao and such principal Peking associates as Chou En-lai and Liu Shao-ch'i were creating a viable central apparatus. It took them a while to structure an obedient, orderly bureaucratic apparatus, and state power did not yet extend on a sustained basis into all local institutions, particularly into villages. This was an era of consolidating power and creating viable institutions. Mao sought to rally the populace around his ideology, which was propagated with great intensity, and he launched several of the major campaigns. But in the main, Mao was accruing power for the eventual push towards collectivization of agriculture and nationalization of industrial and commercial enterprises; the accrual was completed with the dismantling of the regional agencies, and the creation of stronger central Party and government organs in 1954–55.

Mao in Command, 1955–59. Historians are likely to record this era as the halcyon years of Mao's reign in terms of his power and the efficacy of his rule. Except for the 1957 contraction, an increasing state budget yielded sufficient revenues to undertake new economic development and welfare programmes. The expansion made the competition for scarce resources less intense, as everyone could get a piece of the growing pie. Having proven his insight by hastening collectivization in 1955, most of his associates were reluctant to defy his policy recommendations until the failure of the Great Leap. To be sure, Mao complained that he did not obtain a wide range of choices from his economic specialists, and as any strong leader, he encountered limited opposition from his associates on such policies of his as encouraging open criticism of the Party in 1957, or his embarking on the Leap. But he prevailed with power to spare.

The bureaucracies were in place, centralized planning got underway, and a state statistical network was grinding out reliable data on which Mao's associates and their bureaucratic subordinates made informed decisions. Seeking to bar overreliance on bureaucratic modes of policy implementation, Mao successfully balanced the enhanced strength of the bureaucracies by continually launching campaigns in various realms.

112

The search for proper forms of local institutions continued, but the periodic reorganization of basic level institutions in effect prevented routinization at the grass roots. Mao obtained a flood of reports from below on model units worthy of emulation, which he then publicized in books and articles.

To be sure, elements of the system disturbed him, particularly the potential of the bureaucracy turning into an agency of oppression. Certain substantive problems also concerned him, particularly lagging agricultural production and the slowness with which traditional values were being transformed. But on the whole, so satisfied was Mao with the overall performance of these years that he contemplated his succession with equanimity and he willingly reduced the level of his everyday involvement in the policy process.

A Weakened Monarchy, 1960–65. The failure of the Great Leap, the creation of viable local institutions, and the emergence of an entrenched bureaucracy rather swiftly altered the political landscape. The deep economic depression eroded the authority of the regime *vis-à-vis* the populace, damaged Mao's standing among his colleagues, and temporarily deprived him of some of his self-confidence. His associates from Yenan days began to move away from him, in part because of his Great Leap blunders, in part because his vindictive behaviour at Lushan revealed his ugly side. Further, as Mao aged, the issue of succession increasingly came to the fore, and his associates began to scurry and to build independent bases of power that would provide them the capacity to survive after the chairman's death. In addition, a natural, evolutionary process occurred whereby his associates gradually became immersed in the problems, mores and causes of the bureaucracies over which they presided. To some extent, Mao's erstwhile colleagues began to embody the interests of their bureaucratic constituencies. It was a slow, almost indiscernible process, but it meant that the links between Mao and his policy-specifiers weakened, while the ties between them and the bureaucratic arenas became stronger.

In addition, the Great Leap impressed upon bureaucrats the limited utility, indeed the dangers of, campaigns. It also may have taught them political skills for preventing, constricting and subverting campaigns. As Mao concluded from the results of his effort to launch the Socialist Education Campaign in 1963–64, a much greater effort was needed on his part to take issues away from regular bureaucratics of implementation and make them the object of campaigns.

But perhaps most significantly, the entire political system was becoming institutionalized. Local political institutions – Communes, brigades, and teams in the countryside, wards, neighbourhoods, and lanes in the city – had jelled. Predictable career patterns had taken shape. The post-Leap era witnessed a significant return to the economic organizations, planning practices, and budgeting procedures of the 1950s. Life was settling down. And with it, the revolutionaries who throughout the 1950s had been exhilarated by the challenge of remoulding a society and creating a new political order now found themselves administering what they had wrought. They had to live within the confines which they had erected for others. And unlike the 1950s, a shrinking budget brought on painful choices over which programmes to reduce, and which to eliminate. The competition over scarce resources intensified.

All this was particularly frustrating for Mao, who misinterpreted the root cause of his decreasing power. He attributed the loss to the sabotage of his colleagues, most of whom loyally tried to reconcile his commands with their own bureaucratic imperatives. In fact, the chairman's power was being curtailed through the emergence of a stable society.

Fostering a Revolution from Above, 1966–69. Disturbed that the stable social order would eventually yield a new, oppressive ruling class and perturbed by the seeming disloyalty of many of his associates (a perception fed by their rivals), Mao sought to dismantle the very political order which he had helped create. At the age of 72, he tried to orchestrate an attack on the system: the Cultural Revolution. In rapid though not well-planned sequence, and with considerable assistance, Mao undertook these measures: (1) the purge of many policy-making associates and the elimination of several policy-specifying bodies, particularly the Party secretariat; (2) the re-invigoration of the campaign arena through the tapping of generational tensions and the mobilization of youths into the Red Guards; (3) the use of the Red Guards to disrupt bureaucratic routine and literally drag

114

office-holders into the streets (4) reluctantly, the use of the army to undertake the necessary unifying and co-ordinating functions previously performed by the Party and government; and (5) the creation of more democratic local communities to be obtained through the promotion into local leadership positions of younger cadres who demonstrated their understanding of and loyalty to Mao through the course of the Cultural Revolution. In a way, Mao attempted to recapture portions of the system of the CCP's guerrilla days and the early 1950s: Mao, loyal associates unencumbered by ties to the bureaucracy, and campaign head-quarters scattered over the country directing a political move-ment.

For reasons too complex to summarize here, Mao failed even to approximate his goal. The Red Guards escaped his control. Unbridled power struggles occurred at each level of the hier-archy. And the nation approached a state of civil war. Aware of the internal chaos, Mao imposed order by dispatching troops to the centres of rebellion and by turning to the bureaucracies to once again establish routines.

Dying Embers: The End of an Era, 1969–76. While Mao was able to reimpose domestic tranquillity, at the age of 76 and suffering from a debilitating illness, he was unable decisively to shape the system which emerged after the Cultural Revolution. His last successful political manoeuvre, the elimination of Lin, gained temporary policy advantages but did not enable him to remould the system. Mao was an ageing monarch. Chou En-lai, the chief minister to whom he turned in 1970, soon became afflicted with cancer. And all the others saw what loomed ahead and plotted. The political system after the Cultural Revolution was clearly a temporary arrangement, its end to be marked by the death of Mao.

Under these uncertain conditions, none the less, the bureau-cracies reconstituted themselves with alacrity. The leadership of local communities was often bifurcated, with a cleavage be-tween the older cadres and the younger ones who arose during the Cultural Revolution. None the less, these local institutions also for the most part functioned well, the one exception being in the educational sphere, where the Cultural Revolution left schools and universities in political shambles. Real power

115

during 1969–76 gravitated towards the economic bureaucracies and local communities. Court politics in Peking determined the content of the media and Western headlines focused on the top, but the real story was elsewhere: in the planning apparatus, the provinces, factories and farms.

In the capital, the weakening Mao proved unable to check factional strife among his associates. Mao could not nor did he wish to totally eliminate the "inner court" whom he had used to direct the Cultural Revolution. They gave him uncomfortable leverage over those associates such as Teng Hsiao-p'ing who were restored to high office. The "inner court" and the "outer court" – the top leaders of the Party, army and government – girded for their inevitable clash, and sought to initiate and bend such campaigns as "Criticism of Lin, Criticism of Confucius" to their advantage.

Mao's ebbing strength depended upon the loyalty of the military to their dying chief. After Lin's fall, none moved precipitously in support of the various civilian rivals to the throne. The military chose not to force Teng Hsiao-p'ing upon the recalcitrant chairman after Chou En-lai's death. They allowed him to die quietly, and then they moved swiftly in support of Hua Kuo-feng against the "inner court." Mao had ruled, and then he did not rule but reigned. He had enjoyed the ultimate power to reshape the destiny of his nation and then suffered the total frustration of physical enfeeblement while retaining the mental acuity to see what had befallen him. This complex politician who embodied with such intensity so many conflicting qualities had undergone a full range of human experience.

4

THE SOLDIER

Jacques Guillermaz

With the passing of time, Mao Tse-tung's image as a military thinker and strategist is tending to fade. China has known peace since 1949, excluding the Korean War which ended in 1953, and despite the short-lived military operations on the Indian frontier in 1962 and a few incidents on the Ussuri in 1969. Socialist construction and its political upheavals have overshadowed the purely military problems which have for the most part been relegated to the anonymity of the Military Committee and the General Staff. In the world at large, the era of revolutionary wars is over. Only very rarely, at the time of famous purges such as those of Lin Piao, P'eng Teh-huai and Teng Hsiao-p'ing, is the "military line of Chairman Mao" referred to, or a few episodes from earlier wars recalled or re-written.

The death of Mao leads quite naturally to an evaluation of his work in two areas: that of military thought and the conduct of operations, including, in the period after 1949, national defence. Whilst such an evaluation is necessary, it must also be provisional, since the Chinese Communist Party's military history has so far been written only in a fragmentary and highly unscientific way. We do have from Mao himself an important collection of military writings, drawn from the four official volumes of his work, as well as a few thoughts and sallies drawn from texts generated by the Cultural Revolution. Beyond this we must make do with such anecdotal collections as "A Single Spark Can Start a Prairie Fire" and with memoirs and narratives which are too schematic and embellished to lend themselves to satisfactory analysis. Moreover, Mao appears to be the only military writer of the period. Chu Teh, the commander-in-chief of the Red Army, P'eng Teh-huai, his second-in-command, and all the operational commanders seem to have confined their writings to the technical and tactical spheres. Finally, we must distinguish between the various periods of Mao's military history. Thus his responsibilities varied considerably during the period of the Second Civil War from 1927–34, whilst they were almost consistently absolute after the Tsunyi Conference of January 1935. The future will one day unravel reality from fiction. For the moment we have necessarily to confine ourselves for the most part to official accounts of events, without however abandoning the task of occasionally adjusting their meaning and even correcting their content.

I shall begin by summarizing the development of Mao's military thinking, relating it to the history of the Party. I shall then investigate the essential points (both theory and practice) in a few chosen areas: the philosophy of war, strategy, tactics, organization and logistics, moral strength and the importance of man, the ties between the armed forces and society, the value of Mao's military doctrines and of his military experience outside China, in order to arrive at an overall appraisal.

MAO AND THE MILITARY HISTORY OF THE PARTY

From birth Mao had displayed a strong, fighting temperament and there are numerous anecdotes which confirm this character trait as perceptible from adolescence onwards. All Chinese schoolchildren of his age read *The Romance of the Three Kingdoms* or *Water Margin*. Few of them, however, were so deeply influenced that they actually sought in these books models for their youthful ambitions. Mao was imbued with the spirit of rebellion at a very early stage, and was always marked by it. However, rather paradoxically, unlike many young men of his generation who, from Yen Fu to Lu Hsün and Chiang Kai-shek, must have seen in the modern army and navy the means of saving China and wished to make a short- or long-term career in these services, Mao was not attracted by this profession. In this regard the influence of his father, a former soldier, had if anything a negative effect on him. Only a burst of revolutionary enthusiasm led him to join a regiment at Wuhan in 1911 at the fall of the Empire. He spent six months there, more occupied in following political events in the newspapers than in gaining a proper military training, and later he hardly mentioned this brief experience. He was then 18. Another 15 or 16 years were to pass before circumstances led him to discover personally and at first hand the importance of armed action and to acquire a taste for it. In September 1974 he said to President Georges Pompidou of France: "Circumstances forced me on to the battlefield since it was necessary to wage war." During the Northern Expedition (1926–27) his attention was occupied by the training of peasant cadres and, if one consults his "Report on an Investigation of the Peasant Movement in Hunan," written at the beginning of 1927, one might conclude that he considered the conquest of power as attainable primarily through widespread peasant uprisings.

Then came the break between the Kuomintang and the Chinese Communist Party in 1927. The latter changed its urban and working class character to become a rural and peasant Party, though its leadership always remained in the hands of the intellectuals. At the same time the failure of the Nanch'ang Uprising demonstrated that, given the power of the Nationalist armies, only military action was capable of ensuring the success and development of the revolution. The way lay open for a "Revolutionary War" which Mao was gradually to discover, then systematize and much later set up as a universal model. The Autumn Harvest Uprising in September 1927 was, as is well known, the starting point of his military experience. Badly prepared, badly organized, badly led on the field, it ended in pathetic defeat. Mao reassembled the remaining handful of insurgents at the village of Sanwan in the Yunghsin district of Hunan, at the foot of the Chingkangshan. He had at this time only a few hundred poorly armed men. It was from this slender capital that he was to build the military fortune of his Party.

One year later, two fundamental texts, "Why is it that Red Political Power Can Exist in China?" (5 October, 1928) and "Struggle in the Chingkang Mountains," demonstrated the remarkable extent to which Mao had already grasped and assimilated the essential rules of warfare, adapting them in the process to local geo-political and military conditions. He was already in the process of working out the elements of a strategy, the chief characteristics of which were to create "base areas," to develop the expansion of regular armies, and to work with and

119

organize the local populations. The mobile and flexible tactic summarized in the famous "16 character"[1] formula was already making its appearance.

Undoubtedly Mao owed much of his thinking to some of his associates with a more classical military training, notably Chu Teh, and no doubt, during the same period, the Party was trying hard to set up and ensure the survival of other bases, for example in Hupeh and Shensi. But Mao was to have the distinction of being the first to raise his experience to the level of theory. This theory inspired the Red Army in its early years, and its extension to national application during the Sino-Japanese War (1937–45) and during the Third Civil War (1946–49) established it permanently.

At the end of 1929 and the beginning of 1930 Mao, who had in the meantime been transferred to central Kiangsi, wrote two new texts of cardinal importance: "On Correcting Mistaken Ideas in the Party" (December 1929), and "A Single Spark Can Start a Prairie Fire" (January 1930). The first of these documents deals less with strategy and tactics than with the revolutionary tasks of the army and with its internal political life.[2] The second, which is now said to have been intended to combat the pessimism of Lin Piao, is essential to an understanding of Mao's strategical and tactical ideas. In the field of strategy, he was particularly concerned with placing the Red Army and its potential for development in the general political context of the period. In the field of tactics, a disagreement with the Central Committee enabled him to define and justify the limits of dispersal and concentration of troops. We shall see that the principles of guerrilla warfare are particularly well-defined in this document.

In the six years after the writing of these texts there followed the Li Li-san Offensive of 1930, the five Encirclement Campaigns (1930–34) and the Long March (1934–35). In December 1936 Mao made his voice heard in a remarkable text which is much more general than its predecessors, "Problems of Strategy in China's Revolutionary War." This major text, more than 80 pages long, was offered both as an evaluation of the experience

[1] See below, p. 135.
[2] Sometimes unofficially called "Resolution of the Kut'ien Conference" (Ninth Conference on the Organization of the Party in the Fourth Red Army).

gained during the "Second Civil War" (1927–36), and as an authoritative course, intended for the Academy of the Red Army. Before discussing this, we must remember that at this time, speaking of the purely military sphere, Mao occasionally found himself in disagreement with the Party and even relieved of his responsibilities. Against his own judgment, he took part in the disastrous offensive of the summer of 1930 against Ch'angsha, Nanch'ang and Wuhan. Then the brilliant successes achieved by the Red Army during the first three Nationalist Encirclement Campaigns (December 1930–September 1931) were to establish definitively his reputation as a strategist, even though it was Chu Teh who undertook the actual conduct of operations.

In 1932 the Party leadership began to leave the cover of Shanghai and install itself in Kiangsi. In January a "Resolution for the Victory of the Revolution Firstly in One or Several Provinces" indirectly attacked the arguments of Mao who, in August 1932, at the Ningtu Conference, found himself removed from the chairmanship of the Military Committee. The military line of his enemies in the "28 Bolsheviks" group prevailed for three years and ended in the abandonment of the red base at Kiangsi (October 1934) during the Fifth Nationalist Campaign and in the Long March. The vicissitudes of the struggle between the two military lines go beyond our terms of reference. We should however note that the outcome was fundamental since the Maoist military line, which emerged at the Tsunyi Conference (January 1935), was to ensure Mao's political victory, give an entirely new orientation to the Chinese Communist movement and, finally, much later, free it completely from Moscow before leading to the rivalry with which we are now familiar.

The Sino-Japanese War which began in July 1937 with the Marco Polo Bridge incident, placed Mao, as well as both the Chinese Communist Party and the Red Army, over which his authority was henceforth much stronger, in an entirely new position. The fire-power, mobility and manoeuvrability of the Japanese army made it invincible when facing the under-equipped, ill-trained, motley Nationalist troops whose command was far from being genuinely united despite the prestige of the commander-in-chief, Chiang Kai-shek. That remark also applies to the remainder of the communist forces of which Chu Teh was commander-in-chief, P'eng Teh-huai, second-in-command, and Yeh Chien-ying, chief of staff. Their 40,000 men were organized into three regular divisions: the 115th under Lin Piao, the 120th under Ho Lung and the 129th under Liu Po-ch'eng, to which should be added depots, rear services and training centres, comprising 30 to 50 thousand men, and a few local militias. Mao and the Revolutionary Military Committee understood immediately that there could no longer be any question, as at Kiangsi, of pitched battles in which large units (divisions and upwards), rudimentary but regular, were set against each other, alternately on the defensive and the offensive. Moreover, political objectives, namely the establishment of red bases wherever an opening appeared behind the Japanese lines, also influenced the direction of their military strategy.

From the onset of hostilities, Mao directed the action of the Red Army (now the Eighth Route Army) in accordance with two central ideas, that the war must:

(1) be a guerrilla war; and

(2) necessarily be protracted.

Without in principle abandoning conventional warfare, the emphasis was placed on the action of small units (regiments and below) concentrating independently on the weak points of the Japanese army, according to the rules which Mao recalled in his "Problems of Strategy in Guerrilla War Against Japan" (May 1938). Their correct application should lead to the destruction of a large number of small enemy units in a profusion of small engagements. Thus, gradually, the situation could be turned to the advantage of the Red Army whose adversary would lose initiative and freedom of action. When applied to the scale of the vast region of northern and central China, this guerrilla war was bound to assume such importance in the general context of the war of resistance that, despite the scattered and minor nature of the engagements, Mao considered it of strategic importance.

For geo-political reasons, notably because of China's size, its lack of vital economic centres, and the international situation, the war of resistance would inevitably be protracted. This gave rise to two needs:

(1) to set up "base areas" where the population could be mobilized and resources utilized; and

(2) gradually to change the detachments waging guerilla war into regular units which, when the time was right, could wage a mobile war.

In May 1938 Mao Tse-tung entitled a series of lectures "On Protracted War." In these he expounded his vision of the war of resistance which he divided into three stages: strategic Japanese offensive and strategic Chinese defensive, strategic consolidation of enemy positions and preparation of China for the counter-offensive, and strategic Chinese counter-offensive and strategic Japanese retreat.

Mao often referred to his conception of the future development of operations against Japan: guerrilla warfare, conventional warfare – but on the Chinese model, which he called "guerrilla warfare raised to a higher level" – then regular warfare of the general type.[3] But in reality, the struggle of the communist forces against the Japanese army became so fragmented that it is well-nigh impossible to draw up today a detailed and accurate historical account of military events.[4]

Two important engagements were fought in the autumn of 1937 when the Japanese armies marched on Shansi province. On 25 September the 115th Division, commanded by Lin Piao, fighting in co-operation with the Sixth Government Army Group at the rear of the 21st Brigade of the Fifth Japanese Division, succeeded in surprising and partially destroying it, capturing in the process about a thousand weapons. Less significant tactical victories were achieved in east Shansi a few weeks later by Liu Po-ch'eng's 129th Division and at Yenmenkuan in north Shansi by Ho Lung's 120th Division.

By the end of 1938 the Japanese had occupied the "useful" parts of China and no longer sought to extend their conquests. The government forces were established in a certain number of war zones and confined themselves to holding an almost continuous front. The Communists, for their part, strove to occupy

---

[3] "Problems of War and Strategy," SW, Vol. II, p. 227.
[4] This will be possible one day with the help of Japanese military records and what remains of the surviving communist records which have suffered in the course of several sudden removals.

the regions of northern and eastern China which the Japanese were unable to hold for lack of sufficient troops. There was a continuous development of the process of multiplication of "red bases." Although to be sure the population of these bases was mobilized, the lack of arms only just allowed for the creation of militias or self-defence groups with little potential for action. As for the relatively poorly-equipped regular forces, scattered over enormous areas, they were capable of little more than ambushes and the invader was practically free to pursue mopping up operations wherever he wished.

There was only one military event of note – the so-called "Hundred Regiments" offensive, launched during the summer of 1940. About a hundred small units attacked the Japanese lines of communication in northern China. This fruitless and short-lived operation was attributed, during the Cultural Revolution, to an initiative taken by P'eng Teh-huai without the knowledge of Mao.[5]

The Japanese surrender took place on 15 August, 1945 without enabling the Chinese to emerge from the phase of "strategic defence" defined by Mao. In fact, not until the "Third Civil War" (1946–49), fought against the Nationalist Government, did the Communists proceed to the phase of the preparation for the counter-offensive (1946–47), and then to the counter-offensive itself (1948–49) which was to end in communist victory.

In a very short time the communist military forces which, in 1947, became the People's Liberation Army (PLA), were able to proceed from the guerrilla warfare stage to operations on a grand scale carried out from the autumn of 1947, and especially in 1948 and 1949, with large units: armies, army groups and field armies. The intellectual adjustment of the commanders, general staff and junior military cadres, the organizational changes, the implementation of an overall strategy and new tactics, the use of hitherto unknown supporting arms (artillery), the setting up of the services and logistic procedures necessary to support several million fighting soldiers, were perhaps more to the credit of the military authorities than the

[5] P'eng Teh-huai had been in disgrace since the Lushan Plenum in 1959. It is inconceivable, however, that Mao, chairman of the Military Revolutionary Committee, did not at least ratify the decision.

operations themselves. Mao's part in this has not yet been determined but there is good reason to believe that it must have been considerable, not only by virtue of his office but because these changes had for a long time been included in his forecast of events. In any case, one text, "Concentrate a Superior Force to Destroy the Enemy Forces One by One" (16 September, 1946), showed the extent to which Mao perceived the effects of the change in conditions of warfare as far as fighting methods were concerned. Another still more important text "The Present Situation and Our Tasks" (25 December, 1947) recalled 10 principles of strategy either in use or to be used.

We are better acquainted with Mao's part in the general direction of operations. His role was apparent in a number of directives which he issued in the spring of 1947, primarily concerned with the north-western theatre of war (15 April, 1947), the Liaosi-Shenyang Campaign in Manchuria (September and October 1949) and the Huai-hai Campaign (11 October, 1948), not to mention those texts which testify to his precise knowledge of the general situation. Though Chu Teh remained commander-in-chief, Mao, as chairman of the Revolutionary Military Committee, was in direct communication with the commanders in the theatres of war and stipulated their geographic objectives as well as specifying the time-scale and pulse of the operations themselves. After the removal and death of Lin Piao in September 1971, the official publications emphasized his faint-heartedness and lack of foresight, notably during the Manchurian campaign.[6] Only the military genius of Mao could, it was said, rectify in time some major errors and ensure a victory which was, at all events, overwhelming.

The establishment of the People's Republic of China in 1949 had the effect of reversing the problems of the Party. At the political, economic and social levels it was no longer a question of destruction, but of construction, or reconstruction. At the military level it was no longer a question of gaining power by arms, taking the bitter path of civil war, but of building up a powerful national defence capable of dealing with formidable threats from outside. But even in this entirely new situation Mao

[6] See in particular Peking Review, No. 39 (1974), p. 33, and Peking Review, No. 6 (1974), pp. 14–16.

was unable to divorce his military thought from his own experience and tradition. Moreover the weakness of China and its army in terms of modern equipment, its technical backwardness compared with its potential enemies, tended to recall the situation of the Chinese Communist Party in relation to Japan in the 1937–45 war. For a few years the requirements of the Korean War and the influence which the Soviets exerted in the military sphere as in others, gave rise to a tendency towards "professionalization," towards the development of conventional armed forces copied from the Russian model. P'eng Teh-huai, minister of National Defence from 1954 to 1959, was the main advocate of this line which was followed until 1959. But already, in 1956, Mao's traditional military thinking reappeared. It re-emerged in 1965, just before the Cultural Revolution, in a few famous texts which have never been repudiated, despite the disgrace of their authors: Lin Piao's "Long live the victory of the people's war" and Ho Lung's "The democratic tradition of the People's Liberation Army of China." However, in the nuclear age it was no longer equal to the task of inspiring all Chinese military policies by itself alone. The combination of a people's war waged above as well as below in the spirit of Yénan, a classical war waged on given axes by conventional forces, and eventually a nuclear and thermo-nuclear war, endow the Chinese military doctrine of today with an orginality for which Mao is in large part responsible.

MAO'S MILITARY DOCTRINE

There is no uncertainty as to Mao's general concept of war, in view of his numerous and categorical statements. For him as for Clausewitz, whom he quotes without acknowledgment: "War is the continuation of politics." In Mao's own words: "War is politics with bloodshed."[7] For this reason it is inseparable from the history of peoples and will come to an end only when the development of human society has eliminated classes and states.

[7] "On Protracted War" (May 1938), SW, Vol. II, pp. 152–3. Stuart Schram calls attention to some interesting nuances between Mao's texts before and after 1951; see his Thought, pp. 286–7.

War is the highest form of struggle for resolving contradiction when they have developed to a certain stage between classes, nations, states, or political groups, and it has existed ever since the emergence of private property and of classes.[8]

War is therefore essentially a social phenomenon and not the expression of human nature (individual or collective hatreds). It would be impossible to rid it of its class content. On this point Mao Tse-tung breaks with the Confucian tradition, and still more with the Taoist tradition and even refuses to accept the moral and social limitations which limited ancient warfare.[9] The first consequence is that Mao is led to distinguish between "just wars" and "unjust wars." "All wars that are progressive are just, and all wars that impede progress are unjust."[10] Thus war is not always a scourge. It often contributes to the progress of societies by overthrowing the ruling classes and enabling the people to take power. The second consequence of the political nature of war is the need for a political mobilization at all levels since war is revolutionary in character. In fact the theme of mobilization of the people came to dominate all others, particularly during the War of Resistance, and took on a thousand different forms, from simple propaganda to the application of "united front" tactics.

Whatever his moral and philosophical conception of war may be, Mao is above all a strategist in the sense of general strategy, which transcends purely military action and incorporates, in the relevant place and with the same value, all those factors involved in the conduct of a war, and above all, the political economic, social and moral factors. Thus in "Problems of Strategy in China's Revolutionary War," written in 1936, Mao took great care to define the general conditions surrounding the war: the political divisions in China, the strength of the opposing government forces, the weakness of the Red Army and the control of military operations by the Chinese Communist Party which was simultaneously directing agrarian reform. Similarly, in "On Protracted War," the international and Chinese political

[8] "Problems of Strategy in China's Revolutionary War," SW, Vol. I, p. 180.
[9] "We don't need his asinine ethics" he said, quoting the conduct of Duke Hsiang during a battle in 638 B.C. "On Protracted War," SW, Vol. II, p. 166.
[10] "On Protracted War," SW, Vol. II, p. 150.

context is widely referred to. The same applies to nearly all his military writings which are rooted in their overall political and economic context. Mao thought at the level of a war leader who would combine the offices of Party chairman and head of state, as in fact he had done well before 1949.

China was naturally the prime object of his preoccupations as a strategist. War in general, the revolutionary war of class or nation, is often only mentioned by way of reference, for introductory purposes, or even as warnings. Thus in "Problems of Strategy in China's Revolutionary War" he says that the experience of the civil war in the Soviet Union should not be "mechanically applied." Initially it was not, therefore, a question of following a tradition or even of establishing a model of revolutionary conquest valid for all countries in the process of achieving national liberation. The claim to be a model came only after success had been achieved.

It should also be noted that Mao's military doctrine, whether it be concerned with strategy, tactics, or logistics, always stemmed from experience and was thereby incorporated into his philosophy of knowledge.

A person who has no opportunity to go to school can also learn warfare – he can learn through fighting in war . . . for doing is itself learning.[11]

Mao was often to return to this idea, citing himself as a case in point. In 1968 he said:

I have never attended military school. Nor have I read a book on military strategy. People say that I relied on *Romance of the Three Kingdoms* and Sun Tzu's *Art of War* for my campaigns. I said I had never read Sun Tzu's *Art of War*. Yes, I have read *Romance of the Three Kingdoms*.

. . . later [after Tsunyi] when I wrote about what I called problems of strategy I had a quick look at Sun Tzu's *Art of War*.[12]

The realities of China, the value attached to experience, and perhaps the very sketchiness of Mao's theoretical training explain the extraordinary adaptability of Maoist military thought and action to variations in the general situation. Conventional

[11] "Problems of Strategy in China's Revolutionary War," SW, Vol. I, p. 190.
[12] "Dialogues with Responsible Persons of Capital Red Guards Congress," 28 July, 1968, JPRS *Miscellany*, p. 476.

warfare, guerrilla warfare, mobile warfare and finally large-scale operations and battles, followed in succession under his command or his inspiration without apparently greatly upsetting the communist military system.

The texts and the facts indicate sufficiently clearly that the fundamental elements of Mao's strategic thinking were formed very early on, and were scarcely more than enriched by events. I intend to set out below its most important and characteristic features for the period involving the acquisition of power, from 1927 to 1949.

The revolutionary war in China could only be a people's war. The masses, therefore, had to be mobilized at all levels by means of unremitting and powerful political work, combining propaganda and social measures – primarily agrarian – capable of winning over the greatest number of them, and especially those poor peasants who formed the majority of the population. In order to achieve this, a reliable and effective political power, "a red power" led by the Communist Party, had to be set up as soon as possible at a local level, with the help of Party organizations within the army. This was a difficult task too, owing to peasant conservatism and the instability of the military situation.

In this era, any revolutionary war will definitely end in defeat if it lacks, or runs counter to, the leadership of the proletariat and the Communist Party.[13]

The proletariat is mentioned in the above quotation only on grounds of principle. On the other hand, the role of the peasantry was considerable and Mao himself made use of the significant expression "agrarian revolutionary war." It is doubly justified because military operations cannot do without the moral and material support of the peasants and because the latter provide nearly all the army's manpower.

The reason is that our strategy and tactics are based on a people's war; no army opposed to the people can use our strategy and tactics.[14]

If it is to be effective and lasting, popular support for the military must be active in "base areas" which are "small red areas" established "amidst the encirclement of the White

[13] "Problems of Strategy in China's Revolutionary War," SW. Vol. I. p. 192.
[14] "The Present Situation and Our Tasks," 25 December, 1947, SW, Vol. IV, p. 162.

regime." In the civil war just as in the anti-Japanese guerrilla war these bases provided support for military actions. Without them such actions could not be extended or prolonged and guerrilla warfare would take on an erratic, ineffective character. Communist military power on two occasions was built on these "bases," first in a few of the provinces of central China then, once again, in the whole of northern China. They were eventually to form 20 or so small communist states whose territorial unification was made possible by the Japanese surrender in 1945.

The gradual formation of a Regular Army had been since 1927 one of the principal characteristics of Mao's military thinking, though he was accused of having long given priority to guerrilla warfare.

Fourth, the existence of a regular Red Army of adequate strength is a necessary condition for the existence of Red political power. If we have local Red Guards only but no regular Red Army, then we cannot cope with the regular White forces but only with the landlord levies.[15]

Initially founded in the Kiangsi period (1927–34), this Red Army, which was to become "The chief weapon for the great revolution of the future,"[16] nearly disappeared in the Long March and saw its action overshadowed by that of the partisans who converted their detachments into regular units after the Sino-Japanese war. In the end it was these regular units, reorganized into "large units" (divisions and above) which formed the People's Liberation Army in 1947. This marked the beginning of a new chapter in Chinese military history.

With the exception of special circumstances, short periods of time or the activities of very small units, warfare had to be mobile as dictated by the Red Army's lack of manpower, armament and equipment, and the absence of a stable front. The idea was to find different expression according to the period, the situation and importance of the forces involved: mobile warfare, guerrilla warfare, or war of movement. At all events, the war of movement as described by Mao conveys a general conception of attack and includes other routine concepts: surprise, speed,

[15] "Why is it that Red Political Power Can Exist in China?", 5 October, 1928, SW, Vol. I, p. 66.
[16] "A Single Spark Can Start a Prairie Fire," 5 January, 1930, SW, Vol. I, p. 118.

flexibility, secrecy and initiative. Mobility and quickness of decision-making do not, however, preclude the preparation of carefully deliberated plans or caution in their execution. "Desperate recklessness is military short-sightedness."[17] Although mobile warfare has serious disadvantages in as far as it involves recurrent changes in the location and size of the base areas, Mao wrote of it with unqualified approval:

> Mobile warfare or positional warfare? Our answer is mobile warfare. So long as we lack a large army or reserves of ammunition, and so long as there is only a single Red Army force to do the fighting in each base area, positional warfare is generally useless to us. For us, positional warfare is generally inapplicable in attack as well as in defence.[18]

One of the best examples of Mao's hostility to positional warfare is provided by the Fifth Encirclement Campaign. We know that he opposed a semi-static defence strategy based on internal lines designed to preserve the frontiers of the red zone, as decided by the new military leaders, in favour of a mobile strategy based on external lines, which in his view should force the enemy to abandon its encirclement campaign and transfer its attention to other areas. We also know that the importance of this controversy was considerable since it finally resulted in the return of Mao to the leadership of the communist movement at Tsunyi and was to establish definitively his authority in the military field.[19]

The principal objective of war must be the destruction of the enemy's effective strength. It is not sufficient to rout the enemy or to recapture cities or regions. Mao gives two main reasons for this principle, which the best strategists in history have also subscribed to. The first is the disarray to which the enemy is reduced by the complete destruction of one of its units: "Injuring all of a man's ten fingers is not as effective as chopping off one, and routing ten enemy divisions is not as effective as annihilating one of them."[20] The other reason is the Red Army's dearth of

[17] "On Protracted War," SW, Vol. II, p. 171.
[18] "Problems of Strategy in China's Revolutionary War," SW, Vol. I, pp. 239–40.
[19] On this important question see Hu Chi-hsi, "Hua Fu, the Fifth Encirclement Campaign and the Tsunyi Conference," CQ, No. 43 (July–September 1970), pp. 31–46.
[20] "Problems of Strategy in China's Revolutionary War," SW, Vol. I, p. 248.

equipment. A rich "dragon king" and a "beggar" could not compete in a war of attrition. The destruction of enemy units makes possible the recovery of armament, munitions and equipment which could not be done if the objective were merely to put the enemy to flight:

We have a claim on the output of the arsenals of London as well as of Hanyang, and, what is more it is delivered to us by the enemy transport corps. This is the sober truth, it is not a jest.[21]

as Mao humorously put it.

It goes without saying that Mao often discusses the time-honoured laws of warfare: security, surprise, knowing your enemy, economic deployment of forces, initiative, freedom of action, etc. But these are not innovations in the art of war.

Though it is relatively easy, by means of texts and events, to follow the strategic thinking and attitudes of Mao until 1949, the same does not apply to the period between the founding of the People's Republic and his death. Thought and action were broadly merged with overall defence policy, were clouded by ideological stances of varying sincerity, had to take account of the sometimes very sharp turns in foreign policy – especially developments in Sino-Soviet relations – and finally were dominated by the nuclear hypothesis. Nevertheless, through occasional disclosures of remarks made by Mao, the texts published during the Cultural Revolution lead us a little nearer to his innermost thoughts.

The changes in Chinese defence policy have been outlined above. From the Korean War until 1959 objective constraints led China and, doubtless, Mao himself, to link China's defence policy with that of the U.S.S.R. and follow the Soviet model, though not without occasional reservations.[22] However, from 1956 Sino-Russian ideological and political relations began to deteriorate. On 20 June, 1959 the Soviets informed the Chinese of their refusal to honour the promise made on 15 October, 1957 to provide them with the necessary technical and technological

<hr>

[21] Ibid., p. 249.
[22] "We must not eat pre-cooked food. If we do we shall be defeated. We must clarify this point with our Soviet comrades." Speech at the Group Leaders' Forum of the Enlarged Meeting of the Military Affairs Committee, 28 June, 1958. In Schram, Unrehearsed, p. 129.

data to make atomic bombs. A defence policy concentrating on the concepts of independence and self-sufficiency had to be formulated. There is little doubt that Mao, who shortly before had refused any Sino-Soviet military co-operation, which he considered a form of Russian supervision, was at the root of this policy.[23]

Given the balance of military power between China and both the U.S.S.R. and the U.S., both potential enemies, this policy presupposed a general defensive attitude, a rapid build-up of adequate nuclear deterrents, an ubiquitous mobilization of the people at all levels capable of overwhelming a would-be invader and maintenance of conventional forces on the frontiers and axial routes. This general concept of defence seems logical and realistic, and it reveals the logic and realism which Mao had consistently manifested between 1927 and 1949. However, it posed, in the most serious possible way, the problem of nuclear warfare and, thereby, the views and basic attitude of Mao to this problem, in view of his near absolute power and also the ignorance of an ill-informed population largely unaware of the atomic threat.

It would appear that Mao for a long time minimized and even made light of the nuclear threat. In 1946 he declared to American journalist Anna Louise Strong:

> The atom bomb is a paper tiger which the U.S. reactionaries use to scare people. It looks terrible but in fact it isn't. Of course the atom bomb is a weapon of mass slaughter, but the outcome of the war is decided by the people not by one or two new types of weapon.[24]

In February 1957, while speaking at the Supreme State Conference, he said:

> If the imperialists insist on launching a third world war, it is certain that several hundred million more will turn to socialism, and then there will not be much room left on earth for the imperialists; it is also likely that the whole structure of imperialism will utterly collapse.[25]

[23] See especially *Khrushchev Remembers* (Boston, Toronto: Little, Brown and Company, 1970), Ch. 18.
[24] "Talk with the American Correspondent Anna Louise Strong," *SW*, Vol. IV, p. 100.
[25] "On the Correct Handling of Contradictions Among the People," in: *SR*, p. 473.

During the same year, 1957, in Moscow, Mao spoke with an even greater optimism and the famous phrase which sums up his attitude, "the East wind prevails over the West wind," appeared to incite the Soviets to adopt a more war-like policy. He made remarks to Nehru which cast doubt on the extent to which he understood the formidable effects of nuclear weapons which, in Khrushchev's phrase, make no distinction between classes.

Later on, the Sino-Soviet debate gave the Russians the opportunity to attack the Chinese and Mao over the problem of war and peace. The Chinese denied wanting to make war and their arguments – which Mao could not but sanction at the very least – can be summed up in a few sentences: China does not want nuclear war but imperialism seeks it, and it will therefore be a possibility as long as imperialism survives. If nuclear war occurs it will cause large-scale destruction, but socialism will prevail throughout the world. The threat of nuclear war should not preclude "just wars." This is a Maoist idea of long standing which has already been mentioned.

These arguments remained valid at least until Mao's death. They were reflected in the position of the Chinese Government on the problems of disarmament and in the frequent declarations which followed the success of China's own nuclear experiments from 1964 onwards.[26] These experiments came in rapid succession and Mao himself insisted on the absolute necessity and urgency of equipping his country with an adequate arsenal of nuclear weapons, ballistic missiles, miniaturized weapons, etc.[27]

Yet contrary to the official disdain which he initially expressed with regard to the role of nuclear weapons, Mao began to take the role seriously in 1958. He corrected his statements of 1946 by acknowledging that if the imperialists and reactionaries were "paper tigers" from a strategic point of view, tactically they were "living tigers, iron tigers, real tigers which can eat

[26] See especially the Chinese declaration of 31 July, 1963 and the article entitled "Problems of peace and war."
[27] It is known that China has so far conducted more than 20 nuclear and thermo-nuclear experiments since the explosion of her first atom bomb on 16 October, 1964. The first Sino-Soviet agreement on nuclear physics research dates from 1954.

people."[28] It also seems that, contrary to his official opinions, Mao regarded the threats of "imperialism" without too much anxiety. He said several times that both the socialist and Western camps feared war and that the Americans, entirely taken up with exploiting the economic advantages of their position in the world, would have nothing to gain by it.[29]

During the 1970s, the Chinese claimed to be under threat of Soviet aggression. They initiated a whole campaign of preparation for a defensive war and strove to alert the world. Perhaps one day we shall know whether the origin of this can be traced back to Mao.

Whatever Mao's statements on nuclear warfare may have been, it must be recognized that Chinese foreign policy has been in practice very moderate since the Taiwan Straits crisis of 1958, and the risks taken few in number or non-existent. This applied on the Indian frontiers in 1962 and in Vietnam after 1965. We may rest assured that Mao was, in the final analysis, the real architect of this peacetime strategy which he was to impose as the need arose – the removal from office of Chief of General Staff Lo Jui-ch'ing in 1965 being a good example – and which the Cultural Revolution, despite its radicalism, was not to modify.

During the Kiangsi period Mao, with only scant manpower at his disposal requiring very careful deployment, and in difficulties with the Central Committee over military problems, devoted himself to the tactical utilization of his units. It was then that he devised the 16 character formula which the most uncultured of his officers could remember:

> The enemy advances, we retreat;
> the enemy camps, we harass;
> the enemy tires, we attack;
> the enemy retreats, we pursue.[30]

A few years later, at the time of the Fifth Campaign, he analysed and criticized the tactics proposed by Otto Braun (alias Li Teh, alias Hua Fu), the German military adviser sent to the

[28] "Meeting of the Political Bureau at Wuch'ang on 1 December, 1958." See SW, Vol. IV, p. 99.
[29] See especially a speech delivered at the Supreme State Conference, 5 September, 1958, Wan-sui, (1969), pp. 231–2.
[30] "A Single Spark Can Start a Prairie Fire," SW, Vol. I, p. 124.

Chinese Communists by the Comintern. These consisted of surprise attacks at close range against an exposed enemy and the establishment of a network of secure blockhouses set up along the main routes leading into the heart of the red zone. On the other hand, the special conditions associated with the guerrilla warfare, which finds expression essentially on a tactical level, do not seem to have inspired Mao, who, it is true, thought that this war "has broken out of the bounds of tactics to knock at the gates of strategy . . ."[31] He referred to the subject in detail, however, during the "Third Civil War" through various texts which do not invite immediate comparison with his previous writings. The absolute necessity of having total superiority at the point of attack is the essential feature of such warfare.[32]

Since 1949 Mao does not seem to have expressed himself specifically on the problems of tactics. But the small units of the People's Liberation Army are today infinitely more complex and better equipped than in previous wars and their tactics, which conform to those of modern armies in general, doubtless go far beyond the wisdom of their creator.[33]

Was Mao a good organizer of the human and material resources necessary for war? Yes, by comparison with the frightful inefficiency of the central government. No, if his achievement is to be compared with the range and precision of the West in these matters. Human resources are the least of China's deficiencies and, except at the beginning on the Chingkangshan, in 1927, the mobilization of the masses has never posed a serious problem. At certain times, even in the midst of the anti-Japanese war, a large number of soldiers were demobilized. The originality of the communist system – and if in this regard Mao was not the initiator, he was at least one of its principal architects – lay in its organization of human resources at three levels:

---

[31] "Problems of Strategy in Guerrilla War Against Japan," SW, Vol. II, p. 80. Chu Teh, P'eng Teh-huai, Hsiao K'o and others have also written on this subject, see Gene Z. Hanrahan: Chinese Communist Guerrilla Tactics (New York: Columbia University, July 1952).

[32] See especially "Concentrate a Superior Force to Destroy the Enemy Forces One by One," SW, Vol. IV, p. 103, and "The Present Situation and Our Tasks," SW, Vol. IV, p. 161.

[33] Mao was to say in 1958: "Yet we have been training armies for eight years and have not produced even one book on combat regulation." In Schram, Unrehearsed, p. 126.

(1) regular army
(2) militias
(3) local self-defence forces.

This enabled anyone, according to their inclination, age, strength, social and family position, to find a place easily in a system which was very open and for that very reason lent itself to the ready mobilization of the masses and facilitated the building up of the army.

If the Red Army never lacked manpower, it was always terrifyingly short of arms, equipment and even supplies, from 1927 until the last major battles of the Civil War. Mao gave unremitting attention to this problem and a good many minor operations had as their objectives supply towns and second-rate enemy units, both weak and so easily disarmed. In this respect, however, Mao was no more prominent than the other leaders of the Party and was only obeying the harsh laws of necessity.

Mao's first military task was to unite and transform into a disciplined and politically educated fighting force the very diverse group who had followed him or were to join him on the Chingkangshan and later in Kiangsi. Similar tasks were to lie before him throughout his campaigns, but their underlying principles were established in 1929 at the Kut'ien Conference of which "On Correcting Mistaken Ideas in the Party" was the most important document.[34]

Yet any lasting psychological change in each combatant presupposes a certain conception of man who must be given a central position in the overall system, and the continuous guiding and corrective action of politics, that is to say of the Party within the army. Thus in the military sphere we soon come across Mao's well-known arguments on the importance of man and his almost unlimited potential provided that he remains constantly in a state of "revolutionization." In 1938 he wrote: "Weapons are an important factor in war, but not the decisive factor; it is people not things that are decisive."[35]

The importance of moral strength has certainly not escaped

---

[34] And even before 1929 for the "Three Main Rules of Discipline and Eight Points for Attention" (revised and extended in 1947), which would serve as a reference for all the Red Armies, had been drawn up in the spring of 1928.
[35] "On Protracted War," SW, Vol. II, p. 143.

the attention of military commanders either in China or in the West. However, none has expressed such absolute confidence in the voluntarism which dominates all Maoist thinking and which was precisely what the army was instructed to extol and disseminate throughout the population on the eve of the Cultural Revolution.

In the modern era at least, no one has carried the integration of the armed forces into society so far as Mao. Initially, the army as the instrument of the revolutionary movement could not fail to be linked with, and even to merge with the population which it mobilized spiritually and often materially from within. Army officers and civilian leaders were often the same men and the army could be termed the training ground for the Party and the masses. This partnership was to last for more than 20 years and created a spirit and traditions which continued after 1949; in addition, because of his early differences with the Central Committee, Mao tended to rely on the military machine and the army, which was largely his achievement since he had virtually created it in 1927 with Chu Teh, built it up again after the Long March and given it a body of theory. This is what happened in Kiangsi, at Tsunyi and on the eve of the Cultural Revolution.

Once the army had ceased to be an insurrectionary body, no longer lived amongst the population, and had undergone modernization, it moved, after 1949, towards a professionalism on the Soviet model. Still, after 1959 and especially after 1962, general political developments soon brought it into contact with a society which Mao was striving to change and for which it would serve as a model and guide until the years of the Cultural Revolution when it took over from ineffectual political, economic and even cultural institutions and hierarchies.

The army served as a model not only in the moral and ideological field (civic and revolutionary virtues such as unselfishness and a capacity for spreading Mao Tse-tung's thought and exemplifying collective life) but also in the field of organization, method and work style. The leading article in the *People's Daily* of 1 February, 1964, entitled "The whole country must learn from the People's Liberation Army," found its application in the "May 7th Directive" of 1966, which was to inspire the "May 7th Schools." The army soon dominated the nation's entire activity, for which it provided (as indeed it still does to a great extent) all the essential machinery.

In economic affairs, especially at times of major production drives, the participation of the armed forces was of great importance. This took the form of aid to agriculture, industry and transport, as well as the army's own undertakings, and also the transfer of cadres.

Finally, through its newspapers and direct intervention the army came to exert a vigorous influence on cultural change and to inspire new revolutionary themes. In the field of education it provided a model in the form of the Anti-Japanese Resistance University, founded at Yenan during the 1935–45 war.

One might have supposed in the years 1966–71 that Chinese society was undergoing a process of militarization and was moving towards a kind of military communism in which army, Party and population were intimately linked, inspired by the tradition of Yenan and thus by the thought of Mao. This vision was destined to fade as a result of the Lin Piao affair, also doubtless because it was scarcely in harmony with older Chinese traditions, and finally because it did not meet the demands of the development of modern societies. It is a fact, none the less, that it was part of Mao's most authentic politico-military thought and that its effects will remain deep-rooted and lasting.

Since 1949 the "Chinese Way" towards the conquest of power has been offered as a model to countries struggling for their national liberation and to the revolutionary movements of the Third World. A united front, leadership by (and building up of) the Party, the primary role of the peasantry, the creation of rural guerrilla bases from which regular military forces can be gradually developed, these are the principal characteristics of this "Chinese Way" in which Mao's military thinking is naturally the determining factor. In 1965 Lin Piao wrote: "Comrade Mao Tse-tung's theory of people's war ... has not only been valid for China, it is a great contribution to the revolutionary struggle of the oppressed nations and peoples throughout the world."[36] Of the whole of this theory, Lin Piao particularly emphasizes the

[36] "Long live the victory of the people's war." *Peking Review*, No. 36, 3 September, 1965, p. 23.

139

importance of establishing revolutionary bases in rural areas and of encircling towns from the surrounding countryside, and above all the popular nature of the war. Finally he does not fail to draw a strong contrast between this people's war and the bourgeois line of the Soviets whose military strategy, relying on the overwhelming might of nuclear weapons, for that very reason "demoralizes and spiritually disarms revolutionary people everywhere."

However, although Mao's revolutionary thinking broadly speaking inspired several revolutionary movements in the world, his military thinking does not seem to have been similarly applied. It had quite extensive influence in the two Vietnams and through them Cambodia and Laos. Some Maoist underground forces remained active with varying degrees of success in the Philippines, in Burma and in Malaysia. On the other hand it had little effect in Black Africa, Latin America and nearly everywhere else. Contrary to the hopes of the foreign well-wisher, China did not become for the world what Yenan was to China from 1937 to 1949. We should not be too surprised. The general conditions of the Chinese world and of the Chinese revolution are rarely encountered elsewhere. Finally, we should not forget that the Sino-Japanese War from 1937 to 1945 was the major event which enabled Mao and the Chinese Communist Party to transfer and extend the Kiangsi experience to the national dimension and, as it entailed considerable growth in the Red Army (almost defunct in 1936), put them in a position to meet and then defeat the enemy, the Kuomintang. An exactly comparable situation was unlikely to be found again except in Indochina.

As for the policy of national defence followed by China and Mao after 1949, it continued to be determined by objective factors peculiar to that country and to its international environment and could not really act as a genuine model for any other nation, even where the ideological positions were closely allied.

It is far from easy to say what historical importance will attach to Mao as a man of war. The man himself and the situation of his country defy any comparisons or parallels. Neither a Napoleon, nor a Bolivar, Mao Tse-tung is not a great military leader in the accepted sense like these earlier figures, and yet his ambition to be the architect of a new Chinese society went far beyond that of the "Libertador" who was above all concerned to liberate and unify Spanish America. As regards China between the 1920s and the 1950s, it remains, by virtue of its internal and external situation, a unique case further complicated by the weighty heritage of a totally original but long stagnant civilization.

Mao deserves credit probably above all for having a better grasp than all the other Chinese Communists of the correct role and form which military actions should assume in the revolutionary cause as a whole. Because he was less swayed by foreign teachings or influence, he had a better understanding than they of the peculiarly Chinese elements of the problem. This realism, which caused him to be accused at one point of "guerrillaism," prevented him from falling into the rash errors of Li Li-san and Wang Ming, and ensured that he continually weighed up and fully exploited military situations. He might well have adopted the aphorism of Sun Tzu: "Thus a victorious army wins its victories before seeking battle; an army destined to defeat fights in the hope of winning."[37]

This sense of what is possible, this prompt exploitation of new situations, this faculty of adapting rapidly and correctly to all aspects of strategical and tactical reality, are the chief characteristics of the wartime leader of any nation in any epoch. Even though he was not always appearing as a "god of battles" and confined himself to general directives usually drawn up at the level of Military Committees, even though he left the details of campaigns to the commanders-in-chief (most frequently Chu Teh) or to the regional commanders, Mao the military thinker also possessed all the attributes which make good generals.

It should be noted, moreover, that Mao had not only an instinct for military action, but also had such a taste for it that people have spoken of his "military romanticism"; this taste also made an epic poet of him, a rarity in China. He expressed, albeit in classic verse, the exaltation of victory:

[37] Sun Tzu: The Art of War, translated by Samuel B. Griffith (Oxford: Oxford University Press, 1963), p. 87.

141

A million courageous warriors cross the great river,
The Universe is in turmoil, we are all exalted and resolute.[38]

Though he had no real military training in either the classical or
the modern tradition, he was acquainted with China's military
past as told by its historians, and it was through these writers
that he learnt something of the great military authors such as
Sun Tzu. This knowledge exerted hardly any influence on his
theories. There could be no question of routing the enemy and
then allowing him to escape, or of resorting to stratagem and
counter-stratagem instead of combat. The enemy must be
destroyed in the open and victory carried through to the very
end. In this respect Mao is a modern, drawing inspiration from
the West.

Mao, military thinker and war leader, knew how to make
himself accessible to all. As is fitting in a revolutionary people's
war in which cadres and the rank-and-file, often uncultured
and illiterate, fight in isolation and are often left to themselves,
he used a simple language sprinkled with images, summed up
in short phrases which are easy to remember and therefore to
apply. For this very reason Mao is not a great military writer
from a literary point of view. His exposition of theory, always
related to concrete fact, is rarely thorough and systematic, his
account of military events is often over-simplified or ambiguous
and usually discourages the military historian concerned with
precision and accuracy. On the other hand, the summation of his
military thinking in a popular form contributed greatly to his
authority in China and to his prestige in the outside world.

From a military point of view Mao remains and will remain
the man of an era and of a country. His unparalleled genius
was demonstrated when he applied himself to the creation,
development and operations of the Red Army, on which he
bestowed his own discipline, spirit, and strategical and tactical
theories. He was supremely at ease in the conduct of wars which,
through lack of weapons, shortage of equipment and absence of
transport (railways, lorries), were reduced to infantry man-
oeuvres and battles, and which were more reminiscent of the

[38] "The People's Liberation Army Captures Nanking," (April 1949); in Schram,
Mao, p. 244.

wars conducted at the end of the last century than those of today. His admirable handling of the political weapon, his recourse to the masses, eventually gave him a decisive advantage over an enemy who was indifferent to the support or hostility of local populations and who waged a war in every respect different from his own.

All these factors were overtaken by the Party's accession to power, and the old problems were overshadowed by those arising from a modern policy of national defence directed against threats from abroad, a policy which required more industrially produced modern equipment. The people's war by itself can no longer provide a definitive answer to an aggressor determined to resort to strategic and tactical nuclear weapons, or even by means of conventional weapons to destroy a vulnerable economic infrastructure, or to occupy regions which, by virtue of their geographical features and distribution of population, do not lend themselves to defence by the people.

Mao quite rationally adopted a policy combining nuclear deterrents, conventional weapons and people's war. This policy, which appears to favour people's war, is directly related to Maoist military thinking. Born of objective constraints it has in fact only a transitory value until such time as China has a strike force capable of retaliation on a world scale. When this happens, China will be "sanctuarized" to the same degree as the U.S. and the U.S.S.R., and will move permanently into the general category of super-power; that is when Mao's unique military genius will no longer be seen to apply.

Fundamentally a theoretician of revolutionary war and people's war in underdeveloped countries, Mao still lives on this reputation, but it could perhaps be said that the substance of his originality and renown was lost in 1949 with his victory.

5

THE TEACHER

Enrica Collotti Pischel

The problem of education was deeply felt by Mao Tse-tung during his whole life, not only as an intellectual and political issue, but also as a personal experience. The information provided by Mao about his personal life is in the end, alas, rather scanty, in spite of the autobiography which he related to Edgar Snow and in spite of the short glances which we can cast into his world through reading and interpreting his poems.

We are, for instance, in the dark about the cultural influences which played a crucial role in the formation of his knowledge and of his extraordinary dialectical perspective. He does tell us that his mother was a Buddhist and that he was compelled to go through the texts of the Confucian tradition. Here and there he lets people know that he had more than an occasional knowledge of Spinoza, Kant, Hegel, "the ancient Greeks" and Rousseau.[1] To French visitors he liked to quote French 18th century writers, amongst them Lamettrie. We know, through documented evidence, that Russell posed problems to him which were important in his ideological development,[2] and we can resort to some witnesses, such as the brothers Hsiao,[3] to find confirmation of the influence which Rousseau had on the young Mao. All these, however, constitute scattered data and Mao never provided us anything which could be compared to an "intellectual autobiography." There is only one exception: the information concerning his experience as a pupil and as a teacher. Obviously the dialectical relationship of teacher–pupil

[1] Edgar Snow, Red Star over China (New York: Grove Press, 1968), p. 95.
[2] Schram, Thought, p. 296; Unrehearsed, p. 239.
[3] Emi Siao, Mao Tse-tung, His Childhood and Youth (Bombay: People's Publishing House, 1953); Siao Yü, Mao Tse-tung and I Were Beggars (Syracuse: Syracuse University Press, 1959).

or, if one prefers, pupil–teacher was felt by Mao as one of the most important in human life.

From the biography related to Edgar Snow in 1936 to the most recent speeches published by the Red Guards, we can notice that when Mao refers to a really personal experience it is usually an experience in which he was involved either as a pupil or as a teacher; also he tends to speak about such an experience in rather technical, properly pedagogical language. Thus we learn that his first Chinese teacher "belonged to the stern treatment school"[4] and that his father "was a severe taskmaster"[5] but a very bad "politician," because "in the end the strictness of my father defeated him. I learned to hate him and we created a real united front against him. At the same time it probably benefited me. It made me most diligent in my work . . ."[6]

Here the implications about the role of the teacher are very important and – as it always happens with Mao – dialectical and ambivalent: "diligence," the capacity for painstaking work and the will to accomplish one's job thoroughly, was always highly considered by Mao. Could it be taught by a teacher who, being "hated," could not fully perform his role? This problem was certainly not perceived by Mao when he was a pupil or a young son: it was only in 1936 that his deep "teacher's conscience" stirred him to see the development of his own personality in terms of pedagogical problems.

Of course in the story of his life we find episodes which were probably true and which marked his subsequent attitude as a teacher, such as his reading popular romances at school and "covering them up with a classic when the teacher walked past"[7]: when an old leader, he would state that a good teacher should simply allow pupils to do openly what he – both as a pupil and as a teacher – knew they always did secretly.[8] The same is true with his personal experience of the discrimination which peasant children undergo in school,[9] but also of the role which school can play in putting peasant children in touch with world problems.

But the most interesting remarks in Mao's autobiography relate to his choice of teaching as a profession: at the time of this

[4] Snow, Red Star, p. 131. [5] Ibid., p. 132. [6] Ibid., p. 133. [7] Ibid., p. 133.
[8] Schram, Unrehearsed, p. 205. [9] Snow, Red Star, pp. 137–8.

choice Mao was already a grown-up youngster, and his political development had gone through a profound, though confused, experience during the 1911 revolution and his enrolment as a soldier. If we read what he told Edgar Snow, we learn that, when demobilized in 1912, he actually did not look for a *job*, but for a *school*, which could enable him to fulfil the role for which he was longing: namely a school to teach him something which would enable him to help save China. Here again we find a statement which has two sides. Mao tells us about his problems as a young man, uncertain, confused, patriotic, wanting nothing else but to fight for a cause which was worth-while, but unable to find it. This Mao sounds much truer than the one concocted later on by those who put forward the image of the innate wisdom of a man intellectually born in 1926 as a more or less perfect Marxist. On the other hand, Mao as a teacher draws a devastating picture of the school situation in China around 1912.[10] From what he says, we understand that in 1936 he felt that creating a new type of school was an absolute essential for the Chinese people and one of the most important tasks of the revolution.

The emphasis which Mao places on the problems of schooling in framing his own personality seems to be rather exceptional if compared with other Chinese revolutionaries: actually Mao may have been led to discuss more deeply the problem of finding the school which could best suit him, because, as a son of a peasant (though a peasant who managed to become a merchant), he faced no predetermined choice as far as school was concerned. His father seems to have been uncertain whether to make him a mandarin or an accountant; for a son of literati there would have been only one possible choice: to become one of them himself, even at the price of endless unemployment, self-sacrifice and misery. Mao had to give much thought to the choice of a school, but it seems that his meditation had gone deep enough when he decided to leave the First Provincial Middle School in Changsha "to read and study alone"[11] in the Hunan provincial library – a decision which in 1964 he still recorded as one of the most important in his cultural development.[12] Actually one of the distinctive features of Mao's pedagogy is his belief that a pupil must essentially learn by himself, the teacher's role being

[10] *Ibid.*, p. 143.   [11] *Ibid.*, p. 144.   [12] Schram, *Unrehearsed*, p. 213.

primarily to show him how to learn. Mao, the revolutionary leader, would later state more precisely that man can learn only by himself, but he cannot learn if he is alone and aloof. Men can and must learn together, through social revolutionary practice. He could not of course have clearly drawn such a conclusion when he fell on the announcement of the Hunan Normal School, which – by the way a very good one – obviously suited his frame of mind. It provided a response to the problems of a man who – by now approaching 20 – had already experienced personal intellectual growth. In this development the "school problem" played a very important role.

Mao seems to have been happy, though critical, in the Hunan Normal School. All through his life he seems to have owed his classical Chinese culture, uncommon for a contemporary Chinese revolutionary, and his exceptional command of the Chinese language to this school. But he certainly owed much more to the Western philosophical culture of Yang Ch'ang-chi, his "ethics" teacher. In his personal reminiscences, Mao constantly portrays Yang as one of the few male elders whom he entirely respects and admires.[13] True, "he was an idealist": as a Marxist, Mao perceives the political limitations of Yang's idealism. Yet he praises him as a man of "high moral character," one who "tried to imbue students with the desire to become just, moral, virtuous men, useful in society"; he seems to imply that whatever the specific content of Yang's "doctrine" (which was later rejected by Mao), he satisfactorily played the moral role of a teacher towards his pupils. It is instructive to compare Mao's utterances towards his father as "teacher" and his judgment of Yang: the father was a "severe taskmaster," who did after all teach him diligence (a virtue Mao always appreciated), but "was defeated" because he made himself hated. Yang by contrast was obviously loved and accepted by Mao as a model teacher, because he showed to the young Mao the way of believing in a set of values which went beyond and above the "private contingency" of the individual.

It is difficult to say what specific ideological inheritance Mao took over from Yang: when Mao says that in 1920 he became a Marxist, he means also that he spurned (or by-passed) Yang's

[13] Snow, *Red Star*, p. 146.

idealism. Many of the ideas and ideals propounded by Yang were the very ideas which Mao later denounced as hindrances typical of Chinese bourgeois intellectuals. In 1964 Mao said that at one time he had "believed in Kant's dualism, especially his idealism."[14] Though he overcame that particular ideological attitude, it seems difficult to say that Mao completely denied the fundamental point of Kant's morality, namely that a human act can be morally justified only if it is motivated by a universal principle. Of course, since he became a Marxist, Mao was obliged to think that in a class society a "universal principle" is simply impossible, but there was always in his perspective an appeal to work "for the majority," for the "oppressed" who are the "largest majority of mankind" – something like an aspiration towards a world where the largest majority could come very close to "universality." In putting forth the idea of *ta t'ung* Mao rightly used a Confucian concept, but can we completely deny it is reminiscent of some of the Kantian ideals of his youth?

All this is just to say that for Mao, Yang seems to have been the embodiment of a good teacher, one who could appeal to pupils to rise above the mean behaviour of private greed and personal benefit. In a different perspective, in a new ideological setting, he was very much Yang's pupil when he wrote "In Memory of Norman Bethune" and "Serve the People!" It is not true that the whole of Mao is in these two articles; it was a political mistake by Lin Piao to set them apart and identify them as the loftiest expression of Mao's moral doctrine. There is something more – more contradictions, more links with social life – in Mao's moral perspective as a whole than is contained in these two articles. But certainly Mao thought that these articles were the kind of appeal which a revolutionary teacher could reasonably address to his "pupils": thus we can say that for Mao no proper educational process (and hence no proper political development) can go forward if there is no strong moral link between the teacher and his pupils, the leader and the masses. Abstract "ethics" is not enough. Mao did consider Yang a good and a real teacher, but a somewhat "unfinished" one, since he taught "ethics" within the limits of the purely intellectual perspective of bourgeois

---

[14] Schram, *Unrehearsed*, p. 213.

culture.[15] Mao saw himself in a different role as a teacher: a teacher of revolutionary practice, whose aim was to teach all the Chinese people to learn how to change society. Yet he seems to have felt that without a strong moral choice and a deep inner motivation nothing can be learned, nothing can be taught.

If the need for moral motivation in political action and even more in the teacher–pupil relationship was felt by Mao very early, his ideas on teaching and learning were worked out very slowly in connection with his political experience. Only a series of glances through his (official and unofficial) works can give a picture of this development.

His first known work, the article on the role of physical education, is not just an article on education, as Stuart Schram in his introduction amply demonstrates,[16] but there are in it some very interesting remarks which allow us to see how early Mao developed some of his ideas on education and school. He tells us for instance that teachers and principals are prisoners of old-fashioned habits, people prone to labour over details, but unable to see the real problems.[17] From what he says, we can understand how early Mao noticed that most teachers were extremely mean and stupid men. Here he already says what he will repeat in 1964, that school is too heavy and in any case not very useful, all too often just a prison for young bodies. He deems this intellectualistic contempt of movement not only bad for one's health, but also for one's moral and intellectual development.[18] Physical education is already seen as a form of "practice," though obviously not yet of "social practice." However, in this early work we can also see that in 1917 Mao was still very much a student of a "normal school": he focuses the problems of education on the children who are at school, without discussing the problems of those who are not allowed to go to school or the role of "physical education" for the people at large.

Mao's next work, the article "The Great Union of the Popular Masses,"[19] is also interesting as an early document of Mao's

[15] In 1964 Mao stated clearly that what he had learned at the Normal School was "just the usual bourgeois stuff."
[16] Mao Ze-dong, *Une étude de l'éducation physique* (Paris: Mouton, 1962).
[17] *Ibid.*, p. 45.
[18] *Ibid.*, p. 47.
[19] Edited by Stuart Schram in CQ, No. 49 (January–March 1972), pp. 76–87.

attitude to the problem of teaching. Mao singles out students and primary school teachers as the basis for two of the groups of oppressed people, on a par with peasants, workers, women, policemen and rickshaw boys. Here again we find complaints against the physical constraints which traditional schools imposed on children: in his description, schools are very similar to prisons. This situation is seen as a burden not only for the body, but also for the mind as well – a very serious danger for the country, since the students who are brought up are stupid and "feeble minded."

It would be interesting to inquire into the cultural origin of these statements. One of the elements is certainly Mao's own appreciation of the physical movement of the human body amid things as an irreplaceable source of perceptions and hence of knowledge: here Mao's own experience was probably the most important factor. Another one could reasonably be seen in the role which Rousseau assigns to "nature" in the intellectual and moral development of man. It is noteworthy, by the way, that this article is one of the few texts of Mao's where Rousseau is cited as the prophet of a new kind of education, which could free the pupil from the repressive influence of traditional culture and teaching methods. Mao seems to have felt deeply the impact of Rousseau's ideas: not so much of his conception of the state and of political institutions (which were strictly related to the situation of the lower classes in 18th century France and could lead only to a political perspective akin to that of Marat, Robespierre or Saint Just – clearly unsuitable for Mao's problems) but his conception of education. Rousseau saw education as an achievement which every man had to win by himself, with the help of a teacher, whose role was mainly to prevent interference by society and to train the pupil to use his own capacity. Of course, Mao's ideas on education did not stop at what Rousseau said: when he became a Marxist, Mao chose to go beyond Rousseau's perspective. Yet his way of denouncing the intellectual damage of repressive education is typical of the author of Emile.

It is also remarkable that in quoting Rousseau, Mao, in his "Great Union," singles out "self-instruction" as Rousseau's best "invention," but goes on to interpret it as a collective endeavour by students to save themselves from the "ocean of suffering" which the traditional school is.[20] This is obviously not what Rousseau meant, since Jean-Jacques was portrayed bringing up Emile in absolute seclusion, although material things and a rich "natural" background were supposed to be essential. The theme of "self-education" is typical of the Western democratic tradition: Rousseau greatly enhanced this democratic tradition with his ideas on education, but the practice of "self-education" as supported by Mao was developed after the French Revolution, in the late 19th century, by the socialist organizations. There is something else which seems remarkable: Mao's insistence in denouncing a school where even furniture is made just for reading and listening, thus playing a distinctive repressive role, is strictly reminiscent of one of the most popular texts on education by John Dewey.[21] Must we infer that Mao was at that time somewhat familiar with the ideas on education put forward by Dewey?

Another point could be added: the "Great Union" denounces the situation of primary school teachers for the same reasons. The prison in which the children are shut up is no better for teachers, who are, however, even more unlucky, because they are poor (their economic straits are denounced much more bluntly than the situation of peasants and workers) and they are obliged to live far from their beloved wives. "Primary school teachers are in all respects slaves and that's all there is to it! If we want to cease to be slaves, there is no way save to unite with others like ourselves and to realize a primary school teachers union!"[22]

Thus it seems possible to state that many of Mao's ideas on education grew even before he became a Marxist: the problem of schooling still had priority for him in 1920 when he wrote the letter to Ts'ai Ho-shen on Russell and on education, whose importance has been stressed by Stuart Schram.[23] Later this problem was to recede only apparently into the background for Mao: this is evident for instance in the "Report on Hunan," where he over-stresses the spontaneous capacity of the masses for

[20] "Great Union," p. 81.
[21] Namely the speeches and writings of 1896–1903 which were later collected and edited with the title School and Society, 1917.
[22] "Great Union," p. 82.
[23] Schram, Thought, p. 296.

151

revolutionary action. The problem of education – or, if one wishes, the problem of the relationship between the Party-teacher and the masses-pupils – is therefore less important than in later texts. But the problem is nevertheless present. Mao states for instance that "Even if ten thousand schools of law and political science had been opened, could they have brought as much political education to the people, men and women, young and old, all the way into the remotest corners of the countryside, as the peasant associations have done in so short a time? I don't think they could."[24] A few pages later Mao shows how distant he now is from his attitude of 1919: he stresses primarily class relations as the source of peasants' lack of education:

> In China education has always been the exclusive preserve of the landlords, and the peasants have had no access to it. But the landlord's culture is created by the peasants, for its sole source is the peasants' sweat and blood. In China 90 per cent of the people have no education and of these the overwhelming majority are peasants. The moment the power of the landlords was overthrown in the rural areas, the peasants' movement for education began. See how the peasants who hitherto detested the schools are today zealously setting up evening classes.[25]

Here we also find the first of the autobiographical reminiscences which are typical of Mao's statements on education:

> In my student days, when I went back to the village and saw that the peasants were against the "foreign style schools," I, too, used to identify myself with the general run of "foreign style students and teachers" and stand up for it, feeling that the peasants were somehow wrong. It was not until 1925, when I lived in the countryside for six months and was already a communist and had acquired the Marxist viewpoint, that I realized that I had been wrong and the peasants right . . . Now the peasants are enthusiastically establishing evening classes, which they call peasant schools. Some have already been opened, others are being organized . . . The peasants are very enthusiastic about these schools and they regard them, and only them, as their own.[26]

Then Mao goes on with the very optimistic tone which is typical of the "Report" seeing tens of thousands of peasant schools springing up everywhere in the near future.

Mao's attention was to be caught up by military problems in

[24] Report on an Investigation of the Peasant Movement in Hunan," in SW, Vol. I, p. 47.
[25] Ibid., p. 53. [26] Ibid., p. 54.

the next few years, but the problem of education was never absent from his writings. So he sees in "democratic political training"[27] one of the characteristics of the Red Army; again, when discussing the experience of the Chingkangshan strong-hold, political training is seen as the only solution to cope with the problems created by too many soldiers from the lumpen-proletariat.[28] Mao now sees the Party clearly in the role of a teacher, whose capacity for transforming man can go very deep, because of the social and political context in which soldiers of the Red Army live and fight.

The same theme comes up in the resolution of December 1929 (which was one of the favourite texts of Lin Piao's group during the early phases of the Cultural Revolution). The task of the Red Army is "not to confine itself to fighting . . . it should shoulder such important tasks as doing propaganda among the masses, organizing the masses, arming them, helping them to establish revolutionary political power and setting up party organiza-tions.[29] Here the soldiers-pupils turn teachers to the masses in a real endeavour of mutual education and self-education. Note what Mao says about the impact of the habits of lumpen-proletarians and vagrant peasants in the Red Army:[30] all the bad tendencies which are a consequence of the lumpen-proletarian origins of the soldiers can be corrected through political educa-tion. Can we infer that Mao thinks that education cannot change class characteristics in man but that it can help the exploited to understand the true origin of faults which prevent them from fully playing their revolutionary role and thus to overcome them?

Later in the economic texts of 1933–34,[31] Mao's educational ideas seem to take one step forward. The gist of these works seems to be that the role of the Red areas is primarily to educate the masses, to support education, but that no education or polit-ical training can persuade the masses to set aside their funda-mental requirements, that is, revolution must give better condi-tions to the majority of the masses: it must improve their lot from

[27] "Why is it that Red Political Power Can Exist in China?" in SW, Vol. I, p. 66.
[28] "Struggle in the Chingkang Mountains" in SW, Vol. I, p. 81.
[29] "On Correcting Mistaken Ideas in the Party" in SW, Vol. I, p. 106.
[30] Ibid., pp. 109–14.
[31] "Pay Attention to Economic Work," SW, Vol. I, pp. 129–36; "Our Economic Policy," pp. 141–5.

the material point of view. This is the condition which makes political education possible.

In 1936, just after he had given Snow his autobiography so rich in pedagogical hints, Mao wrote "Problems of Strategy in China's Revolutionary War,"[32] one of the highlights of his thought on education, since here significantly the central theme of research is "how to study." One of the first statements by Mao is that specific and not general problems must be studied and solved. We are not surprised, having followed the development of Mao's educational thought from its beginning, that he holds "manuals" in a very low esteem, because they are "wholly copied from abroad"; this seems to be more or less true also with Soviet manuals since "if we copy and apply them without allowing any change we shall also be cutting the feet to fit the shoes and be defeated."[33] Here we find one of the first echoes of Mao's denunciation of "compradore culture" extended to the wholesale import of culture from the Soviet Union, which became one of the typical features of his thought after 1956.

One of the most important paragraphs (the one which was singled out in 1965 to be reproduced in the Selected Readings for Cadres) states that "the important thing is to be good at learning." Mao puts forth his deep pedagogical belief: "to learn is no easy matter and to apply what one has learned is even harder ... to become both wise and courageous, one must acquire a method ... to be employed in learning as well as in applying what has been learned."[34] Then Mao goes on to describe how "a commander's correct disposition stems from his correct decisions, his correct decisions stem from his correct judgments and his correct judgments stem from a thorough and necessary reconnaissance and from pondering on and piecing together the data of various kinds gathered from reconnaissance":[35] strategy is thus seen primarily as a problem of learning, though what one could call "moral virtues" are also necessary, because "an experienced military man" will be good at learning, "provided he is modest and willing to learn." Anyhow learning strategy is not a purely

---

[32] SW, Vol. I, pp. 179–254.
[33] Ibid., p. 181.
[34] "Problems of Strategy in China's Revolutionary War," SW, Vol. I, pp. 186–7.
[35] Ibid., p. 188.

intellectual process: "reading is learning, but also applying is learning and the more important kind of learning at that. Our chief method is to learn warfare through warfare. A person who has had no opportunity to go to school, can also learn warfare – he can learn through fighting in war. A revolutionary war is a mass undertaking; it is often not a matter of first learning and then doing but of doing and then learning, for doing is itself learning."[36] At this point Mao's ideas on learning seem to have come to their full development: he added new themes and new experiences later, but the hard core of his pedagogy was already clearly outlined in December 1936. It seems worthy to note that Mao chose strategy – the most dialectical field of human culture – as the context in which to state in full his line on education.

Mao's two most celebrated texts of philosophy, "On Practice" and "On Contradiction," do add something to these pedagogical themes, but they are not the most significant sources to analyse Mao's educational ideas. Of course, if knowledge comes from social practice, true education can be brought about only by social practice. How is the teacher to involve pupils in social practice? Has the school a specific proper role to play? Can education be attained only through participation in social practice? In "On Contradiction" Mao states that the particularity of contradictions is very important. Hence education must enable the pupil to go deep into the research of particular contradictions. Vague concepts are all too often dogma. Any teacher must fight against "lazybones" who just repeat dead dogma. Education must enable people to master a dialectical vision of men and things, must train people into a very hard intellectual exercise demanding a resilient mind as well as a consistent will and an aptitude to painstaking, thorough research and – last but not least – also some imagination.

In the short article "Combat Liberalism" Mao sees ideological struggle as a typical educational activity. "Liberalism" in Mao's eyes is a mistaken attitude of those who, for opportunistic reasons, refuse to educate persons "who have clearly gone wrong,"[37] – refuse, so to speak, to be their "severe taskmasters." The struggle against liberalism demands a sound principled stand such as a responsible rejection of gossip and personalism,

[36] Ibid., pp. 189–90. [37] SW, Vol. II, p. 31.

but even more of laziness and of any disposition to let things drift. Mao sees liberalism as a very serious danger in that it encourages people to give up the struggle to solve contradictions. In this text Mao puts forth a strong appeal, which – though in a Marxist context, of course – is strongly reminiscent of Rousseau's appeal to struggle against *amour propre* in the name of the rightful *amour de soi*.

A communist should have largeness of mind and he should be staunch and active, looking upon the interests of the revolution as his very life and subordinating his personal interests to those of the revolution; always and everywhere he should adhere to principle and wage a tireless struggle against all incorrect ideas and actions, so as to consolidate the collective life of the party and the masses, he should be more concerned about the party and the masses than about any private persons and about others more than about himself. Only thus can he be considered a communist.[38]

True, this text asks more questions than it answers: who, for instance, will be the "teacher" of such a Communist? Who will imbue him with such sublime virtues? The Party, the masses, social practice or he himself? Is there no danger of a philistine attitude in this moralistic perspective? These questions are not abstract ones, since in the course of the subsequent history of the Chinese revolution every one of these assumptions was at one time accepted and later discarded.

During the War of Resistance against Japan, Mao the teacher and Mao the leader seem to have merged for good. This is evident in the report "The Role of the Chinese Communist Party and the National War,"[39] where the problem is that of the relationship between the Party and the masses which was due to become the crux of the educational debate in Mao's wartime works. Were the Communists to be the teachers of the masses or their pupils? Mao seems to answer that they are primarily teachers but also pupils:

It must be realized that the communists form only a small section of the nation and that there are large numbers of progressives and activists outside the party with whom we must work. It is entirely wrong to think that we alone are good and no one else is any good. As for people who are politically backward, communists should not slight or despise

[38] *Ibid.*, p. 33.   [39] *Ibid.*, pp. 195–217.

156

them, but should befriend them, unite with them, convince them and encourage them to go forward. The attitude of the communists towards any person who has made mistakes in his work, should be one of persuasion in order to help him change and start afresh and not one of exclusion, unless he is incorrigible. Communists should set an example in being practical as well as far sighted. [But can a teacher fail to be also a pupil?] Communists should therefore set an example in study; at all times they should learn from the masses as well as teach them. Only by learning from the people, from actual circumstances and from the friendly parties and armies and by knowing them well, can we be practical in our work and far sighted as to the future.[40]

Here we find very clearly stated a contradiction which was going to become deeper and deeper in Mao's thought and political practice especially after 1957 and during the Cultural Revolution. In the first sentence it looks as if the Communists were already the "owners" of a well defined truth, which they would teach with forbearance, tact and intelligence to pupils who could be somewhat reluctant, but who seemed for the most part willing to accept the political and pedagogical role of the teachers. In the second sentence the "truth" still needs to be found or completed, and the Communists need help to accomplish their task. The contradiction is not solved here, and it never will be in Mao's perspective; we could only ask whether it is only the Communists who have the capacity to work out a political perspective (though with the aid of the masses) or whether the "masses" or somebody else could replace the Party in this role. This is probably the most momentous political question in Maoism, which was to have the most serious political consequences, because Mao was never able to point at a specific solution or at least to a well defined behaviour to face this contradiction, however hard he strove to come to grips with the problem. It is not a purely political problem: it has obvious "pedagogical" relevance. It was not by chance that the Cultural Revolution had such deep pedagogical undertones: Mao had to try to solve this contradiction in terms of school organization and political education of young people, once revolutionary power had been set up.

This set of questions came up very soon for Mao, though he

[40] *Ibid.*, p. 198.

157

was at the time less outspoken than after 1957. In the article "The Orientation of the Youth Movement"[41] the problem of education is set against a historical background, namely the evaluation of the whole course of the Chinese revolution since the May Fourth Movement: here Mao says for the first time very clearly that manual work plays an indispensable role in education. Political integration and participation in armed struggle are essential in the building up of a youth movement, but they are not enough: "You have been learning the theory of revolution and studying the principles and methods of resisting Japan and saving the nation. You have been carrying out the campaign for production and have reclaimed thousands of *mou* of waste land."[42]

This education through manual labour is contrasted with the Confucian ideal of education. Confucius is bluntly attacked for his ignorance, due to his contempt of manual work. But it is not only youth who must be educated: intellectuals also are to be educated or re-educated to integrate themselves with the masses. In 1939 the 20th anniversary of the May Fourth Movement gave Mao the opportunity to state his policy towards the intellectuals: actually the passionate engagement of the intellectuals in the resistance movement against Japan posed the Communist Party a problem which was hardly perceived in the Kiangsi Soviet. The role of the intellectuals in the United Front is one of the main subjects of Mao's analysis during the Second World War: the problem is primarily a political and social one, but it has also an educational aspect. "The intellectuals will accomplish nothing if they fail to integrate themselves with the workers and peasants. In the final analysis, the dividing line between revolutionary intellectuals and non-revolutionary or counter-revolutionary intellectuals is whether or not they are willing to integrate themselves with the workers and peasants and actually do so."[43] This is a highly dangerous sentence whose citation would later be applied to any contingent need of policy towards intellectuals and even become instrumental in personal denunciations, but it is clearly in agreement with the whole of Mao's social and political perspective.

[41] *Ibid.*, pp. 241–51. [42] *Ibid.*, p. 248.
[43] "The May 4th Movement," in *SW*, Vol. II, p. 238.

What is to be done to get the intellectuals effectively integrated with the masses? In the resolution of the Central Committee of December 1939,[44] Mao tries to put forward specific suggestions to overcome the "sectarian" attitude of Party members towards the intellectuals. A few months later the problem is taken up again – amongst others – in the directive "On the Question of Political Power in the Anti-Japanese Areas": the leading role of the Party in the organs of political power is to be secured by correct policies and by "the example we set by our own work to convince and educate people outside the party, so that they willingly accept our proposals."[45] "Ruling by example" has a well-known long tradition in China: here it seems that it is primarily the Party members who must be "educated to overcome the narrowness manifested in their reluctance and uneasiness in collaborating with non-communists": one could say that they are to be educated in order to enable them to educate others. Mao rejected the contents and the methods of Confucian education, as much as he rejected the role of the ruling class supported by the Confucian bureaucrats. He took over from the Confucian tradition, however, its emphasis on education as a means for ruling, that is first for selecting the rulers, then to enable them to rule through education. The people to be educated, together with the aims and the content of education should be changed, but not the role of education.

The whole of the *cheng-feng* movement in 1942, though focused primarily on proper political and ideological problems, had deep educational implications. For instance the preface to Mao's village investigation[46] is a typical document of his ideas on teaching. He relates how he gathered data and material through questioning different kinds of people (whose alignment with the revolution could not at all be taken for granted), then he adds: "They made me conscious of many things I did not know before . . . [these people] were my respected teachers."[47] This

---

[44] "Recruit Large Numbers of Intellectuals," in SW, Vol. II, pp. 301–3.
[45] SW, Vol. II, pp. 417–19, namely p. 418.
[46] "Preface and Postscript to Rural Surveys," in SW, Vol. III, pp. 11–16 and also Boyd Compton, Mao's China (Seattle: University of Washington Press, 1966), pp. 54–8.
[47] SW, Vol. III, p. 12; Compton, Mao's China, p. 56.

statement tells us as much about the role of the teacher in Mao's opinion: a teacher must first of all enable his pupil to become conscious of what he does not fully perceive. We cannot verify which were the specific intellectual sources of this statement of Mao's: it seems to imply once again a long familiarity with philosophical and educational texts, but it can also have been the result of a long educational experience by a very intelligent teacher.

Anyhow the whole document is a short treatise on education: it is here that Mao tells us better than anywhere else that "investigating" is the highest form of learning and that his own role is first of all to teach militants how to investigate.

Sufficient time must be given, an outline for investigation has to be determined and we, ourselves, must ask the questions and do the recording; in addition we must open discussion with those who come to the meetings. Thus, if we are not completely sincere, if we are not determined to look downward, if we do not have a thirst for knowledge and do not put aside foul conceit and show a willingness to act as primary school students, nothing can be done and our performance will be poor. We must understand that the masses are truly heroic and we ourselves are often immature and ridiculous. If we do not understand this point, we cannot achieve the least knowledge. These investigations are even more necessary for all who understand only theory but not reality; in no other way can we relate theory and reality. 'If you have done no investigation, you have no right to speak.' Also though this phrase has been ridiculed as 'narrow empiricism,' I still haven't rejected it today. Not only I have not rejected it: I still insist that there is no right to speak without investigation.[48]

Here Mao is in his full self-appointed role: he teaches "how to learn."

The problem of education is central also in "Reform our Study,"[49] although somewhat superseded by the complicated question of the so-called "sinification of Marxism." Mao restates some of the ideas on education: research must be pains-taking hard work; Marxism–Leninism is "science and science is serious learning"; carelessness is in complete opposition to Marxism; dogmatic teachers are bad teachers of bad students who "develop an abnormal outlook: they have no interest in Chinese

[48] Ibid., pp. 56–7.
[49] SW, Vol. III, pp. 17–25; Compton, Mao's China, pp. 52–68.

problems and pay no heed to Party instructions; their inclination is to regard what they have learned from their teachers as never changing dogma." Mao thinks, as did Hegel, that knowledge must not aim to seize a static truth: truth is constantly made up by gradually approaching it. "We should start with actual conditions within and outside the country . . . and derive, not concoct, the inner regulating laws, which means that we should find the inner-relationships in the happenings around us and make them our guide to action; if we are to do this, we must not rely on subjective thought, enthusiasm or books, but on objectively existing facts and on an intimate knowledge of materials, drawing correct conclusions from these facts and materials. These conclusions are not an A–B–C–D arrangement of phenomena, nor are they essays of excessive length filled with hot air: they are scientific conclusions."[50]

The educational themes come up once more at length in "Rectify the Party's Style of Work,"[51] the only difference being that the focal point here is not "how to learn" but "how to apply" what one has learned: the students of the Party school must be able to master both doctrines and methods of Marxism and to apply them, the application being the sole object of mastery. Schools usually give no real knowledge to students and the display of abstract knowledge by intellectuals is harmful and obstructs their progress. In this speech Mao sketches his interpretation of the sources of knowledge, which he was to take up again in the "First Ten Points" in 1963: "One type of knowledge is knowledge of the struggle for production; the other is knowledge of the class struggle. What knowledge is there apart from this? There is none."[52] (In 1963 Mao added "scientific experiment" as a source of knowledge.)[53] This means that book knowledge is not knowledge at all and that schools produce only "half-intellectuals."

All this could already be taken for granted, given the development of Mao's thought on education, but something is

[50] Compton, Mao's China, p. 66.
[51] In SW, Vol. III, pp. 35–51; Compton, Mao's China, pp. 9–32.
[52] Ibid., p. 15.
[53] In R. Baum and F. Teiwes (eds.), Ssu-ch'ing, the Socialist Education Movement (Berkeley: Center of Chinese Studies, University of California, 1968), pp. 58–61, namely p. 58.

added here, that is the condemnation of the parasitic role of the intellectuals who hold books in their hands and "receive millet from the public." This is not the only point which makes this speech remarkable, because here Mao analyses also the danger of "practical knowledge without any theoretical elaboration," saying that this is no scientific knowledge either. To be satisfied with one's limited experience is a serious danger which must be overcome. In reading Mao's pages we come to feel that after all he deems it easier to overcome this fault than the haughty attitude of the dogmatic intellectuals: he loves better the cadres of working class origin who must struggle against their lack of theoretical ability, since this is merely a consequence of their poverty: nevertheless he says very clearly that this condition must be changed. The problem became very important immediately after 1949 when a large number of peasant cadres were faced with the problems of ruling China at least at the intermediate levels.

When reading these pages we sense that the texts of the cheng feng movement are the ones in which Rousseau's impact on Mao seems strongest. In "Oppose Stereotyped Party Writing,"[54] we find an interesting remark by Mao about language and linguistic education. Though opposed to abstract schooling, Mao was always definitely in favour of a good, even refined, linguistic development for students: this proved true even when he discussed school problems in the wake of the Cultural Revolution. Here he once again criticized those schools which "leave the language insipid and poor, divorced both from the living language of the masses and from the efficient language of the past." This implies that studying literature can be useful in as much as it gives a full possession of a pertinent and efficient linguistic tool.

As the cheng-feng movement drew to a close, the formulation of Mao's ideas on education seems to have attained completion, at least for the phase of the struggle for installing revolutionary power. A new spell of research was inaugurated by Mao around 1962–64 when he sought ways to save socialist society from involution and tried to outline an educational policy for that need.

[54] In SW, Vol. III, pp. 53–69.

The relationship between leaders-cadres-Party members on the one hand and the masses on the other continued to be modelled on the "educational" relationship between teacher and pupils in the new context created by the final struggle against the Kuomintang after 1945. Now Mao tells us that political education and debate must not reach only a narrow elite of cadres and militants, but the broadest masses: it is a serious political mistake if one fails to mobilize the masses by teaching them. "The journalist's job is to educate the masses, *to enable the masses to know their own interests*,[55] their own tasks and the Party's general and specific policies."[56] During the final years of the struggle against the KMT, Mao stressed again and again that political education and mass mobilization were just one and the same process, which had to be undertaken both within the Party (between the secretary and the members of every committee, the secretary being at the same time the teacher and the pupil of the members[57]) and in the country at large, through the rearing of cadres from among the masses, namely the soldiers of the People's Liberation Army.[58]

This discussion can seem inappropriate or exaggerated in the West: yet, the workers' movement in Western Europe had from its start very strong educational implications and it did play (at least in Italy) a vital role in changing educational levels and the very perception of the meaning of education. It is doubtful whether this role will continue in the conditions of neo-capitalistic society: anyway the formation of an "alternative leadership" in the ranks of the working class has long since been one of the aims of the socialist and communist parties in Europe. We must not wonder that Mao faced the same need: but in China the problem of education was not identical to that in Europe, since in China education had been the very method of selection of the ruling class: neither noble birth, nor land, nor possessions, nor money (at least not in principle, of course) could grant the entry into the world of rulers and leaders. If a revolution had to succeed in China, the Communists had to evolve a new way to

[55] Emphasis added.
[56] "A Talk to the Editorial Staff of the *Shansi-Suiyuan Daily*," in SW, Vol. IV, p. 243.
[57] "Methods of Work of Party Committees," in SW, Vol. IV, pp. 377–81.
[58] "Turn the Army into a Working Force," in SW, Vol IV, pp. 337–9.

select those who were to rule the country: knowledge could not be the condition, unless one was to recruit just another class of "non-Confucian" mandarins, but knowledge was a requirement which could not be overlooked when recruiting those who were to rule China and lead its people to modernization.

This was one of the biggest problems for Mao. It became more acute as the communist seizure of power approached: it was to obsess him after 1957 when he took full measure of the failure of the Russian Revolution in creating a new society. But already on the eve of the seizure of power by the revolutionary forces, Mao showed himself very worried about a possible reversal of the politico-educational process: he sensed the danger of a corrupting "counter-education" exercised by "the enemy," playing on the moral weakness of the revolutionaries. In the Maoist vision of dialectics, no process can ever be regarded as safely accomplished, no result taken for granted: any success which has been achieved can turn into failure, any balance can and must be offset. The same is true with education: education can be both acquired and lost. Thus in a much celebrated quotation, which was to become more and more relevant as time went by, Mao foresaw that the Communists could have to undergo a process of "dis-education":

> With victory certain moods may grow within the Party—arrogance, the airs of a self-styled hero, inertia and unwillingness to make progress, love of pleasure and distaste of continued hard living. With victory the people will be grateful to us and the bourgeoisie will come forward to flatter us. It has been proved that the enemy cannot conquer us by force of arms. However, the flattery of the bourgeoisie may conquer the weak-willed in our ranks. There may be some Communists who were not conquered by enemies with guns and were worthy of the name of heroes for standing up to these enemies, but who cannot withstand sugar-coated bullets: they will be defeated by sugar-coated bullets. We must guard against such a situation.[59]

Though a deep educational conscience, which reveals itself in small remarks here and there, never failed Mao, in the first years after Liberation he was more preoccupied with other social and political problems than with education. He did pay attention to

[59] "Report to the Second Plenary Session of the Seventh Central Committee of the Communist Party of China," in SW, Vol. IV, pp. 361–75, namely p. 374.

school organization[60] and asked for exchange of experience between schools, factories and agricultural co-operatives;[61] he remarked once again that teachers were ignorant and arrogant, that they had primarily to educate themselves.[62] In 1957 he stated bluntly that Stalin was after all a bad teacher, since he was a "metaphysician" who brought up people with a tendency to metaphysics.[63] In Wuhan in April 1958 he ascribed Stalin's faults and mistakes to his having been brought up in a religious school, in a very dogmatic environment.[64] The problem of the moral and political development of the new generation must have been close to Mao's mind and heart, as is clear from the deep emotion in Mao's speech to the Chinese students in Moscow: "The world is yours, as well as ours. But in the last analysis, it is yours. You, young people, full of vigour and vitality, are in the bloom of life, like the sun at eight or nine in the morning. Our hope is placed on you."[65] This sentence seems to be the embodiment of Mao's feelings towards youth: obviously optimistic and yet tainted with doubt, typical of his conception of the teacher unable to know for certain his students' future will and bearings.

After 1957, as the struggle for new policies became fiercer both within the Chinese Communist Party and in the international communist movement, Mao went back more often to themes linked with education. Thus he discussed once more the birth of a new revolutionary Chinese culture in contrast both with Western bourgeois tradition and with Soviet cultural work: his call for the construction of an independent Chinese revolutionary culture, which could make good use of the cultural products of other societies, posed educational problems.[66] Mao's perspective and propositions here seem far richer and more "open" than the cultural policy which was later to be supported by the left-wingers during the Cultural Revolution.

[60] "Speech to the Central Committee of the Chinese Communist Party on 6 June, 1950," in Mao Tse-tung, Textes 1949–1958 (Paris: Editions du Cerf, 1975), pp. 28–34.
[61] "Speech to the Conference of Secretaries," January 1957, Textes, p. 267.
[62] "Intervention in the National Conference on Propaganda Work," 12 March, 1957, Textes, p. 348.
[63] "Conference of the Secretaries of Municipal and Provincial Committees," January 1957, in Textes, p. 276.   [64] Textes, p. 515.
[65] Ibid., p. 432, very often quoted in Red Guards materials after 1966.
[66] For instance "Talk to the Music Workers," in Schram, Unrehearsed, pp. 84–90.

The theme of technology was also "crammed" with educational implications. As soon as the break with the Soviets faced the Chinese Communists with the necessity of an independent economic and technological development, Mao indulged again and again in the analysis of the problems of technological education for the widest masses. Here it is necessary to dispose of a legend which has been somewhat persistent amongst European "Maoists," that is that Mao had some misgivings about technological development and favoured an "un-industrialized society." This could be the feeling of rebels who have grown up within industrial society, but could never be entertained by a revolutionary from a "colonized" country, a victim of imperialist domination, such as Mao was. Mao was always entirely in favour of technological development: the quicker, the better. He wanted however, real technological development and no "counterfeit development," no myth forged by a small group of privileged people (be they engineers, workers or politicians) to delude the whole country into a non-existent perspective or just to extort money from the peasants.

No wonder that Mao wanted the stress laid on technology and science in education at every level; he always put the emphasis on the broadest circulation of technological and scientific knowledge among the masses and especially the young peasants; he clearly favoured practical technology and science, against abstract elaboration or dogmatic imitation. In 1958, in connection with the Great Leap Forward when writing the draft resolution known as the "Sixty Points of Working Methods,"[67] he stressed the need to learn technology as a precondition to any economic breakthrough. The Chinese revolution had to fulfil the historical task of a great technological revolution and the Communists had once again to start by "learning": "Those who have no practical knowledge are pseudo-red, empty-headed politicos. We must unite politics and technology . . . Compare the advanced with the backward under identical conditions and encourage the backward to catch up with the advanced."[68] Cadres, especially cadres at the centre, must "leave their offices

[67] See Jerome Ch'en (ed.), Mao Papers (London, Oxford University Press, 1970), pp. 57–70.
[68] Ibid., p. 65.

for four months every year to investigate and study at a lower level and attend meetings at various places":[69] then Mao continues with specific prescriptions of methods for gathering materials, analysing data and checking information, for writing documents "precisely, clearly and in a lively manner," stating once again the political need to acquire a good linguistic capacity.[70] Though the text published by the Red Guards is unfortunately incomplete here, it is interesting to remark that the points 39 to 50 propose a general outline of a school programme: social sciences, technology, history and language are all equally important in Mao's view.

Given Mao's conception of the role of practice,[71] what seems more interesting is Mao's demand that schools become self-sufficient from the economic point of view:

All secondary technical schools for technicians should if possible experiment in setting up workshops and farms to attain complete or partial self-sufficiency by engaging in production. Students should do part-time study and part-time work. Under favourable conditions, these schools can take on more students but should not at the same time cost the country more money. All the industrial colleges should try to set up laboratories and workshops for teaching and research and also for production. In addition, their students and teachers may sign contracts with local factories to take part in their work. All agricultural schools, apart from productive work on their own farms, may sign work contracts with local agricultural co-operatives . . . Under favourable conditions, universities and urban middle schools may jointly set up factories or workshops and they may sign contracts with factories, work sites or service industries . . .[72]

This attitude was prompted not only by Mao's well known mistrust of abstract intellectual education, but also by the economic necessity of lowering the cost of education, keenly appreciated by Mao who knew very well how the cost of educating the students was being borne by the majority of the Chinese people, that is by the peasants.

In the next few months Mao was to stress again his ideas on the interchanging of roles between schools and factories: "schools should have factories and factories schools" and on "part-time school and part-time work."[73] Both ideological and economic

[69] Ibid., p. 67.   [70] Ibid., p. 72.   [71] Points 49 and 50 in ibid., p. 74.
[72] Ch'en, Mao Papers, pp. 73–4.   [73] Ibid., pp. 84–5.

167

requirements justified this choice, though the problem of eliminating the gap between manual and intellectual labour became more and more pressing for Mao as he pursued the analysis of the birth and development of the "new class" in the Soviet Union. At the same time more traditional problems of mass education did retain his attention: in 1958, at the Chengtu conference, during the Second Talk he saw the elimination of illiteracy as one of the aspects of the struggle against agricultural backwardness during the Leap Forward,[74] while during the Third Talk he went back to an old favourite theme of his, the creativity of young people with little schooling:

in history it is always those with little learning who overthrow those with much learning ... ever since ancient times, the people who founded new schools of thought were all young people without much learning; they had the ability to recognize new things at a glance and, having grasped them, they opened fire on the old fogeys.[75]

Here however Mao seems to have been fired by over-enthusiasm in ascribing great inventions to ignorant people, to the point of mistaking Fleming for a laundryman and in depicting Franklin as an ignorant "newspaper boy." His aim was to attack intellectual and social conservatism: he was waging a political struggle, not suggesting an educational programme. As an "educational planner" Mao was always very careful: giving the utmost attention to particular problems, whereas here he just wanted to stress the need of political engagement:

Of course some things can be learnt at school; I don't propose to close all the schools. What I mean is that it is not absolutely necessary to attend school. The main thing is whether your direction is correct or not and whether you come to grips with your studies. Learning has to be grasped. As soon as they grasped the truth, the young founders of new schools embarked on discoveries, scorning the old fogeys. Then those with learning oppressed them ... When we started to make revolution, we were mere twenty-year-old boys, while the rulers of the time ... were old and experienced. They had more learning, but we had more truth.[76]

The political meaning of these utterances of Mao's becomes clear when we read his speech of September 1959: here we find

[74] Schram, Unrehearsed, p. 104. [75] Ibid., pp. 118–19. [76] Ibid., p. 120.

again Mao's usual call to study, hard study, serious study, though study of useful things only:

All of us without exception must study. What shall we do if there is not enough time? If there is not enough time, we must squeeze in the time. The problem lies in cultivating the habit of study; once we have done this, we will be able to go on studying. I say these things first of all for the benefit of those comrades who have committed errors, but my words are also directed to all of us comrades, including myself. There are many things I haven't studied. I am a person with many shortcomings, I am by no means perfect. Very often, there are times when I don't like myself. I have not mastered all the various domains of Marxist learning. And, for example, I do not know foreign languages well, either. I have only just begun recently to study economic work. But, comrades, I study with determination and I will go on studying until I die. When I die it will be the end of it. In sum, as long as I am alive, I shall study every day.[77]

These lines and the following page on the relationship between swimming and the knowledge of water seem to stand out as Mao's testament on education. Understanding is seen as a process, gradually gaining both in width and in depth. The importance of experience (historical as well as scientific) lies in that it broadens one's knowledge. The gradual acquisition of knowledge is a political aim which must be pursued by any Communist, yet narrow-minded learning and the dogmatic repetition of old ideas are an intellectual and social evil.

This is the message which Mao restated again and again in the following years, as he deepened his criticism of Soviet society: obviously he saw in the Soviet school system one of the roots of the "degeneration" of the revolutionary society. For instance the well-known remarks about "Where do correct ideas come from?" does not seem to improve much on what had been written in "On Practice" or during the cheng-feng movement: what is more astounding is that this epistemological analysis introduces a resolution on rural work which is an appeal not to forget class struggle.[78] Actually this brief sketch of Mao's ideas on knowledge and school, having been widely published in the Selected Readings for Cadres in 1965, was to become one of

[77] Ibid., p. 154.
[78] R. Baum and F. Teiwes (eds.), Ssu-ch'ing, the Socialist Education Movement, p. 58.

the passwords of the students' rebellion, in China and elsewhere. Thus it seems that, facing a severe intra-Party struggle after 1962, Mao was very much concerned to give the widest possible circulation to his ideas on education in order to mobilize youth to support his policy. This explains also the strong moralistic flavour in many of his statements on education. Typical for instance is the instruction of December 1963 "against complacency and conceit,"[79] one of Mao's texts where Rousseau's influence is most clearly seen though systematically corrected by the appeal to class struggle and mass control. As Soviet policy came to be perceived by Mao to be a "total betrayal" of revolution, as he grew more apprehensive about the emerging of "revisionism" within his own Party, he tended to place all his hopes on youth, whose moral engagement was felt as essential in the struggle to defend the revolution.

In the three talks with Mao Yuan-hsin[80] the discussion on education is totally merged with the elaboration of new policies against "revisionism": in Mao's mind the need to "bring up successors" had by that time become identified with the need to save the state born in the revolution from the danger of a "change in colour." This did not mean that Mao, in the wake of the Cultural Revolution, left out technical educational details: on the contrary we find in the writings of 1964–65 some of the most detailed prescriptions ever given by Mao on the methods of teaching.[81] Now he proves himself really "red and expert" in didactics; it is evident that he was interested in the practical problems which every teacher faces. For instance, he recommends that lecture notes are given to the students in advance, in order to substitute a question-and-answer dialogue for traditional "lectures"; he deals once more with the problem of language, especially technological language, with the different course of the historical development of science and the inner order of scientific concepts, and suggests general and bold experimentation. But the most important problem for him is still

[79] Ch'en, Mao Papers, p. 86.
[80] Schram, Unrehearsed, pp. 242–52.
[81] Here some caution seems necessary: the bulk of unofficial Mao texts come from Red Guard publications. Red Guards were primarily interested in school problems.

the problem of the teachers: "If one wants to educate others, the educationist should first be educated."[82]

Mao's crucial interest seems, however, at this time to have gone far beyond the strict problems of school and teaching methods: his battle is now the Cultural Revolution. It is impossible here to deal with the turns and twists of the Cultural Revolution: though the pedagogical elements in it were strictly intermingled with social and political processes, the fight for a new school, for a new conception of education, did play a decisive role. And not only in China, since one of the widest and deepest repercussions of the Cultural Revolution in the West was precisely to challenge the old educational order which was in some ways and in some places far more outdated and old-fashioned than in People's China. The new conception of education – more properly of permanent and general political development for young and old, cadres and masses, soldiers and workers, peasants and students – which Mao wanted to enforce, is evident in the well-known May 7th Instruction:[83] this manifesto of the Cultural Revolution symbolized and summed up but also oversimplified Mao's long elaborated approach to the educational problem, his ideal of the political formation of man as a militant. Actually Mao remarks rather pertinently that this instruction is "neither new nor original . . . Our army has been working in this way for decades": what is new is rather the generalization of this practice as a policy for the whole of Chinese society.

In the early stages of the Cultural Revolution the educational programme merged with political struggle and became the front line of the fighting: this is plain for instance in the resolution of 8 August 1966[84] as well as in Mao's letter to the Red Guards.[85] Here Mao's reference to Marx clearly reminds the young Red Guards of the need to undergo further political education in order to learn how "to emancipate mankind as a whole," that is how to unite with other groups of oppressed: a programme which goes well beyond the problem of school and teaching methods and which was to fail in the course of the Cultural Revolution. In the

[82] "Talk at the Report Meeting" (24 October, 1966), in Schram, *Unrehearsed*, p. 264.
[83] Ch'en, *Mao Papers*, pp. 103–4.
[84] Ibid., pp. 117–27.   [85] Ibid., p. 115.

later stages of the movement, after the army's intervention into school affairs[86] and the widespread development of students' factionalism, Mao went back again to more specific problems of teaching methods: now he tended to stress the role of the proletariat as a force to lead the students both to a proper vision of class struggle and to technological and scientific education.[87] Generally speaking, in the summer of 1968, when factionalism and factional strife were spreading far and wide in China, Mao was once more deeply concerned with educational problems, which had come to the forefront of political struggle. Unlike the speeches of 1964–65, this material is rather scanty, however, and we know Mao's bearing only by short citations in articles by other leaders. Still later the demands of the international situation and the evolution of inner-Party struggle probably took up most of the energies of the ageing revolutionary.

Mao seems to have been the political leader most concerned with education in modern times: for him the problem of "bringing up revolutionary successors" merged with the problem of preventing the degeneration of the social regime created by the revolution into the more or less despotic power of a "new class." His appeal "never to forget the class struggle" in a socialist society was the root of the turbulence in China since 1958, but also one of the reasons which made "Mao's China" so very different from any other country, especially from the Soviet Union and from those countries whose "failure" prompted Mao's research for a new road.

All his life Mao wanted to be a "teacher" – not a "master"; just a teacher. Actually his contribution in outlining a strategy for revolution in China and in "teaching" the Chinese people the ways of carrying it out could hardly be exaggerated. We can properly wonder whether, without Mao, the Chinese people could have overthrown the old order and achieved a substantial change in their living conditions. Thus far we can say that Mao was a very successful teacher: he was able to single out the problems which his generation faced and to show a way out, not

[86] Mao's instructions to PLA for action in schools, in Ch'en, *Mao Papers*, pp. 133 and 136.
[87] See for instance the instructions of 21 July, 1968 setting the Shanghai Machine Tool factory as an example, or the instruction of 27 August, 1968 in Ch'en, *Mao Papers*, pp. 154 and 155.

only to an elite of militants but to the "great majority" of the Chinese: and he did that for at least 40 years. Very few teachers ever had so many pupils or – after all – such good ones. But Mao demanded more, both of himself and of his pupils: he would have liked to enable them to solve the coming problems, to see them fit enough to solve new problems with the boldness which was typical of Mao and his comrades. Born at a time in which exceptional circumstances combined to bring up that extraordinary group of men who led the Chinese revolution, Mao hoped to leave China to a youth which could compete with his own generation in the will, skill and decisiveness to go on changing China and the world, for the benefit of the majority of mankind.

In this he probably deluded himself: the very success of the revolutionaries could well sap the energy or at least the abilities of the coming generation. Men usually act out of their own pressing needs, not out of the teaching they receive, however good the teacher. Thus it is possible that Chinese youth will sooner or later reject Mao's teaching or just pay dogmatic lip-service to it, which would be tantamount to rejecting it. The "new class" lurks on and the old Mao seems to have sensed its approach and its inevitable self-assertion.

In the long run, however, more people – in China and outside China – could go back again to what Mao wrote and said to search for analyses, methods and perspectives to help them solve their new, as yet unforeseen problems. Their way of reading and interpreting Mao could very well diverge from Mao's idea of his own role. But Mao has been one of the few men in our time to speak plainly of the human need to pursue the "quest for truth"; a quest which was never reassuring. Personally Mao was actively engaged (rather satisfied) in that quest: "My wish is to join all the comrades of our Party to learn from the masses, to continue to be a school boy."[88] A highly dialectical (contradictory, if one prefers) ideal for a leader, but one which can be taken as typical of Mao, with all the unsolved contradictions of his "historical experience" – "the Party," "the masses," "the teachers," "the school-boys": every term with all its implications – whose results are necessarily unforeseen.

[88] Ch'en, Mao Papers, p. 115.

173

6

THE ECONOMIST

Christopher Howe and Kenneth R. Walker

INTRODUCTION

This essay attempts to understand Mao Tse-tung in the context of China's economic development. During Mao's political lifetime China's economy was transformed. Traditional economic institutions were swept away and replaced by socialist systems of ownership and control; and, from a negligible base, modern industry developed dramatically in scale, in composition and in quality. Many of these changes began before 1949 but most of them accelerated and took decisive shape after that year. In what follows we ask two main questions: first, how did Mao perceive the process of economic change and the role of political leadership in it and secondly, when and with what effect did he actively involve himself in economic policy? Since our main sources are Mao's writings and speeches, the former question is the easier to answer. The latter involves many difficulties, since the history of Mao's career still requires much research by historians and political scientists; but even at this stage there are several important points which can be made with reasonable confidence. Where the facts remain inadequate and confusing, we draw attention to some of the issues at stake.

Although the approach adopted is mainly chronological, within this framework the analysis focuses on certain themes of particular interest to economists. These are: the nature of economic institutions and planning, the speed of development, incentives, trade and technology. The conclusion summarizes our findings and suggests the nature of the economic legacy bequeathed by Mao to the leadership that follows him.

THE ECONOMY BEFORE 1949

The economy of Mao's youth was predominantly rural. At least four-fifths of the population lived in villages or in small country towns and agriculture was the chief determinant of living standards. Technically the characteristics of this rural economy were that it was small in scale, required intensive and skilful use of manpower, and involved negligible application of modern agronomic techniques or of mechanical power. Institutionally the nature of tenancy and ownership varied from place to place. In parts of south and east China landlordism was a serious economic and social evil, while evidence for parts of north China suggests that these problems were not equally common throughout China. On the whole, agriculture's performance from the 1920s was inadequate: growth was marginal, incomes from it were unequal and precarious and it did not supply the food and raw materials required by the development of industry, by the cities and by foreign trade.

China's industrial growth made a significant advance during the First World War and development continued down to the mid-1940s. Thus before 1949 there was a substantial light industrial system in Shanghai, while in north-east China (Manchuria) Japanese investment produced a sizeable base of modern, heavy industry. Despite these developments the following industrial weaknesses remained: the number of people employed in industry never exceeded three million; the geographical concentration of industry limited its economic and social impact, and its structure reflected the preferences of foreign investors and traders rather than Chinese needs. The weaknesses of agriculture and the lack of effective national government impeded improvements in this situation.

One may argue that many of China's pre-war economic problems were due to the unfavourable international economic climate and to the direct effects of the civil and anti-Japanese wars. This may well be so, but China's fundamental problem was how to transform a vast economic, geographic and cultural entity which, for more than a century, had failed to accommodate itself to the growth of its population. China did not have all the handicaps facing contemporary underdeveloped countries, but at this time the potential inherent in China's history of economic, political and administrative achievements was unexploited. Indeed, this history seemed to reinforce stagnation rather than to stimulate improvement.

MAO'S EARLY ECONOMIC WORK AND IDEAS

Mao's contact with the pre-1949 economy occurred at three overlapping levels. As a theoretician he sought a basic explanation of China's backwardness. As a revolutionary he was concerned with the economic dimensions of revolutionary work. And as a leader in the localized communist governments Mao had direct experience of economic problems – experience on which he was to draw in later years.

As a theoretician, Mao consistently emphasized the stifling economic effects of the class structure. This structure, he declared in 1926, was dominated by "landlords and compradors" who were themselves "vassals of the international bourgeoisie, dependent upon imperialism for their existence and development. These classes represent the most backward and the most reactionary relations of production in China and hinder the development of her productive forces. Their existence is incompatible with the objectives of the Chinese Revolution."[1] Mao clearly anticipated that the removal of these classes and the dissolution of their domestic institutions and international links would release new economic energies. This confidence in the economic effects of political and institutional change persisted in various forms throughout Mao's career.

In 1927 Mao undertook his famous investigation into the peasant movement in Hunan province. For the most part his Report on this experience analyses the movement's revolutionary potential and hammers home the message that "every revolutionary comrade should know that national revolution requires a profound change in the countryside."[2] However, the spirit and content of the Report illustrate vividly attitudes that play an important part in Mao's subsequent economic work. For

[1] "Analysis of the Classes in Chinese Society," SWL, Vol. I, pp. 13–14.
[2] "Report of an Investigation into the Peasant Movement in Hunan," SWL, Vol. I, pp. 21–59.

example Mao stressed not only the stifling effects of the class system but also the liberating effects of smashing the "super-structure" of its religious and cultural systems. Mao also described the revolutionary possibilities inherent in the poverty of the poorer peasants whose debts "pile up like the load on the back of draught oxen." In the "High Tide" of 1955–56 he returned to the theme that the poor have nothing to lose by revolutionary change. But above all, Mao stressed the speed and violence with which rural change could occur. He likened the peasant movement to a "tornado" and a "tempest" and revelled in the "mess" which it had created. Similar sentiments were to occur in the "High Tide" of 1955–56, the Great Leap Forward of 1958 and the Cultural Revolution of 1967–70. Thus at the very beginning of his career Mao discovered the importance of the rural areas and the exhilarating effectiveness of wave-like advances.

Mao's early career also illustrates his ability to alternate upsurges of optimistic advance with calculated retreats and cold pragmatism. One reason why flexibility and pragmatism were so important was the tendency of Mao's comrades to implement orthodox Russian Marxism without making allowance for important differences between Russian and Chinese conditions. Mao complained of such colleagues that "what a man has learnt in Yenan [in theoretical classes] he doesn't know how to apply in Fu county."[3] And in 1941, in a postscript to his Hunan Report, he revealed that "my assertion 'no investigation, no right to speak' [at meetings] has been ridiculed by some people as 'narrow empiricism'. Yet even now I do not regret having said it and what is more, I still stick to it."[4] Related to his pragmatism was a virulent dislike of bureaucracy. As early as 1933 he described bureaucracy as a "great evil" which "must be thrown into the cesspool";[5] and later, in the Border Regions, Mao initiated a campaign to "simplify" organizations which was a precursor of many such movements that continued down to his death.

Among more specific economic principles adopted by Mao before 1949, one of the most important was that of "self-

[3] "Reform our Study," SWL, Vol. IV, p. 15.
[4] "Preface and Postscript to 'Rural Survey'," SWL, Vol. IV, p. 9.
[5] "We Must Attend to Economic Work," SWL, Vol. I, p. 135.

reliance." This required that the Border Regions should be able to produce the range of products needed to support life and military activity and, where possible, that individual units of the economy and army also be self-sufficient. To some extent this policy reflected the particular needs of a particular time. It also reflected Mao's wider confidence that, given proper government, China would not have to depend economically on foreign countries. "It is sheer nonsense," he wrote in 1937, "to say that a country with such a vast territory and a huge population can be financially and economically helpless."[6] He was, however, always careful to speak fulsomely of the importance of Soviet aid. On Stalin's 60th birthday, for example, Mao wrote a short article in which he emphasized[7] the guidance given by Stalin to the Chinese Communists and the fact that "the Soviet Union alone has helped us with aeroplanes and supplies."

Another important way in which Mao displayed his pragmatism was in his acceptance of a "mixed" economy in which private and various types of public ownership co-exist. Mao perceived that premature socialization of the economy would be harmful and he therefore allowed private enterprises to exist and grow, and even spoke[8] of the need to encourage capitalists to migrate to the communist areas from other parts of China. Flexibility on these matters is reminiscent of Lenin's willingness to employ foreign capital and skills and to allow the private sector to flourish during the New Economic Policy of the 1920s. In Mao's case this policy became embodied in his plans for the New Democratic period – the stage through which China was to pass on the way to socialism.

MAO'S PREPARATION FOR THE TAKEOVER OF
THE ECONOMY IN 1949

Three documents reveal how Mao predicted he would deal with China's economy when he won power: "On New Democracy" (1940); "On Coalition Government" (1945); and "On the

[6] "The Policies, Measures and Perspectives of Combating Japanese Invasion," *SWL*, Vol. II, p. 63. "Our Economic Policy," *SWL*, Vol. II, pp. 141–6; Edgar Snow, *Red Star over China* (London: Victor Gollancz, 1963), p. 254.
[7] "Stalin is the Friend of the Chinese People," *SWL*, Vol. III, p. 103.
[8] "On Policy," *SWL*, Vol. III, p. 222.

People's Democratic Dictatorship" which was written in July 1949, three months before the establishment of the Chinese People's Republic.

"On New Democracy" opens with a sweeping account of China's history in which the Opium War of 1840 is identified as the turning-point in the modern period. Mao describes it as the point when China began to change from a feudal to a semi-feudal, semi-colonial society. In this article Mao distinguished between the Democratic Revolution which was already in progress and the Socialist Revolution which was still a distant prospect. He emphasized that, because of China's backward condition, the Democratic Revolution would be completed only after considerable time, and moreover that it would need the support of a broad section of the Chinese people.

The economic component of this strategy involved first and foremost a land reform that would satisfy the demands of the peasantry. "The New Democratic politics," he wrote, "is virtually the granting of power to the peasants."[9] He also argued for the continuing existence of a private industrial and commercial sector that would be subject to the leadership of the public sector. He outlined these proposals in the language of Sun Yat-sen, obviously attempting to demonstrate that the Communists were the true heirs of Sun and the only group in China likely to implement his ideas.

In his speech "On Coalition Government," Mao expanded his conception of the New Democratic stage of the Chinese Revolution. Here, he saw it as a stage that "may last for several decades," and he now made detailed proposals for agrarian reform and for the establishment of an economic system that would safeguard the interests both of the working class and of private capital. This speech is particularly interesting because it shows that Mao saw China's economic future in terms of large-scale industry and big cities:

In the future tens of millions of peasants will go to the cities, to factories. In order to build up powerful industries of her own and a large number of modernized big cities China will have to undergo a continuous process of transforming the rural inhabitants into urban inhabitants.[10]

[9] "On New Democracy," SWL, Vol. III, p. 138.
[10] "On Coalition Government," SWL, Vol. IV, pp. 294–5.

This passage shows that Mao's experience of a small-scale economy geared to guerrilla warfare had not led him to conceive the future in these terms – terms which would have imposed a pattern of socialist industrialization that differed radically from the Soviet Union.

Mao's article "On the People's Democratic Dictatorship" draws these strands together. It contains his last statement on economic policy before he came to power. By this time there was no need to think in terms of a political coalition and he therefore went out of his way to stress the dictatorial qualities of the government he was about to form. He confirmed that socialism remained a distant objective. On the private sector he stated:

China must utilize all urban and rural factors of capitalism which are beneficial and not detrimental to the national economy and the people's livelihood and unite with the national bourgeoisie in a common struggle. Our present policy is to restrict capitalism and not to eliminate it.[11]

In this article Mao faced a new problem: that of defining the role of foreign assistance and trade in China's development. His response to this problem was ambivalent. While he recognized that "a long time is required for China to realize true economic independence and become free from reliance on imperialist nations,"[12] he also made the well known assertion that China must "lean to one side." By this Mao meant that China would look to the Soviet Union and to the Socialist Bloc for guidance and material support. Thus he acknowledged the need to develop foreign economic links (at least for a period) but he did not seem entirely clear about where these links would have to be made.

THE BUILD-UP TO THE FIRST FIVE-YEAR PLAN

The state of the economy in 1949 reflected both a long-term economic crisis and the impact of war. Industrial and agricultural output were below their previous peaks and war finance had produced a hyper-inflation. These short-term problems were to dominate the economy for three years.

[11] "On the People's Democratic Dictatorship." Translated in Conrad Brandt, Benjamin Schwartz and John K. Fairbank, *A Documentary History of Chinese Communism*. (London: George Allen & Unwin, 1952), p. 460.
[12] *Ibid.*, pp. 459–60.

One of Mao's first acts after taking power was to fly to Moscow to discuss with Stalin the question of Soviet aid to the Chinese economy. After nine weeks of negotiation Mao returned home in February 1950 with the promise of repayable credits worth $300 million. By any objective criterion this support was minuscule. It bore no resemblance either to Soviet support to Eastern Europe or to American aid to Europe under the Marshall Plan. For China the outcome was that, for the time being at least, she was on her own. Mao later referred to economic relations with Stalin as like getting "a piece of meat from the mouth of the tiger."[13]

In this context the government adopted pragmatic and conservative policies. Land reform was to be implemented cautiously, with care being taken not to impede the recovery of agricultural output by attacking the "upper middle" strata of peasants. Private industry and commerce were encouraged to "flourish" and inflation was to be controlled by drastic, centralized fiscal measures. There is no evidence that Mao disagreed with these policies. On the contrary, in June 1950 he outlined a three-year programme of rehabilitation and recovery in which he openly supported[14] all of them. This is not surprising. A tactical de-radicalization of land policy was consistent with his record, and encouragement of the private industrial sector was an integral part of the New Democracy. During the Cultural Revolution, critics of Liu Shao-ch'i alleged that there had been a serious dispute at this time between Mao and Liu concerning agrarian issues.[15] They argued that Liu had won and that it was his victory over Mao which led to the implementation of a conservative land reform, and to the official acceptance of the view that there could be no substantial progress towards collective farming before industry was developed and agriculture mechanized.

[13] "Summing up Speech at a Conference of Provincial and Municipal Party Secretaries," January 1957. Wan-sui (1969), p. 85.

[14] Mao Tse-tung, Wei cheng-ch'ü kuo-chia ts'ai-cheng ching-chi chi-pen hao-pien tou-cheng. (Struggle to Achieve a Basic Turn for the Better in the Nation's Financial and Economic Condition.) (Secretariat of the South China Bureau of the Central Committee of the Chinese Communist Party, No Place, 1950.) This speech was made at the Third Plenum of the Seventh Central Committee which met 6–9 June, 1950.

[15] Important articles in this controversy are in Survey of China Mainland Magazines, 633, No. 4, 1968. These articles quote Mao's and Liu's views to reconstruct a long history of the controversy.

But the evidence for this interpretation is unimpressive. As examples of Mao's views at this time Liu's critics quoted statements from "On Coalition Government" and "On the People's Democratic Dictatorship." They also cited Mao's speech to the Second Plenum of the Seventh Central Committee of March 1949. Their quotation from "On the People's Democratic Dictatorship," however, includes the sentence: "And to carry out the socialization of agriculture a powerful industry with State-owned enterprises as the main component must be developed." This makes Mao's argument consistent with Liu's view. And in his speech to the Second Plenum, Mao had said merely that the rural sector "must be developed prudently, progressively and positively in the direction of modernization and collectivization." This does not suggest pressure for rapid socialization and, again, accepts the Liuist link between modernization and socialization.

In October 1950 China entered the Korean War. This placed strains on the economy and led to a series of campaigns to repress "counter-revolutionaries" and to stop corruption. Among the people killed in these campaigns (estimated at between one and three million) were many rural and business leaders. These campaigns undoubtedly had Mao's support and in May 1951 he observed that the large numbers of criminals under suspended death sentences constituted a useful potential labour force.[16] This idea later flowered in the system which involved camps for people sentenced to "labour reform" and to "education through labour."

The economic effect of the campaigns were serious. They led to rising urban unemployment and eventually to the paralysis of normal economic life. Thus, from the second half of 1952 the government was forced to end the terror and take steps to stimulate the economy. It was apparent, however, that within a few months the economy would again be pressing at the limits of full capacity and that stimulation of the private sector (which still accounted for about half of all industrial and handicraft production) would lead to problems.

By the spring of 1953 agricultural policy was also encounter-

[16] "Resolutions of the Third National Security Conference," 15 May, 1951, *Wan-sui* (1969), pp. 5–6.

182

ing difficulties. The land reform had left inefficiencies and class differences in the countryside, and a drive to increase mutual aid and co-operatives had not been successful. As a result the government found itself with serious problems in grain procurement, and with a migration of peasants to the cities that threatened rural work and promised to increase urban unemployment.

THE FIRST FIVE-YEAR PLAN AND THE TRANSITION TO SOCIALISM

Against this background some basic questions of economic strategy had to be decided. These may be summarized as follows:

(1) At what speed should the economy develop?

(2) What sort of institutional and planning system should the Chinese economy adopt, i.e. should China continue indefinitely with a system of mixed, public and private ownership in the cities and individual peasant farming in the countryside?

(3) What balance should there be in the allocation of resources between agriculture and industry and, within industry, between its different branches?

(4) What proportion of China's national income should be devoted to investment rather than consumption?

(5) What role should foreign trade play in the development process?

Answers to these questions emerged during 1953 in three forms. These were: the decision to go ahead with the First Five-Year Plan; the decision to adopt the General Line in the Period of Transition to Socialism and the decision to renew efforts to accelerate the socialization of agriculture.

Although the First Five-Year Plan was not published until July 1955, first drafts of it dated back to 1951 and the Plan for 1953 called for a huge increase in industrial construction. Between June and August 1953 the National Conference on Financial and Economic Work debated longer-term Plan strategy, and in September agreement on trade credits and assistance was reached with the Soviet Union. These agreements, covering plans for 141 major projects, made it possible to reach basic decisions on industrial growth for the period to 1959.

Adoption of industrial plans was followed by a meeting of the Politburo in October at which the General Line for the Transition to Socialism set the political and institutional guidelines within which China's industrialization drive was to be conducted. Parallel to these decisions came a climax to the debate on agriculture which led, in December 1953, to the adoption of the *Decisions on the Development of Agricultural Producers' Cooperatives.*

In terms of the five questions listed above the strategy incorporated in these decisions may be described as follows:

(1) The economy was to grow at high speed.
(2) There was to be a decisive step forward in the socialization of the economy and in the economic leadership of the public sector.
(3) The strategy committed most of the nation's investment (and nearly all of the public sector's investment) to the development of heavy industry and transportation at the expense of light industry and agriculture.
(4) The rate of investment was to be approximately 20 per cent of national income at the outset and a rising share thereafter. This rate was equal to that achieved in the Soviet Union's First Five-Year Plan, at which time Soviet incomes were considerably higher than those in China. Compared to the pre-1949 performance the new rate represented at least a tripling of investment effort.
(5) China was to depend almost totally on imported machinery, equipment and technical assistance from the Soviet Union and Bloc countries.

In sum these decisions marked a turning-point in China's economic history and it is not surprising that they were the subject of fierce controversy. Several schools of thought participated in this, but the main debate was between those who favoured the adoption of the fast, heavy industry, socialist strategy to be adopted and those who argued for a slower pace of development, more resources for agriculture and light industry and long-term reliance on the Soviet Union for industrial goods, rather than a short-term dash for industrial independence.

Those who supported the latter strategy believed that it entailed less risk, would yield more stable growth and would allow larger rises in living standards than would otherwise be possible.[17]

Where did Mao stand in these arguments? To judge by the materials currently available, he spoke relatively infrequently in these years and it is possible to interpret this as an indication that he opposed what was decided, or perhaps was uncertain. But he himself subsequently stated that, in spite of excessive adherence to the Soviet model, the Plan had been "basically correct."[18]

We think, therefore, that Mao was a supporter of the strategy adopted and that if he had reservations he kept them to himself. To begin with, the strategy had several points of continuity with his past thinking. Institutional change, rapid advance and emphasis on heavy industry had all been advocated by Mao in earlier contexts. The main inconsistency between the 1953 plans and his earlier views arose from the fact that he now believed that solutions to China's economic problems would only be found if the timetable of development was speeded up. The main casualty of this change was his earlier account of the stages through which he had argued that the Chinese revolution would have to pass. For, whereas 1949 had previously been seen as a point in the development of the New Democratic Revolution, in October 1953 he made important speeches in which he explained that 1949 had actually been the year in which the transition to socialism had begun.[19] Thus the New Democratic

[17] "The improvement of livelihood must be subordinated to the development of production," Jen-min jih-pao (The People's Daily), 16 December, 1953; Ts'eng Wen-ching, "Why must we give priority to heavy industry?" Hsüeh-hsi (Study) (1953), No. 11, pp. 12–16.

[18] "Examples of Dialectics," no date. Wan-sui (1967), p. 150. However, in his "Speech to an Enlarged Central Work Conference," 30 January, 1962, Wan-sui (1969), p. 416, he also commented that the Plan "lacked creativity."

[19] We have no full text of Mao's speeches at this time, one of which was made in the Politburo. Commentators do however quote key sentences from them. Jen-min shou-ts'e (The People's Handbook) (1955) (Peking: 1955), p. 343; Li Wei-han, "Speech at the National Congress of the All China Federation of Industry and Commerce," Jen-min jih-pao, 10 November, 1953. Mao later confirmed his view that 1949 marked the completion of the Democratic Revolution in "Reading Notes on the Textbook of Political Economy," Wan-sui (1967), pp. 168–9 (hereafter "Reading Notes").

stage (in which the private sector was to have a role for "several decades") was now said to have been completed four years previously![20]

Further evidence of Mao's support for the Plan strategy is in Li Fu-ch'un's *Report on Consultations with the Soviet Union Concerning Questions of Aid for Our Country's Economic Development*.[21] This Report was published side by side with Mao's telegram of thanks to Malenkov – the text of which concluded with a statement that Soviet proposals would enable China to avoid "many errors and false roads." In his speech Li spoke as follows:

> According to Chairman Mao's instructions our basic tasks are first, to concentrate strength on the development of heavy industry in order to establish the basis of our country's defence, modernization and industrialization; then to increase appropriately and train construction manpower; then to develop communications and transport, light industry, agriculture and commerce; and then to implement the reform of private industry and commerce while using correctly the positive functions of individual handicrafts and agriculture and of private industry and commerce.

"All these measures," said Li, "are to guarantee the progressive domination of the socialist sector of our country's economy and to guarantee, on the basis of rising production, a gradual rise in the material and cultural levels of our people." It is difficult to believe that Mao would have allowed these plans to be described as his "instructions" if they were not. In the case of agriculture there is additional evidence of Mao's role. In October 1953, speaking at the National Conference on Agricultural Mutual Aid and Co-operation Work he is reported to have urged the case for socialization and to have said:

> If socialism does not occupy the rural front line then capitalism will. And you can't say that it won't go one way or the other.[22]

[20] Wang Hui-te, "On the two stages of the Chinese Revolution," *Hsüeh-hsi* (1954), No. 1, pp. 3–5. In this definitive account, Wang had to draw attention to errors made only two months earlier, i.e. "Are the tasks of the first stage of the Chinese Revolution completed?" *Hsüeh-hsi* (1953), No. 11, pp. 24–5.
[21] For Li Fu-ch'un's Report see *Chieh-fang jih-pao* (*Liberation Daily*), 16 September, 1953.
[22] Chen Po-ta reported this statement in his explanation of the "Draft Resolution on Agricultural Producers' Co-operatives," *Jen-min shou-ts'e* (1956), p. 93.

This was language which he was to repeat in the summer of 1955 and it seems probable that, as in 1955, Mao was advocating the radical policy against more cautious colleagues.

THE FIRST LEAP FORWARD: 1955-57

The disagreement on economic policies which continued until the summer of 1955 must have forced Mao to clarify his own economic thinking for, when he intervened to put an end to the argument, he was able to put forward detailed plans for the economy based on his own distinctive economic principles.[23] The impact of his new economic proposals was immediate and far-reaching. A "High Tide" of socialist reform in agriculture, industry, handicrafts and commerce in 1955 was followed in 1956 by a leap in production and construction. This upsurge of economic activity was followed in 1957 by an equally big contraction. The origin and characteristics of this cycle merit close attention because it was to be repeated, with remarkable similarity, twice within five years.

Mao's intervention was the result of (a) his desire to correct the conservative, rightist outlook of the leadership and (b) his belief that the time was right for a rapid transformation of the economy both in ownership and production (which he considered closely related). The poor performance of the economy, especially in

[23] These plans and principles may be found in the following six documents: (i) "On the Question of Agricultural Cooperativisation," 31 July, 1955, SR, pp. 389–420. (ii) "Summing up Speech at the Sixth Expanded Plenum of the Seventh CCP Central Committee," September 1955, Wan-sui (1969), pp. 12–25 (hereafter "Summing up Speech, 1955"). (iii) "Talk Opposing Right-Deviation and Conservatism," 6 December, 1955, Wan-sui (1969), pp. 25–7. (iv) Preface to The Upsurge of Socialism in China's Countryside, Peking, 1956. Mao's preface was written in December 1955. (v) 1956 nien tao 1967 nien ch'uan kuo nung-yeh fa-chan kang-yao (ts'ao-an) (1956–1967 Draft Outline Plan for the Development of the Entire Nation's Agriculture.) Jen-min jih-pao, 26 January, 1956. This was known as the "Forty Articles" and will be called this hereafter. A detailed analysis of Mao's role in the formulation and implementation of this plan is available in Parris H. Chang, Power and Policy in China (University Park and London: Pennsylvania State University Press, 1976). (vi) "On the Ten Great Relations," 25 April, 1956, Wan-sui (1969), pp. 40–56. Mao put this before senior ministers in December 1955. The approach, he said, "made a start on proposing our own line for construction" (i.e. appropriate to Chinese conditions and independent of the Soviet Union). See "Talks at the Chengtu Conference," March 1958, Wan-sui (1969), p. 163.

1954 and the spring of 1955, cannot be divorced from the disagreements over economic policy. In spite of the adoption of the *General Line* and of a broad, long-run economic strategy, the government had not yet adopted or published detailed targets for the First Five-Year Plan and the implementation of agricultural policy was indecisive.

In 1954 a second attempt to set up co-operatives on a broad front had encountered opposition from the peasants, many of whom were not yet convinced that they would receive real economic benefits by joining. The peasants had also reacted[24] strongly to the burdens imposed on them under the government's Unified Purchase and Supply scheme for grain. (This scheme set consumption, tax and sales quotas.) As peasants' incentive to produce declined, output fell back and there were mounting deaths of pigs and draught animals. In an economy without tractors, and in which pigs were the chief source of fertiliser, this had serious implications. Also the decline in output of cotton and major grain crops in 1953 and 1954 directly affected industrial production and construction, and must have indirectly affected the credibility of any high targets being proposed for future industrial growth. All this led to pressure from influential people such as Teng Tzu-hui (head of the government's rural work department) to "get off the horse"[25] – i.e. to abandon any plans for the speedy collectivization of agriculture and to concentrate instead on increasing material incentives for the peasants. During the spring of 1955 Chekiang province had already "dismounted" by dissolving 20,000 co-operatives in an atmosphere described by Mao as one of "terrified confusion."[26] This dangerous situation was the context of Mao's decision to give a rigorous lead in economic policy in 1955 and early 1956. His economic analysis is considered under four headings:

(1) *Institutional Reform, Planning and the Rate of Growth.* Mao believed that rapid growth could be achieved by a new combination of firmer central direction balanced by an increase

[24] Mao made several references to this. A particularly vivid account is found in "Talks at the Nanning Conference," 11–12 January, 1958. *Wan-sui* (1969), p. 153.
[25] "On the Question of Agricultural Cooperativisation"; also "Summing up Speech, 1955."
[26] "On the Question of Agricultural Cooperativisation."

in certain types of local initiative. This change was to be brought about by the socialization of agriculture, handicrafts and industry, and by reform of the planning system. Failure to create a dynamic socialist economy would, Mao thought, lead to prolonged economic stagnation. He saw ample evidence for this thesis in the recent performance of both agriculture and industry.

The plan for agricultural collectivization was first described in his speech of 31 July. In this he called for a new campaign to establish semi-socialist co-operatives to be followed by fully socialist collectives at a later date. Emphasizing the importance of transforming agricultural organization in stages (he argued that their hasty collectivization would have an adverse effect on production and incomes) Mao envisaged the completion of the *first stage* (semi-socialist co-operatives) by 1960. Fully socialist collectives were to be introduced *gradually*. These targets represented a speedier transformation of agriculture than that laid down in the First Five-Year Plan[27] (published three weeks earlier), and they themselves were totally surpassed by Mao's revised targets of December 1955.[28] By then, it was clear that his July speech had already set the "High Tide" in motion and he concluded that semi-socialist co-operativization could be accomplished during 1956 and full collectivization in 1959–60. Elated by his success, Mao then went on to argue that the "High Tide" in agriculture made it possible and necessary to socialize industry, handicrafts and commerce. In this way the non-agricultural sectors could be planned to respond to the growth unleashed by co-operativization.

At this time Mao's optimism[29] about China's future economic development was tremendous, and in 1955 he put before the nation his predictions (not simply targets) of the levels of production that would be achieved by the end of three five-year plans, that is by 1967. Grain output was to double, cotton output

[27] Chung-hua jen-min kung-ho fa-chan kuo-min ching-chi ti ti-yi ko wu nien chi-hua, 1953–57. (Chinese People's Republic First Five-Year Plan for the Development of the National Economy, 1953–57), Peking 1955.
[28] Preface to The Upsurge of Socialism.
[29] "Tremendous changes and immense productive forces have appeared. It is like discovering a new continent. The continent was there all the time but we did not see it." "Talk Opposing Right Deviation," Wan-sui (1969), p. 25.

was to quadruple, and steel output was to rise to six times its 1955 level.[30] To set the economy on the path to attaining these heights he launched an immediate drive:

We must go faster; every item of work must be faster, greater and better. Achieve better results within a shorter period of time.[31]

This was China's first leap forward and it was based on one of Mao's most consistent principles – that economic development is achieved by rapid, wave-like movements. He opposed a gradualist approach which tries to eliminate tension, arguing that "imbalance is normal, balance is temporary."[32] This was for Mao the "law of advance." He accepted that wave-like motions created imbalance or "contradictions" (for example in the form of shortages due to uneven development between sectors) but saw these as a stimulant to progress. The problems created would be solved, leaving the economy in a better position than before. Mao actually envisaged three such waves in China during the winters of 1955–56, 1957–58 and 1958–59.

This approach to economic development contained some elements of contradiction. On the one hand he advocated the attainment of socialization in stages, which suggested some degree of smoothness; but on the other hand he also believed that growth was the product of shocks or waves. As in later years, Mao tried to cover himself by qualifying what at first seemed to be clear-cut. Thus he called for both a leap in production and a socialization campaign during 1956, commenting:

Either too slow or too fast is no good. Both are called opportunism.[33]

And at the same time as he attacked the rightist tendencies prevalent in 1955 he warned that "left deviation" was also possible.[34]

Another inconsistency is that between Mao's advocacy of imbalance and decentralization, and his belief in the virtues of "overall" planning with strong central direction. Thus on the

[30] "Summing up Speech, 1955," pp. 14–15.
[31] "Talk Opposing Right Deviation," Wan-sui (1969), p. 26.
[32] Ibid., p. 27, where he also stated "with eternal calm, mistakes are inevitable."
[33] "Summing up Speech, 1955," Wan-sui (1969), p. 18.
[34] Ibid., p. 23.

one hand, he described the need to extend regional power[35] in order to encourage enthusiasm and independence. On the other hand, he complained that "some comrades delight in decentralization and love to set up independent kingdoms,"[36] and insisted that only central planning could create the "national balance," without which "the country would be in great chaos."[37]

(2) *Priorities Between Economic Sectors*. It was during this period that Mao began to reconsider the relative priorities that should be given to heavy industry, light industry and agriculture. While reaffirming that heavy industry was still to be the "key sector," he directed that "appropriate adjustments" be made in the allocation of investment in favour of light industry and agriculture. Mao's passage on this theme in the "Ten Great Relations" is particularly interesting for the extraordinary lengths to which he went in justifying the fact that he had raised the question at all.[38] He appeared to argue that the proposed redistribution of investment away from heavy industry would in fact increase its rate of development. But in reality he was advocating greater production of consumer goods. We must note, however, that Mao did not direct heavy industry to structure its output around the needs of agriculture. At this stage agriculture was still to grow primarily on a basis of traditional inputs and reforms in organization.

(3) *Consumption and Incentives*. In the course of 1955 and 1956, Mao stressed the importance of financial incentives for both industrial workers and peasants in promoting production. But although he favoured raising workers' wages because their labour productivity had increased, [39] he did not comment on its possible implication – that the gap between workers' and peasants' incomes would widen. Mao also warned against squeezing the peasants by imposing high rates of taxation, procurement and investment in the collectives.[40] He proposed that peasants'

---

[35] "On the Ten Great Relations."
[36] "Summing up Speech, 1955 " Wan-sui (1969), p. 21.
[37] "Speech at an Enlarged Conference of the Politburo of the Central Committee," April 1956, Wan-sui (1969), p. 38.
[38] "On the Ten Great Relations," Wan-sui (1969), pp. 41–3.
[39] Ibid., Wan-sui (1969), p. 47.
[40] Ibid., p. 48.

incomes should, wherever possible, increase every year and that price policy should be an instrument in achieving this end.[41]

(4) The 'Wave' of 1956. Although Mao's economic speeches included some conservative statements, to the cadres his message was unambiguous: production and investment must be increased dramatically. Memories of the 1954 purge of Kao Kang and the 1955 campaign against counter-revolutionaries compelled cadres to repudiate rightism by adopting Mao's most ambitious proposals. Thus, for the first six months of 1956 the pace was frantic. In industry, shortages of raw materials, fuel and power were widespread. In agriculture, Mao's stages of reform were swept aside. Full collectivization was carried out in most provinces by June 1956 and in the process basic rights of peasants were violated.[42] In an attempt to attain targets of the Twelve-Year Plan within a year or two, rural labour was mobilized throughout China to build water conservation works, carry fertilizer and move earth. Much of this endeavour was ineffective and involved a deterioration in the health of peasants. Pigs and draught animals were killed by peasants or died of hunger and neglect. People were forced to pull ploughs and harrows. Harvests failed because peasants were ordered to grow inappropriate crops using inappropriate methods. This upsurge lasted until June 1956 when it was called off (according to Mao) in a People's Daily editorial entitled "We must oppose both conservatism and hastiness."[43] Mao considered the editorial to be an attack on himself[44] and there can be little doubt that his

[41] Mao advocated a narrowing of the "scissors difference" in his "On the Correct Handling of Contradictions Among the People," 27 February, 1957, SR, pp. 432–79. See also "Summing up Speech at a Conference of Provincial and Municipal Party Secretaries," January 1957, Wan-sui (1969), p. 90: "The price of marketed grain should be raised by 5 per cent at a certain time . . . If we want to increase the amount of marketed grain but the price is too low, who will till the land? I am not saying that we should raise the price right now but that price policy requires research."
[42] For example: privately owned pigs, poultry, tools and trees were compulsorily collectivized even though government regulations stipulated that such collectivization must be on a voluntary basis; collectives allocated no private plots (although provided for by the regulations). Peasants were fined for doing "inadequate" collective work.
[43] Jen-min jih-pao, 20 June, 1956, p. 1.
[44] "Talks at the Nanning Conference" January 1958, Wan-sui (1969), pp. 151–2.

mismanagement of the economy in 1956 did affect his standing as an economist.

As so often, the pendulum then swung to the opposite extreme, and for a year China pursued more liberal economic policies. Central planning was relaxed, wages were increased, incentives for livestock production were introduced and peasants were given bigger private plots with the opportunity to sell in small free markets. Mao gave his blessing to all these reforms and although he had been stung by the criticisms of the leap, his optimism concerning China's economic future does not appear to have been shaken.

Neither the "High Tide" nor the liberalization provided immediate solutions to China's major economic problems. For example, in spite of two years of fairly rapid growth in grain production, grain consumption was proving difficult to control. A serious imbalance between government acquisition and supply had arisen in 1954–55 and then, in the second half of 1956, rising peasant consumption forced the government to use stocks to meet a procurement deficit. Nevertheless Mao still felt confident enough in January 1957 to state that in two years' time "there will be no competition with the people for grain."[45] And in his famous speech "On the Correct Handling of Contradictions Among the People," he attacked those who stirred up a "miniature typhoon" against the collectives and grain rationing system, describing the problems of the collectives as "not serious."

As the First Five-Year Plan period drew to an end, despite considerable success in industrial development (particularly in heavy industry) agricultural production was failing to grow fast enough. And while collectivization had not reduced output, it had not raised it at the rapid rate envisaged by Mao. To a considerable extent, China's economic difficulties were due to rapid population increase. This was reflected in rural and urban unemployment, in low consumption of food and other basic commodities and in serious problems in the provision of housing and welfare services. Mao, however, still regarded China's

[45] "Speech at a Conference of Provincial and Municipal Secretaries," January 1957, Wan-sui (1969), p. 79.

big population as an "asset"[46] and, in the last analysis, appears to have been more worried about the dangers of slow, unplanned, market-orientated economic growth than of the problems created by leaps. The "rightists" had gained ascendancy during 1957 and Mao felt compelled to react sharply. By this time, moreover, his experience and ideas had matured. He therefore felt impelled to launch the Great Leap Forward.

THE GREAT LEAP FORWARD OF 1958

The build-up to the Great Leap Forward took six months. During the summer and autumn of 1957 the government issued a number of important directives which initiated mass movements centred on water conservation, irrigation and fertilizer collection. Rectification and socialist education campaigns were also organized to put an end to the attacks on many aspects of economic policy during the "Hundred Flowers" period. Directives announcing the decentralization of industry and the sending down of cadres from the higher levels of administration in later 1957 and early 1958 were further indications that a new economic strategy was being formulated. On the eve of the second leap, Mao did not make a dramatic intervention comparable with his 1955 speech on co-operativization. Instead he toured China, urging local cadres to set the leap in motion. Documents and speeches of spring 1958 provide rich evidence of Mao's economic thought at this turning point in Communist China's history. Mao's general analysis was the same as that on the eve of the first leap in 1955; it was necessary to restore "confidence" in the future and to banish rightist thinking; the initiative of the masses, who were demanding a new "upsurge," must be unleashed; development was only to be achieved through waves of activity.[47] Answering those who opposed

---

[46] "On the Correct Handling of Contradictions Among the People," p. 461.
[47] Preface to "Sixty Points on Working Methods (Draft) of the General Office of the Central Committee of the Communist Party," 19 February, 1958. In the preface (dated 31 January, 1958) Mao wrote: "As I see it now, there has never been such an upsurge of enthusiasm and initiative among the masses of the people on the production front." "The Sixty Points" are translated in Jerome Ch'en, *Mao Papers: Anthology and Bibliography* (London: Oxford University Press, 1970), pp. 57–76.

a new leap, and remembering the events of 1956, Mao said:

Water conservation, rectification, anti-rightism, six hundred million people engaged in a great campaign. Isn't this "craving for greatness and success"? In setting advanced production norms aren't we "being impatient for quick results"? Unless despising the old system and the old reactionary production relationships, what do we think we are doing? If we do not have faith in socialism and communism, what do we think we are doing?[48]

Compare this, however, with his insistence that targets must be realistic. For example, Honan had adopted a 1958 target of three tons per hectare for grain (the six-year average yield for 1952–57 was only 0·9 tons per hectare). Mao considered that this target should not be published since the kind of competition it would create was bound to produce "crude" work and the masses would be "over-tense."[49] How then is the following to be interpreted?

The appearance of disorder contains within it some favourable elements; do not fear disorder.[50]

Was this the real Mao? The restoration of the slogan "more, faster, better and more economically" and publication[51] of a revised "Forty Articles" on agricultural development represented Mao's defeat of those who had swept them away in 1956. Given his prestige and the political context in which cadres (including provincial leaders) were being purged for opposing the new leap, Mao's cautious words on high targets were bound to be ignored and he must have known this.

To some extent the theoretical basis of the Great Leap Forward of 1958 was the same as that of the 1956 leap. Its core was Mao's conception of social and economic change as something that occurs unevenly, in cycles. He rejected the smooth, orderly view of development expounded by Soviet theorists, describing it as, "out of touch with the wave-like form taken by advances in the

[48] "Talks at the Chengtu Conference" (1958), Wan-sui (1969), p. 178.
[49] Ibid., p. 166: "If everyone is striving to be first, the country may be thrown into confusion."
[50] Ibid., p. 171.
[51] Jen-min jih-pao, 26 October, 1957.

development of socialist production."[52] In the "Sixty Points on Working Methods" he put this in its most abstract form:

Disequilibrium is a general objective rule. The cycle, which is endless, evolves from disequilibrium to equilibrium and then to disequilibrium again. Each cycle, however, brings us to a higher level of development.[53]

By 1958 he had added two new elements to this theory. The mechanism underlying wave-like progress was, in Mao's view, the fluctuating imbalance between (a) the development of production and the social relations of production and (b) the social relations of production and their "superstructure" of ideology and culture. These imbalances, he later argued, should "serve as the key to the study of the economic problems of socialism."[54] Many of Mao's colleagues still believed that only the lengthy and systematic development of production would create the right conditions for a socialist culture and for highly collectivized economic institutions. Mao, on the other hand, took the view that if the immediate establishment of such institutions were to be combined with an intensive inculcation of socialist ideas and values, a dramatic acceleration of economic development would follow.[55] Later, after the Communes had been established, he was thus able to envisage an "unlimited" growth in grain production and also to propose plans for steel output by which the "world will be shaken."[56] Mao's new emphasis on the "superstructure" was particularly important. In the first round of socialization he had believed that changes in ownership and organization were all that was necessary to liberate economic forces:

[52] "Reading Notes," Wan-sui (1967), p. 207; ibid., pp. 202–4.
[53] "Sixty Points on Working Methods," p. 66.
[54] An important discussion of this is included in Richard Levy, "New Light on Mao," CQ (March 1975), No. 61, pp. 95–117.
[55] See particularly "Reading Notes," Wan-sui (1967), pp. 179–80, pp. 182–3 and pp. 206–9. A comprehensive and authoritative account of Mao's thought at the time of the Leap is: Ch'en Po-ta, "Under the banner of Chairman Mao," Hung ch'i (Red Flag) (1958), No. 4, pp. 1–12.
[56] In May 1958 Mao envisaged an output of 40 million tons of steel in 1964, and catching up with United States output by 1966. "Speech at the Conference of Heads of Delegations by the Second Session of the Eighth Party Congress," Wan-sui (1969), p. 225, 18 May, 1958. Tao Chu, "Refute the theory that there is a limit to increasing grain output," Hung ch'i (1958), No. 5, pp. 1–4.

In the past [before the Great Leap Forward] we did not know how to make a socialist revolution. We thought that after the co-operativization [1955] and after the introduction of public-private management [1956] everything would be resolved.[57]

The events of 1956 and 1957 had shown that matters were far from being resolved and that even under socialist organization there was still "struggle between factions among the people."[58]

The second new element in Mao's thinking was that he had now abandoned his theory of development by discrete stages in favour of a theory of "permanent revolution" in which the stages are merged. Its application to China justified the immediate adoption of economic institutions appropriate to a communist society.[59]

Mao's theory of the Leap embraced two other interesting ideas. First, he saw both the leaders and the led embroiled in a process of struggle: struggle against nature, struggle against social forces and struggle against ideas. And it was from this idea of struggle that Mao developed his military approach to economic problems, an approach that he later admitted to be simplistic.[60] Secondly, Mao's theory of the Leap underlined the significance of ignorance. Unlike the Soviet theorists, who believed that the organization and allocation of resources in the Soviet economy obeyed known "laws" of socialist develop-ment, Mao claimed that the Party's understanding of such laws was fragmentary and could only be improved as a result of trial and experiment. As he later wrote:

[57] "Reading Notes," Wan-sui (1967), p. 244.
[58] Ibid., p. 199. The debate about the superstructure reached a climax in the Cultural Revolution. Liu Chien-hsün (Honan's First Party Secretary) was attacked for allegedly arguing "At present, the productive forces have not developed in the way we had originally expected so that premature change in the system of ownership would be harmful to production." Noted in Facts about Liu Chien-hsün's Crimes. Pamphlet published by General Command Headquarters of Revolutionary Rebels of Organs of the CCP Honan Provincial Committee, 12 March, 1967. Attacks on Liu Shao-ch'i emphasized his history of opposition in both organizational and ideological transformation as a means of accelerating the base of production.
[59] This is discussed in the introduction to Stuart R. Schram, La "Revolution Permanente" en Chine (Paris: Mouton, 1963).
[60] "Speech at a Conference of Provincial and Municipal Party Committee Sec-retaries," 2 February, 1959, Wan-sui (1969), p. 278. In this Mao commented, "In economic construction we were as children, lacking experience: unfamil-iar with tactics or strategy we made war on the earth."

197

Only in practice and struggle do we recognize objective reality and what the plans and ratios [should be] . . . Only by going through with the Great Leap did we find the [correct] way.[61]

The significance of ignorance was not restricted to social and economic matters. Mao also argued that even in a socialist society the discovery of the laws of natural science and their application to production were hampered by "academic authorities" and by bureaucrats.[62] This belief led him to stimulate the economy by decentralizing power, by encouraging the abolition of "irrational"rules in economic organizations, by promoting the growth of small-scale (and therefore unbureaucratized) enterprises and by initiating the vast campaign for backyard furnaces which involved all of these measures.

From these remarks it will be clear that Mao's unfolding conception of the Leap led to several departures from the economic strategy he had supported in 1953. These may be summarized as follows: at the institutional level it led to the establishment of large, highly collectivized People's Communes and to a radical decentralization of economic and financial planning.[63] At its most extreme the latter created a situation where the economy was subject to central control only to the extent that it responded to direct appeals by Mao and others. Thus the policy of moving gradually towards socialist institutions and of adopting Soviet planning techniques, was abandoned.

Mao also rejected Soviet resource allocation policies. He anticipated that the Leap would provide a solution to the problem of how to create the correct balance between agriculture and industry, between different types of industry and between small-scale and large-scale industry. A combination of rapidly

[61] Ibid.

[62] "Reading Notes," Wan-sui (1967), p. 202. "First Speech to the Second Session of the Eighth Party Congress," May 1958, Wan-sui (1969), p. 192.

[63] The decentralization of finance was particularly important. Mao had criticized Finance Minister Li Hsien-nien's technical approach as early as 1956: see "Report on the 1957 budget out-turn and the draft estimate for 1958." Hsin-hua pan yüeh k'an (New China Semi-monthly) (1958), No. 5, p. 5. A theoretical discussion of Maoist financial policy is found in Ch'en Pao-sen, "Chairman Mao's 'On the Correct Handling of Contradictions Among the People' guides the reform of financial codes and conventions," Ching-chi yen-ch'iu (Economic Research) (1958), No. 7, pp. 10–15.

growing output, new institutions (such as the Communes) and a decentralized financial system, would enable the economy to achieve higher rates of investment than ever before. This higher investment could be ploughed back, stimulating agriculture, ensuring full use of all resources and promoting the high-speed growth of both the modern and the small-scale indigenous sectors of industry. This was Mao's policy of "walking on two legs."[64]

Finally, Mao's belief that he could tap vast Chinese resources of effort and creativity found expression in a move to diminish reliance on foreigners and to establish a policy of "self-reliance." This change in his thinking was rapid. In 1956, he was still supporting the policy of depending on the Soviet Union.[65] By 1957 he had adopted a more cautious approach, pointing out that it was only necessary to learn from the Soviet Union "selectively."[66] By 1958, however, Mao wanted to go it alone. This reflected both his optimism about China's domestic prospects and his worries about the outside world. For Mao saw not only that relations with the Soviet Union were deteriorating but also that "the West may possibly fall apart."[67] Although Mao regarded 1958 as the point at which China embarked on self-reliance, foreign trade actually remained at peak levels during the leap itself. Indeed, in the case of steel, imports were higher in 1958 than in any year between 1949 and 1968.

In more concrete terms, the essence of the Great Leap Forward was found in the plans for steel and agriculture. Mao became obsessed with overtaking Britain in steel production. In March

[64] "Talk at the Symposium of Hsin, Lo, Hsu and Hsiu-sen Local Committees," 21 February, 1959, Wan-sui (1967), pp. 3–7; "Speech at the Conference of Provincial and Municipal Party Secretaries," 2 February, 1959, Wan-sui (1969), p. 277.

[65] Mao said, "We still do not know how to design a big plant. Who, at present, would come and do it for us? . . . Imperialists want to keep their technology secret . . . Economically, we are still not independent." "Instructions at a Discussion Meeting for a Section of Delegates Attending the Second Session of the First Committee of the All-China Federation of Industry and Commerce," 8 November, 1956, Wan-sui (1969), p. 63.

[66] "Summing up at a Conference of Provincial and Municipal Party Committee Secretaries," January 1957, Wan-sui (1969), p. 84.

[67] "Second Talk with Directors of Some Regions of [Economic] Co-operation," 12 December, 1958, Wan-sui (1969), p. 256.

1958 he suggested[68] that by 1962 China should produce 20 million tons (compared with five million tons in 1957). He later confessed[69] that he had, at one time, favoured a target of 100–120 million tons. Agricultural production, too, was to leap forward to such an extent that the targets laid down by the "Forty Articles" for 1967 were to be achieved in eight years at most and perhaps in two to five years.[70] Mao called for an immediate rise in collective investment and, associated with this, he directed that private farm activity should be curbed in order to direct the peasants' "enthusiasm" into the socialized sector.[71] Deep ploughing, close planting, the use of more steel ploughs and chemical fertilizers, together with a massive improvement in water conservation, were to be the main sources of faster agricultural growth.

The new upsurge of activity was even greater than that of 1956. Local authorities, with their new powers, unearthed "hidden potentialities" in their quest to industrialize every corner of China. Central planning as it had been previously practised disappeared and targets from above soared into the realms of fantasy. In agriculture the mobilization of labour was on an unprecedented scale, involving the creation of large work brigades which embraced more than one collective. This in turn was accompanied by the merger of collectives, but the Communes were not mentioned until summer. In July the government began to announce the attainment of "miracle" targets. Mao accepted these claims almost entirely and this was to have catastrophic consequences. Thus, in September 1958 he stated that grain output had doubled and referred to the possibility of

---

[68] "Talks at the Chengtu Conference" (1958), *Wan-sui* (1969), p. 171. Having proposed this target Mao asked: ". . . will it throw everything into confusion?"

[69] "Speech at the Sixth Plenum of the Eighth Central Committee," 19 December, 1958, *Wan-sui* (1969), p. 264.

[70] The plan to attain the targets in eight years was given in Mao's "Speech at the Supreme State Conference," 28 January, 1958, *Wan-sui* (1969), p. 154. By March he had reduced the period to between two and five years: "Talks at the Chengtu Conference," *Wan-sui* (1969), p. 166. In September, however, Mao wondered whether the targets had already been achieved. "Speech at the Supreme State Conference," September 1958, *Wan-sui* (1969), p. 228.

[71] "Sixty Points on Working Methods."

its doubling again in 1959.[72] He raised (not for the first time)[73] the question of how China might use all this grain, concluding that, after all needs had been met, some could be burned as fuel, and he even suggested that China should plan to reduce grain production after 1959.[74] Thus, for a few months Mao led the Chinese people to believe that miracles had happened in agricultural production. Communes acted as if grain was available in unlimited amounts; rationing was abolished, grain was distributed free, on a basis of need, not work, and large amounts of food were wasted by the new Commune mess-halls.

Against this background the *People's Daily* proposed a new system of land use.[75] Known as the "three-three" system, it involved allocating a third of the arable land to crops, a third to horticulture and the rest to lie fallow: the new, high yields reported for 1958 would more than compensate for the reduction in the area under grain. The *People's Daily* attributed this "revolutionary measure" to Mao. Of course, the change was to be implemented "over time" or "when appropriate," but in the circumstances it was not surprising that cadres immediately reduced the sown area of grain for the 1959 harvest. Meanwhile, the campaign for smelting steel in small, "backyard" furnaces reached its climax during the autumn of 1958. This diverted labour away from agriculture and the decline in the farm labour force was further accelerated by the migration of millions of peasants to towns and cities in response to the industrial boom. As a result, not all of the 1958 harvest was collected. The economic situation was, in short, chaotic to an unparalleled degree.

It was not until the end of November that Mao began to voice even tentative doubts about the state of the economy. People, he said, were "a little tense" over Commune organization and the steel campaign.[76] Commenting on the lack of verification of

[72] "Speech at the Supreme State Conference," September 1958, *Wan-sui* (1969), p. 228.
[73] "Chairman Mao comes to Hsüshui." *Jen-min jih-pao*, 11 August, 1958.
[74] "Speech at the Supreme State Conference," September 1958, *Wan-sui* (1969), p. 240.
[75] "Revolutionary measures in agricultural production." *Jen-min jih-pao*, 24 October, 1958.
[76] "Talks with Directors of Some Regions of [Economic] Co-operation," *Wan-sui* (1969), p. 252.

grain output, he wondered whether total grain output for 1958 was perhaps only 350 millions instead of the 375 million tons claimed. He still predicted that grain production would rise by 40 per cent in 1959, bringing the total to 525 million tons (compared with 185 million tons in 1957). But one wonders if he really believed this since he also said:

> Next spring will there be areas where people cannot eat three times a day? . . . At the moment we are groping for a firm basis regarding the question of whether or not we should eat somewhat less now and more later. All areas should discuss it.[77] . . . [Mao also commented frankly at this time on the unreality of his targets for steel production]: at that time I was only concerned with the question of whether we needed it or not . . . and did not pay attention to the question of possibilities. This year the production of 10·7 million tons has tired us out and thus raises problems concerning possibilities. Next year 30 million tons, the following year 60 million tons and, in 1962, 120 million tons, these are false hopes, neither realistic nor possible. We must now shorten the time and reduce the target to 18–20 million tons.[78]

His reservations about the Leap led him to propose that the Central Committee's resolution (on the current situation) should not be published immediately, so as "to avoid certain unrealistic ideas which were produced in the Great Leap Forward . . ."[79] But, although Mao alluded[80] to the possibility of China's becoming like a "reinless horse," beset by "confusion and anarchy," there is no firm evidence that he yet fully understood the gravity of the situation. It was not until the spring of 1959 that the crisis broke, and Mao's prestige as an economic thinker and strategist suffered a further setback from which it was never to recover.

MAO'S IMMEDIATE RESPONSE TO THE GREAT LEAP FORWARD

Did the course of events in China during the Great Leap Forward lead Mao to revise his economic thinking? He certainly suffered a temporary loss of confidence but he did not abandon his basic view of economic development. He did, however, call for an

[77] Ibid., pp. 253–4.
[78] "Speech at the Sixth Plenum" (December 1958), Wan-sui (1969), p. 264.
[79] Ibid., p. 264.
[80] Ibid., p. 262.

urgent revision of some specific policies: the government, he said, must issue some "proclamations to pacify the people."[81] His response to the economic effects of the Leap is considered in three sections:

(1) *Planning and Growth*. Mao soon realized that the speed of development would have to be reduced in 1959. This, he said, was perfectly consistent with the wave-like character of economic change and, indeed, was to be expected by those who understood this law. In other words, Mao went near to professing that he had foreseen the need to slacken the pace when initiating the Leap:

... sometimes a horse gallops a little faster, sometimes a little slower. Sometimes one has to mount the horse and at other times one has to dismount. This situation is completely possible because, in the first place, we are inexperienced; secondly, because our economic construction has to be changed according to circumstances ... The progress of economic construction is wave-like ... that is to say there is balance which is upset and, having been upset, another balance is restored. Of course the wave-like advance cannot be too big or it will suddenly become a reckless advance and then suddenly a conservative [withdrawal]. But it is inevitable that progress in development will follow the law of waves. If you acknowledge this point then it will not worry you when, having advanced a bit hastily this year, you pull back somewhat next year.[82]

Having committed himself to a policy of retrenchment, he stressed yet again the importance of fixing realistic targets, directing cadres at all levels to ignore "those stipulations made in the instructions from higher levels. Ignore them and simply concentrate on practical possibilities."[83] Only a year earlier he had called for the achievement of several long-term goals within a few years, but now he told the people to take a longer view:

What is greater, what is faster? These must be viewed from practice. Now we are proposing to build a great socialist country with modern

[81] "Talks at the Chengchow Conference" (February–March 1959), *Wan-sui* (1967), p. 26.
[82] "Examples of Dialectics," *Wan-sui* (1967), p. 149–50.
[83] "Intra-Party Correspondence," 29 April, 1959, *Wan-sui* (1969), p. 292.

industry, modern agriculture and modern science and culture, in 15 years. If this is impossible, then increase the period a bit.[84]

The slower pace should, in Mao's view, be accompanied by a return to some kind of central, overall planning, if for no other reason than to allow for the formulation of consistent targets. On the question of the relations between the central and local authorities in the planning process, he made his usual vague references to the need for "proper initiative . . . proper independence . . . All that can be centralized should be, must be centralized; all that cannot be centralized should not be . . . Localities should strive for these powers and not fear being dubbed with the 'hat' of localism."[85] He made more concrete proposals, however, about the planning of the Communes, where excessive centralization had already affected incentives and production. The details of his directives on this subject are given in section three.

(2) *Balance between Sectors.* The experience of 1958 forced Mao to consider more deeply the relationship between rapid economic growth and "proportional development." Mao, we have argued, above all favoured rapid growth and saw virtue in the imbalances which this would create. Correct "proportional development" also involved a consideration of the balance between sectors from the standpoint of the living standard which, in turn, affected the growth and composition of production. The technical imbalances created by the Great Leap Forward were probably much more disruptive than Mao had expected. Moreover the imbalance between investment and construction on the one hand and the supply of consumer goods (including basic essentials such as grain) on the other, was greater than in any year since he had assumed power. Mao confessed his ignorance:

In regard to the question of the planned, proportionate development of the national economy, I am not very clear, and research is needed . . . We must study, understand, grasp and become accustomed to objective laws. Stalin spoke about this question at length but he did not follow

[84] "Speech at a Conference of Provincial and Municipal Committee Secretaries," February, 1959, *Wan-sui* (1969), p. 279.
[85] "Examples of Dialectics," *Wan-sui* (1967), p. 151.

through. He did not abide by the ratios and had a large industry with a small agriculture. He emphasized the big and scorned the small. We are now doing it differently: from 1956 we began to create the dual growth and leap forward in industry (including transport and communications) and agriculture; and we began to find the way towards the principles of planned, proportionate development.[86]

Mao believed that one of the "major lessons" to be learned from the Great Leap Forward was that the Chinese economy was still not "walking on two legs." By this he meant that China was still over-emphasizing heavy industry relative to light, and all industry compared with agriculture. In an attempt to solve the problem of "correct proportions" he advocated the setting of "national ratios" for the three main balances in the economy: balances within agriculture (between crop and animal production etc.), between branches of industry and between industry and agriculture. But he did not specify what these "national ratios" should be. Of great interest, however, is the fact that he now questioned the validity of the national order of sectoral priorities – heavy industry, light industry and agriculture:

Henceforth we may have to reverse the order.[87]

(3) *Consumption and Incentives.* By the spring of 1959 Mao realized that the policies implemented in 1958 had reduced the standard of living of the peasants to a dangerous level, and that failure to take swift remedial action would result in "tens of thousands of cases of dropsy."[88] He painted a vivid picture of the "great panic"[89] among the peasantry over the "communist wind," the advent of which he called a "great adventurist mistake."[90] The Communization of private plots, pigs and household goods, the reallocation of draught animals between brigades, the dispatching of labour from one brigade to another and the equalization of income between rich and poor brigades, had, he argued, driven peasants to conceal grain, kill pigs and poultry, and abandon or destroy their crops. China, said Mao,

[86] "Speech at a Conference of Provincial and Municipal Committee Secretaries" (1959), *Wan-sui* (1969), pp. 276–7.
[87] "Several Important Instructions," 29 June–2 July 1959, *Wan-sui* (1967).
[88] "Speech at a Conference of Provincial and Municipal Committee Secretaries" (1959), *Wan-sui* (1969), p. 278.
[89] "Talks at the Chengchow Conference," *Wan-sui* (1967), p. 19.
[90] *Ibid.*, p. 26.

was on the point of committing "Stalin's error" in handling the peasants – an error that would retard agricultural development for 30 years. The struggle between Commune cadres and peasants had clearly involved violence. Mao called for the punishment, even execution, of those guilty of serious crimes against the peasants whose action, in defending the "fruits of their labour," he described as "rational."[91]

Reform of the Commune system was outlined by Mao in his draft Sixty Articles of March 1959. One of the most important clauses directed that the production brigade (equivalent to the former collective) should replace the Commune as the basic level of ownership and accounting. In addition, a private agricultural sector, similar to that provided for in the collectives, was to be restored. Mao advised the leadership not to rely on the peasants in any attempt to speed up the transition to communism:

> Before last autumn it seemed as if the peasants were running ahead of the workers, but after autumn they were immediately concealing output and dividing it privately among themselves. These, then, are the two sides of the peasantry: peasants are still peasants.[92]

He nevertheless predicted that full communism would still be achieved in agriculture after four, or at most, 10 years. And despite his dire warning over the critical state of agricultural production, he was prepared to state that, with mechanization planned for completion in 1969, "after eight or 10 years of struggle the grain problem can be solved."[93] We may note that, in 1977, some 16 years after Mao's forecast, the mechanization of agriculture has barely begun and the grain problem has still not been solved.

MAO UNDER CRITICISM: 1959–62

Any possibility that Mao's economic reforms would be implemented was precluded by P'eng Teh-huai's attack, in the summer of 1959,[94] on the Great Leap Forward and, more impor-

[91] Ibid., p. 13.   [92] Ibid., p. 12.

[93] "Intra-Party Correspondence," Wan-sui (1969), p. 293. Mao's inconsistency at this time is quite bewildering. Only a few weeks before this he had argued "Don't say that we shall have solved the grain problem even in 10 years."

[94] Full documentation of this remarkable episode is found in Union Research Institute, The Case of P'eng Teh-huai 1959–1968, Hong Kong, 1968.

tantly, on Mao himself. At first sight, P'eng's analysis of the economic situation appears to be little more than a restatement of Mao's own views, as expressed at the Chengchow Conference in February. But it also contained criticism of Mao. For example, P'eng identified Mao with the "three-three system" of land use and other "slogans" which, he argued, had involved leftist mistakes. He also refuted one of Mao's cherished principles:

> In the view of some comrades, putting politics in command could be a substitute for everything ... Putting politics in command is not a substitute for economic principles, still less for concrete measures in economic work.[95]

And perhaps most pointed of all, he suggested that Mao should not be held personally responsible for the serious state of the Chinese economy.[96]

At first, Mao's response was quite conciliatory. Admitting that the Great Leap Forward had been a "partial failure,"[97] he accepted personal responsibility for the "great catastrophe"[98] of the backyard steel campaign. However, Mao then criticized T'an Chen-lin for Communizing agriculture too quickly and also criticized the planners.

> I should not make excuses and yet I shall, because I am not the head of the Planning Commission. Before last August my main energies were devoted to revolutionary matters. I am a complete outsider when it comes to economic construction and understand nothing about industrial planning.[99]

He insisted that the excesses of the Great Leap Forward had already been curbed, and urged the Party "not to waver at this critical time." He was obviously determined not to allow another campaign to unfold against "bold advance," comparable to that of 1956. Not surprisingly, therefore, the counterattack on P'eng was swift and fierce. The Central Committee's resolution[100] of August portrayed P'eng as "opposed to the high-speed development of the national economy ... to high yields, steel, the people's Communes and politics in command" – that is, opposed to all the main strands in Mao's economic thinking.

[95] Ibid., p. 12.
[96] "Speech at the Lushan Conference," 23 July, 1959, Wan-sui (1967), p. 276.
[97] Ibid., p. 274.   [98] Ibid., p. 275.   [99] Ibid., pp. 273–4.
[100] The Case of P'eng Teh-huai, pp. 291–305.

Within a few weeks of P'eng Teh-huai's attack Mao's moderate line had disappeared, and instead he spoke in terms that were the opposite of those contained in his speeches of the spring. He argued that the main problem was to oppose the right, not the left – a shift that carried far-reaching economic implications. Having previously stressed the need to increase incentives, he now scorned the preoccupation with living standards:

... it was all vegetables, pork, grain in a number of areas, soap and even umbrellas ...[101]

The 12,000 workers who had built the Great Hall in Peking in record time were singled out for praise:

Did they need material incentives? Did they want a few extra yüan ... They did not want it ... they were striving for a common cause.[102]

In the autumn of 1959 Mao initiated a campaign to "scatter the anti-leftists." It was directed against those who desired a more moderate economic policy based on slower growth, more balance in the economy and more financial incentives. The campaign, described by Liu Chien-hsün as a "brutal struggle and a ruthless blow,"[103] prolonged the Great Leap Forward in town and country with many of the worst economic characteristics of 1958, but with much more severe economic consequences.

Figures in Table 1 summarize the changes in the Chinese economy during the crisis years which followed.

The main point illustrated by Table 1 is that rapid growth in industrial output continued until 1960, when it was halted as a result of falling agricultural production. With grain output declining by 17 per cent in 1959 and a further 12 per cent in 1960, malnutrition (partly manifested in dropsy) and even starvation affected many areas of rural China. Famine was serious in Shantung, Honan and Kansu. For the first time since the early 1950s China was forced to import grain. The published documents of the time blamed the effects of "unprecedented natural

[101] "Speech at the Enlarged Session of the Military Affairs Commission and External Affairs Conference," 11 September, 1959. Mao referred scathingly to those who had described the shortage of umbrellas as a "maladjustment of priorities," Wan-sui (1969), p. 314.
[102] A different version of the same speech, Wan-sui (1967), p. 100.
[103] See Facts about Liu Chien-hsün's Crimes.

Table 1. Economic Indicators for 1957–62

	Grain	Cotton million tons	Steel	Index of Industrial Production
1957	185	1·64	5·35	100
1958	205	2·00	11·08	145
1959	170	1·80	13·35	177
1960	150	1·02	18·67	184
1961	160	0·88	8·00	108
1962	170	1·03	8·00	114

Sources: Grain: Chao Kang, *Agricultural Production in Communist China, 1949–1965*. (Madison: University of Wisconsin Press, 1970), p. 260. Cotton: *Ibid.*, p. 270. Steel: *China: A Reassessment of the Economy*, A Compendium of Papers Submitted to the Joint Economic Committee, Congress of the United States, 10 June, 1975 (Washington D.C.: U.S. Government Printing Office, 1975) (hereafter referred to as *JEC 1975*), p. 276. Industrial Production Index: *JEC 1975*, p. 149.

calamities," but secret documents, including Mao's own speeches, admitted that errors in economic policy were also a decisive factor. The "communist wind" blew again. Technical errors associated with water conservation, deep ploughing and close planting created crop failures and, more serious in the long run, large areas of soil became saline and alkaline, unfit for agriculture. The incentive measures in the Communes called for in the "Sixty Articles" of March 1959 were not implemented. Egalitarian income distribution, high rates of grain procurement and various forms of coercion all induced the peasants to reduce production. And although detailed figures are not available, press reports show that draught animals and pigs declined rapidly.

In January 1961, as a result of the decline in agricultural output, much of China's industrial production and nearly all of her constructional activity was suspended. This policy was explicitly approved by Mao in a speech to the Central Committee.[104] The reversal of sectoral priorities forecast by Mao in 1959 was officially announced, putting agriculture first and heavy industry last. The most pressing need was to promote agricultural production through the provision of appropriate incentives. In December 1960 the Central Committee had issued an "urgent directive on rural work" (the "Twelve Articles"), which

[104] "Speech to the Ninth Plenum of the Eighth Central Committee," 18 January, 1961, *Wan-sui* (1967), pp. 258–66.

repeated the main measures contained in the "Sixty Articles."[105] But seven years of Mao's directives which had oscillated, often suddenly, between "left" and "right," had left the rural cadres bewildered and demoralized. Now, in 1961, they simply did not know what represented the correct line. It needed an intensive education campaign to convince them that the clauses of the "Twelve Articles" and "Sixty Articles" (a revised version of which was issued in March 1961)[106] were to be implemented. Some cadres opposed the sending down of the accounting and ownership unit on the (valid) grounds that it would increase income inequality; others were afraid to allocate private plots which, they considered, would encourage capitalism, contrary to Mao's wishes. In Honan province, T'ao Chu, first Party secretary of Kwangtung, rebuked cadres who were reluctant to introduce a system of loaning land to peasants who would farm it on an individual non-collective basis, commenting that they were "afraid of capitalism but not of dropsy."[107] Liu Chien-hsün further agreed:

If we have to eat grain imported from capitalist countries why can't we have loaned land?[108]

Throughout the crisis years Mao was attacked from high and low for his handling of economic affairs. Some of the indirect criticisms borrowed Mao's own metaphor of the horse with great effectiveness. For example, Liu Chien-hsün was accused of having described Mao's leadership in the Great Leap Forward as that of a "blind man riding a blind horse,"[109] while the following is attributed to Lu Yü:

It is said that when one horse runs at the head, ten thousand horses

---

[105] *Union Research Service*, Vol. 28, pp. 200–1. Union Research Institute, Hong Kong.
[106] *Chinese Communist Party, Central Committee rules and regulations for the operation of the rural people's communes* (draft), March 1961 (Taipei: Research Department Bureau of Investigation of the Ministry of National Defence). The revised draft of September 1962 was reprinted in May 1965 by the Chinese State Security Bureau, Taipei.
[107] "Individual operations in Honan, How did the black wind start?" *SCMP*, Supplement 193.
[108] *Facts about Liu Chien-hsün's Crimes*.
[109] *Ibid*.

will follow it. Now ten thousand horses have followed the one at the head but have broken their legs.[110]

The peasants and their relatives in the army were more direct:

At present what the peasants eat in the villages is even worse than what dogs ate in the past. At that time dogs ate chaff and grain. Now the people are too hungry to work and pigs are too hungry to stand up. Commune members ask: "Is Chairman Mao going to allow us to starve to death?"[111]

Mao's reaction to these attacks was muted and defensive. Isolated from senior officials,[112] he actually made a self-criticism before the Central Committee in June 1961 but no record of its content is available.[113] He offered three non-climatic explanations for China's difficulties: (1) the "communist wind" of 1959–60 had been forced on the country by P'eng Teh-huai:

At the Lushan Conference the problem for correcting leftists had not been made clear but P'eng Teh-huai forced us to accept the challenge.[114]

(2) Soviet revisionism had diverted the Party's attention from economic affairs during 1960.[115] (3) His own policies had not been implemented. Mao pointed out that he had been advocating the simultaneous development of industry and agriculture (his own "two legs" policy) for five years "but it has not been implemented."[116] He further claimed that cadres had ignored his instructions to conduct "investigations and study" at basic levels of production.[117] Mao took an unusually pessimistic view of China's prospects at this time:

[110] "Thoroughly distorting the inside story of the Ch'ang Kuan Lou counter-revolutionary incident." SCMP, No. 4001.

[111] "Comrade Wang Tung-hsing's report on ideological conditions in the central garrison." Bulletin of Activities, 1 January, 1961, translated in The Politics of the Chinese Red Army, J. Chester Cheng (ed.) (Stanford: Hoover Institution, 1966), p. 13.

[112] Note Mao's revelations on this subject in "Talk at a Report Meeting," 24 October, 1966, Wan-sui (1969), p. 655.

[113] "Speech at an Enlarged Central Work Conference," 30 January, 1962, Wan-sui (1969), p. 406.

[114] "Speech to the Ninth Plenum" (1961), Wan-sui (1967), p. 259.

[115] "Speech to the Tenth Plenum of the Eighth Central Committee," 24 September, 1962, Wan-sui (1969), p. 432.

[116] "Speech to the Ninth Plenum (1961), Wan-sui (1967), p. 266.

[117] Ibid., p. 262.

But China has a large population, meagre resources and a backward economy so that in my opinion it will not be possible to bring about a great development of her productive power and to catch up with, or overtake, the most advanced capitalist countries in the world, in over a hundred years.[118]

During 1961 and 1962 agriculture began to recover as the liberal reforms were implemented. Once they had been persuaded about the correctness of the "Sixty Articles," however, cadres allowed an unprecedented increase in semi-private farming to occur. In some areas this led to a severe decrease in collective grain production.[119] Peasants withdrew draught animals and tools from the Communes to engage in household and individual agriculture. And although this was later condemned by Mao as the work of capitalist roaders such as Liu Shao-ch'i, it should be emphasized that Mao's own "Sixty Articles" contained clauses that were bound to undermine collective farming. For example, private plots, land specifically allocated for growing fodder and privately reclaimed hill land could, in all, amount to 15 per cent of the arable land. Moreover, the output of these categories of land was exempt from government tax procurement. There is no way of knowing whether Mao approved of contracting production to households as a short-term expediency. The speeches he made in 1959 on the correct treatment of peasants (and on what could be expected from them) are certainly consistent with the proposition that he did agree to such a measure. It is clear, however, that by the summer of 1962 Mao considered that the "wind of individual farming" had swept away too much of the collective activity in the Communes and had undermined central planning.[120]

[118] "Speech at an Enlarged Central Work Conference" (1962), Wan-sui (1969), p. 413. Contrast this with the following: "Judging from this, it will probably take less time than previously estimated for our industry and agriculture to catch up with that of the capitalist powers. In addition to the leadership of the Party, a decisive factor is our population of 600 million. More people means a great ferment of ideas, more enthusiasm and more energy ..." "Introducing a Cooperative," 15 April, 1958, SR, pp. 499–501.
[119] "Implementation of the resolutions of the Tenth Plenum of the Eighth Central Committee on strengthening the collective economy and expanding agricultural production" (1962). Translated in C. S. Chen and C. P. Ridley, Rural People's Communes in Lien-chiang (Stanford: Hoover Institution, 1969), p. 101.
[120] "Speech at a Central Work Conference," 28 December, 1964, Wan-sui (1969), pp. 598–602. In this speech Mao refers to the prevalence of san tzu yi pao

The situation was in some respects similar to that of July 1955 when Mao had first set China on the road to collectivization. Now, seven years later, he brought to a head the same issue of which "road" should be followed in agriculture: that of socialism or capitalism? At meetings of the Central Committee held in Peking and Peitaiho during September 1962, he argued in favour of adopting measures to strengthen the collective economy, against those who maintained that if agricultural work was not contracted to individual households it would take from 8 to 10 years for production to recover.[121] It was the same sort of argument which had been adduced against speeding up collectivization in 1955, and Mao rejected it. And so began another round in the continuing search for a system which would provide the right combination of central control, adequate flexibility and local initiative, and in which production would increase as rapidly as possible without adversely affecting the interests of the poor and lower middle peasants.

MAO'S ECONOMIC THOUGHT AFTER 1962

By the mid-1960s output in most sectors of the economy had regained the levels reached between 1958 and 1960. Mao's role in the economy during this recovery was an indirect one. Situated in the "second line" of the Politburo's Standing Committee, he was not involved in day-to-day handling of the economy and he did not attend the important meetings at which Liu Shao-ch'i, Ch'en Yun and Po I-po established the economic strategy of the 1960s. Mao used his freedom to concentrate on the broad issues of revisionism and the dangers of a "capitalist" revival. In particular, he directed his attention to the Socialist Education Campaign by which the Party was trying to eliminate the abuses of authority, corruption and excessive private economic activity that had sprung directly from the liberalization of 1960 and 1961.

Between 1964 and 1966, China's Third Five-Year Plan was
(three freedoms and one contract) in 1962. The "freedoms" were (a) the extension of private plots, (b) of free markets, and (c) an increase in the number of small enterprises with responsibility for their own profits and losses. The "contract" was between the commune and peasant households.
[121] *Ibid.*, p. 599.

formulated. The Plan was never published but we do have Mao's comments and advice to the planners on what the Plan should be like. This material provides almost our only firm evidence of Mao's thoughts on economic matters in his old age. (He was 71 in 1964.) Notably absent from Mao's remarks at this time is any discussion of the inevitability of "waves" and "leaps." Instead Mao advocated cautious, realistic and incremental progress. He warned the planners:

Order plans in accordance with our grasp of the objective, propor-tionate relationships in the economy . . . Don't make rash advances. Improve quality, scale and specifications. Make the quantity of output rise gently, don't rush. Then [our enemies] will be worried.[122]

All this was not only a rejection of his earlier approach to growth, but it also spelled the end of China's experiment with the Soviet method of planning by material balances. Mao called this "a revolution" in planning, which indeed it was. He pointed out that under the Soviet method the starting point was the fixing of targets for steel and other industrial commodities. From these, further targets for coal, electricity, transport, urban growth, wage and welfare expenditure, etc., were all deduced. Mao called this the "method of the calculator" and he criticized it for making no allowance for what the "Lord of Heaven" might do to disrupt the Plan by sending natural disasters to lower agricultural output. He argued that the correct approach was to base the Plan on probable grain output – to be estimated by assuming one good, two average and two poor harvests every five years. In short, the plan for industry should be a function of the plan for agriculture – a complete reversal of the inflexible, industrially orientated planning of the 1950s.[123]

Mao's understanding of the role of agriculture did nothing to weaken his belief that the dynamic factor in China's economic modernization had to be industry. He proposed that the main priorities be given to steel, machinery, chemicals and petro-leum. These choices reflected imbalances that had developed in the 1950s and also considerations of defence. On industrial matters, Mao remained very ambitious. Asked by China's two

[122] "Ku Mu and Yü Ch'iu-li Report Mao's Directives at the Time of Planning Work," January 1965, Wan-sui (1969), pp. 605–6.
[123] "A Talk on the Third Five-Year Plan," 6 June, 1964, Wan-sui (1969), pp. 497–9.

leading planners whether China should try to surpass international standards in industrial and defence technology, he replied:

Yes . . . whatever the country, whatever the missiles, atomic bombs, hydrogen bombs, we must surpass them.[124]

In 1964 and 1965 China began to fuel the industrial revival with imported plant. Preparations were also made for a further expansion of imports when the economy could afford it. Mao's attitude to this approach seems to have been somewhat critical; while he was happy to compare the Russians unfavourably with China's new imperialist suppliers, he continued to insist that any form of dependence was "dangerous." Similarly, while he seems to have been prepared for some further loss of self-reliance in industry, he was adamant that food imports should be stopped as soon as possible:

Strive for several years so that we shall no longer have to import grain and use the foreign exchange saved in this way to buy more technological equipment and materials.[125]

In the event, this proved harder than Mao anticipated, for 10 years after his statement, imports of grain were as large as ever and considerably more expensive.

CONCLUSIONS

Mao's involvement in China's economic affairs was lengthy and complex. A flexible politician, he oscillated between the utopian and the pragmatic, between advance and retreat and between being in charge and being an isolated outsider.[126] As a result, he left behind a record from which it is difficult to abstract either a core of Maoist principles or a clear history of his own role in economic decisions. This makes difficulties for scholars but will surely suit his successors, since they will be able to justify almost any course of action by reference to a Maoist precedent. In spite of this, we think that there are certain lines of consistency and development in Mao's economic work

[124] "Ku Mu and Yü Ch'iu-li."
[125] A Talk on the Third Five-Year Plan."
[126] A fascinating analysis of psychological aspects of Mao's relations with his colleagues is to be found in Chapters 10–11 of Lucian W. Pye, *Mao Tse-tung: The Man in the Leader* (New York: Basic Books, 1976).

and that we can identify strengths and weaknesses in China's economic performance for which he was responsible.

At the most general level we have stressed Mao's conception of economic development as something involving discontinuity, struggle and endless experiments with the unknown. In policy terms, these premises led Mao to accelerate key economic sectors in the belief that they would pull the rest of the economy behind them. They also explain Mao's willingness to use violence and coercion and his distrust of expert, centralized economic administration. After the Great Leap Forward Mao modified his emphasis on wave-like development by trying to combine it with an appreciation of the need for "proportionate" but still rapid growth. This reflected his dissatisfaction with the "unbalanced" strategies of both the First Five-Year Plan and the Leap, which had created many serious problems. Perhaps he came to regard these strategies as incorrect, and was converted to the alternative policy of balanced, slower growth. It is interesting to record that in his later years, and especially after the Cultural Revolution, there is little evidence that he continued to expound the theory of waves.

Another theme on which Mao developed his ideas as a result of experience was the analysis of the relationships between the development of production, the pattern of ownership and organization and the "superstructure" of ideas, values and modes of behaviour. Up to the early 1950s, Mao argued that the conditions for complete socialization of the economy would appear only after a long period of economic and technical progress. In 1955, he reversed this by arguing that only an acceleration of socialization could bring about a transformation of production. And in 1958 he added that it was essential to combine socialization with a campaign of political education that would transform the superstructure. Articles published during the Cultural Revolution suggest that towards the end of his life, the transformation of the superstructure became his main preoccupation. And he envisaged that such a transformation would produce rapid economic development.

CHINA'S ECONOMIC PERFORMANCE UNDER MAO

The main achievements of the economy under Mao's leadership were a dramatic rise in the rate of investment and the development of a modern industrial base. By comparison with pre-1949, the investment rate in the 1970s had at least quadrupled and, in spite of the depression caused by errors in the Leap and the withdrawal of Soviet support, the long-run rate of industrial growth averaged 11 per cent per annum. This growth occurred in most branches of industry and included particularly impressive advances by the machine-building and oil industries. Industrial growth was not, however, as rapid as Mao had anticipated. Leaving the hopes of the Leap entirely on one side, the shortfall is indicated by comparing Mao's 1955 estimates for the output of six industrial commodities in 1967 with actual output in that year. This is done in Table 2. The data show that, apart from chemical fertilizer, Mao's plans were unfulfilled by a substantial margin.

In addition, the steel industry, which Mao had insisted was the most important indicator of an economy's modernization, performed erratically. In recent years output faltered, efficiency declined and imports of steel rose. These failings can be traced directly to Mao's policies. In 1958 he abandoned the Soviet plan for the industry and pushed forward with ideas that were technically impracticable. Also, despite Mao's obsessive determination to promote iron and steel he failed, over a long period, to take realistic account of the complementary development needed in mining and other sectors.

One area in which Mao appears to have been responsible for unusual and successful innovations is the control of fertility, population movement and city size. Mao was a reluctant convert to fertility control. Throughout most of the 1950s and especially in 1958, he emphasized the positive advantages of a large population. Even in 1957, when he was on the defensive, he was only prepared to admit that the advantages of a large population had to be qualified by awareness of "difficulties" associated with it. During the 1960s, however, he came to a more realistic understanding of the population problem and in the early 1970s he moved decisively to support a programme of population limita-

Table 2: **Production in 1955 and 1967 Compared with Mao's Predictions of 1955**

	1955	Predicted for 1967	1967 achieved	1967 output as % of Mao's prediction
	MILLION TONS, UNLESS OTHERWISE STATED			
Grain	175	(a) 300	230	(a) 77
		(b) 437		(b) 53
Cotton	1·5	(a) 6·0	1·9	(a) 32
		(b) 4·5		(b) 42
Steel	2·9	18–20	12·0	63
Coal	98·3	280	190	68
Cement	4·5	16·8	14·2	85
Chemical fertilizers	0·4	7·5	8·1	108
Oil	1·0	18	13·9	77
Electric power (b.kw.h.)	12·3	73	45	62
Tractors (thousands)	nil	183	43	24

Sources: all 1955 figures except chemical fertilizers are from *Wei ta ti shih-nien (Ten Great Years)*, Peking, 1959. Chemical fertilizer production is from R. M. Field, "Civilian industrial production in the People's Republic of China," *JEC 1975*, pp. 146–74. The 1967 predictions (including (a) figures for grain and cotton) are in Mao's "Summing up Speech" of September 1955. The (b) figures for grain and cotton were implied by Mao's "Forty Articles" and cited by Liao Lu-yen in his "Explanation of the Twelve-Year Plan," (*Hsin-hua pan-yueh k'an*), 1956, No. 4, pp. 6–9. The grain and cotton figures for 1967 are from A. G. Ashbrook: "China: Economic Overview 1975," in *JEC 1975*, pp. 20–51. Other 1967 data are from Field, "Civilian industrial production."

tion,[127] a programme believed to have had dramatic success.[128] Moves to control population movement and to stop the wild growth of cities started in the 1950s received great impetus from Mao's speech "On the Correct Handling of Contradictions Among the People." He continued to press this policy.[129] In the 1960s

[127] Mao's enthusiasm for a large population peaked in the two great economic upheavals led by him: The "High Tide" of 1955 and the Great Leap of 1958. See, "Talk Opposing Right Deviation," (1955), *Wan-sui* (1969), pp. 25–8; "Talk at the Conference of Heads of Delegations to the Second Session of the Eighth Party Congress," 18 May, 1958, *Wan-sui* (1969), p. 225.

[128] See data on fertility decline between 1970 and 1975 in Central Intelligence Agency, *People's Republic of China: Handbook of Economic Indicators* (Washington, 1976), p. 7.

[129] "Reading Notes," *Wan-sui* (1969), p. 226.

the draft Third Five-Year Plan called for further migration to the cities, to which Mao's reply was "no way."[130] The net result was that, in some respects, China has avoided the worst effects of excessive urbanization which are common in other developing countries.

UNRESOLVED PROBLEMS

There were three major problems that Mao was unable to resolve satisfactorily. These were (i) the problem of decentralization; (ii) the problem of the relationship between economic development, living standards and the distribution of income; and (iii) the problem of reconciling "self-reliance" with the development of modern industry.

(i) *The question of decentralization*. Mao had powerful reasons for wishing to decentralize the economy in the sense of giving scope for initiative to both local planners and individual units of production. To begin with, he was convinced that the central bureaucrats were too isolated to understand real problems: "Real knowledge comes from plants, from co-operatives, from stores and from schools," he wrote. "The higher you go, the less knowledge you get . . . Peking is not a good place to acquire knowledge."[131] He also distrusted the bureaucrats' education which he regarded as over-sophisticated and inappropriate. He went to extremes on this point, asserting that "an illiterate person could be the Prime Minister" and "Even those who cannot read may discuss economics."[132] Apart from these reservations, Mao was one of the first to see the practical impossibility of incorporating China's vast, small-scale economy into a centrally directed planning system. We must remember that in this Mao was facing unique problems. No socialist country in the world provided a precedent for planning such a backward economy. Yet, once Mao had decided on complete socialization, a solution had to be found and it had to include some form of decentralization. The problem was that Mao wanted the economy to be decentralized and still remain responsive to his

[130] Interjections at a Briefing by Four Vice-Premiers, May 1964. *Wan-sui* (1969), p. 495.
[131] "Interjections at a Conference of Provincial and Municipal Party Committee Secretaries," January 1957, *Wan-sui* (1969), p. 80.
[132] *The Case of P'eng Teh-huai*, p. 19.

plans. He attempted to achieve this by impregnating China with an ideology that would render administrative controls unnecessary. The results of this policy were disappointing, particularly in the countryside. In rural China, following a radical decentralization of the Communes, the "Four Clean-ups" revealed corruption, hostility to socialism and widespread disintegration of the collective economy.[133] In a pessimistic moment during 1964, Mao was forced to admit that a third of the power in China was controlled by his enemies, and that a Party secretary could be bribed with a few packets of cigarettes. "And there's no telling," he added, "what one could do by marrying one's daughter off to such people."[134] This was a predictable outcome of a situation in which a great deal of production and distribution could be handled by individual or household units. We are not arguing that socialization and controls constitute an error, since a number of favourable consequences followed from them. But, once undertaken, tension between private interests and the collective economy were an inescapable result that Mao found impossible to accept.

(ii) The standard of living and the distribution of income. Any appraisal of the development of the Chinese economy under Mao would wish to establish what had happened to the level and distribution of personal incomes, over the period of 27 years. No accurate report of this is possible, but the following propositions summarize the position:

(1) Average consumption per head of food, clothing and housing increased only marginally. In the crucial case of grain (which accounts for around 80 per cent of all calories) if we compare average output per head in the first few years of the 1970s with that in the 1950s, we find that it was almost identical. This was not what Mao had anticipated when promoting institutional, technical and ideological programmes. A solution to the "grain problem" (so often mentioned by Mao) has yet to be found. Consumption of welfare services (i.e. health, education, recreational facilities, etc.) rose substantially.

[133] The best account of this campaign is by Richard Baum, Prelude to Revolution: Mao, the Party and the Peasant Question, 1962–1966 (New York and London: Columbia University Press, 1975).
[134] "Talks on Problems of Philosophy," 18 August, 1964, Wan-sui (1969), p. 55.

(2) Rural living standards were static in the 1950s, fell steeply in the early 1960s and increased by a small but perceptible margin since then, especially in relatively backward areas.

(3) Urban living standards which had increased rapidly up to 1956, remained constant on average right up to Mao's death, but declined for the higher-paid workers.

(4) Inequalities between rural and urban populations and within the rural and urban sectors were larger than is often supposed, but not as large as those found in some other developing countries in which private ownership of land and capital has been retained.

(5) A system of tight controls ensured that all members of the population received a minimum quantity of food grain in all but the years 1959–62.

Mao's attitude to income growth and distribution was ambiguous. In the 1950s he was anxious that rural incomes should rise in order to encourage the peasants to enter and support the co-operatives. He is also on record as saying that the 1956 wage reform (which raised the average wage and increased inequality) was broadly correct, and in the aftermath of the Leap he supported the revival of incentives in agriculture and industry. Against this, Mao clearly became critical of the graduated wage system and increasingly preoccupied with the possibility that rising personal incomes would have undesirable political consequences. In his comments on Stalin's *The Economic Problems of Socialism*, he went so far as to criticize Stalin for arguing that steadily rising wages were an important measure of the superiority of socialism over capitalism. Later in the 1960s, he made several references to the corrupting effects of rising incomes and this theme was re-echoed in the campaigns against Lin Piao and Teng Hsiao-p'ing during the 1970s.[135]

There can be no doubt that Mao's attitude found few supporters, and that the industrial labour unrest in China during 1974 and 1975 was a response to rigid control of living standards and to a campaign, probably inspired by Mao, to abolish the eight-grade industrial wage system. Moreover, Mao's attitude to the

[135] Mao supported the 1956 wage reform in the "Ten Great Relations"; important comments on this theme are in "Reading Notes," sections 39 and 42, *Wan-sui* (1969); also "A Talk on the Third Five-Year Plan," *Wan-sui* (1969).

wage system must be seen as part of a life-long campaign against bureaucracy. Thus, while Mao consistently wanted China to develop large-scale, modern economic institutions, he could not accept that this would also involve the establishment of structured incentives and organization.

(iii) Foreign trade and technology. The other area in which the policy of economic modernization clashed with Mao's political and nationalistic preferences was foreign trade. During the First Five-Year Plan his policy was (a) to rely on the Soviet Union, and (b) to regard the Soviet programme as a once-for-all transfer after which China would be basically "independent." When the Soviet link collapsed, Mao formulated his concept of "self-reliance" – described by one commentator as his "fundamental" economic thought.[136] Even so, in the mid-1960s imports of industrial technology grew and by the mid-1970s had become very large. The evidence is indirect, but it seems that Mao's ambivalence persisted. Campaigns against foreign technology in 1975 and 1976 appear to echo many of his feelings on the subject.

Mao's cautious policy towards foreign trade was beneficial to the extent that it enabled China to avoid unmanageable foreign debts, and encouraged the planners to avoid excessive dependency on individual industries. On the other hand, the accessibility of cheap foreign technology is potentially a key to the acceleration of China's economy and it would be illusory to imagine that "catching up" can be a once-for-all achievement. Mao grew up in a country where anti-foreign feeling was an entrenched emotional force, and his formative years were passed before the lessons of the second- and third-generation industrial revolutions had been appreciated. It was therefore difficult for him to appreciate fully the opportunities which foreign technical progress made available to the Chinese economy, or to accept the implications of taking advantage of these. In so far as his successors are not bound by these limitations, the future prospects for the Chinese economy will be that much enhanced.

[136] Ch'ien Chia-chü, "An appreciation of some guiding ideology based on the study of Chairman Mao's economic and financial policies," Ching chi yen ch'iu (1960), No. 9, pp. 34–41.

7

THE PATRIOT

Frederic Wakeman Jr

Mao Tse-tung's first conscious political concern was the salvation of his country.[1] By the time he had left Shaoshan Primary School at the age of 13 to work on his father's farm, Mao had grown acutely aware of China's national jeopardy. Reminiscing 20 years later, he told the American journalist, Edgar Snow, that in 1906:

> I began to have a certain amount of political consciousness, especially after I read a pamphlet telling of the dismemberment of China. I remember even now that this pamphlet opened with the sentence: "Alas, China will be subjugated!" It told of Japan's occupation of Korea and Formosa, of the loss of suzerainty in Indo-China, Burma and elsewhere. After I read this I felt depressed about the future of my country and began to realize that it was the duty of all the people to help save it.[2]

Before that dismemberment began, the Ch'ing empire had stretched for nearly 4,500 kilometres. Its borders had encompassed much of the Asian land mass, reaching the Sea of Okhotsk in the far north and the shores of Lake Balkhash in the far west. Manchuria, Mongolia, Sinkiang and Tibet were all directly ruled by the emperor of China. The monarchies of Korea, Vietnam and Nepal considered themselves tributaries of Peking. In 1800 the Ch'ing dynasty of Manchus controlled more people and land than had any government in Chinese history.

By the early 20th century, however, China had become the sick man of the Orient. During every decade but one since the 1840s China had fought a major war, either with Japan or with a Western power. In each case, the Chinese and their Manchu

[1] I would like to express my thanks to Irwin Scheiner and Carolyn Wakeman for suggestions to improve this essay, and to the staff of the Center for Chinese Studies at Berkeley for helping with its preparation.
[2] Mao Tse-tung, quoted in Edgar Snow, *Red Star over China* (New York: Grove Press, 1961), p. 131.

rulers were defeated. The imperial capital had been twice occupied by allied expeditions. More than 20 treaty ports had been opened to foreigners, who enjoyed extraterritoriality and economic privileges. Province-sized portions of territory had been ceded to Russia and the lush island of Taiwan had been lost to the Japanese. Along the coast five major leaseholds – each a foreign zone of occupation – had been granted to the British, French, Germans, Japanese and Russians. Even from young Mao's perspective in landlocked Shaoshan, it was obvious that Western and Japanese imperialists were relentlessly pushing their way into the heartland of China, forcing the proudly anti-foreign Hunanese to admit them to their provincial capital in Changsha.

Mao Tse-tung's generation of Chinese was certainly not the first to espy an emergency. In fact, Mao's patriotic determination to restore China to the Chinese was nurtured by two earlier traditions of national defence: the Confucian elite's conception of individual loyalism and patriotic statesmanship, and a more popular notion of heroic protest against injustice and of mass resistance to the presence of foreigners in China.[3]

The elite's primary commitment was to defend a cultural tradition rather than a nation or race, but the Confucian loyalist heroes in their opposition sometimes seemed ethnic patriots as well. After the Manchu conquest a few Chinese scholar-officials actually took issue with the conventional idea that any group – regardless of race – could adopt universal Confucian culture. A Hunanese philosopher, Wang Fu-chih, wrote in the 17th century that barbarians had cultures of their own and were unsuited to take on the trappings of Chinese civilization. Wang also emphasized the importance of distinguishing the different categories (lei) of being, and of segregating species of things. Although his works were not widely read at the time he lived, Wang Fu-chih's sociological justifications for ethnicism later profoundly influenced radical intellectuals and nationalists like Mao. In the high culture of the Ch'ing, the patriotism of the literati was stripped of its particular commitment to Chinese values, and instead defined more abstractly as the elite's obligation to defend the Confucian heritage which Manchu emperors

---

[3] Jerome Ch'en, Mao and the Chinese Revolution (London: Oxford University Press, 1965), pp. 6–8.

could share with Han (native Chinese) mandarins. By the early 19th century, the only visible signs of purely ethnic patriotism were to be found in more popular manifestations.

Among the "black-haired masses" of China there existed an almost legendary history of popular resistance to foreign invasion. Since at least the 14th century, when White Lotus rebels overthrew the Mongol Yuan dynasty, sectarian movements had been strongly imbued with anti-foreign sentiments.[4] During the Manchu conquest of China in the 1640s, there were numerous instances of peasants, sometimes led by marginal elements like bandits or smugglers, fighting against the invaders. Particularly angered by the Manchus' insistence that the Chinese copy their tribal custom of shaved heads and plaited queues, Chinese peasants formed militia specifically to attack the Ta-tzu (Tartars) in their midst.[5] Even after the Manchus had pacified south China, there continued to be uprisings to expel the barbarians and restore Han rule. Especially after the turn of the 19th century, the Triads of Fukien and Kwangtung provinces revolted repeatedly against Ch'ing officials in the name of the native Ming dynasty.

Because the object of the secret societies' hatred was the ruling elite of China, the Chinese literati who served the Ch'ing dynasty did not find it possible to identify their own commitment to the defence of the culture with the popular tradition of anti-foreign resistance. In fact, secret society revolts helped convince members of the gentry that they had more in common with an alien emperor who was their cultural ally, than with Triad "riff-raff" (wu-lai) who were their social enemies. The domestic opposition between the two different traditions of scholarly cultural loyalism and popular ethnic anti-foreignism was only reconciled by the appearance of a new external enemy. It was thus the growing presence of Westerners in China that provided an opportunity for these two forms of patriotism momentarily to merge.

[4] Yūji Muramatsu, "Some themes in Chinese rebel ideologies," in Arthur F. Wright (ed.), The Confucian Persuasion (Stanford; Stanford University Press, 1960), pp. 250–3.
[5] Hsieh Kuo-chen, Ch'ing ch'u nung-min ch'i-i tzu-liao chi-lu (A Compilation of Documents on the Peasant Uprisings of the Early Ch'ing) (Shanghai: Hsin chih-shih ch'u-pan she, 1956), pp. 122–6.

The Opium War of 1839–42 saw the temporary fusion of the elite's sophisticated determination to defend the empire and the peasants' outraged passion to expel the barbarians. Wartime leaders like Commissioner Lin Tse-hsü tried both to equip their conventional forces with new weapons to oppose the aggressors, and to encourage rural militia to attack the British troops *en masse*.[6] By the end of the Opium War, and even despite the Ch'ing dynasty's submission to the British, many Chinese were convinced that, with proper leadership, patriotic gentry and zealous peasant irregulars together possessed the capacity to drive off European invaders.[7]

During the Taiping rebellion the momentary alliance between gentry and peasants began to dissolve. The Taiping movement was an extremely complex social phenomenon, which left its own tradition of primitive communism for later revolutionaries like Mao to look back upon with pride and self-identification. At the time of their uprising in Kwangsi, the rebels drew deeply upon the strong anti-Manchu feelings of the nativist secret societies of south China. Yet the movement also acquired a certain foreign air because its major leader, Hung Hsiu-ch'üan, was seminally influenced by Christianity. The Taipings' anti-foreignism was thus directed not against the Westerners, who had so recently invaded China, but against the Manchus. Selecting the ruling house as its target at a time when the Ch'ing Government was still allied with Han officials against European invaders, the Taipings aroused the avid opposition of cultural champions who believed the rebels were inspired by an alien doctrine to challenge the Confucian elite's right to rule China. Thus, the very same statecraft writers who had enthusiastically applauded Lin Tse-hsü's support of popular movements against a common enemy now strongly endorsed leaders like Tseng Kuo-fan who called for a new heroic Confucian commitment against the massed rebels.

Mao was a youthful admirer of this kind of heroic Confucianism. As a schoolboy he seemed to identify more readily with Confucian paragons like Tseng Kuo-fan, the imperial offi-

[6] Lin Tse-hsü, *Lin wen-chung kung ch'üan-chi* (*Complete Works of Lin Tse-hsü*) (Taipei: Wen-hai ch'u-pan she, 1963), p. 1:3b.

[7] Frederic Wakeman Jr, *Strangers at the Gate: Social Disorder in South China, 1839–1961* (Berkeley and Los Angeles: University of California Press, 1966), pp. 11–21.

cial who defeated the Taipings, than with the rebels themselves.[8] One reason for Mao's identification with Tseng Kuo-fan may have been that the latter stood for a much larger group of tough-minded administrators mainly from Mao's native province of Hunan. These men had spearheaded the effort to restore order to central China and, while destroying the Taipings, had at the same time strengthened China against external enemies by trying to advance the military modernization programmes initiated by Lin Tse-hsü. Like Lin, Tseng Kuo-fan equated the resurgence of Chinese national strength with the revival of Confucian moralism. In Hunan, where the province's reputation for anti-foreignism and cultural conservatism was a source of great pride, native writers were vaunted and their works printed under official rubric. Tseng, for instance, sponsored the publication of the collected works of Wang Fu-chih in 1864–66, thus helping revive the latent tradition of high cultural ethnic patriotism associated with Ming loyalists. Hunanese pride and interest in Wang's writings would continue to grow in decades to come. By the time of the May Fourth Movement in 1919 there was a Wang Fu-chih Study Society (Ch'uan-shan hsueh-she) in Changsha, and Mao attended its meetings on more than one occasion.

Even though Tseng Kuo-fan's or Li Hung-chang's regional armies were originally formed to suppress the Taiping rebellion, they were also conceived as a line of defence against foreign aggression. After the internal rebels were quelled, therefore, some of these well-equipped armies (and especially Li Hung-chang's Huai Army) were kept under arms to thwart Western encroachment. The latter grew to be more of a threat just as popular anti-foreignism and elite patriotism again converged to preserve the native culture. When the Taipings were finally defeated, this putative union between elite and popular champions of Han culture was even more fully realized as an alliance against Western missionaries and their converts.

Meanwhile foreign encroachment on China intensified. Although Japan was forced by Russia, France and Germany to drop some of the more onerous provisions of the Treaty of Shimonoseki in 1895, the Chinese were still profoundly shocked by the magnitude of their defeat in the war with Japan.

[8] Schram, Mao, p. 51.

Most aroused were younger literati – and especially those who were convinced that fundamental political reform was now necessary. Beginning in 1895, young gentrymen throughout the empire formed reform clubs and study societies dedicated to further self-strengthening and to defending the country. The leading figure in this movement was a Cantonese scholar named K'ang Yu-wei. He and his major disciple, Liang Ch'i-ch'ao, recommended, in a series of memorials addressed to the throne and journalistic pieces addressed to the literate public, that reforms be implemented as rapidly as possible. Their hope was to persuade the Kuang-hsu Emperor (reigned 1875–1907) – who had recently taken full charge of the throne from his aunt, the empress dowager – to order changes in the organization of the government by abolishing sinecures, drastically modifying the examination system, creating new schools, carrying out full-scale military modernization, and initiating assemblies to give the gentry a legitimate political voice.

Hunan was a major centre of reform because the provincial governor, judicial commissioner and director of studies all favoured some measure of educational and administrative change. Even more important, young Hunanese literati like T'ang Ts'ai-ch'ang and T'an Ssu-t'ung were eagerly engaged in building up a network of local clubs to take the lead in revising the educational system, in undertaking economic projects, and in urging the gentry to mobilize popular support. T'an Ssu-t'ung was especially eager to broaden his contacts with the peasantry by joining popular religious sects and by participating in secret society-style martial arts groups.[9] There was thus in Hunan an especially conscious effort to fuse together the elite tradition of Confucian commitment to cultural preservation with popular ideals of peasant resistance to invasion.

The imperial government was slow to accept any proposals for reform, and certainly very cautious about encouraging these local clubs to lead provincial political movements. What kept the reform movement alive, and led K'ang Yu-wei to revive his organization in the capital, was the critical international situation faced by China. If the country had been helpless in 1894–95 to resist Japan's demands, China was even more impotent in the

[9] T'an Ssu-t'ung's religious activities have been studied by Richard Shek, whose research on this topic has not yet been published.

228

face of the series of diplomatic ultimatums that were delivered by the other great powers in 1897–98. In quick order, Germany demanded and got special concessions in Shantung, as did Russia in Liaotung, Great Britain in Shantung and in the New Territories, and France in the far south. This "scramble for concessions" understandably led many Chinese to believe that their country was being "carved up like a melon" by the imperrialists.

Fearful now that he might actually lose his throne, the Kuang-hsu Emperor expressed interest in K'ang's reform memorials, and, beginning in June 1898, launched the "Hundred Days of Reform." After consultations with K'ang Yu-wei and some of the other reformers, the emperor issued a set of decrees which ordered a fundamental reorganization of the bureaucracy, the army and the educational system. But the fiats were never fully implemented. Reasserting her authority over the emperor in the autumn of 1898, the empress dowager moved back into the palace and ordered the reformers purged. Six prominent reformers (including the Hunanese, T'an Ssu-t'ung) were actually executed, and the abortive "Hundred Days of Reform" came to an abrupt end within China. However, the two most important leaders of the movement – K'ang Yu-wei and Liang Ch'i-ch'ao – managed to escape abroad. In years to come they would continue in exile to symbolize the spirit of patriotic gentry reform.

Indeed, 12 years later they still represented that spirit to 16 year-old Mao Tse-tung, then enrolled in Tungshan Higher Primary School in Hsiang-hsiang.

I was reading two books sent to me by my cousin, telling of the reform movement of K'ang Yu-wei. One was called the *Journal of the New People*, and was edited by Liang Ch'i-ch'ao. I read and re-read these until I knew them by heart. I worshipped K'ang Yu-wei and Liang Ch'i-ch'ao . . . I considered the emperor as well as most officials to be honest, good and clever men. They only needed the help of K'ang Yu-wei's reforms.[10]

A year later, in 1911, Mao enrolled in middle school in the provincial capital of Changsha. There he learned of the anti-Manchu uprisings fomented by the Revolutionary Alliance (T'ung-meng hui) under the nominal leadership of Sun Yat-sen.

[10] Mao Tse-tung, quoted in Snow, *Red Star*, pp. 133–4.

At first Mao confused these revolutionary activities with the reformist programme of K'ang Yu-wei, perhaps because both seemed designed to save the country.

I learned also of Sun Yat-sen at this time, and of the program of the T'ung-meng hui. The country was on the eve of the first revolution. I was agitated so much that I wrote an article, which I posted on the school wall. It was my first expression of a political opinion, and it was somewhat muddled. I had not yet given up my admiration of K'ang Yu-wei and Liang Ch'i-ch'ao. I did not clearly understand the differences between them. Therefore in my article I advocated that Sun Yat-sen must be called back from Japan to become President of a new Government, that K'ang Yu-wei be made Premier, and Liang Ch'i-ch'ao Minister of Foreign Affairs.[11]

Mao Tse-tung's chagrin at having failed to see the distinction between Sun and K'ang is certainly understandable. By the time Mao posted his article on the middle school wall a great gap had grown between the two men. This gap represented what had since 1898 become nearly a chasm between higher and lower traditions of patriotism in China.

The split in China between patriotic reformists and nativist masses was painfully apparent during the Boxer uprisings of 1899–1900. The Boxers formed an anti-imperialist movement as socially diverse as the villages and towns of north China itself. They were loosely organized into bands led by sectarians and boxing masters, and united as a whole by their common belief that magic would protect them against European weapons as long as they proceeded to destroy all signs of the Western presence in China. Their elemental anti-foreignism seemed to the empress dowager – then desperate for popular support as anti-Manchu uprisings were again occurring in the south – a sure sign of her subjects' eagerness to close ranks behind the dynasty against the great powers. To many of her own officials, however, the Boxers appeared at worst to be chiliastic sectarians like the White Lotus rebels, and at best hapless peasants deluded by fanatic leaders who were just as capable of overthrowing the government as they were of murdering Christian converts. Especially at the provincial level, the reformist gentry was beginning to feel that its own nationalistically inspired self-strengthening projects would be jeopardized by the more primi-

[11] Ibid., p. 135.

tive anti-foreignism of the masses. All Chinese could agree upon the importance of restoring China to its proper place in the world. But what provincial reformers regarded as instruments of modernization crucial to national development (railroads, telegraphs, new schools) appeared to the Boxers as alarming signs of Westernization.

The cultural split between elite patriotism and mass nativism became all the more pronounced after 1901 when the Boxers were defeated and the empress dowager was encouraged to launch a second and eventually more effective dynastic reform movement. As the central government sponsored new local schools, chambers of commerce, native industry, new army units, and national railroads, the gentry became more deeply involved in provincial political and economic activities. The abolition of the examination system in 1905 eventually severed the gentry's dependence upon Peking for ultimate social status, and made it possible for wealth and a Western education to become determinants of elite status. The gentry thus dramatically altered its cultural outlook, preferring to educate its progeny in the new schools, and hopefully to send sons (and even daughters) abroad for higher training. Because modern schools and education abroad cost so much more than traditional tutors, entry into the new elite became much more difficult.[12] 50 years earlier, a young boy like Mao Tse-tung (whose father, after all, was a part-time rice broker with liquid assets of $2,000–3,000) might have hired a teacher in hopes of becoming an "aspirant" (t'ung-sheng) or "flourishing talent" (hsiu-ts'ai) in the examination system. Now, he could barely afford to leave home to attend a Western-style school in the nearby country seat.

One of the profoundest impulses of the student associations organized in Japan in the early 1900s was to get back in touch with the people of China. It is perhaps some measure of the students' distance from the peasantry that they turned so quickly to a man whose own mass support consisted largely of fund-raising contacts with the petit bourgeois communities of overseas Chinese dwelling in South-east Asia, the Americas and Europe. Yet Sun Yat-sen, product of an American missionary school in Hawaii and Western-style medical training, did

[12] Martin Bernal, Chinese Socialism to 1907 (Ithaca and London: Cornell University Press, 1976), p. 131.

populistically promise access to the global network of secret
societies (the Triads, *Chih-kung t'ang* and so forth) that supposedly led back through San Francisco or Singapore to the
inhabitants of south China.

Not all exiles identified the secret societies' cohorts as authentic peasant revolutionaries. Sun's rival, Liang Ch'i-ch'ao,
viewed them as congeries of "gamblers and swindlers" — as
"riff-raff" whose fanatic anti-Manchu "racialism" (*min-tsu
chu-i*) was opposed to the unitary "nationalism" (*kuo-chia
chu-i*) of responsible patriots like himself.[13] Liang's elite-
sponsored "nationalism," however, did not promise to gain the
students' popular support for a political revolution in China.
Sun Yat-sen, on the other hand, could at least guarantee that
anti-Manchu "racialism" was potentially a strong bond between
secret society nativists and young republican revolutionaries.
Thus, Sun Yat-sen's voice prevailed when the Revolutionary
Alliance (*T'ung-meng hui*) was formed in 1905 in Tokyo and, at
least in the very beginning, his strategy led to a series of abortive
secret society uprisings that brought his name to the young
Mao's attention in Changsha. Yet as the Revolutionary Alliance
gained visibility in students' eyes, it may have sacrificed respec-
tability in the view of the reformist gentry.

The reformist gentry had responded vigorously to the throne's
proposals for reform after 1901, and eagerly sponsored modern
schools, banks, local railways, industrial enterprises, and so
forth. However, these projects all cost a great deal of money. The
central government was already deeply in debt to foreign bankers and had pledged some of its most important sources of
income to pay off the ruinous indemnities resulting from its
military defeats. Virtually the only way to pay for the urban
gentry's reform projects was to increase the taxes upon the
peasantry, mainly in the form of increased salt taxes and higher
excise taxes levied upon farm goods brought into market towns.
The tax burden, which was both visible and onerous, was also
clearly associated in the public's mind with the gentry-
sponsored modernization projects then being carried out.[14]

[13] Bernal, *Chinese Socialism*, pp. 160, 189.
[14] Winston Hsieh, "Triads, salt smugglers and local uprisings: observations on
the social and economic background of the Waichow revolution of 1911," in
Jean Chesneaux (ed.), *Popular Movements and Secret Societies in China,
1840–1950* (Stanford: Stanford University Press, 1972), pp. 160–1.

It was just such a situation in Changsha that precipitated the rice riots of 1910. As Mao later explained to Edgar Snow:

Outside the little Chinese school where I was studying, we students noticed many bean merchants, coming back from Changsha. We asked them why they were all leaving. They told us about a big uprising in the city. There had been a severe famine that year, and in Changsha thousands were without food. The starving sent a delegation to the civil governor, to beg for relief, but he replied to them haughtily, "Why haven't you food? There is plenty in the city. I always have enough." When the people were told the governor's reply, they became very angry. They held mass meetings and organized a demonstration. They attacked the Manchu yamen, cut down the flagpole, the symbol of office, and drove out the governor . . . [After the rebels were executed,] I felt that there with the rebels were ordinary people like my own family and I deeply resented the injustice of the treatment given to them.[15]

What Mao could not have known, being at the time in Hsiang-hsiang, was that during the mélée in Changsha, conservative gentry – opposed to the measures of modernization introduced by the reformist elite – helped direct the rioters towards the edifices that either contained foreign goods, were rented by foreigners, or were associated with the reformers' proposals. What had begun as a classic grain riot, in other words, turned into a forceful demonstration against the urban gentry's reform effort, with mobs attacking government schools, foreign missions, foreign-connected shops, foreign-style hotels, foreign steamship lines, and so forth. The most important targets were the schools. Five of the new government schools, the very symbol of Westernization and of the reform gentry's new expensive projects, were burned.

Mao may not have known about the burning of Western-style schools in Changsha; but he certainly must have sensed the implicit connection between this lower-class economic resentment and anti-foreign feelings, which were often directed most strongly against the "foreign slaves" (yang nu) who had taken on Western ways. In fact, one of the teachers in his own school at Hsiang-hsiang incurred such attacks.

Another notable thing [Mao told Snow,] was that one of the teachers was a returned student from Japan and he wore a false queue. It was quite easy to tell that his queue was false. Everyone laughed at him and

[15] Mao Tse-tung, quoted in Snow, Red Star, pp. 130–1.

called him the 'False Foreign Devil'. . . Many of the students disliked the 'False Foreign Devil' because of his inhuman queue, but I liked hearing him talk about Japan.[16]

The custom of plaiting men's hair into a pigtailed queue had been forced upon the Han Chinese by their Manchu conquerors in the 17th century. By Mao's time the population had grown so used to wearing the queue that most people thought it was their own native custom. To Mao and his schoolmates, not to have a queue was not to be Chinese; it was to be foreign. To the Westernized schoolteacher, on the other hand, the old-fashioned and Manchu-imposed queue represented both cultural backwardness and racial humiliation. Though now obliged to wear a false queue to avoid arrest by the Ch'ing authorities, he had cut his queue in Japan as a sign of his cultural enlightenment and his nationalistic identity. Back in Hsiang-hsiang, however, his action was taken to be a symbol of despised Westernization. Pigtail-shorn, he was ridiculed for slavishly imitating foreign customs, so that his false queue ironically became a symbol of Mao's teacher's loss of Chinese manhood.

This misunderstanding was not an isolated example in China at the time. Mao's favourite modern writer, Lu Hsün, later published a very famous novella called *The True Story of Ah Q* which was set in the period of the Revolution of 1911. The "hero" of the serial, Ah Q, was an illiterate roustabout – "riff-raff" despised by nearly everyone who knew him – who none the less felt superior to a "fake foreign devil" in his village just like the teacher in Mao's higher primary school.

From the distance approached another of Ah Q's enemies. This was Mr. Ch'ien's eldest son whom Ah Q thoroughly despised. After studying in a foreign-style school in the city, it seemed he had gone to Japan. When he came home half a year later his legs were straight and his queue had disappeared . . . What Ah Q despised and detested most in him was his false queue. When it came to having a false queue, a man could scarcely be considered human . . .[17]

---

[16] Mao Tse-tung, quoted in Snow, *Red Star*, pp. 132–3. As Professor Schram points out, Mao rallied his First Normal School soccer team against the Westernized Chinese players from Yale-in-China with the cry, "*Yangnu!*" See Schram, *Mao*, p. 73.

[17] Lu Hsün, "The true story of Ah Q," translated in Gladys Yang, *Silent China: Selected Writings of Lu Xun* (London, Oxford and New York: Oxford University Press, 1973), p. 25.

Much of the irony in Lu Hsün's novella rests upon Ah Q's chagrin when he finds out that this "fake foreign devil" is one of the local leaders of the victorious revolutionary movement he, Ah Q, wishes to join. Consequently, Ah Q and the rest of the villagers discover to their surprise that cutting the queue signifies revolutionary opposition to the Manchu regime.

In much the same way and on the eve of the 1911 revolution, Mao Tse-tung also experienced the symbolic reconstruction of the queue. Now in middle school in Changsha, he noted that:

> The students in my school became more and more agitated. They demonstrated their anti-Manchu sentiments by a rebellion against the pigtail. One friend and I clipped off our pigtails, but others, who had promised to do so, afterward failed to keep their word. My friend and I therefore assaulted them in secret and forcibly removed their queues, a total of more than ten falling victim to our shears. Thus in a short space of time I had progressed from ridiculing the False Foreign Devil's imitation queue to demanding the general abolition of queues. How a political idea can change a point of view![18]

The popular reformulation of the symbolism of the queue was an apt metaphor for the momentary reunion of elitist and popular traditions of political engagement during the initial stages of the Revolution of 1911. Anti-Manchuism thus provided the temporary bridge between Westernized leaders and the nativist populace, but only for a transitional moment. All too soon the span was gone. With their common Manchu enemy overthrown, the reformist gentry in the cities and the peasantry in the countryside lost the patriotic animus they had held in common. In Hunan, for example, the rift began even before the Manchu dynasty had surrendered the throne to the republic. The reformist elite in Changsha, led by the speaker of the provincial assembly, T'an Yen-k'ai (a former Hanlin Confucian scholar), quickly grew disturbed by the prospect of Revolutionary Alliance demagogues arousing tax-burdened peasants or secret society elements to carry out a social revolution. When the radical leader, Chiao Ta-feng, began to take charge of the revolution in Hunan with the help of secret society elements, T'an became alarmed, and "spoke to the people of their higher duties":

[18] Mao Tse-tung, quoted in Snow, *Red Star*, pp. 135–6.

235

A civilized revolution is different from country banditry. It is only possible with the co-operation and dedication of the great families and ancient clans, and the military officers.[19]

Consequently, as Chiao Ta-feng took over the governship (tu-tu) of Hunan in the name of the Revolutionary Alliance, T'an Yen-k'ai turned to the army for help. Mao, not yet in the thick of things himself, observed from the sidelines that:

The new tu-tu [Chiao Ta-feng] and vice-tu-tu [Ch'en Tso-hsin] did not last long. They were not bad men, and had some revolutionary intentions, but they were poor and represented the interests of the oppressed. The landlords and merchants were dissatisfied with them. Not many days later when I went to call on a friend, I saw their corpses lying in the street. T'an Yen-k'ai had organized a revolt against them, as representative of the Hunan landlords and militarists.[20]

Thus, after the initial uprisings in October 1911, many of the T'ung-meng hui revolutionaries were displaced by members of the upper gentry. And less than five years later the reformist gentry had been removed from power by military men. After 1916 the generals ruled most of China, and it was obvious to nearly everyone that the Revolution of 1911 had turned out to be the destruction of an ancien régime rather than the construction of a new nation-state. By sweeping away the old Confucian monarchy, however, the revolutionaries did create the potential for dramatic future changes. In this sense, 1911 opened an era of political possibilities and social opportunities.

For Mao, coming of age with the revolution meant a brief stint in the revolutionary army of the young Wuhan militarist, T'ang Sheng-chih. Then, after some hesitation about choosing a career when he left the army, Mao enrolled in Changsha's prestigious First Normal School, where he was to spend the next five years. During that period he was to come the closest to being part of that local urban elite dominated by men like T'an Yen-k'ai. At the Normal School, Mao soon became a prominent student leader: chairman of the local student association, and by his senior year author of an article published in Ch'en Tu-hsiu's pace–setting magazine, New Youth (Hsin ch'ing-nien). For a while, Mao even contemplated study abroad. Helping organize a programme for work-study in France, Mao's own rural roots

[19] Esherick, Reform and Revolution in China (Berkeley, Los Angeles and London: University of California Press, 1975), p. 202.
[20] Mao Tse-tung, quoted in Snow, Red Star, pp. 137–8.

were attenuating. It seemed natural, then, for Mao to leave Changsha and go to Peking with a contingent of Hunanese students preparing to sail for Europe. Ultimately, Mao decided not to go abroad, perhaps because he found the study of French and English too difficult. He told Snow later that he had felt that he "did not know enough about [his] own country, and that [his] time could be more profitably spent in China."[21] Whatever the reason, this decision kept Mao from temporarily severing his strong provincial ties. After a brief three-month stint working in the Peking University Library, Mao returned to Hunan.

He was thus in Changsha, teaching in a primary school, when the May Fourth Movement erupted in 1919, beginning as a student protest in Peking against Japanese demands on China—demands which were supported by the Western powers and agreed to by Chinese warlords. As the movement spread across China, students, merchants and workers together called for national unity against imperialism. Mao strongly shared the emotions of the protesters. Organizing a very successful anti-Japanese boycott in Changsha, Mao eloquently appealed for a "great union of the popular masses" in a stirring article published in July 1919, in the *Hsiang River Review* (*Hsiang-chiang p'ing-lun*):

In reality, for thousands of years the Chinese people of several hundred millions all led a life of slaves . . . Today things are different, and in every domain we demand liberation. Ideological liberation, political liberation, economic liberation, liberation [in the relations between] men and women, educational liberation, are all going to burst from the deep inferno where they have been confined, and demand to look at the blue sky. Our Chinese people possesses great inherent capacities! The more profound the oppression, the greater its resistance; that which has accumulated for a long time will surely burst forth quickly. I venture to make a singular assertion: one day, the reform of the Chinese people will be more profound than that of any other people, and the society of the Chinese people will be more profound than that of any other people. The great union of the Chinese people will be achieved earlier than that of any other place or people. Gentlemen! Gentlemen! We must all exert ourselves! We must all advance with the utmost strength! Our golden age, our age of glory and splendour, lies before us![22]

As Stuart R. Schram has pointed out, this newspaper article reveals a Mao who has not yet become a Marxist – a Mao who is

[21] *Ibid.*, p. 149.
[22] Mao Tse-tung, "The Great Union of the Popular Masses," translated in Stuart R. Schram, CQ, No. 49 (January–March 1972), p. 87.

above all a nationalist.[23] Yet one can also detect the first stirrings of Mao's conviction that China would remake herself, and that this change would occur precisely because the country had become so oppressed. Mao had begun to perceive that oppression had created a counter-force, the will of the people, who, liberated through struggle, would unite together to build a new golden age in Chinese history.

This new belief in mass action, as part of a generally patriotic commitment to the recovery of national strength and independence, was influenced by Marxist theory. Mao's initial exposure to Marxism had mainly been through the writings of Li Ta-chao, whose "Victory of Bolshevism" celebrating the Russian October Revolution was used by Mao as a text when he lectured on Marxism in Changsha in 1919. Li's revolutionary vision was global, so that China's struggle for liberation was viewed as part of a new stage in world history. He preached a romantic reunion of city and countryside – a China transformed by the nationalistic solidarity between the urban youth and the rural masses.

> . . . we ought to work in the fields . . . Then the atmosphere of culture will merge together with the shadows of the trees and smoke of the village chimneys, and those quiet, depressed old villages will become transformed into lively, active new villages. The great unity of the new villages will be our 'Young China.'[24]

Three years later, however, Li Ta-chao did accept the need for social conflict and forcefully identified the "proletarian nation" of China with the socialist world revolution as such. Invoking the popular tradition of peasant protest, Li claimed that the Triads and the Taiping rebels represented a national history of class warfare that was directly linked to the Marxist global struggle. Quite of its own accord – though "under the leadership of Sun Yat-sen" – the Chinese national revolutionary "tide" had "entered onto the correct track of world revolution in order to carry out a gigantic reconstruction of human history."[25]

Mao Tse-tung was deeply impressed by Li Ta-chao's theory of national struggle. The most immediate effect of Li's influence

---

[23] Stuart R. Schram, "From the 'Great Union of the Popular Masses' to the 'Great Alliance,'" CQ, No. 49 (January–March 1972), p. 94.
[24] Maurice Meisner, Li Ta-chao and the Origins of Chinese Marxism (Cambridge, Mass.: Harvard University Press, 1967), p. 88.
[25] Ibid., p. 225.

may have been Mao's growing commitment to the new United Front between his own fledgling Chinese Communist Party and Sun Yat-sen's populistic Kuomintang.[26] Many Communists originally opposed plans for an alliance on the grounds that the larger "bourgeois" Kuomintang would engulf their tiny "proletarian" Party. Yet despite their misgivings, some members of the Chinese Communist Party retained enough of their initial commitment to a national revolutionary movement, and to patriotic unification, to accept even the idea that a bourgeoisie – the merchants supporting the Kuomintang – might lead the struggle against the warlords and imperialism. Mao was one of those who welcomed the United Front by arguing in July 1923, that:

The present political problem in China is none other than the problem of the national revolution. To use the strength of the people to overthrow the militarists and foreign imperialism, with which the former are in collusion to accomplish their treasonable acts, is the historic mission of the Chinese people. This revolution is the task of the people as a whole ... but because of historical necessity and current tendencies, the work for which the merchants should be responsible in the national revolution is both more urgent and more important than the work that the rest of the people should take upon themselves.[27]

The United Front thus allowed Mao nationally to perpetuate the position taken provincially during the campaign to oust Chang Ching-yao from Hunan. Once again, he was cast in the role of an intermediary between a reformist elite and the masses whose support was needed to oppose the warlords. During the interim, however, Mao had acquired invaluable organizational experience, while coming to identify national liberation with social revolution.

Mao's role became increasingly ambiguous within the United Front – as was well illustrated in his article on class analysis

[26] The populistic qualities of Sun Yat-sen's Kuomintang probably stem from his earlier Revolutionary Party (Ke-ming-tang), which has been described as an "inclusive elite single party" which proffered "a sort of fraternal paternalism" to the "vulnerable and ignorant" poor. Edward Friedman, Backward Toward Revolution: The Chinese Revolutionary Party (Berkeley, Los Angeles and London: University of California press, 1974), p. 26.
[27] Mao Tse-tung, "The Role of the Merchants in the National Revolution," in Schram, Thought, pp. 206–7.

which appeared in *The Chinese Peasant* (*Chung-kuo nung-min*) in February 1926. Here Mao unequivocally declared that the Chinese revolution had so far failed because its leaders had not always been able to tell their true friends from their enemies. In the case of China, this meant that revolutionaries had not always been aware that the "big bourgeoisie" (big landowners in the countryside; big merchants, bankers and industrialists in the cities) was their class enemy, while portions of the vacillating "middle bourgeoisie," along with the "petty bourgeoisie" (peasant landholders), the "semi-proletariat" (part freeholders and part labourers) and the "proletariat" (agricultural labourers) were their class allies. Mao thus singled out portions of the reformist elite – and certainly those who were large landholders – as class enemies of the revolution, and yet at the same time continued optimistically to call out for national unity with "our true friends" whom he believed to constitute 99 per cent of the Chinese population.[28]

The Northern Expedition was cast in the metaphor of a mass revolutionary tempest then sweeping across China to smash warlords and imperialists. As Mao put it a few months later in his famous "Report of an Investigation into the Peasant Movement in Hunan" (February 1927):

> In a very short time, several hundred million peasants in China's central, southern, and northern provinces will rise like a tornado or tempest – a force so extraordinarily swift and violent that no power, however great, will be able to suppress it. They will break through all the trammels that now bind them and push forward along the road to liberation. They will send all imperialists, warlords, corrupt officials, local bullies, and evil gentry to their graves.[29]

To T'an Yen-k'ai and "bourgeois" provincial gentry like him, this stormy image initially summoned up the old high cultural ideal of the enlightened gentry mobilizing popular militia during the Opium War. Their elite populism emphasized the importance of moral leadership guiding the people's zeal against outsiders (imperialists, warlords, corrupt officials) and against traitors in their midst (local bullies and evil gentry). T'an

---

[28] Mao Tse-tung, "Analysis of all the Classes in Chinese Society," in Schram, *Thought*, pp. 210–14.
[29] Mao Tse-tung, "Report of an Investigation into the Peasant Movement in Hunan," in Schram, *Thought*, p. 250.

Yen-k'ai's own perspective was faithful to Sun Yat-sen's personal belief that his programme for improving the "people's livelihood" (min-sheng) was a politically administered prophylactic to forestall future economic ills. The Kuomintang's prescriptions for economic reform, in other words, were supposed to be a national socialist solution to the horrors of class warfare that the Chinese had observed in the industrialized West.

After his death in 1925, Sun's priority for the national revolution continued to be underscored by the Kuomintang leader, Hu Han-min, who argued that while the motive force of imperialism was individual profit-seeking, Marxism merely substituted class selfishness for the individual's self-interest. National unity demanded that such particularisms be put aside; class struggle would only weaken their common struggle against imperialism.[30] In October 1926 Mao proceeded to Shanghai to take charge of his own Communist Party's Peasant Department, and by December could be found in Hunan investigating the peasant movement there. Mao soon discovered that the most active and vigorous peasant associations were those in which the poorer peasants had taken control and were directing their struggle against the power of local landlords.

After the peasants had organized themselves, action ensued. The main targets of the peasants are the local bullies, the evil gentry, and the lawless landlords; they also hit out against various patriarchal ideologies and institutions, corrupt officials in the cities, and evil customs in the rural areas . . . The dignity and prestige of the landlords are dashed to the ground . . . The broad peasant masses have risen to fulfil their historical mission, [and] the democratic forces in the rural areas have risen to overthrow the rural feudal power. *The overthrow of this feudal power is the real objective of the national revolution.*[31]

By identifying the ultimate aims of the national revolution with a social revolution against the supposed integument of landlord-warlord-imperialist interests, Mao had forcefully moulded a conflict model of history. Class struggle, he was to declare in the future, was the key to everything: the mass line,

---

[30] Arif Dirlik, "Mass movements and the left Kuomintang," *Modern China*, Vol. I, No. 1 (January 1975), p. 62.

[31] Mao Tse-tung, "Report of an Investigation into the Peasant Movement in Hunan," pp. 250–2. (Emphasis added.)

proletarian consciousness, military mobilization and national revolution. It was in class conflict that Mao discovered the means towards the ultimate "great union" that he had written about eight years earlier. As he observed in Hunan, the peasant movement was more than just *jacquerie*. Social struggle created its own forms of political participation. Encouraged to vent their wrath on local landlords, the poorer peasants' rage brought them to the fore, so that they took charge of their associations, "rais[ing] their rough, blackened hands and lay[ing] them on the heads of the gentry."[32] The peasant associations momentarily displaced the rural government of the landlords, and the peasants' anger was expressed in popular tribunals which tried the worst of the gentry for their excesses. If only momentarily, the "riff-raff" ruled the countryside.

Mao's own declaration in 1927 that the national revolution was, after all, a social revolution, partly reflected the immediate events he had witnessed. It also marked a momentary political reaction to the unitary nationalism of United Front conservatives like Hu Han-min. At a deeper level, however, Mao's peasant report expressed his personal decision to abandon the elitist populism of T'an Yen-k'ai and to identify himself with the Chinese peasant tradition of rural protest. His was thus a commitment to join the Ah Q's of China, the "riff-raff": these people, who used to go around in worn-out leather shoes, carry broken umbrellas, wear blue gowns and gamble . . . [and who have] now dared to raise their heads."[33]

Those words from Mao's own peasant report were echoed later in his remarks to Edgar Snow about his days at the school in Hsiang-hsiang when "many of the richer students despised me because usually I was wearing my ragged coat and trousers."[34] But we must remember that in spite of his own memory of ragged clothing, Mao had once been a student and, at least in passing, a member of the intellectual elite of China. His rural background and marginal identity as an intellectual may have eased his unconscious identification with the poor, but there was certainly a conscious transformation as well when he embraced the lower classes to become more like them. In his

[32] *Ibid.*, p. 254.
[33] *Ibid.*
[34] Mao Tse-tung, quoted in Snow, *Red Star*, p. 132.

Yenan talks on art and literature in 1942, Mao made it very clear that he had resolved the contradiction between elite and popular cultural traditions by a form of social trans-valuation which rejected the elite altogether. Li Ta-chao had urged his students to go to the masses. Mao now told his intellectual followers to become members of the masses themselves.

I began as a student and acquired the habits of a student; surrounded by students who could neither fetch nor carry for themselves, I used to consider it undignified to do any manual labour, such as shouldering my own luggage. At that time it seemed to me that the intellectuals were the only clean persons in the world; next to them, the workers and peasants seemed rather dirty. I would put on the clothes of other intellectuals, because I thought they were clean, but I would not put on clothes belonging to a worker or peasant, because I felt they were dirty. Having become a revolutionary I found myself in the ranks of the workers, peasants, and soldiers of the revolutionary army, and gradually I became familiar with them, and they with me. It was then and only then that a fundamental change occurred in the bourgeois and petty-bourgeois feelings implanted in me by the bourgeois schools. I came to feel that it was those unreconstructed intellectuals who were unclean as compared with the workers and peasants, while the workers and peasants are after all the cleanest persons, cleaner than both the bourgeois and the petty bourgeois, even though their hands are soiled and their feet smeared with cow dung. This is what is meant by having one's feelings transformed, changed from those of one class into those of another.[35]

By identifying with the masses, Mao not only adopted the social customs of the lower classes; he rejected as well the cultural manners of the Westernized bourgeoisie. Class struggle and patriotic struggle were thus reconciled in his decision to revive that part of himself attuned to lower-class culture, thereby embracing the peasantry's nativism.

For 16 years, ever since discovering that the "fake foreign devils" of China were actually political patriots, Mao Tse-tung had belonged to the urban world of the bourgeoisie. By 1927, however, he had come to identify the upper classes with the enemies of China's national liberation; to be bourgeois was to be at once both a member of an oppressive class and an ally of imperialism. The story is told of Mao's encounter in Shanghai

[35] Mao Tse-tung, "Literature and Art in the Service of the People," in Schram, *Thought*, p. 362.

with a former schoolmate who had returned from study abroad. Mao, who was dressed in old Chinese clothes, stared at his friend's Western suit and advised him to exchange it for native wear. "Why?" asked the friend. Mao's answer was to lead his old classmate to the municipal park in Shanghai and point to the sign which read: "Chinese and dogs are not allowed."[36] In Mao Tse-tung's eyes, the Westernized bourgeoisie had socially and culturally betrayed China. His revolutionary identity thus became a new form of national identity.

Mao subsequently made a strong connection between the class question and the national question. As a Communist, he could not ignore the importance of international class struggle. As a patriot, he had to relate that struggle to the recovery of Chinese national unity and strength. He told Agnes Smedley in 1937 that:

> The Communists absolutely do not tie their viewpoint to the interests of a single class at a single time, but are most passionately concerned with the fate of the Chinese nation, and moreover with its fate throughout eternity . . . The Chinese Communists are internationalists; they are in favour of the world Communist movement. But at the same time they are patriots who defend their native land . . . This patriotism and internationalism are by no means in conflict, for only China's independence and liberation will make it possible to participate in the world Communist movement.[37]

By the time he and his comrades had won the civil war against the Kuomintang, Mao had managed to subsume the identity of the social revolution under the banner of national liberation. On the eve of communist victory, therefore, many Chinese were inclined to share Mao's confidence, that, "We have a common feeling that our work will be recorded in the history of mankind, and that it will clearly demonstrate that the Chinese, who comprise one quarter of humanity, have begun to stand up."[38]

Mao's contribution to national recovery ultimately stemmed

---

[36] Schram, Mao, p. 73. The estrangement between revolutionary nationalism and bourgeois cosmopolitanism is thoughtfully explored in Joseph R. Levenson, Revolution and Cosmopolitanism: The Western Stage and the Chinese Stages (Berkeley, Los Angeles and London: University of California Press, 1971), pp. 1–9, 45–55.

[37] Schram, Mao, p. 201.

[38] Mao Tse-tung, "The Chinese People Has Stood Up," in Schram, Thought, p. 167.

from this conception of class struggle. His patriotism, after all, was a form of egalitarianism. By urging fellow Communists to become one with China's masses, Mao Tse-tung helped transform elitist populism into a unique belief in national class transformation. This egalitarian emphasis upon changing one's class feelings made a "proletarian nation" possible. When in 1965, on the eve of the Cultural Revolution, André Malraux visited China and paid his respects to Mao in the Great Hall of the People, Mao spoke of the ongoing struggle to change China's traditional customs into revolutionary ones, based upon the daily travail of the people. The new China, he declared, would be a society which mixed together the elite cadre and the broad masses.

While Mao spoke, Malraux was reminded of the emperors of China's past – and yet of something more. No one since Lenin had so profoundly shaken the world. The European era of world power seemed to be dissipating, and a Chinese epoch beginning. Thinking of world conquerors, Malraux told Mao that he believed the China of the future would be the China of the great empires. Mao answered slowly that he was not sure this was true:

I don't know, but I do know that if our methods are good – if we tolerate no deviation – China will remake herself. But in this struggle we are alone. I am alone with the masses. Waiting.[39]

Since then Mao Tse-tung has made his "final report to Marx." Now the masses must wait, and struggle without him.

[39] André Malraux, Antimémoires (Paris: Gallimard, 1967), p. 551.

8

THE STATESMAN

John Gittings

Ten years before the death of Mao Tse-tung, the choice of this title would have been inconceivable to most Western experts on Chinese foreign policy who were writing at the time. The only statesman generally acknowledged to exist within the Chinese leadership was Chou En-lai: Mao's own record of lively interest and activity in Chinese foreign affairs had been obscured by the accumulation of Cold War myths. He was mostly regarded as a man who knew little of the world, who understood less, and who had pushed his country into a disastrous split with the Soviet Union.

In the condolences of leading world politicians 10 years later, from President Ford of the United States to President Marcos of the Philippines, the label of "statesman" was attached to Mao without a second thought. Most of them had met the chairman in the past few years and, either dazzled by the experience or out of diplomatic prudence, had already remarked on his exceptional grasp of international affairs. Most of them now found his anti-Soviet passion very much to their liking; many claimed to have established a special rapport if not with the chairman himself at least with Chou En-lai – viewed before his own death more as the executor than the initiator of Chinese foreign policy.

Switches of this sort in Western attitudes and scholarship towards China are nothing new. For lack of any well-defined criterion in judging the "statesmanlike" qualities of a world leader, it is not surprising if these should be measured by the congruence of his policies with the interests of Western diplomacy. We may be sure that if Mao had chosen before his death to retilt the balance of Chinese foreign policy towards the Soviet Union, his record would have been more critically viewed.

It is another matter to make a lasting judgment on the

achievements and failures which resulted from Mao's influence upon his country's external affairs, and to do so in a principled way. For we may do so according to three very different sets of criteria – although the first two may under present conditions overlap:

(i) by measuring Mao's contribution to "world peace," or to the maintenance of some sort of international stability preserving the present order;

(ii) by measuring the contribution to the building up and strengthening of the socialist state in China, with well-defined interests and a social and political system secure from outside interference; or

(iii) by measuring Mao's contribution to the building of socialism not only in China but abroad, and to advancement of the proletarian revolution.

The first and second criteria are those which have been generally applied by Mao's fellow-"statesmen" in the West, and by which in his declining years he was judged most favourably. But it is in the contradiction between "socialism in one country" and proletarian internationalism that the real interest and the important questions about Mao's statesmanship reside, and it is upon these that I shall focus in this essay.

It is not unusual for politically aware people in the countries of the exploited world to grasp early on that the future depends on their exploiters – unless they can get rid of them. "When elephants fight, the grass is trampled" is an aphorism which has been attributed with equal plausibility to President Nyerere of Tanzania and Prince Sihanouk of Cambodia. Several decades earlier, writing in 1923, Mao had put it more pungently: "If one of our foreign bosses farts, they [the foreigners' allies in China] say it is a fragrant perfume."[1] More decorously he would argue in 1940 that "the history of modern China is a history of imperialist aggression, of imperialist opposition to China's independence and to her development of capitalism."[2]

This sort of statement was a commonplace for millions of young Chinese in the early decades of the 20th century, many of whom had been politicized by the anti-foreign struggles which helped spark off the 1911 Revolution, which in the May Fourth

[1] "On the Cigarette Tax," translated in Schram, Thought, p. 210.
[2] "On New Democracy," SW, Vol. II, p. 354.

Movement of 1919 helped usher in a new stage of social and cultural revolution, and which in the boycotts and strikes of the 1920s helped to create a militant Chinese proletariat. It was not defeatism but common sense to recognize that, however hard the Chinese people struggled, the shifting alliances among the imperialist powers would strongly affect the nature and degree at any given time of aggression against China. This became particularly evident as the Western grip weakened and Japan supplanted the older imperialists. "China is already intimately connected with the rest of the world," argued Mao in 1938. "The Sino-Japanese war is a part of the world war, and the victory of China's war against Japan cannot be separated from the world."[3]

In theoretical terms Mao had developed early on in his career in the Communist Party a very sharp perception into the relationship between imperialism and the Chinese revolution, summed up in the phrase that China was "both a semi-colonial and a semi-feudal country." What was striking was not the phrase itself but the use which Mao made of it to point the way forward and encourage revolutionary optimism. As a "semi-feudal" society, China's weaknesses had exposed the nation to foreign imperialism. But the geographical vastness of China coupled with the rivalries of the foreign powers meant that it could not be swallowed up by one imperialist country alone – hence it was "semi-colonial." Both Stalin and Sun Yat-sen, from their different perspectives, had seen this as indicating China's position to be even more dire than that of an outright colony. Mao on the contrary saw China's semi-colonial state as providing a vital opportunity for the Chinese people to outmanoeuvre the semi-colonizers, and as allowing at the same time the revolutionary section of the Chinese people to press the struggle against their own ruling class. For they could exploit not only the contradictions arising between the imperialists in their struggle for China, but those which the latter inspired by proxy among the rival groups within China who were thus incapable of establishing unified rule. Put crudely, as Mao argued it in 1928–30 from his mountain retreat on Chingkangshan, it was in such no-man's-land between the territories of the rival warlords

---

[3] "On the New Stage," October 1938, MTC, Vol. VI, p. 234.

of China, themselves supported by rival imperialists, that the "Red power" of the Chinese revolution could not only survive but flourish.[4]

If one asks whether a revolutionary high tide is imminent in China, the answer can only be found by making a detailed investigation into whether the contradictions, that will bring on the "High Tide," are developing or not. We must see correctly that the international contradictions between imperialisms, between imperialisms and the colonies, and between imperialism and the proletariat have all developed. Imperialism consequently needs more urgently than ever to struggle for China. As this struggle becomes more intense the contradictions between imperialism and China as a whole, and among the imperialists themselves, develop within China's boundaries at the same time; consequently there arise within China's ruling classes chaotic wars that spread and intensify with every passing day, while the contradictions among them grow.[5]

Already there existed in Mao's analysis two salient features which would distinguish his view of the world right up to the 1970s and the arrival of Mr Nixon in Peking. They were also features which were not shared at the time by the majority of the CCP leadership – nor did they conform to the Comintern line laid down by Stalin – and would also meet with opposition again in the future. First was the sheer weight attached by Mao to China's external relationships, which represented, so he argued, the principal contradiction faced by his nation and which, according to his theory of semi-colonialism, dominated the shape of the class struggle within China. As his colleague Ch'en Po-ta wrote later on, Mao at this time "had perceived that the contradiction between imperialism and the Chinese nation (a characteristic of semi-colonial China) *would precipitate or influence the development of other contradictions.*"[6] Second was Mao's early insistence upon the crucial fact that the external powers threatening China were themselves divided, and that

---

[4] The two crucial documents where Mao argued his case are (i) his report to the Second Border Area Congress at Maoping, 5 October, 1928, and (ii) his "Letter to Comrade Lin Piao" dated 5 January, 1930. Both are in *MTC*, Vol. II. The *SW* versions are very different. The original letter to Lin Piao has been translated by Bill Jenner in *New Left Review* (London), No. 65.
[5] "Letter to Lin Piao," p. 62.
[6] Ch'en Po-ta, *Notes on Ten Years of Civil War* (Peking, Foreign Languages Press, 1954), pp. 29–30. (Emphasis added.)

their own inter-imperialist contradictions should be studied, analysed and exploited. (In October 1928 he referred to the "irreconcileable positions" of the Western powers). Mao's views clashed directly with the Comintern line after the break-up of the United Front in 1927 that the main target of the revolution must be its "internal enemies" – including the national bourgeoisie who were now lumped together with the "feudal regime" in Nanking – while there was no essential difference between the imperialists in their China policies. In 1929 the CCP was actually reprimanded by the Comintern for having suggested that there might be some conflict between American Far Eastern policy and the interests in China of Britain and Japan.[7]

Mao's approach made much better sense to his colleagues, and to Stalin, after the Long March and as Japan moved further into China. The conflict which this provoked with the other Western powers became more evident; so did the opposition of the national bourgeoisie within China. It also chimed with the mood of Popular Frontism in Europe, officially endorsed by the Comintern. Few would dissent when Mao wrote in 1937 that "the contradiction between China and imperialism in general has given way to the particularly salient and sharp contradiction between China and Japanese imperialism."[8] Some of Mao's fellow-leaders (notably the Comintern's own representative Wang Ming) wished to go even further than he did in promoting A Second United Front with the bourgeois Nationalist Government of Chiang Kai-shek to join forces against Japan. Mao now became effectively the CCP's spokesman on foreign affairs, writing lengthy commentaries (of which very few have been reprinted in his *Selected Works*) and speaking on the subject with impressive authority to the foreign visitors who, led by Edgar Snow, began to make their pilgrimage to Yenan. The flow of visitors ceased in the early 1940s as the communist border areas came under blockade, but resumed in 1944–47 when not only journalists but American Foreign Service officials came, saw, and were usually captivated by Mao's impressive grasp of international affairs. He was, wrote Edgar Snow, "the student of

---

[7] See further John Gittings, *The World and China, 1922–1972* (London: Eyre-Methuen, 1974), pp. 46–51.

[8] "Tasks of the Chinese Anti-Japanese United Front under Present Conditions," 3 May, 1937, MTC, Vol. V.

world events and the political analyst" who settled down every evening with a huge pile of radio dispatches, "from the battle front in Shansi, from all over China, and from countries abroad."[9] Mao held forth with authority to his guests, noted Nym Wales. He "was regal and pontifical in his pronouncements, always taking the long view."[10]

During this decade of war in China and the world, Mao was grappling essentially with the same problem throughout, that of how to correlate developments on the shifting international stage with the interests of the Chinese nation and the Chinese revolution. Britain and France, already regarded with extreme suspicion as attempting to promote "a Munich in the Far East," soon became irrelevant to the Chinese situation, which was dominated by the twin poles of the Soviet Union and the United States. Mao did not of course refer to them as the "super-powers," and he drew a clear distinction between the imperialist U.S. and the socialist U.S.S.R. Yet it is already possible in the late 1930s and 1940s to detect a trace in Mao's attitude of the tendency which he would develop later on (i) to view the whole international scene as a function of "super-power" activity, and (ii) to judge the performance of each international giant primarily by reference to how each behaved towards China. Furthermore although Mao did his best to make his pronouncements conform with the letter of Soviet policy, in spirit they often diverged – a fact of which the Russians themselves were well aware.

The basic principle guiding Mao's attitude was stated by him, without reference to proletarian internationalism, in his first reaction to the announcement of the Nazi-Soviet Pact in September 1939. Unlike the Russians he did not feel obliged to put a moralistic gloss on the Pact, but interpreted it quite candidly as a case of supping with the devil to save one's skin, and argued that China should do likewise:

In the field of foreign relations we regard those who assist us as our friends and those who aid the enemy as our foes . . . Germany and Italy for instance have helped the enemy in the past, and for that reason Wang Ching-wei's demands for rapprochement with those two nations are wrong and treasonable. Should Germany and Italy cease aiding the

[9] Edgar Snow, Scorched Earth (London: Left Book Club, 1941), Vol. II, p. 270–1.
[10] Nym Wales, My Yenan Notebooks (Madison: mimeographed, 1961), p. 132.

enemy we would not be opposed to improving our relations with them in order to weaken Japan. Should Britain assist our enemy, then we should abandon all hope of aid from her and vigilantly guard against being caught by any traps she might set to endanger our war of resistance.

As for the Soviet Union, we must strengthen the friendship between our country and her and form a true united front of the two great nations; and thus get even more aid and strengthen our position. The same should be our attitude in general towards America.[11]

Two weeks later Mao apologized – perhaps under pressure from his more orthodox colleagues – for having bracketed the United States together with the Soviet Union as a source of aid for China. But he continued to argue that, whatever might be happening in Europe (where he now observed the Soviet line that there was nothing to choose between the different imperialist powers), as far as China was concerned "The enemies of our enemies are our friends."[12]

Mao's extreme sense of realism also led him to forecast the possibility that one day it might serve Soviet interests to enter the war on Germany's side, if the Allies looked likely to defeat Germany and move next against Russia. A united front with Germany would then become "a war of advantage to the socialist nation."[13] Mao even contemplated, in an interview with Edgar Snow, the prospect of a Russo-Japanese rapprochement, perhaps leading to a non-aggression treaty. This he described as a "Leninist possibility" (i.e. as being justified, like the Treaty of Brest-Litovsk, as a necessary tactic in defence of the Soviet Union) though he added, probably for the sake of appearance, the condition that such a treaty should "not interfere with Soviet support for China." But in general Mao took care to discount the likelihood of large-scale Soviet aid to China, judging quite correctly that the Chinese war theatre was increasingly marginal to Moscow's concerns.[14]

It is beside the point to argue whether Mao was fundamentally

---

[11] "On the Present International Situation," 1 September, 1939, *MTC*, Vol. VII, pp. 15–16.

[12] See further Gittings, *The World and China*, pp. 78–81.

[13] "The Identity of Interest Between the Soviet Union and all Mankind," 28 September, 1939, *MTC*, Vol. VII, p. 62. This passage, like most others quoted here, was omitted from the *SW* version.

[14] Gittings, *The World and China*, pp. 76–7.

"loyal" to the Soviet Union or demonstrated his "independence," in this formative period of the 1930s and 1940s. Throughout his life Mao acknowledged the October Revolution as the source of revolutionary inspiration to 20th century communism. He also acknowledged that the Soviet Union, by surviving alone as bulwark of socialism for nearly 30 years before other revolutions succeeded, had shouldered a very heavy burden. "How fortunate for our world," he wrote in 1939 on Stalin's 60th birthday, "to have the Soviet Union, the Soviet Communist Party, and Stalin, to make things easier to deal with."[15] But Mao clearly reckoned as well with the fact – which those of his colleagues who were less critically "loyal" found hard to accept – that mistakes would be made by the "great leader" and (even more importantly from a theoretical perspective) that there need not and probably could not be identity of interests between different revolutionary forces faced with different sets of contradictions in their separate struggles for survival. Nor did he see any reason why the first revolution to succeed should either be a model for those which came afterwards nor why it should be regarded as embodying a richer form of experience. This was the burden of the cheng-feng (rectification) movement in Yenan in 1942–43, and also of Mao's response to the dissolution of the Comintern in May 1943.

The CCP has gone through three revolutionary movements, one after the other without a pause and all extremely complex in their nature. One could go as far as to say that they have been even more complex than the Russian Revolution. In the course of these movements the CCP has acquired its own body of experienced and excellent cadres. Since the Seventh World Congress of the Comintern in 1935, it has not interfered in the internal affairs of the CCP, which during the whole period of the Anti-Japanese War of National Liberation has done its work extremely well.[16]

The problem of the divergence of interests between the Soviet state and the Chinese Communist Party came to a head after the war with Japan ended and civil war approached in China. Stalin's attempt to dissuade the Chinese Party from embarking

---

[15] "On Stalin," 21 December, 1939, MTC, Vol. VII, translated in Jerome Ch'en, Mao Papers (London: Oxford University Press, 1970).
[16] Report on dissolution of Comintern, Chieh-fang jih-pao (Liberation Daily), 28 May, 1943.

on war with the Kuomintang is now well known – he "tried to prevent the Chinese revolution by saying that we must collaborate with Chiang Kai-shek. Otherwise the Chinese nation must perish" (Mao to the 10th Plenum in 1962).[17] At that time the Soviet interest lay in the maintenance of a world balance of power with a United States which had a monopoly of the atom bomb and was economically much stronger, while a civil war in China might lead to American intervention and the loss of a vital buffer to the Soviet East, unless Russia also intervened with unforeseeable consequences. (Stalin, Chou En-lai later recalled, "was worried about the outbreak of World War III.")[18]

What is less well known is how Mao justified Soviet behaviour to those of his own colleagues who were alarmed by it, but doing so in a way which asserted the right of the CCP as well as of the Soviet state to pursue its own path in accordance with its own interests. The vital document, available even now only in what is probably an edited version, was written by Mao as an internal Party memorandum dated April 1946. First he argued that the danger of a third world war did exist, and that the Soviet Union was fully entitled to reach "compromise on many issues, including certain important ones" with its potential enemies. But, Mao continued,

Such compromise does not require the people in the countries of the capitalist world to follow suit and make compromises at home. The people in those countries will continue to wage different struggles in accordance with their different conditions.[19]

Secondly, Mao was not content with assigning to the different forces of revolution different tactical tasks, so to speak, in their struggles with imperialism. In a line of analysis which would become of crucial importance again in the 1960s, Mao actually assigned to the Chinese revolution – and by implication to other colonial and semi-colonial struggles – the key position on the battlefield. The real action, Mao explained in his famous "paper tigers" interview with Anna Louise Strong (August 1946), took place on the intermediate ground which lay between the two

[17] "Speech to 10th Plenum," 24 September, 1962, Wan-sui (1969), pp. 430–6.
[18] Chou En-lai "Criticism of Liu Shao-chi," SCMP, No. 4060.
[19] "Some Points in Appraisal of the Present International Situation," April 1946, SW, Vol. IV, pp. 87–8.

great powers. He illustrated his argument with a long line of teacups to show the vast intervening space between them, including China. "Under such conditions," Mao concluded in his exposition of what in the 1960s would become known as "the theory of the intermediate zone," "will the masses of the peoples of these countries wait to be subjugated? Certainly not. They will rise and resist."[20] The argument also implied that China was one of the most important teacups in the series, if not the most important one. The "dominant political contradiction" on the international scene, it was claimed in an official CCP pronouncement, was "not between the capitalist world and the Soviet Union and also not between the Soviet Union and the United States." It consisted instead of the internal contradictions within the capitalist world and, significantly, of "the contradiction between China and the United States."[21]

It was ironically not with Soviet diplomacy but with that of the United States that Mao co-operated in 1946–47, supposedly to prevent a civil war though by this time effort by the American ambassador in China, General Marshall, was mostly for the sake of form. The same realism which led Mao to write off Soviet aid had made him a persuasive advocate of American support to the CCP – or at least American neutrality between the CCP and the Kuomintang – since he first found an audience in the journalists and members of the U.S. Army Observer Group (the "Dixie Mission") who arrived in Yenan in July 1944. In his interviews with Edgar Snow and other foreigners in the late 1930s Mao had welcomed foreign aid to China as a whole. He had even, perhaps not with complete sincerity, painted for Snow a warming picture of a China with a genuine "people's government" which would one day seek foreign loans and approve of "legitimate" foreign business interests.[22] In 1944–45 Mao again invited American intervention – this time on behalf of "democratic" China which the CCP alone now claimed to represent. Though the "democratic" rhetoric of Roosevelt's vision for a post-war world may have had some effect, Mao was moved above all by

[20] Interview on 25 August, 1946. Anna Louise Strong, "World's eye view from a Yenan cave," *Amerasia* (New York), April 1947.
[21] Lu Ting-yi, "Explanation of several basic questions on the post-war international situation," January 1947, translated in the Department of State, *United States Relations with China* (Washington D.C., 1949), pp. 710–19.
[22] Edgar Snow, *Red Star Over China* (New York: Grove Press, 1968), p. 104.

the evident fact that the U.S. was now the only foreign power that counted in China. As he told the young American Foreign Service official John Service on their first meeting:

America has intervened in every country where her troops and supplies have gone. This intervention may not have been intended, and may not have been direct. But it has been none the less real – merely by the presence of that American influence.[23]

Mao's approach to the impressionable Americans was a characteristic mixture of engaging frankness and of improbable blandishment – the same concoction which he and other Chinese leaders would use to good effect upon the foreign leaders who flocked to Peking in the early 1970s. There is no point in denying, he told Service in the same interview, that "the chief importance of your coming is its political effect on the Kuomintang." Yet in a second interview he spoke quite unashamedly the language of the New Frontier (later to be known as neocolonialism) in trying to tempt American interest:

America needs an export market for her heavy industry and these specialised manufactures. She also needs an outlet for capital investment. China needs to build up light industries to supply her own market and raise the living standard of her own people. Eventually she can supply these goods to other countries in the Far East . . . America is not only the most suitable country to assist this economic development of China: she is also the only country fully able to participate.[24]

The story of the early flirtation with Washington was buried or played down by Western China scholarship for two decades when it hardly chimed with the dominant interpretation of Mao as implacably hostile to the United States, only to be disinterred amid a good deal of "If only . . ." speculation when Nixon travelled to Peking and the Chinese were discovered to be diplomatically flexible after all. It had reached a brief and unsatisfactory climax in January 1945 when Mao and Chou put their names forward for an immediate visit to Washington to meet President Roosevelt. This proposal, also ignored for years

[23] "Interview with Mao Tse-tung," 23 August, 1944, Foreign Relations of the United States (China), 1944 (Washington D.C.: Department of State, 1967), pp. 602–14.
[24] "Memorandum of conversation," 13 March, 1945, Foreign Relations of the United States (China), 1945 (Washington D.C.: Department of State, 1968), pp. 272–8.

although it was in the public record, ran foul of internal disagreements among American officials over China policy which, at the end of the day, would more naturally favour – though with reservations – the political and economic status quo offered by Chiang Kai-shek in China. We may still read some significance into the fact that Mao offered to visit the U.S. five years before he eventually arrived in the Soviet Union to conclude the Sino-Soviet Treaty with Stalin.[25]

Patient as ever, Mao was prepared to stay nearly two months in Moscow in December 1949 to February 1950, in order to secure an alliance which, in the changed situation of cold war and the defeat of Chiang, was essential to defend a socialist China against the hositility of American imperialism. It is hard to measure the additional strength of the bond between Mao and Stalin of shared ideological commitment, but perhaps this counted for more as circumstances brought the CCP and the Soviet Union closer together. With his usual realism Mao also accepted that Stalin had most of the cards, and he was prepared to compromise when pushed to the point:

> In 1950 I argued with Stalin in Moscow for two months. We argued about the Treaty of Mutual Assistance and Alliance, about the Chinese Changchun Railway, about the joint-stock companies. Our attitude was like this: "If I disagree with your proposal I shall struggle against it. But if you really insist, then I shall accept it." This was because we took into account the interests of socialism as a whole.[26]

The part played by Mao in the conduct of Chinese foreign affairs from 1949 until his death was intermittent but crucial. For the whole of the 1950s he refrained from public utterance, except for a few formal greetings and messages issued under his name. He received few foreign visitors until the 1960s. But it was only after the Cultural Revolution, in a strange after-glow of the passion he had shown during the original revolution for international affairs, that he became once again the entertainer and

[25] The story of Mao's offer to visit Washington was told by Admiral Leahy (chairman of the Joint Chiefs of Staff at the time) in his memoirs I Was There (London: Gollancz, 1950), p. 100. See later, Barbara Tuchman. "If Mao had come to Washington: An essay in alternatives," Foreign Affairs. No. 50, October 1972.
[26] "First Speech to Chengtu Conference," 10 March, 1958, Wan-sui, pp. 159–64. Translated in Schram, Unrehearsed, pp. 96–103.

dazzler of pilgrims from abroad, until his faculties began to fail and his last interviews began to pain and embarrass.

Clearly Mao did not have a sustained interest in Chinese diplomacy, nor did he concern himself with the details. In foreign as in domestic affairs, he would intervene at critical moments – as he perceived them – in the course of China's development, grasping the nettle or (in his phrase) "seizing the hour" to ensure that difficult decisions were not fudged. Three major turning-points of this kind stand out in the record of post-1949 diplomacy: China's entry into the Korean War, the Sino-Soviet dispute, and the opening to the West in the early 1970s. In each case Mao's hand was on the helm. Mao's speeches and writings after 1949, now reasonably well known to us through the various "unofficial" collections which have appeared since the Cultural Revolution, reveal the same eclectic style and selective pre-occupation with the outside world. At major moments of crisis he picked out the main features of the scene, dwelling most of all on the behaviour of the same two great powers which had pre-occupied his attention during the revolution. The rest of the world was seen largely by reference to the two giants. It was entirely reasonable for Mao to continue to chart his course by reference to the stars, evil or otherwise, of Washington and Moscow, the two countries which dominated the international environment and leant particularly closely upon his own.

In February 1950 Mao had succeeded in buying a breathing-space for the new China, at peace for the first time in 12 years, through the Sino-Soviet Treaty. It would, he said in June, "enable us freely and more rapidly to carry forward the reconstruction work within our country."[27] But before the month was out the Korean War had begun, forcing Mao within weeks to take the decision – apparently opposed by some of his colleagues – to intervene and prevent American power from crushing socialism in Korea and ruling up to the Yalu.[28] But although reconstruction continued, the Korean War disastrously affected China's relations with both great powers, leading to total isolation from the United States and increased dependence upon the Soviet Union. The greater part of China's diplomatic effort for the rest

[27] "Report to Party plenum," 6 June, 1950, People's China (Peking), No. 12, 1950.
[28] I have discussed the circumstances in The World and China, Ch. 9.

of the 1950s and 1960s would be directed towards adjusting these imbalances.

Already by 1955–56 Mao was arguing strongly against the tendency, encouraged by dependence, to copy the Soviet model without discrimination. "When we raised the slogan of learning from the Soviet Union," he said in December 1956, "we never meant that we should learn from their backward experiences."[29] And in the previous year, battling with critics of his proposal to speed up the Agricultural Co-operative Movement, he returned to the argument, which he had already voiced during the Revolution, that the Chinese experience was in many ways richer than that of the Soviet Union.

> We have the experience of more than 20 years in the revolutionary bases, and the training of three revolutionary wars; the whole experience is extremely rich. Before victory we gained experience from every point of view, going to the Left and to the Right a good number of times, so we could organize the State quickly and complete the task of revolution. (The Soviet Union set up a state from scratch, and at the time of the October Revolution it had no army, no government, and not many Party members) . . . Let us not always make comparisons with the Soviet Union.[30]

Mao must already have known that Soviet leaders, in conversation with Western politicians at the various summit meetings from which China was excluded, were putting distance between themselves and Peking. ("Help us to cope with Red China!" said Khrushchev to Chancellor Adenauer in September 1955.)[31] By this time China was seeking to spring the trap of isolation, but not very successfully since the United States, while prepared to talk about détente with Moscow, refused at the ambassadorial talks with China in 1955–57 to contemplate any practical steps to open relations with Peking. By 1958 it was clear that this road was blocked until China could come to the negotiating table with better cards to play. The desire to improve China's economic position and force the West to concede respect and equality of relations, was in fact one of the mainsprings of the Great Leap Forward. "In the past," said Mao, "others looked

[29] "Instructions to Federation of Industry and Commerce," 8 December, 1956, Wan-sui, pp. 62–6.
[30] "On Opposing Right Tendencies and Conservatism," 6 December, 1955, Wan-sui, p. 27.
[31] K. Adenauer, Erinnerungen 1953–55 (Bonn, 1966), pp. 527–8.

down on us mainly because we produced too little grain, steel and machinery. Now let us do something for them to see!"[32] The same motive also lay behind the decision to develop an independent nuclear capability which was taken on the eve of the Great Leap Forward.

The years 1958–62 constituted another turning point in China's relations with the two great powers which Mao negotiated with his customary analytical sharpness and dislike for half measures. In terms of strategy towards the United States, Mao once again counselled the faint-hearted not to be intimidated by the alliances and warships with which Washington was trying to encircle China. The ships, he pointed out, could not come on land; the alliances papered over deep cracks in the "so-called unity of the West":

> There is unity of a kind, and Dulles is working hard for it right now. But he wants unity under the control of the United States; he wants his partners, big and small, to depend on the United States under the shadow of the atom bomb, to kowtow and declare allegiance – this is what the Americans mean by unity. This kind of situation must inevitably lead to the reverse of unity, to a complete shambles. Comrades, look at the world today and see who it really belongs to![33]

As he had done in the past, Mao advised his colleagues to sit back and watch the contradictions between the major imperialist power and its subordinates work themselves out. From the Suez war in 1956 to the Middle East crisis of 1958, Mao saw nothing but disunity – and on his own doorstep the Offshore Islands crisis (which so alarmed the Russians) was yet another demonstration that the United States was at odds even with Chiang Kai-shek and the more so with its Western allies. He never imagined that "a few shots at Quemoy and Matsu" would have stirred up such a storm. "This is because people are afraid of war and of the U.S. going around everywhere and making trouble."[34]

Mao in the late 1950s revived not just the "paper tigers" concept which he had formed a decade before to rally his Party at a previous time of isolation for China, but the underlying view of

[32] "Speech to Military Affairs Committee," 28 June, 1958, *Chinese Law and Government* (New York), Vol. I, No. 4.
[33] 25 November, 1958, *Wan-sui*, p. 245.
[34] 5 September, 1958, "Speech to Supreme State Conference," *Wan-sui*, p. 233.

international politics which went with it. Then he had regarded the Soviet Union as relatively immune from the attentions of the United States which would be preoccupied for years to come with trying to mop up and occupy the vast zone of peoples and countries (including China) which lay between. In 1958 he revived this theory of the "intermediate zone," but this time including China in the safe area of the "socialist camp."

My opinion has always been that its main purpose is to be tyrant of the intermediate zone. As for our part of the world, unless the socialist camp is beset by great disorder, the U.S. won't try to grab it . . . What one might call real anti-communism would be to take up arms against us and the Soviet Union. But I don't think these people are so stupid. They only have a certain number of troops to move around."[35]

The irony was that by the late 1950s, when China and Mao in particular were regarded generally in the West as implacably hostile and belligerent, he took a relaxed, almost dismissive, view of the strength of imperialism in the long-term (although, as he had explained from his "paper tiger" interview onwards, one should still pay proper respect in the short-term to its capacity for making mischief). America's affairs were like those of the big family house in *The Dream of the Red Chamber* – "a big house has big problems" – and the dynasty of Mr Dulles and his successors was as doomed as the clan of Chia in that famous Chinese novel.[36]

But while the decline of imperialism and the collapse of capitalism in the West was only a matter of time (and here Mao took a strictly determinist view) there was no such certainty about the triumph of socialism and the attainment of communism in those states which had already embarked upon the "socialist transition." On the one hand Mao could cheerfully thumb his nose at the American threat ("What a pity there is only one American imperialism. If there were 10 more it wouldn't be worth talking about . . ."[37]), but on the other hand he would become increasingly pessimistic about the growth of revisionism in the Soviet Union and the chances of avoiding it in China. "The sword of Stalin has now been abandoned," he had

[35] 8 September, 1958, Wan-sui, p. 239.
[36] 2 March, 1957, "Speech to Supreme State Conference," Wan-sui, p. 99.
[37] 17 May, 1958, "Speech to Second Session of Party Congress," Wan-sui, pp. 196–7.

commented as early as November 1956. "As for the sword of Lenin, has it too now been abandoned to a certain extent by some leaders of the Soviet Union?"[38] During the Great Leap Forward Mao made a systematic study of the latest Soviet textbook on political economy. His own notes on the book, which were circulated among Party cadres in the aftermath of the Great Leap Forward, clearly illustrate his preoccupation and frequent uncertainty.[39] "In our work of socialist construction," he would say in 1962, "we are still to a very large extent acting blindly. For us the socialist economy is still in many respects a realm of necessity not yet understood."[40] But the thrust of his notes on the Soviet book led to a conclusion which – although never made explicit in official Chinese anti-Soviet polemics – helped to widen the gap and make it even more difficult to see any redeeming feature in the current Soviet leadership. For in the last analysis, it had to be acknowledged that the roots of Khrushchev's revisionism were firmly lodged in the soil which had been prepared by Stalin, and that what had happened under both leaders could not be regarded as a temporary deviation but as a fundamental deformation of the proto-socialist system occurring over a long period of time.

Mao's analysis of the problems of the socialist transition, and his attempts to tackle them in Chinese society, certainly show a far greater political sensitivity than any Soviet leader (including Lenin) had ever achieved, though in fairness Mao had the advantage of learning from the negative features of the Soviet experience. Largely thanks to Mao and to the road taken by the Chinese – however defective in its execution – from the Great Leap Forward onwards, it is now generally understood among Marxists throughout the world that socialism is not simply achieved by creating a heavy industry and bringing the means of production into public ownership. Future revolutions will no doubt draw lessons in turn from the further problems which have emerged from the Chinese experience. Yet this principled basis for serious ideological differences with the Soviet leadership does not

[38] 15 November, 1956, Speech to Second Plenum of Eighth Central Committee, quoted in "Leninism or Social-Imperialism," *Peking Review*, 24 April, 1970.
[39] "Notes on the Soviet textbook *Political Economy*," *Wan-sui*, pp. 319–99.
[40] 30 January 1962, "On Democratic Centralism," translated in Schram, *Unrehearsed*, p. 175.

explain the exceptional bitterness shown by Mao to them, and which one may reasonably expect to be alleviated after his death. Here one suspects that the memory of Soviet behaviour during the Revolution – a period to which Mao now turned increasingly to seek historical reference points for current policies – added several degrees of distortion. Just as Mao had been prepared to fight the civil war without the support of either great power, so he was prepared to see China isolated in the 1960s until (as he correctly predicted) at least one of them was forced to come to terms. By January 1962 he had decided that the Soviet leadership had been "usurped by revisionists"; by June 1964 he was declaring that "the present-day Soviet Union is a dictatorship of the bourgeoisie, a dictatorship of the big bourgeoisie, a dictatorship like German Fascism." They were already to be regarded as China's major enemy. "We dared to struggle with imperialism and we defeated imperialism. Why cannot we defeat Khrushchev too?"

Mao rejected proposals by neutral Communist Parties, including those of Romania and Japan, for a truce in the open polemics and later for the formation of a common front to assist the Vietnamese struggle against American aggression. In doing so, he appears to have acted against the wishes of most of his colleagues whom he abused on one famous occasion as "you weak-kneed people in Peking."[41] Only after the Cultural Revolution would Mao's assessment of the Soviet leadership as (a) social-imperialist, and (b) a bigger threat to China than the United States, become openly declared official policy, although it would still lack a proper analysis of why and how this should be so. (Mao's close intellectual confidant, Ch'en Po-ta, was said, during the Cultural Revolution, to be working on an explanation of the social basis for Soviet social-imperialism, but he was removed from power in 1971 without any indication that it had been completed.)

By the end of the 1960s the basic assumptions of Mao's previous strategy at last produced the desired result when the United States, held at bay in Vietnam, was forced to seek a diplomatic way out requiring accommodation with China. China's refusal since the late 1950s to compromise on minor issues with the

[41] See M. Yahuda, "Kremlinology and the Chinese strategic debate," CQ, No. 49, (January–March 1972) pp. 32–75.

United States before agreement on basic principles now paid off. The price of Mr Nixon's ticket to Peking was the abolition of the trade embargo and tacit acquiescence in China's entry to the United Nations. Verbally at least the Americans also discarded, in the Shanghai communiqué which Nixon signed, the concept of "two Chinas."

It is probable that, whether or not Mao had still been alive, some response would have been made by China to the overtures which the Americans began to extend after Nixon took office. But it is also probable that relations with the Soviet Union would not have been so uncompromisingly cut, and hence that the process of U.S.–China accommodation would have been lengthier and more equivocal. The speed with which the Chinese acted, the decision to invite Nixon himself (and not be content with his secretary of state) and the warmth with which he was received, suggests that Mao supervised and even initiated the new opening to the West. No doubt it was partly to allay domestic criticism that this policy was attributed to "Chairman Mao's revolutionary diplomatic line," but it also bore his personal mark. It was as if Nixon was paying a return visit to balance the one which Mao himself never managed to make in 1945. Doubting Communist Party members in China were referred back to Mao's advocacy in the early 1940s of a tactical accommodation with the other imperialist powers against Japan.[42]

It was a magnificent victory for the Chinese nation, but with Nixon arriving in Peking less than two months after his savage bombing of Hanoi and Haiphong, it would be hard to describe it as a socialist foreign policy. Here we come to the paradox of Mao's last years. One of the world's greatest revolutionary leaders now led his nation in pursuit of state-to-state relationships at the expense of other people's revolutions. Various rationalizations were offered by the Chinese but the only potentially convincing one depended upon acceptance of the major premise that Soviet "social-imperialism" was the principal threat not only to China but also, for example, to the people of Chile – who to their astonishment saw Peking extend aid to General Pinochet's military junta. While it was reasonable for China to wish to open diplomatic relations on a broad front after so many

[42] For example "United the people defeat the enemy! A study of On Policy," Peking Review, No. 35, 1971.

years of isolation, the task was pursued to the point of obsession, so that Peking even asked for British help (but was refused) in seeking to develop relations with the Sultan of Oman.[43] It was also reasonable for China to warn those who wished to listen of what in Peking's estimation were Soviet intentions, but this too was carried to extravagant lengths – with the Chinese press in 1975 taking the side of CIA-backed factions in Angola and applauding the deaths of what it described as Cuban "mercenaries." The argument that China had to deal realistically with those who held power was a fair one to make in the majority of cases when official visitors were entertained from the growing range of countries with whom Peking had relations. But did this apply to politicians out of power, from Nixon on his second visit – now no longer president – to Herr Franz-Josef Strauss, whom Mao received apparently in preference to attending the National People's Congress in January, 1975?

Whatever explanations might be offered, the overall line of Chinese foreign policy in the last five years of Mao's life ran counter to the very clear priorities laid down for the conduct of a socialist foreign policy in the "Nine Comments" of 1963–64, where Khrushchev had been castigated for precisely the same tendency to place national interest above proletarian internationalism.

There are two attitudes towards the national democratic revolutionary movement. The first is to maintain good relationships with the Western countries, giving little or no support to the national revolutionary movement. The second is to support the national revolutionary movement as a general principle, with the possibility of having some contacts with the Western countries but only for secondary reasons . . . While we may have some contacts with the Western countries, we shall never let these contacts gain the upper hand.[44]

It appears to have been criticized by Lin Piao before his downfall and death (which occurred significantly soon after the deci-

[43] See Fred Halliday, "Marxist analysis and post-revolutionary China," New Left Review, No. 100.
[44] "Several important problems concerning the current international situation," Kung-tso T'ung-hsun (PLA Work Bulletin), translated by J. Chester Cheng, The Politics of the Chinese Red Army (Stanford: Hoover Institution, 1966), p. 483. See also the nine anti-Soviet polemics of 1963–64, especially Editorial Departments of Jen-min jih-pao, and Hung ch'i, 12 December, 1963, "Peaceful co-existence – two diametrically opposed policies."

sion to invite Nixon), though this aspect of the case was only hinted at in the official Chinese accounts. It also ran counter to the rather sporadic efforts made during the Cultural Revolution to redefine Chinese diplomacy, even if these were as much concerned with questions of working style (whether or not Chinese diplomats abroad should throw parties, etc.) as with policies. The question which needs to be considered here is why Mao was not, as far as we know, at all sensitive to these problems and instead lent his authority so wholeheartedly to the new diplomatic line, personally receiving the most contentious visitors – including Nixon for the second time only a few months before his death.

CONCLUSION

As a Chinese statesman, defending the interests of the Chinese revolution and state, Mao displayed an ability to grasp the essence of the international contradictions surrounding his country, and to seize the right moment for decisive action or shift of policy, which by the early 1970s had brought China to the end of 130 years of humiliation and dependence. It was this ability, coupled with his energetic anti-Sovietism, which so impressed the leaders of conservative governments, from Heath of Britain to Kukrit of Thailand, who visited him in his last years and awarded him the title of "statesman."

But was Mao a world statesman, and did he have any interest in being one? The answer to both questions must be no. Though Mao looked forward to the day when China would be taken seriously as a great power, nowhere in his speeches and writings does he claim a special role for his country which would be commensurate with a world vision. Occasionally he spoke of China being the "centre of world revolution" but in a rhetorical sense which was never matched by action. Though Mao wrote and spoke at great length on foreign matters during his career, he never showed that capacity to move easily between the general and the particular – from the global theory to the individual case – which is the mark of someone playing an active role on the international stage. Almost the entire world – the "intermediate zone" of which he had first spoken in 1946 – was seen mainly by reference to and in the shadow of the two great powers. Unlike Chou En-lai he showed no great interest in the internal politics and class struggle of individual countries. When these problems were discussed, for example in some interviews in the early 1960s with non-governmental visitors from the Third World, Mao more often than not would fall back on the Chinese experience in order to illustrate his thinking. Thus a question about the formation of a united front against imperialism and neo-colonialism in Africa in the 1960s was met by a lengthy discursion on the united fronts with Chiang Kai-shek in the 1920s and 1930s. The specificity of the Chinese experience (which Mao had recognized so brilliantly at the time) was now overlooked; nor did he appear to have any feel for the very specific features of neo-colonial control in Third World countries today which have no opportunity to reproduce China's "semi-colonial" circumstances.

The question of forming a united front is the question of who opposes imperialism and who does not. All those who oppose imperialism must get united. If we want to categorize the bourgeois democratic revolution, the question is whether or not it is anti-imperialist. As for establishing a real socialist state (not just in name), and an economy under state or collective leadership under the leadership of the proletariat, that is quite another matter. This does not just clash with interests of imperialism but with that of the bourgeoisie.[45]

This is the basis for Chinese advocacy of a broad united front against imperialism (now including the Soviet Union) based solely on the criterion of "who opposes imperialism and who does not," deferring the question of building socialism to a second stage. It is not even an exact description of the Chinese experience, where a proto-socialism was developed in the communist-led areas even during the anti-imperialist united front. It fails to grapple altogether with such problems as the emergence in the Third World today of sub-imperialist systems which display a degree of "anti-imperialism" in defence of their own interests (Iran – with whom China has developed cordial state relations – is an obvious example, but so, nearer home, is Japan). The very real and difficult question of how to correlate the class struggle and the anti-imperialist struggle is side-stepped altogether by saying, as Mao does, that they are two entirely different things.

[45] 18 June, 1964, "Conversation with Zanzibar Expert M. M. Ali and his Wife," *Wan-sui*, pp. 511–12.

Writing in 1976, one finds it hard to recall that 10 years ago China was being roundly accused (by the Soviet Union as well as by the Western powers) of claiming the leadership of the "world revolution." The charge was literally true. Already in his notes on the Soviet textbook on political economy, Mao had claimed in 1960 that the mandate of Marx had shifted east to China – carrying Lenin's own argument a stage further:

> It can be seen from the history of revolution in the past that the centre of revolution has been shifting from the West to the East. At the end of the 18th century the centre was in France . . . In mid-19th century the centre of revolution shifted to Germany, where the proletariat mounted the stage and gave birth to Marxism. In the early 20th century it moved to Russia, where it produced Leninism . . . By the middle of the 20th century the centre of world revolution has shifted again, to China. Of course in the future it may still move again somewhere else.[46]

Claims for the general validity of "The Way of Mao Tse-tung" were first made in 1945, and reached their apogee in Lin Piao's famous essay "On people's war" 20 years later, but it is not at all clear whether the Chinese, or Mao, had ever thought out the implications of assuming a leading role in the world revolutionary process. At the height of the Cultural Revolution, Mao had this to say: "Not only is China the political centre of the world revolution; it will also become the military and technological centre . . ."[47] But his remarks to a delegation from the Palestine Liberation Organization in 1965 conform more closely to the general run of Chinese policy:

> There are some foreigners studying military science in China. I advise them to go back, and not to study too long. A few months is enough. There are only lectures which are of no use. The most useful thing to do is to go back and join in fighting. Some truths need little or no explanation. Stay most of the time in your own country or don't leave it at all, then you can do it there all right.[48]

Thus the Way of Mao Tse-tung essentially placed the onus for making revolution on those who were actually in the field, with the minimum of external aid. When in the 1970s China

---

[46] "Notes on the Soviet textbook *Political Economy*," Ch. 3.

[47] September 1967, "Our Strategy," translated in *Chinese Law and Government* (White Plains, New York: International Arts and Science Press), Vol. II. No. I, pp. 3–12.

[48] March 1965, *Wan-sui*, pp. 614–15.

developed a more active state-to-state diplomacy, it was possible to justify the apparent sell-out of revolutionary interests by reference to this doctrine of revolutionary self-reliance. At the same time the Way of Mao Tse-tung imposed, so to speak, a patent upon the revolutionary process which seems to have diminished Mao's and China's interests in the possibility that other roads might exist. Alternatives as diverse as those of Allende in Chile and Guevara in Bolivia could be dismissed with a lamentable lack of enquiry – let alone of solidarity.

Though Mao has never used the phrase "socialism in one country," he has been above all concerned with the strengthening of socialism in a country which he regards historically as being the centre of world revolution and inheriting the mandate of Marx. It is reasonable therefore to assume that Mao himself accepted the claim widely made by Chinese supporters abroad that the defence of the Chinese socialist state is of primary importance. As shown above, Mao himself found this a reasonable position for Stalin to adopt in 1946, justifying to his colleagues the necessity for the Soviet Union to "make compromises" with imperialism. The same sort of justifications were circulated among Chinese Party members at the time of the Nixon visit in 1971–72. One may also suspect that when Mao re-defined the concept of the "intermediate zone," in the early 1960s, he placed China in the same position that the Soviet Union had occupied in the 1940s. Then China had been one of the teacups in the vast zone separating the leader of the socialist camp (the Soviet Union) from its main enemy (the United States). Now China's own position as "centre of the world revolution," adopted through the default of Soviet revisionism, must logically place her at the same pole of the international contradiction between socialism and imperialism (while Moscow itself has moved to the opposite pole). This sort of global vision, in which the position of countries in the rest of the world is defined primarily by reference to the two poles rather than to relationships within the intermediate zone itself, also helps to reinforce Mao's and China's relatively undifferentiated vision of the component parts of the zone. The teacups may be of different sizes, but they all have the same job to do.

Mao's global approach to international affairs must be considered finally in the light of his view of war – itself seen as a global process in which particularities are easily submerged. For all Chinese nationalists of Mao's generation it was common ground that the development of their consciousness and the weakening of the imperialist grip upon China had been assisted by the First World War. When the Second approached, Mao (unlike the Soviet Union and the Comintern) positively welcomed the prospect. "This war will be the last in history. From then on there will be no war but permanent peaceful development. This is to say that world socialism will be realized in this war and this includes all countries, on condition, of course, that victory is on the side of the revolution."[49]

Mao was too optimistic, but by 1949 he could legitimately conclude that the second great imperialist war had at least opened the door to socialism in China if not yet in the rest of the world. It was entirely consistent with this view for him to argue another decade later that even a nuclear war would further the socialist cause. "It will sweep the world clean of imperialism, afterwards we can rebuild again, and from that time onwards there can never be another world war."[50] By the year of Mao's death, it was official Chinese policy that a world war was likely "sooner than later" and almost certainly within the next 30 years.[51]

Mao and his colleagues must be credited with a degree of realism which in the West is confined to a small and powerless body of protesters at the growing likelihood of nuclear war. Yet once again Mao's very breadth of vision somehow inhibits the sort of detailed analysis which would be helpful. Even granting that a nuclear war is "inevitable," how can one try to ensure that it comes "later" rather than "sooner"? (Or is it even possible, as Mao had suggested in a previous formulation after the Cultural Revolution, that the "revolution" might come first on a global scale and pre-empt the "war"?)[52] Mao's views on the Chinese

[49] June 1937, interview with American visitors, version in Nym Wales's *Yenan Notebooks*, pp. 128–32, 133–5.
[50] 17 May, 1958, "Speech to Second Session of Party Congress," *Wan-sui*, p. 208.
[51] "William Hinton on China's world view," in *Background Articles for a Discussion of the International Situation*. (New York: Ad Hoc Committee for a Conference on the International Situation, 1976).
[52] "With regard to the question of world war, there are but two possibilities: one is that the war will give rise to revolution and the other is that revolution will prevent the war," quoted by Lin Piao in his report to the Ninth Party Congress, April 1969.

bomb were also inconsistent and tinged with chauvinism. "China did not want a lot of bombs," he told Edgar Snow in January 1965, yet in an internal discussion in the same month he set his sights rather higher: "Yes, we need them. No matter what country it is, what bombs they are, atom bombs or hydrogen bombs, we must overtake them!"[53]

Mao's death leaves his successors with a world view which is global in the sense that it encompasses the broad issues of war and revolution which most governments prefer to side-step or postpone. But it is also an extremely partial view, rooted in China's own experience to a degree which makes it extremely hard to comprehend by people outside China and of limited relevance to their own tasks and struggles. By a series of bold and decisive steps, Mao had guided China to attain its present position of equality and respect on the international stage. But for China this has also had negative consequences, particularly in relations with the Soviet Union where some adjustment is bound to follow the "freeze" which owed a great deal to Mao's anti-Soviet passion, and in a lack of flexibility and understanding for the very complex problems of neo-imperialism and the politics of the developing world. With great respect for the man who brought China, against enormous odds, to a position of national independence and international equality, these aspects of Mao's statesmanship still need to be studied.

[53] Edgar Snow, The Long Revolution (Harmondsworth: Penguin Books, 1972), p. 210; Wan-sui, pp. 605–6.

9

THE CHINESE

Wang Gungwu

If heaven had feelings it would have aged!
People now talk of green fields risen from the sea.[1]

The most Chinese thing about Mao Tse-tung was his poetry and
his loyalty to its traditional forms. Despite all attempts by his
admirers to give his poems a profound Marxist–Leninist meaning, the above lines, as with the dozens of others similar in style
and phrasing, stir something in every literate Chinese simply by
evoking the past masters of this art. But the poems also have a
different significance. They remind us how near we still are to
the times when every Chinese who could, would have tried his
hand with similar lines, images and clichés, and known no
better way to probe his own deep sense of being Chinese. They
warn the historian that he is observing only the first lifetime of
radical change in China. He is recording the life of a man who
grew up when being Chinese was obvious and taken for granted,
but who had redefined Chineseness partly by his own lifework
so that, when he died, it had become hard to tell what was
Chinese.

For most writers on Mao, it has become almost obligatory to
pursue his Chinese roots. It is assumed that there is a Chinese
cultural heritage, a complex and multi-faceted combination of
all that had made up China prior to the 20th century, a deep, rich
and massive pre-Western lode just below the ground which only
needed cultural historians and archaeologists acting as miners
to expose its wealth and significance. With this kind of effort,
with digging and sifting, Mao would become knowable in all his
stratified layers as we follow his progress, as he might have us

[1] From "The occupation of Nanking by the PLA" (April 1949). There are many
editions of Mao Tse-tung's poetry and several translations. Unless otherwise
stated, the translation is my own.

do, from feudal student to semi-colonial petty-bourgeois nationalist to socialist philosopher to the new sage of communism.

The task of so sifting Mao's thoughts and actions has begun and it will occupy many for a long time. Why should this be so? No one surely could mistake Mao for anyone but a Chinese. To write about Mao the Chinese would seen like writing about his whole life. Is it so important that he was a Marxist–Leninist as well? Of course, there are Chinese today who argue that he used an alien ideology to destroy great traditional values along with some of the finest cultural achievements of China and that this was the work of a traitor; only ignorant foreigners would call him a Chinese. There are also foreigners who would acclaim Mao as the great internationalist revolutionary leader and not a mere Chinese, but many more, who are not necessarily ignorant, are fascinated by his apparent Chineseness. For the latter, the difficulty is only in defining what is Chinese and in determining how Chinese he was.

Despite his fondness for traditional shih and tz'u poetry, Mao came to reject that part of the cultural heritage associated with the dominant literati elites. He was openly political about his preference for the values and aspirations of the majority, mostly the poor, illiterate, under-privileged, oppressed, and he preferred them because he thought that it was from this majority that the potential revolutionaries of China would come. As a Marxist–Leninist he believed that he must be on the side of the majority. And as this majority was, is and shall always be unmistakably Chinese to him, it followed that there was no contradiction between being Chinese and a dedicated Marxist–Leninist at the same time. The conscious will of the majority of Chinese could never be anything but revolutionary in his eyes, therefore identifying with such Chinese meant there was nothing disembodied about his thoughts and actions on behalf of revolution.

Let me clarify this further by making some brief comments on some other prominent Chinese figures of this century. Sun Yatsen (1866–1925), for example, was only too conscious of the foreign origins of most of his political ideals and struggled all his life to try and make them more Chinese and comprehensible. He made a great effort at each stage of his career to fuse the disparate parts of his programme so that the alien nature of much of his early thinking could be disguised or blurred. Chiang Kai-shek (1887–1975) had a different kind of start and could only really comprehend the traditionalist elements of the Kuomintang heritage. He, therefore, embraced Methodism to try to overcome his obscurantist image to his Western friends, but this act remained baffling and meaningless, almost irrelevant, to the Chinese themselves. Among intellectuals, Hu Shih (1891–1962) was a dedicated modernizer and appealed to all Chinese who wanted to create a modern China. But his modernism was regarded by most Chinese as academic, even superficial, and he never converted more than a handful of the urbane and the sophisticated. Even Ch'en Tu-hsiu (1879–1942), the first communist leader, was unable to overcome his ambivalence, something he seemed to have shared with the American-educated Hu Shih. The steep jumps he made from reformism to science and democracy and then to Marxism–Leninism and even a sort of "Trotskyism" revealed a series of bold but mainly cerebral decisions. Despite the modernity he espoused, he remained in practice something of an enlightened literatus. As for Lu Hsün (1881–1936), the only literary man Mao Tse-tung admired, he succeeded in marrying a fierce alien scepticism to a Chinese sensibility, but it was a unique achievement that did not endear him to many Chinese in his lifetime. He needed, after his death, someone like Mao Tse-tung to endorse his kind of "rebelliousness" before he could be thrust upon the Chinese majority.

I suggest that Mao's achievement was different from those of the eminent Chinese mentioned above. It is difficult to find exact analogies in the Chinese past to explain his emergence. Perhaps we can point to the following: he was less unintegrated than Hung Hsiu-ch'üan (1813–64) and the Taiping rebels; he was more enlightened than the Boxer leaders and more plebeian than K'ang Yu-wei (1858–1927) or even Yen Fu (1854–1921); he was not corrupted as were Yuan Shih-k'ai (1859–1916) and Li Hung-chang (1823–1901) by their imperial experience; nor was he as brutalized and hypocritical as Feng Yü-hsiang (1882–1948) and the southern warlords. But he shared something with all of these that few of his other great contemporaries did: he never wasted time worrying about his Chinese identity or about the decline and fall of Chinese civilization. He was effortlessly and supremely confident about being Chinese, almost the way Churchill was about being English, and never suffered the agonies and self-doubts which paralysed so many Chinese of his generation. And it was this freedom from genteel sensitivities that gave him the single-mindedness to bring Marxism–Leninism to the Chinese people as if it were the most natural thing for him to do.

This confidence and single-mindedness may be found in his earliest writings, his essay on physical exercise, for example, which he published in 1917 when he was 23 years old.[2] There are no flashes of brilliant insight here, none of the sudden enlightenment that came upon most of his youthful contemporaries, merely the earnestness of the intellectually underprivileged, with all the ponderousness of a barefist pugilist explaining the joys of training in Miltonic prose. But as a Chinese, he was doing something original: he was addressing the literate in their language on the virtues more common among the illiterate and the outlaws of the hills and marshes. And he was not afraid of stating the obvious carefully and patiently, as in his concluding section on the six kinds of exercises he recommended, a quality that he was to display often the rest of his life. It was the quality of the self-taught man with a justifiable pride in what he had taught himself, whether it be about peasant landholdings, military strategy, world affairs or Marxism–Leninism.

Mao was already 26 years old when he formed his own Socialist Youth Corps in Hunan; this qualified him to be one of the founder-members of the Chinese Communist Party the next year. For six years, he read and wrote and worked hard both for the CCP and for the KMT when all CCP members were urged to join the latter. These were very formative years, as can easily be seen from the vast contrast between what he wrote in 1917 or 1919 and his earliest efforts at class analysis in 1926.[3] But the most striking feature of this change was that it seemed to have come so gradually. Mao seemed to have put his head down to learn how hard it was to be a revolutionary.

He was, of course, not alone in his work. There were numerous young men around him both of the KMT itself and of the CCP

[2] MTC, Vol. I, pp. 35–47.
[3] MTC, Vol. I, pp. 161–73; the translation of the revised version is found in SWL, Vol. I, pp. 13–20.

who played their part. The difference was that he was among the very few at the top of both parties who had never been abroad, who knew no foreign language and whose reading of each Marxist work and Leninist directive or resolution from the Comintern was in translation and was largely done in direct connection with some propaganda work he had to do or some group of peasants he had to study, organize or lecture to. At every point, therefore, there was little danger of his being merely theoretical. His knowledge of theory was limited but he absorbed without difficulty each bit of theory that could be seen or shown to be relevant to the Chinese people he was trying to rouse or train, and once absorbed became fully Chinese and was to remain deeply embedded in him. There is no better evidence of this than his famous essay "Analysis of the Classes in Chinese Society" published in early 1926. In this, he confidently asserts that:

> The attitudes of the various classes in China towards national revolution are almost completely the same as those of various classes in Western capitalist countries towards social revolution. This appears rather strange but it really is not, because the revolutions of today completely share the same goals and methods, that is, the goal of destroying international capitalist imperialism and the method of uniting the oppressed peoples and oppressed classes in a common struggle. This is the biggest difference between revolutions today and all previous revolutions in history.[4]

But when he summed up the classes in China in a table, it read as shown in the table opposite.[5]

Clearly Mao did not allow his earlier comparison with the West to divert him from setting out some un-Western categories. Although he was later to realize how extraordinary some of his classifications were and did not insist on his estimates of the size of each class, the essay as a whole demonstrates his ready fusion of Marxist–Leninist concepts with his direct experiences. When he discovered that about 245 millions would serve the revolution directly and another 150 millions could be made to support the cause, he must have been greatly encouraged. For now, he was able to call out "Unite, you 395 millions!" Against them, the

---

[4] MTC, Vol. I, p. 162; this passage was deleted in the revised version.
[5] MTC, Vol. I, pp. 172–3; this table was deleted on revision. I have simplified it by leaving out Mao's judgments on how revolutionary he thought each class was.

five millions who may be considered as enemies need hardly be feared. Obviously, Marxist–Leninist concepts provided the key he needed to unlock the secrets of power and revolution, and from the moment he could actually see a Chinese application of these concepts, Marxism–Leninism was no longer alien. I would

Class	Numbers
Big bourgeoisie	1,000,000
Middle bourgeoisie	4,000,000
Petty bourgeoisie	
1. Those with surplus – right-wing	15,000,000
2. Those self-supporting	75,000,000
3. Those with declining incomes – left-wing	60,000,000
Semi-proletariat	
1. Semi-tenant peasants	50,000,000
2. "Semi-self-supporting tenants?"	60,000,000
3. Poor peasants	60,000,000
4. Handicraftsmen	24,000,000
5. Shop assistants	5,000,000
6. Peddlers	1,000,000
(Sub-total	200,000,000
Proletariat	
1. Industrial proletariat	2,000,000
2. City coolies	3,000,000
3. Agricultural proletariat	20,000,000
4. Lumpen-proletariat	20,000,000
Total	400,000,000

suggest that at this stage of his life, it became no less part of his mind and personality than the words of the Hunan patriot, Wang Fu-chih (1619–92), the military writings of Sun Tzu (4th century B.C.) or the heroic stories of Shui-hu chuan (Water Margin), and even superior in his eyes because it was more progressive and useful.

The point made above that his adoption of some features of Marxist–Leninist analysis did not make Mao any less Chinese raises again the question of what was "Chinese," in this case what was "Chinese" in the 1920s. Let me, for the sake of comparison, take a rather extreme example. Was the American-educated engineer who subscribed to Jeffersonian democracy and loyally served the Canton Government under Sun Yat-sen any less Chinese than Mao? The answer for the 1920s would have to be "No." There is nothing absolute about being Chinese, and being Chinese in the 1920s was probably more relative than at any other period of Chinese history. It was still a decade of wide-open choices for the Chinese people: nationalism, socialism, anarchism, liberalism, communism, fascism; even modified forms of restored Confucianism were not unthinkable. There was no orthodoxy, only the multifarious quest for some new successful orthodoxy to replace the old one. Everyone who cared for and identified with China could claim to be Chinese. Only those who explicitly rejected China, or abandoned their homes to live abroad, could not qualify and this was largely because they wished to disqualify themselves, and they were very few indeed. It was a decade of maximum freedom bordering on anarchy and no one had any right to determine who was or was not Chinese. Thus being "Chinese" was easier than being almost anything else, for the Chinese people were still struggling to find their new identity.

This condition, as the whole of Chinese history attests, was not one the Chinese people were comfortable with. It was identified with *luan* or disorder, a condition which was expected to be temporary and one that had to be followed by *chih* or order, and that was but a short step to orthodoxy. For the period of disorder, however, almost everything was possible except perhaps a determined effort to preserve the state of disorder – that would have been clearly un-Chinese! And as the next decade was to show, Westernized liberals and anarchists who were suspected of partiality for disorderly freedoms were the first to be attacked for their alien beliefs.

Thus the fact that Mao was no less Chinese for being a Marx-ist–Leninist in the 1920s was not remarkable. Every other Chinese was modified in some way or the other. The interesting questions about being Chinese became more important only in the 1930s. After the KMT victory in 1927 over warlords as well as their leftist partners in the Northern Expedition, a condition of partial order had been established. The KMT leaders demanded the right to define who and what was Chinese. Soon the "party" and the "nation" were hardly separable in the eyes of the Nanking Government and indeed being Chinese should have meant a willingness to accept such a development. It was therefore only logical for the "party-nation" government to control publications and the media, to ban those who seemed to favour *luan* over *chih* and ultimately to try to define more positively what values it recognized as "Chinese." Hence the misnamed New Life Movement, more like a Confucian restoration, that was launched about the time of the great campaigns to exterminate all the communist bases in south and central China. This was appropriate to the right-wing of the Kuomintang because it had long condemned the CCP as alien, unpatriotic and destructive of the great Chinese values. Had the KMT united the country successfully, no doubt a new orthodoxy would have reigned, one that would have had greater continuity with the Confucian state than any offered by Mao and in the CCP, but new nevertheless in its strong nationalist rhetoric and slogans.

I suggest that Mao's Chineseness was called into question during the period 1927–36: for taking orders from Moscow, for using Marxist jargon to reject the Chinese heritage, for not submitting to *cheng-t'ung* (legitimacy). After the CCP was nearly crushed following the April 1927 killings in Shanghai, Mao was largely on the run as a "bandit," as the Nanking Government described him and his comrades. At the same time, the remaining CCP leaders depended more than ever on the new orthodoxy that Stalin had created in the Soviet Union; even their Sixth Party Congress had to be held in Moscow because there was nowhere safe for them in China. The pressure on Mao to be "Chinese" à la Nanking or "internationalist" à la Moscow remained great for the ensuing decade. Fortunately, the legitimacy of both was widely challenged for the whole period and Mao remained far enough from both capitals for him to learn in his own way from Marxism–Leninism and from rural China.

This period was in many ways Mao's bleakest and most unfruitful. His only comfort was his faith in the peasantry which he had begun to study in detail in his home province in early 1927, just before the disaster to the Party.[6] He was able to satisfy himself that peasant attacks on landlords, "local bullies and bad

[6] "Report of an Investigation into the Peasant Movement in Hunan," *MTC*, Vol. I. pp. 207–49; *SWL* Vol. I, pp. 21–59.

gentry" constituted revolutionary actions and thus confirmed that the seeds of revolution were already in Chinese soil. He reported that there were 7,000 or so peasant associations in Hunan with 1,307,727 members and estimated that there might have been a mass following of some 10 millions. Whether these figures were realistic or not, his conviction that poor and middle peasants constituted 80–90 per cent of rural populations, and the utterly impoverished some 20 per cent, encouraged him to lodge all his revolutionary hopes where the numbers were. This remained his greatest safeguard against Nanking and Moscow, a safety in numbers that combined a Chinese traditional respect for size and the progressive idea of working on behalf of the majority. And through the years of survival around his Ching-kangshan base to the years of defence in the Kiangsi Soviet Republic (1931–34), he continued to study peasant society with intense care, personally compiling several reports examining every feature of the new village organizations which he and his comrades had devised.[7]

Thus Mao remained immovably Chinese by placing himself on the side of the peasants. Even the most conservative Confucians could not fault him, for such primary producers were highly regarded in Confucian rhetoric. The KMT's attack on the CCP's treacherous links with a hostile foreign power was partly blunted by Mao's stance and his practical and realistic attempts to proletarianize the peasantry only as fast as most of them were willing to go. He was less than comfortable with Stalin's men in the CCP's Central Committee, especially after they moved to Juichin when he became subject to their ideological control and his policies were vetted by them. Fortunately, the pressure of events helped him overcome some of the embarrassment of being patronized by the young Bolshevik cadets and their Comintern advisers. On the one hand, Japanese imperialism did not spare the Nanking Government just because it was anti-communist. It continued to tread on Chinese sovereignty and the Manchurian incident of 18 September, 1931 gave Mao and

[7] Notably his "Report on Hsing-kuo" (26 January, 1931), MTC, Vol. I, pp. 185–252; "An Investigation into Ch'ang-kang Village" (15 December, 1933), Vol. IV, pp. 125–71; "An Investigation into Ts'ai-ch'i Village" (1933), Vol. IV, pp. 175–96; "How do we Work in the Village Soviets?" (10 April, 1934), Vol. IV, pp. 337–53.

the CCP a chance to voice their patriotism as good Chinese. On the other, Russian anxieties about Japanese ambitions in Siberia eventually spurred Stalin and the Comintern to approve a wide-ranging United Front policy in China to unite all the Chinese people against Japan. Together, they enabled the CCP to present itself as a patriotic party and Mao as a patriot, and what could be more Chinese than that?

Another matter helped the cause of Mao: after the Kiangsi Soviet had been abandoned and during the Long March, Mao turned the tables, at the Tsunyi meeting in January 1935, on those who had failed to defend the Republic. He was thus the man to lead the remnants of his army into Yenan at the right time and place for his united front call to carry weight. That he and the CCP were now close to the northern front line with the Japanese and showed willingness to fight them cleared most of the doubts people still had about the CCP's Chineseness, and even more about Mao's, for many credited Mao with the Chinese image the CCP now began to have.

The years of frustration for Mao were clearly over. One only needs to compare his various writings in the 1929–34 period, his village and land reports, his drafts of laws, regulations and resolutions on behalf of the Kiangsi Soviet, with the spirited analytical writings in 1936–37, planning strategy and excoriating enemies, to see a new man. The most obvious reason for the contrast was the plain fact that he was, after 1935, beginning to be the real leader of the Party. He could now speak with increasing authority on national and international subjects, he had more time to devise new policies and strategies to meet the new situations and he could begin to test his arm in the area of Marxist–Leninist studies, albeit carefully and modestly.

But there was probably another deeper reason for this new authority: something partly due to the heroic perceptions of his destiny and partly to the intensity of the Chinese experiences that coloured the historic role he saw himself as having to play. His traditional poetry reveals this more clearly than his prose, and his later poems more openly than the poems of this period. But as early as 1929, he writes of his successes in western Fukien while "the warlords renew their battles":

281

WANG GUNGWU

A part of the realm has been recovered
And the land is being actively redistributed.[8]

He uses the imagery of the faultless golden bowl for the realm in combination with some down-to-earth words reflecting the "divide land!" slogans of almost every peasant rebellion in Chinese history. In this context, even his several references to the red flags unfurling in the wind and reddening a patch of battleground recall the peasant scarves of many a great rebellion in the past.[9] Also his millions of worker-peasants are t'ien-ping or "heavenly hosts," so are his 200,000 troops marching into Kiangsi, all on the side of the majority, on the side of Heaven, seeking the mandate:

> The heartening Internationale,
> like a hurricane,
> Whirls down on me from heaven.[10]

Such sentiments had sat uncomfortably with the well-trained "internationalists" among his comrades who were better tuned to the messages they were receiving from Stalin. But all this was changed in Yenan. The Chinese struggle in 1936 had become an independent part of the international struggle, the vision of a special role for China was now legitimate and there was a need to appeal not to world socialist approval so much as to Chinese public opinion. For this new task, Mao was psychologically well-prepared, now that he was unchained from his internationalist limitations and fighting entirely on his home ground.

From this time on, Mao's confidence in his Chinese application of Marxist–Leninist theory was unshakeable, nor was his Chineseness among Chinese and foreigners alike seriously in doubt again. It is therefore of particular interest that it was in 1937 that Mao began to venture seriously into Marxist

---

[8] From "The War between Chiang (Kai-shek) and Kwangsi (Warlords)" (autumn 1929). I have used here the translation by Michael Bullock and Jerome Ch'en, in J. Ch'en, Mao and the Chinese Revolution (London: Oxford University Press, 1965), p. 326, under the title, "Advance to Fukien."

[9] See "New Year's Day" (1929); "On the Road to Kwang-ch'ang" (February 1930); "Against the First 'Encirclement'" (spring 1931).

[10] "From Tingchou Towards Ch'angsha" (July 30). The translation is that of Bullock and Ch'en, Mao and the Chinese Revolution, p. 329, under the title "Attack on Nanch'ang."

philosophy. He drafted his two famous essays "On Practice" and "On Contradiction" for lectures which he gave to Party cadres, and the next year he circulated his lecture-outline on "Dialectical Materialism."[11] His quality as a philosopher and a Marxist have been examined by others and I shall not touch on the question of what Chinese roots lie behind his philosophy and modified his Marxism. What is specially relevant here is why he blossomed forth into theory at this time, at the age of 43. A number of explanations are possible but one is specially relevant to the theme of this essay: Mao the Chinese. When he said in 1938 that "my lecture notes are also not good because I myself have only begun to study dialectics,"[12] he felt the need to prove that he could explain Marxism–Leninism better than his Moscow-trained colleagues who had all succeeded in making the subject profoundly difficult to understand. He simply had to demonstrate that anyone could learn theory; there was no advantage in going to Moscow, the important thing was to study it in the context of revolutionary practice and this could, in fact, be done within China. He was also laying the foundations to challenge those comrades who habitually turned to Soviet theoreticians and quoted Russian textbooks to overawe their colleagues with the imprimatur of Stalin. As a major national figure, admired for both his patriotism and his concern for social justice in the countryside, it could not have been a better time for him to show that such a Chinese could not only understand Marxism–Leninism but was also able to place it in the Chinese context. Thus 1937 was a wonderful opportunity to seek actual and ideological leadership of a national Marxist–Leninist movement.

Related to this question of national leadership was the chance Mao had, through the United Front against Japan, to reopen the question of what was "Chinese." I have suggested that, in times of chih or order, China was inclined to orthodoxy and those who ruled China were only too ready to try and define this orthodoxy as soon as possible. The new order of the Nanking Government

---

[11] The two essays "On Practice" and "On Contradiction" were not published until 1950 and we do not know how different our version is from the drafts in 1937; SWL, Vol. I, pp. 282–97; 298–338. The lecture-outline he circulated in 1938 has now been reprinted in MTC, Vol. VI, pp. 265–303.

[12] MTC, Vol. VI, p. 303.

since 1928 had tried to determine such an orthodoxy. Had it been fully established and accepted, the foreign-supported Communist Party would have become so heterodox that even Mao would have ceased to be "Chinese." The United Front in 1937, however, postponed the issue of orthodoxy and gave Mao and the CCP a second chance to become fully Chinese. Once again, it was possible to be many kinds of Chinese: the modified "Confucian" nationalist was not superior to the Westernized liberal, the Marxist–Leninist, and varieties of socialistic worker-peasant democrats, or even the "Trotskyites," as long as they professed unity against the Japanese enemy. In reality, the struggle was soon reduced to that between the KMT and the CCP as both prepared their armies for the eventual showdown after Japan was defeated by the Western allies. But Mao and Chiang Kai-shek were perhaps among the few to grasp the all-or-nothing nature of the competition. In this mighty struggle, Mao was certainly no less Chinese than Chiang; what conditioned them was the Chinese tradition that the winner would have the right to determine the new orthodoxy and the parameters of the new Chinese identity. Mao clearly understood what was at stake when he wrote these famous lines:

> Such is the beauty of these mountains and rivers
> That has been admired by un-numbered heroes –
> Pity Ch'in Shih-huang and Han Wu-ti
> For their lack of literary skill,
> And T'ang T'ai-tsung and Sung T'ai-tsu
> For their weakness in style,
> And the prodigious Gengis Khan
> Knowing only how to bend his bow and shoot at vultures.
> All are past and gone!
> For men of vision
> We must seek among the present generation.[13]

This leads me appropriately to the time when the man of vision won an almost complete victory over Chiang Kai-shek in 1949 and established, under the label of "New Democracy," the new orthodoxy. Such an orthodoxy was something that the majority of Chinese had always expected to be established once the condition of order had been restored and, whatever it might

---

13 "Snow" (February 1936). I follow, with slight modifications, the translation by Bullock and Ch'en, *Mao and the Chinese Revolution*, p. 340.

have started as, it was by definition Chinese and, if sustained, would be seen as the replacement for state-Confucianism. The alternatives had been systematically reduced in the 1930s and 1940s. Now the CCP, in full control, was able to proclaim that it was the KMT in Taiwan which represented a treacherous heresy that had to be exterminated. The People's Republic of China strengthened its majority status by also drawing into its fold most of the non-communist traditionalists, nationalists, liberals and social democrats and fitted them loosely into the new order. The question may be asked: how new, how Marxist–Leninist, how Chinese was this orthodoxy and what was Mao's contribution?

I should say at the outset, however, that the influence of Chinese ideas and traditions on Mao's actions and decisions and on the policies of the People's Republic Government was so extensive that it would be meaningless to point to every occasion when that influence can be detected. There were also continuities of inherited obligations both written and unwritten, conscious and unconscious, too varied and subtle to try to sift out in a short essay. The important point about Mao was that, after 1949, he tried to rid himself of the obvious traditional values which had served him well as a "united front" leader during the Sino-Japanese War and even during the civil war that followed. He saw himself as being responsible for the task of moving the Chinese people firmly towards seeing themselves as part of the world and accustoming them to being in a world that could be explained by the use of Marxist–Leninist terms. Fraternal relations were now called for, not only with the Soviet Union but also with the workers, peasants and patriots of all other anti-imperialist countries. The time had come to wind down the nationalist phase and prepare for the socialist one.

Thus he began in 1949 by doing what might appear to have been a most un-Chinese thing. He declared that China would lean to the side of the Soviet Union and proceeded to develop the closest possible relationships that China had ever had with any single country. This could, of course, have been justified on strategic grounds alone, but he went much further and stressed the internationalist bonds that linked the Chinese revolution to the Soviet Union. Mao was confident enough of his Chinese image among most Chinese to know that he could do this without serious doubts arising about his patriotism. Most Chinese would have interpreted the decision as a tactic necessary for the time and were probably surprised to learn over the years how serious Mao and his comrades were about learning from the Russians. Indeed, Mao was serious and for good reason. The Soviet Union was the only model of socialism there was and Stalin was the only person alive that Mao might have considered his superior. China needed help to salvage its broken-down economy, defend itself against possible imperialist counterattacks and to industrialize without having to depend on the capitalist countries for equipment and highly specialized skills. The Chinese in him made sure that there was no loss of sovereignty. China's size and spectacular triumphs made sure that China would not be treated like one of the East European satellites, or like Mongolia. Ultimately, he expected to use the Soviet Union to make China strong, but as a Marxist–Leninist, that was for a good cause, for the consolidation of the socialist camp and for the advance of world revolution.

The death of Stalin put the Chinese in Mao to a great test. Between that event and Khrushchev's secret speech of 1956 demystifying Stalin, he would have seen himself as inheriting the mantle as the most successful socialist leader in the world. His Chinese comrades would have seen that there was certainly no one in the Soviet Union to match him for revolutionary experience and world reputation. But when he was not even consulted before Khrushchev prepared his speech to the 20th Party Congress of the Soviet Communist Party and when many of his own comrades seemed too ready to follow Khrushchev uncritically, Mao must have had much to think about. He continued in public to say that China must learn from the Soviet Union, but in private he began to warn against being too imitative.[14] He began also to express his doubts about going too far and neglecting matters in which Chinese methods and experiences were better, especially in areas like agriculture and light industry. But most of all, he saw that Khrushchev did not believe

[14] As in his "Talk at the Enlarged Politburo Meeting (April 1956)," *Wan-sui* (1969), pp. 35–40; "On the Ten Great Relationships," *Wan-sui* (1969), pp. 40–59, translation in J. Ch'en (ed.), *Mao* (Englewood Cliffs, N.J.: Prentice-Hall, 1969), pp. 66–85; and in "Talks at the Chengtu conference (a) Talk of 10 March," *Wan-sui* (1969), pp. 159–65; translation in Schram, *Unrehearsed*, pp. 96–103.

in fraternity and equality within the socialist camp and that the Soviet Union insisted on leadership whatever the quality of its own leaders.

Whether it was Mao the socialist who was disillusioned with Khrushchev's failures, especially in Hungary and Poland, or whether it was Mao the Chinese who believed that there should be only one sun in the socialist sky and that he be the one is still a matter of interpretation. What is not in doubt is that he began to challenge the Soviet way and this thrust him back onto his Chinese resources. That Mao the Chinese would inevitably have contributed towards a Sino-Soviet rift, just as the long vulnerable borders between the two countries and the respective histories and cultures would have placed great strains on that relationship, is clear. It is less clear, however, that the final break in relations and the intensity of the conflict between the two was due only to this Chineseness. I think that such an interpretation would be a serious underestimation of Mao's dedication to Marxism–Leninism. It would lead to the rather simplistic view that external relations brought out the Chinese in Mao, and that would be just as simplistic as the opposite view, that internal problems made him more consciously Marxist–Leninist.

Within the People's Republic, Mao recognized from the start that his Chineseness could be taken for granted and did not need proving. The really mammoth task was to move his people towards a full understanding of the Marxist–Leninist foundations of the new China. The clearest evidence of how conscious Mao was of his new internationalist responsibilities may be found in the editing of his war-time writings for the first three volumes of his *Selected Works* published in 1950–52. The best example of this was his treatment of the small textbook on "The Chinese Revolution and the Chinese Communist Party."[15] Mao very carefully removed all the parts of the original 1939 version that smacked of Chinese imperialism, taking out the references to tributary states and omitting the list of such states (Korea, Annam, Ryukyus, Burma, Bhutan and Nepal) from the new edition. Another example was the way he added to the descriptions of "peasant rebellions and peasant wars" the clause, "these class struggles of the peasants."[16]

[15] *MTC*, Vol. VII, pp. 97–135; *SWL*, Vol. III, pp. 72–101.
[16] *MTC*, Vol. VII, p. 105, p. 102. Cf. *SWL*, Vol. III, p. 78; p. 76.

It was not, however, enough to change words or add new revolutionary messages to old texts. He had to reach the minds of hundreds of millions of people, and especially the millions of intellectuals who saw Mao as a great national leader but were unwilling to move away from their traditional heritage. He found the latter especially difficult to influence. A perfect example of his dilemma was his careful attempt to inject a bridging sentence into the 1939 text which would help his readers see how much Chinese history was part of world history. This was the sentence which he added:

> As China's feudal society developed its commodity economy and so carried within itself the embryo cf capitalism, China would of herself have developed slowly into a capitalist society even if there had been no influence of foreign capitalism.[17]

This was deliberately inserted to give authority to the view which would have logically followed the use of Marxist–Leninist social and historical categories for China. It strongly supported one of the basic tenets of historical materialism which Mao had reaffirmed in 1939 as follows:

> The development of the Chinese nation (chiefly of the Han nation) was the same as that of other great nations in the world: it went through tens of thousands of years of life in an equal and classless primitive communist society, and when this primitive communist society collapsed, its social life was transformed into class life and passed through (the stages of) slave society, feudal society for five thousand years until now.[18]

It should not, therefore, be surprising to assume that China would also have developed into a capitalist society "of herself." The surprising thing was that the newly inserted sentence was greeted with much excitement as one that reflected Mao's latest thoughts on an important phase of Chinese history. For the next half-dozen years, thousands of writers and scholars combed the literary and historical sources for evidence to prove what Mao had merely inferred. A great deal of time and energy was spent on arguing whether the "embryo" (more literally translated as "young shoots") of capitalism had appeared in the Early or Late

---

[17] SWL, Vol. III, p. 77.
[18] My translation of the original version in MTC, Vol. VII, p. 98 is slightly different from that in the official translation, SWL, Vol. III, p. 73.

Ming, or Early Ch'ing, dynasties, or much earlier, in the Sung or even the T'ang dynasties. The results of all this feverish inquiry need not concern us here. The question is, did Mao seek to open such a difficult and rather formless debate ranging over at least a thousand years of history, or was he misunderstood? Mao would have welcomed the re-interpretation of Chinese history along Marxist–Leninist lines, but he was carefully vague as to what might have been and did not say that the "young shoots" of capitalism could be located in the Chinese past. There was certainly no hint of boasting veering on the chauvinistic in what Mao actually said – if read together with all the corrections, omissions and additions he had made in editing his pre-1949 writings, the sentence is matter-of-fact and conforms with all other textual changes made to fit Chinese society and history into a Marxist–Leninist framework. The only value judgment implied here that moved a Chinese audience long accustomed to shame at China's inferiority was the idea that the Chinese were as good and progressive as the Europeans. This aroused much chauvinistic pride and led to interpretations which Mao did not reject but probably did not expect.

All the same, the episode revealed some of the ambivalence that underlay Mao's own position between the Soviet-type party he led and the millions of Chinese who saw him as their national leader. He himself, as I have argued earlier, saw no difficulty in being a good Chinese Marxist–Leninist. He had grown into one through the interplay of theory and practice in his long experience of revolution and I believe he found it effortless to talk and write as he did and was no longer consciously Chinese or Marxist–Leninist. But this, of course, was not the condition of the majority of the people in the 1950s for whom Marxism–Leninism was still mainly learnt through textbooks, lectures and study meetings, and through efforts to practise what they had been told. And for most of those who were beyond their 'teens, there were two parts to Mao; the Chinese, and the bearer of victory through a secret weapon that was impressive but no less alien for that, and it was much easier to respond to Mao the Chinese.

It must therefore have been tempting for Mao to do what most Chinese expected him to do: to act the Chinese ruler. Had he not been a Marxist–Leninist, it would be hard to see why he did not do just that. Of course, he was not an entirely free agent. He led a tightly-knit Party, China needed Soviet aid and he could not afford to offend Stalin. But the evidence of his revisions of earlier works, his speeches and writings and all his actions show that the idea of not being Marxist–Leninist never occurred to him. On the contrary, in terms of the traditional heritage, he was iconoclastic as only someone who was wholly confident about his own identity could have been. In his writings and lectures, and especially in his Party discussions, he would interpose now and again remarks that were obviously intended to shock his bourgeois listeners and amuse his worker-peasant audiences. He would deliberately re-interpret some common sayings, giving them new twists and even making them mean the opposite of their original meanings. He grew specially fond of quoting Confucian phrases to show what hypocrites the followers of Confucius had been. For example, he was very concerned to attack conservatism and superstition, and his attacks ranged from serious criticisms of the idea that "Heaven does not change; the Way does not change"[19] to laughing at those who would not eat dog-meat by pointing to Mencius' reference to the dog-eating ancient Chinese.[20] At another level, he recommended the romanization of the Chinese language and mocked the idea that "Chinese characters are the best in the world."[21] But he reserved his sharpest barbs for Confucians and ultimately, the more he found that the older intellectuals resisted his calls for radical change, the more openly critical he became of Confucius himself.

Confucius seemed to have posed a particularly knotty problem for Mao the Chinese. The attacks against Confucius would seem to be a rejection of much of the Chinese past and its values. The Westernized liberal Chinese, the Christians, Marxist–Leninists and other types of radicals and revolutionaries had, since the May Fourth Movement, attacked Confucius as the symbol of all that was out-of-date and backward about China.

---

[19] "On Dialectical Materialism," MTC, Vol. VI, p. 285; also in "On Contradiction," SWL, Vol. I, p. 300.
[20] "Talk at the Supreme State Conference (13 October, 1957)," Wan-sui (1969), p. 140.
[21] "Talk at the Conference on the Problem of Intellectuals Called by the CCP Centre (21 January, 1956)," Wan-sui (1969), p. 31.

But at first Mao was properly cautious, especially during the United Front period. He did not hesitate to quote Confucius with approval, as, for example, the well-known "Learn without being satiated; instruct without being wearied" and he strongly advocated that cadres be chosen by merit, echoing the Confucian observation that good and wise rulers chose their ministers and officials according to merit.[22] At the most, Mao was only mildly critical of Confucius as when, for example, he commented on the fact that Confucius' disciples did not work with their hands – at least Confucius did not place himself above the peasant and the vegetable gardener!

When his [Confucius'] disciples asked him about how to plough fields, he said, "I don't know, I am not as good at that as the peasants." And about how to plant vegetables, he also said, "I don't know, I am not as good at that as the vegetable gardeners."[23]

In the 1950s, Mao began to deflate Confucius' reputation, but it was not until the late 1950s, after the "Hundred Flowers" and "Anti-Rightist" campaigns, that he really attacked fiercely. For example, in ridiculing the traditional idea that "gentlemen gather but do not form factions," he quoted the case of Confucius ordering the execution of Shao-cheng Mao and declared that Confucius himself practised factional politics.[24] But, by this time, he had grown so sensitive to the way Confucian values permeated much of the idioms and literary allusions in the Chinese language that he became quite defiant and turned Confucius around by asserting, "What you do not want others to do to you, you shall do to others!"[25] Finally, in the 1960s, as China became isolated from both Western and Soviet ideas and values,

[22] "The Role of the Chinese Communist Party in the National War" (October 1938), *MTC*, Vol. VI, p. 262 and *SWL*, Vol. II, p. 261. As for "employing the worthy," this may be found in the same text, *MTC*, p. 251 and *SWL*, Vol. II, p. 252.

[23] "Speech at a Meeting in Yenan to Commemorate the 20th Anniversary of the May Fourth Movement" (4 May, 1939), *MTC*, Vol. VI, p. 337; *SWL*, Vol. III, p. 20 (under the title "The Orientation of the Youth Movement").

[24] "Talk at the Supreme State Conference (28, 30 January, 1958)," *Wan-sui* (1969), p. 155.

[25] Quoted by Chin Ssu-k'ai, *Mao Tse-tung ssu-hsiang nei-jung yü hsing-shih* (Hong Kong: University of Hong Kong, 1976), p. 166, from a Red Guard paper, *Chingkangshan* (1 August, 1967), reproduced in *Tsu-kuo* (Monthly), Hong Kong, No. 68 (1 November, 1969): "Mao Tse-tung's critique of P'eng Teh-huai."

and its intellectuals began again to look to China's own moral and spiritual resources, Mao had grown so impatient and bitter that he said:

Confucius said, "The benevolent man loves others." Loves which others? All others? No such thing. Loves exploiters? Not all of them, only part of the exploiters.[26]

After that it is easy to understand how some of Mao's most enthusiastic followers after the Cultural Revolution could be so carried away as to publish some of the distortions and absurdities about Confucius and Confucians, especially during the anti-Confucius campaign of 1973–75. The young "radicals" rushed to imitate Mao's style by abusing the past, but their imitations certainly reminded one of the old Chinese saying, "Failing to copy the tiger painting, the picture turned out to resemble a dog."

Despite his frequent iconoclasm, Mao was uneasy about the power of the Chinese past over the Chinese imagination. He realized how complex a problem this was and how much it could become an obstruction to the speed and depth of revolutionary change in China. He was certainly forewarned by the energetic but misplaced response to his comment on "the young shoots of capitalism" in the 1950s. Although there was good response to his call to study the traditional heritage critically and to explain it all in Marxist–Leninist terms, he was keenly aware that the traditional Chinese skill in the use of historical analogies for political purposes could be turned against him and his regime. He was quite skilled himself in the political use of the past, especially in pointing to examples of progressive change which helped him to explain a current policy. The skill was not, of course, peculiar to the Chinese. Mao greatly admired the ways Marx and Engels used the past for both their scholarly studies and their polemical writings, and he recognized the positive benefits such uses of the past could bring to a new revolutionary order. If the Chinese could only learn to use the past in the framework of scientific and dialectical materialism and not, as they have always done, to illustrate moral and personal qualities and even to criticize rulers and

[26] "Talk on Questions of Philosophy (18 August, 1964)," Wàn-sui (1969), p. 550; a slightly different translation may be found in Schram, Unrehearsed, p. 214.

ministers, then the past could be recruited to help with the transformation of China itself.[27]

But the Chinese intellectuals were incorrigibly fond of using historical analogy in the traditional, and popular, ways. The most blatant example of this was Wu Han's study of Hai Jui, which was easily recognizable through this 16th century analogy as an attack of Mao's treatment of P'eng Teh-huai in 1959.[28] Other obvious ones concern the motives of founders of dynasties, the judgments on emperors and the fates of rebels and peasant rebellions. The obsession with Chinese "kings, princes, commanders and ministers" was very hard to cure with heavy doses of Marx, Engels and Lenin who had themselves nothing of interest to say about Chinese history. And all the attempts to fit Marxist historical stages to the Chinese past led only to more disputes and disagreements – the difficulties also easily led to absurdities which must have had a subversive effect on Chinese confidence in Marxist historiography itself.

Thus Mao the Chinese understood a part of China which Mao the Marxist–Leninist could not easily eradicate. Although the use of historical analogies by most Chinese did not necessarily mean a hankering for the past, it did remind the readers of reference points which had once set standards for Chinese political behaviour and social responsibilities. It was therefore symptomatic of other resistant features in Chinese society which could not be speedily removed. In this way, the Marxist–Leninist in Mao became impatient with the Chinese in him – and this was to evolve into what was to turn out to be Mao's most un-Chinese insistence on haste.

This really began with the events leading to the Great Leap Forward, where he abandoned his native caution and insisted on going faster than most of his colleagues wanted and faster than the available personnel and institutions could carry. He mocked and scolded his comrades for walking like "women with bound feet"[29] but the whole campaign failed largely

[27] I have written more fully about this in my article, "Juxtaposing past and present in China today," CQ, No. 61 (March 1975), pp. 1–24.

[28] Wu Han's essays are collected in Ting Wang (ed.), Wu Han and the "Hai Jui pa-kuan" Affair (Documents of the Chinese Cultural Revolution, Vol. 4), Hong Kong, 1969; see James R. Pusey, Wu Han: Attacking the Present Through the Past (Cambridge, Mass.: Harvard East Asian Center, 1969).

[29] Mao had used this phrase earlier in "On the Question of Agriculture Co-operatives" (Report, 31 July, 1955), Hsüeh-hsi, No. 11 (1955), p. 3, but it was equally appropriate in 1957–58.

because of inadequate preparation, the pressure of impossible demands and ultimately the lack of clear objectives. The result was a large-scale disruption of the economy which, aided by three years of bad harvest, slowed down China's development considerably. Mao's first real personal failure in his long career was traumatic for him and for China. Already the two had, in Mao's eyes, become bound together, in the sense that Mao remained convinced that what he wanted was what the majority wanted and was capable of achieving were it not for the Party and government bureaucracies dragging their feet. The economic crisis that caused much suffering throughout the country checked his momentum and also some of his confidence. It was some years before he felt he could take full charge again and this time act the Chinese ruler in the way the people would understand: to do battle with laggard and corrupt ministers and serve the people. Thus he launched the Cultural Revolution to throw aside all those who had treated him like an honoured ancestor.[30] In this original way of attacking the very Party he led, he propelled himself to become the sole arbiter of China's fate, a position not unlike that of an activist founder-emperor of a traditional dynasty. He was Chinese enough to perceive how he would appear to his historically sensitive people: many analogies spring to the Chinese mind, notably Ming T'ai-tsu (reigned 1368–98)[31] and Ch'in Shih-huang (reigned 246–210 B.C.).

If it had to be, he would rather be compared to Ch'in Shih-huang, who had not simply restored an old order but founded a truly new one. The comparison was not at all original. Chiang Kai-shek's propagandists in Taiwan and Hong Kong had long called him that in the hope that his "dynasty" would be equally short-lived. And as early as 1958, Mao had been able to joke about it.

[30] "Talk at the Report Meeting of the Politburo (24 October, 1966)" Wan-sui (1969), p. 655; translation in Schram, Unrehearsed, p. 267.
[31] Ming T'ai-tsu was a commoner who drove off the Mongol conquerors with his peasant-based army. It is interesting that Wu Han had written a biography of him in the 1940s (Chu Yuan-chang chuan) and also wrote a study of Hai Jui where one of T'ai-tsu's successors behaves like a tyrant (see note 28 above). On the nature of Ming "despotism," see F. W. Mote, "The growth of Chinese despotism, a critique of Wittfogel's theory of Oriental despotism as applied to China," Oriens Extremus, Vol. 8/1 (1961), pp. 1–41.

I have debated this matter with the democratic people. I say, you abuse us for being Ch'in Shih-huang, you're wrong! We surpass Ch'in Shih-huang by a hundred times. You say that we are Ch'in Shih-huang, that we are dictators. We admit the whole thing. The only pity is that you don't say enough and we often have to add to what you say.

But he was careful to say "we."

What was Ch'in Shih-huang? He only buried 460 ("Confucian") scholars, we have buried 46,000 scholars.[32]

Whereas, for himself, he had added, "Of course, I also do not approve of taking Ch'in Shih-huang (as an example)." And Lin Piao, by his side, had given the stock Chinese answer, "Ch'in Shih-huang burnt books and buried scholars!"

It was still a joke then because his whole audience could see how absurd it was that they, who represented the majority and who had established a dictatorship of the proletariat, should be compared with a tyrant. After the Cultural Revolution, however, such a comparison was no longer funny. Mao was the sole authority, there were very few people he could trust to do his bidding or give him accurate reports about what the people really wanted. Despite much travelling around the country to meet the people personally, he could hardly be sure that people really told him what they thought. His battle to loosen and democratize the Party had given him victory over his Party but, ironically, his awesome success had so raised him above ordinary mortals that he had become remote, the cool distant father-figure that was the traditional ideal for a great emperor. Of course, Mao did not want to be a Ch'in Shih-huang, who was merely a shrewd aristocrat who used a group of Legalists to establish the first empire in China but was not conscious of the historic role he was playing in the class struggle. Only a post-Marxist analysis could reveal that the First Emperor was the spearhead, and his reign the climax, of the revolutionary struggle between the feudal landlord class and the remnants of the slave-owning aristocratic class who were trying to restore themselves to power.[33] Absurd though this must have sounded to

[32] "Talk at the Second Session of the Eighth Party Congress: First talk (8 May, 1958)," *Wan-sui* (1969), p. 195.
[33] I introduce the beginnings of this analysis in " 'Burning books and burying scholars alive': some recent interpretations concerning Ch'in Shih-huang," *Papers on Far Eastern History* No. 9 (1974), pp. 137–86. A more complete

scholars who had read their documents and sources, this was probably credible to a generation of Chinese brought up on almost nothing else except the class struggle as the key to all history. From Mao's point of view, knowing the deep prejudice the Chinese have had against Ch'in Shih-huang, including himself and Lin Piao as noted above, only a Marxist explanation of Ch'in Shih-huang's place in revolutionary history could have made any comparison with him acceptable. And as long as Mao had control over the new world-view and was a conscious agent of global historical forces, he was clearly superior and there was no danger of his People's Republic suffering the fate of the First Empire.

Mao was also Chinese enough to know that his new orthodoxy would be compared with that of the Confucian state which came to an end in 1911 and which could no longer be successfully restored despite various pathetic attempts to do so. Although Confucius' reputation was more "fragrant" than that of Ch'in Shih-huang and his ideas are considered to have lasted a thousand times longer than Shih-huang's dynasty, Mao probably did not in the end want to be compared to Confucius. Unless he could thoroughly change Chinese thinking about Confucius, he must have realized that he could not but suffer in the comparison.[34] Thus the anti-Confucian campaign would not only have served to cleanse Chinese minds of preconceived notions about Confucius' sageness by branding him as a thorough-going reactionary wanting to restore the power of slave-owning aristocrats, it could ultimately, had it been successful, make it safe to compare Mao with Confucius to Mao's advantage. It would then be seen that Maoism was not only more progressive in its time than Confucianism ever was even at its best, but clearly also so much more far-reaching that it would help to change the world, something which Confucianism never did.

It would be wrong for me to suggest that Mao became more

collection of the 1973–74 campaign articles has been translated in Li Yu-ming (ed.), The First Emperor of China: the Politics of Historiography (White Plains, N.Y.: IASP, 1975).
[34] On the latest effort to change Chinese thinking about Confucius, see M. Goldman, "China's anti-Confucian campaign, 1973–74," CQ, No. 63 (September 1975), pp. 435–62.

Chinese as he grew older and more powerful. I believe that, while he remained Chinese, he was also unswervingly Marxist–Leninist in his mind until the day he died. What overcame his ambitious revolutionary vision was China itself: the 900 millions, the deep political and cultural heritage, the people's pervasive and incorrigible addiction to the country's long history and the urge for order after a century of *luan* which grew stronger with each decade. When one considers what he inherited in 1949, it is, in fact, a measure of his personal success that he managed to move the Chinese as far and as long as he had done. In short, I do not think it helpful to ask whether he might have achieved more if he had been more conventionally Chinese or if he could have acquired a more purist form of Marxism–Leninism. Both China and Marxism–Leninism moulded the growth of his mind and character in inextricable ways. Even though he, as a brilliant, sensitive, thinking man might have been clearly aware from time to time which part of him was more Chinese and which more Marxist–Leninist, there is little evidence that this mattered at the crunch.

Of course, one could still speculate if some other leader who was both Chinese and Marxist–Leninist to a similar degree might not have had a different effect on China and thrust a different China upon the world. The question does force us to consider if the unique fusion that produced Mao's personality and political style actually helped China's progress or obstructed it. It seems to me that his mastery and vigorous use of the Chinese language helped to communicate both the need for radical change and a sense of urgency to his audiences. Most of the time, Marxism–Leninism was made to sound familiar and easy to understand after he had said it. This might not have been good for the original ideas of Marx and Lenin, but it was probably more effective than asking all the Chinese to read the Marxist classics and find the ideas alien and abstruse. If the danger to avoid was to dilute the idea of progress when the Chinese most needed it, I would think that Mao's Chinese expressions and striking use of Chinese analogies did more to avoid that than any text of Marx or Lenin translated into Chinese.

At the same time, Mao's supreme confidence in what the scientific truth of Marxism–Leninism could achieve and how quickly this could be done, and his conviction that he knew what the Chinese would not do or could not do, led him in the end to obstruct China's progress by demanding too much of its people. He simply would not settle for steady progress; nor would he leave the matter to inevitable forces at work in history to guarantee success. Although we should take into account his reading of English and French revolutionary history where reaction and restoration took place and his belief that restoration of capitalism had also occurred in the Soviet Union, it was probably his Chinese fears about what China would do if it became prosperous and strong that determined him not to let the Chinese settle down. Had China had a different history, or had he known less about it, he might have acted differently. But given China's long history of literati-officials or bureaucratic elites, he could hardly not notice how easily some of his comrades enjoyed their hard-won privileges and were prepared to reinstate the meritocracy that had always ruled China. I believe that Mao was not willing to see corrupt Confucian bureaucrats be replaced by corruptible Marxist–Leninist bureaucrats, and therefore would rather see China's progress slow down to allow that to happen without a fight. The majority of the Chinese people probably shared his fears and were prepared to help him create the thoroughly selfless man, but the cost of continuous disruption, the risk of economic stagnation and the difficulty in keeping up living standards combined to throw doubt about whether that could ever be done. And if it could not be done while Mao was alive, what hope is there that it can be done after he is gone?

Despite his mistakes and failures, Mao did achieve the one important thing that he did want as a Chinese: his China has certainly made a great impact on the world. But this is not the old China, nor did he want the world simply to respect and admire the glories and achievements of a dead civilization. His message is that there can be a new China, one that is new because he had helped decisively to turn its eyes towards the world and see the world through his eyes. What he saw may or may not be the reality today, but China will never take the world for granted again, nor will it accept the world's own estimation of itself. The great mistake that Mao made was about the timing of all this. The sentiment at least may be found, most appropriately, in the

following lines written in 1963, in the most Chinese *tz'u* form, to
the tune of *Man-chiang-hung*:

> There have always been
> Many things that were urgent.
> Although the world spins on
> Time is short.
> Millennia are too long:
> Let us dispute about mornings and evenings.[35]

They might be included in the un-Chinese corner of his long and
eulogistic Chinese epitaph.

[35] "Reply to Kuo Mo-jo." I have adopted the translation by Bullock and Ch'en,
Mao and the Chinese Revolution, p. 360.

10

THE INNOVATOR

Edward Friedman

To focus on Mao as a great 20th century innovator, we must first be aware of just how recent are the creative acts which have won him his deserved fame. Had Mao died in 1945, people might still be asking about him, as they still do about China's republican revolutionary, Sun Yat-sen, whether he was or was not a genuine revolutionary. As a rebel in the mountains, Mao, like Sun, in order to survive adopted numerous policies of compromise and reform, incremental change and moderation. Rather than collectivize land and impose new social forms, the rebels merely reduced rent and interest, established a fair and progressive tax system, moved forward on jobs, health and education and kept government as inexpensive and unobtrusive as possible. And, while mistrusting his counter-revolutionary adversaries and even preparing for an ultimate show-down, Mao was open to a share in united fronts, a part in coalition governments. Stalin concluded that Mao was not a real revolutionary but a fake, a mere "margarine communist."

Mao Tse-tung actually was one of the greatest political innovators in human history. His inventiveness, however, was not a matter of sitting quietly in his book-lined study – or before that his cave headquarters in the mountains of north China – and thinking up nice ideas for others to implement. Rather, Mao was almost invariably responding in a uniquely creative and profoundly ethical way to deep political crises. Hence, Mao's social inventiveness cannot be divorced either from political imperatives or his own ethical vision. Had he died in 1945, then, in the heritage of Chinese nationalism, Mao would have been much praised for his anti-imperialism, for his efforts in fighting to throw out of China the brutalizing Japanese invaders of the Second World War. His willingness to co-operate closely with the American side in 1944–45, including an acceptance of U.S. economic aid and investment in China, might – as the U.S. emerged from the War as the dominant global economic power – have led some, however, to question Mao's nationalism. Questions would have been raised about how many of his ethical goals he had compromised in order to share the post-war stage of power in China. This doubt would have been strengthened by the content of the reforms carried out in the Second World War period when Mao's capital was in the town of Yenan.

To keep the revolutionary movement alive and growing, Mao found ways to build an extremely broad united front. People were encouraged to participate in local organizations controlling everything from local government to wiping out opium addiction, prostitution and footbinding. Mao found ways to co-ordinate a large-scale guerrilla and mobile war effort against the Japanese invaders premised on a host of community power reforms. By holding central-local administration to a minimum, promoting agriculture among the troops and keeping rations for army and Party to subsistence needs, taxes were reduced to a modest level. With the exception of the 1940–42 period of economic hardship caused by massive Japanese search and destroy pacification campaigns, by unusually harsh weather and blockade by his domestic Chinese adversaries, Chiang Kai-shek's National Government, Mao brought material gain, democratic reform and anti-imperialist mobilization. But was he a revolutionary?

Of course, in retrospect, Mao's revolutionary credentials are impeccable. Nonetheless, looking even at this one period gives us a clue to a major trademark of all Mao's politics. He believed that if he could survive a dangerous period and keep the initiative, then in the next period he could carry through more socially transforming, socialist-directed policies. The danger never ceased. Consequently, almost any compromise was always legitimate. Hence, at any one time, to others, claiming to be truer leftists, Marxists or revolutionaries, Mao often seemed a traitor to the cause. His united front alliance in this wartime crisis with the National Government of Chiang Kai-shek seemed to such leftists outright betrayal. How ally with Chiang, a murderer of hundreds of thousands of progressive young people, union members and democratic personages, a killer of the friends, loved ones, colleagues and comrades of these, China's revolutionaries? Mao's societal creativeness cannot be divorced from a long view of history and social change and from a double political struggle, against his outright enemies and against his erstwhile friends and allies. One area in which Mao's genius is unquestioned is as a political actor, able to join with various groups at different times, all in the service of an only half-formed vision of the good society, his own quest for the power to shape a better world.

It all would have looked very different had Mao died in the mid-1950s. By 1956, there could no longer be any doubt that Mao was indeed a real revolutionary. The Red Armies had won national power, nationalized industry and collectivized the land. Economic growth seemed to be surging forward with socialism the promised destination. Mao now was both liberator and builder. (These two features were mirrored at the international level where the Chinese revolutionary victory could eventually help inspire fighters from Mozambique to Algeria, from Cuba to Cambodia and also help unite Third World countries in an attempt to build their economies by organizing against control and pricing by industrialized nations.)

To be sure, there were unique characteristics of the Chinese path. Emerging from a protracted war in the countryside and embodying a nationalist cause, it was so popularly rooted that, virtually the antithesis of the Soviet story, its history was full of vibrant life void of purge and fear and murder. Nonetheless, despite its step-by-step advance not too far out of line with popular consciousness, as China borrowed Soviet technology and blueprints, as it stressed rational management and planning, as Party-power became entrenched, it seemed headed on a course not so different from the U.S.S.R. Since numerous theories explain the peculiar inhuman horrors of Stalin's development, it is not surprising that a gentler version of that path should be possible in the very different circumstances of China.

And then in 1955–56 Mao began to go his own way. In retrospect it is easy to find numerous indications that Mao always intended to find alternatives to a Party monopoly of power, alternatives to finding ultimate progress in urban centres, hierarchical forms and technological solutions. He had long insisted that people were the most precious thing in the whole world and that with people every miracle was possible. But no-one could foretell what this would mean in practice, in wrestling with capital shortages and agricultural bottlenecks, in deciding how a weak and poor country could build a just and plentiful society. It was this new and unexpected turn which led Mao to pioneer, to see the need for entering on ground hitherto unexplored in the 20th century. Mao then emerges as the quintessential revolutionary creator.

Once Mao was recognized as a genuine revolutionary, his past was reinterpreted. In like manner, we can be certain that the future Marxists and people of China will re-create and re-interpret Mao to fit their eventual needs of the moment. The Mao who was is yet to be. Consensus, however, will be as impossible then as it is now. There is no way to reconcile the concerns of those who insist that revolution is a senseless blood-letting since the inevitable routinization that follows re-institutes domination and exploitation, with those who see the post-1955 Mao as pioneering a new and hopeful path in which the revolution for social justice continues even after the revolutionaries take power.

Given this latter, more hopeful perspective, the early Mao takes on new contours. The pre-Liberation Mao, the Mao before the formal 1950s break with the Soviet model, is suddenly discovered to have long been moving towards a non-stratified society, to have long been committed to that revolutionary project. What are now magnified are all the earlier, pre-1949 modes meant to destroy hierarchy such as the relatively equal treatment in the red armies of officers and regular soldiers, the equalizing of rations, the opening of the books, the insistence on leadership by moral example rather than command. And even while "copying" the Soviet model, the Chinese moved away from merely putting their resources into high production areas, insisting instead on helping the worst off, on levelling up.

With these features to the fore, one is not upset, as dogmatic Marxists are, that Mao's revolution did not emanate from the urban industrial proletariat. Instead, one takes seriously Mao's insistence that Marx's living message, among many extraordinary social and theoretical contributions, is not in the details of his analysis of the contradictions of 19th century capitalism, but in one's own commitment to make revolution. All those who would act on behalf of human liberation are literally Marx's metaphorical proletariat. To the extent that the force of Mao's example wins back would-be revolutionaries to that central project, his major innovation – accepting the responsibility for making liberation real in one's circumstances – will prove a launching pad for true human explorations and discovery. For Mao, if the lack of an urban proletariat would not prevent him from forging a revolutionary coalition whose goal was socialism, why should limited productive forces impede further movement in that direction once Mao stood at the peak of state power? No obstructive mountain was so large that it could not be cleared away. Every evil had to be reconceived as an opportunity. The crisis imposed by the bad had to be resolved so that the bad was turned into the good, such that danger became possibility. The particulars of such reversals testify to Mao's political and social inventiveness.

In mid-1955 Mao broke with the Leninist logic of his Party and of his Soviet allies and urged China's rural dwellers to collectivize their land even though industry could not yet provide the electricity and machinery to take advantage of larger scale farming units. He would not accept the logic that claimed that social progress had to wait for and follow after technological advance. For a poor country such as China that meant waiting too long. Not only was there an inherent good in more progressive social relations – e.g. a larger unit of income distribution could reduce inequalities frozen into smaller units, some poorer, some richer – but co-operation among a larger number of people in water conservation projects, such as irrigation, dams, canals, and dikes, could stabilize production at higher levels, thereby raising production, improving the standard of living and quality of life (e.g. reducing anxiety about bad times and bad weather) and, most importantly, create genuine popular enthusiasm, a real desire to move on to yet more progressive social relations.

It turned out that Mao was right and the Party wrong on the issue of collectivization. The change occurred with minimal dislocation and real benefits. Thus Mao had a real basis, it seemed, for pushing again in 1958, urging country people to emulate the Communes already created in one northern province, Honan, as part of a Great Leap Forward. Mao and his staff had searched the country over for popularly-devised means which could deal ethically and practically with China's continuing economic crisis.

What was at issue here was one of Mao's great innovations, the notion of self-reliance. The people in the Kremlin threatened to pull out their aid if China broke with the Stalin model which embodied for the rulers in the U.S.S.R. the only way to build socialism. And the American forward containment of China with its blockade and embargo kept China's ruling groups from finding needed aid and trade in Japan and other American semi-dependencies. Mao then built on all the innovations from the periphery which suggested that through multi-purpose, large rural organizations, dubbed Communes, agricultural productivity could leap forward as labour power was liberated and efficiently organized. In addition, the people themselves in their own regions could develop, based on local resources, a small and intermediate technology which would rapidly increase production of steel, fertilizer, electricity, local tools, equipment, etc. These innovations to win maximum independence from the pains of the world market would eventually win the close attention of leaders of other Third World countries faced with similar dilemmas.

While there was much creative wisdom in this attempt to limit dependence on others, while there was originally an enthusiastic popular response to this vision of China saving itself, it was, in the short run, doomed from the outset. Hastened into practice, untested, with great political pressure to produce results, errors were made, co-ordination was impossible, lies replaced data and shortly, with the statistical system in disarray, food production and the will to work plummeted. China barely avoided mass starvation. Mao barely avoided being deposed. From this point on, from the failure of the Great Leap onwards, Mao's innovations, his visions of the self-reliant future building on social reorganization and conscious popular enthusiasm became a basic issue in Chinese politics.

Among ruling groups in China, Mao became far less popular than a reading of Chinese journals might suggest. Of course, anyone who challenges the shibboleths of his or her society is likely to be searchingly scrutinized and doubted, if not ridiculed. The failures of the Great Leap, however, along with the vengeful defeat of his opponents in 1959 and Mao's continual pushing of most unpopular social forms such as communal mess-halls, added to this normal scepticism among Mao's colleagues. Hence by the 1960s, more than ever, Mao's social innovations were invariably entangled with a political struggle against these powerful sceptics who were supported by many of those who suffered from the horrendous consequences of the Great Leap.

Nonetheless, modified and corrected, Mao's ensemble of discovered social forms proved their worth from the 1960s on. Smaller, somewhat less egalitarian Communes, national planning stressing agriculture and not just heavy industry, utilizing all China's local resources for industrial growth of an intermediate type, began in combination to push China year after year to ever higher standards of living.

But, Mao insisted, more was needed. The bond between leader and led had to be retied so that once again the Chinese people would willingly commit themselves to struggle and work and sacrifice for the building of a more just society. While his colleagues worried that it was too soon after the horrors of the Leap to plunge ahead, while they even sabotaged such renewed efforts, Mao moved on. Had Mao died at that point in the early 1960s, all evaluations of his contribution would have been affected by the idea that his vision had failed, as the Great Leap supposedly proved. His peers would most likely have reversed his course.

The innovations of Mao which are usually summed up in the term "Maoism" mostly begin at this moment. Just when others became most pessimistic, Mao, entering his 70s, became most confident of the worth and possibility of his vision. He could joke pointedly about his opponents, ridicule the obstacles to further progress and plot successfully to keep the revolution going.

Investigations showed that most rural cadres had, during the three awful years that followed the Great Leap, often stolen, cheated and otherwise acted corruptly for themselves and their families. What should be done about this? How again make leaders living models, people trustful of the integrity of such leadership? A campaign was launched to involve the populace in cleaning up these corrupt cadres so that they would be persuaded, in Mao's parlance, educated such that the people again would want to work for socialism.

But then Mao drew back from the direction of this campaign. Its harshness contradicted his preferences for never attacking more than a small minority, for always allowing people a way to change and advance, for never choosing methods which would force people to lie and conspire to protect themselves. In place of the campaign to ferret out numerous evil-doers, Mao discovered and had popularized a new positive model of how to deal with these difficulties, that of the village of Tachai.

The people of Tachai, inspired by the leadership of one Ch'en Yung-kuei, had erased doubts about the selfishness of local leaders and liberated enormous popular energies for building a better world by various social innovations which did not require waiting for a higher level of technological development. Responsible local officials were required to spend most of the time out of their offices working with other villagers in the ordinary labours of life. In addition, material rewards were decided not by a complex wage system of precise, fixed monetary incentives but by each person assessing his or her own contribution to the quality of the life of all, with all then voting on a just reward in which social contributions could also be assessed – e.g. helping the sick and infirm, putting in needed extra hours in the worst weather. In opting for this Tachai model, Mao chose to raise people's sights, to focus on affirmative action, to turn away from blaming so many individuals. Hopefully, as with Tachai, it would thus always be possible to close the gap between leaders and led, and create or re-create true dedication for combining material and socialist (i.e. egalitarian and communitarian) progress.

Mockingly, Mao made clear that as higher-level cadres resisted this Tachai model, so in general the sickness of China, which kept it from energetically liberating creative socialist energies, was the soft life of high office-holders, which led them to prefer and justify their special privileges instead of seeing that their complaints only proved that their self-serving attitudes were the real sickness. Said Mao:

I have never before heard of so much high blood pressure and liver infection. If a person doesn't exercise but only eats well, dresses well and lives well, taking a car whenever going out and never walking, of course that person will often be ill. Paying too much attention to clothing, food, housing and transport are the four causes of illness among high level cadres.[1]

Mao then in 1966 launched a Great Proletarian Cultural Revolution to unseat officials on high horses, to undercut bureaucratic power, to incite people to invent means to prevent the recurrence of such illnesses among high-level officials. Particular solutions were devised. The educational system was to be revamped: there would no longer be special schools for the children of cadres, and after high school people would have to work for a couple of years and win the endorsement of their co-workers before being permitted to move on to college and advanced training. Specialists were supposed to work to make experts of working people, colleges having to associate with factories to train workers so that they could become or judge managers, planners and technical personnel. Numerous similar innovations grew in the countryside all directed at making less likely the institutionalization of a new ruling class, as in the Soviet Union, of managers, technocrats and party bureaucrats.

Focusing on the dangers inherent in bureaucratic specialization led to a stress on generalists and para-professionals. Concern that the selfish consequences of isolation in a bureaucratic office meant divorce from the needs of most citizens led to a search for ways to involve officials and specialists with the daily world of the citizenry. One result was the creation of barefoot doctors, para-medics of, from and for the countryside, trained by professional doctors in the cities who now had to spend a part of each year touring the rural areas, upgrading medicine in isolated areas, improving the knowledge of the barefoot doctors, coming to understand the need to have their medical practice serve the primary needs of most people.

In like manner, a method was devised to get all officials to re-dedicate themselves to such service. Places called May 7th Cadre Schools were built. Here, usually in the countryside, officials lived together, raised food, cooked it and lived divorced from the amenities of capital city life. There, reading Mao's works, talking over their job and China's actual conditions, it was hoped they would re-dedicate themselves to the

[1] *Wan-sui* (1969), p. 454. Mao's talk is dated 24 January, 1964.

ideals of revolutionary change, placing true public service – not the illnesses of living high off the hog – as the first priority deserving their closest attention.

In sum, the Party bureaucracy was weakened. The need for responsiveness and accountability to the public was strengthened. Most important, the issue of bureaucratic power as a seemingly neutral technique but actually a form of governance which destroyed participatory, egalitarian élan was brought to the centre of public debate. By so doing Mao made a major contribution to progressive people the world over. Henceforth, criticizing the bureaucratic degeneration of a socialist revolution would not be the sectarian monopoly of Trotskyists. Rather, the problem of the relation of the centralized bureaucratic state to the continued democratization of a society was to be a necessary concern for many more democratically directed people. Perhaps the gap between libertarians and socialists made mammoth by the Marx–Bakunin polemics was narrowed.

And yet, some people insist that the innovations of the Cultural Revolution were, as those of the Great Leap, actually failures, even disasters. The attacks on Party people and officials by students organized as Red Guards were said to treat proven friends of the revolution as if they were counter-revolutionaries. Such people would, it was claimed, afterwards be afraid to take the initiative, become parrots of whatever line seemed safe. In addition, reducing the role of the Party opened up room for military manoeuvre, even a military coup. In 1971 Mao's former ally Lin Piao attempted such a coup. And finally, it was argued that the Cultural Revolution ended in actual failure, meaningless factional squabbling facilitating an attempted power grab by an ultra-leftist whose preachings of utter selflessness left them divorced from the actual consciousness of most people, thereby turning Maoist values into impossible and objectionable demands. This in turn facilitated a return to a more conservative and military power grab to restore order and popular backing. In sum, only worse evils followed from trying to change human nature.

This critique of Mao's Cultural Revolution innovations hardly considers his insistence that not to act was to permit a Party-dominated bureaucratic state of vested interests to take China down the Soviet path with its distant elite, depoliticized population and grey, police-state aura. This is not to suggest that Mao's alternative did not harbour risks but that the other path seemed to him certain to lead China into a bleak, unhappy future.

Whatever the truth of the other criticisms, the egoists who insist that the failures of the Cultural Revolution prove Mao's project impossible because it is impossible to change human nature, as Mao supposedly was attempting, merely show their ignorance of the violent struggle and tremendous forces required to transform we humans into the selfish, alienated creatures who are regularly treated by market-profit societies as the consequence of some genetic code. In fact, from the alienation of the children of the rich in advanced societies to religious revivalism among the offspring of the upper middle class, with the continuing strength of family, ethnicity, religion, culture and other group identities against this materialist individualism, social practice endlessly gives the lie to this imputation that individual people are by biology only competitively self-interested, a conclusion concurred with by all serious anthropology, which reminds us that without mutuality and social co-operation the human species would not have made it this far.

What is really revealed in this critique of Mao's attempt to help create a more just society in China is the irrelevance of much of mainstream political science in the West. The question of how to construct a more just society is relegated by modern political science to the mental gymnastics of supposedly unrealistic political philosophers. Realistic, positivistic, value-neutral political science cannot be bothered with such ethical irrelevances. Mao seems mad to social scientists because to judge him sane would mean to judge themselves, if not immoral or amoral, then pessimists overwhelmed by the crisis of their era – which teaches not only that human problems have no solutions, but that those who insist on actively innovating and seeking answers are dangerous idealists, the kinds of fanatics who make for societal disasters, even world war.

Not seeing that this ultimate pessimism stems from an identification by political science with the deep, insoluble contradictions of the centralized, bureaucratic, military-oriented nation state, political scientists cannot see that Mao's innovations permit them to redefine their professional identity, to abandon statism in the guise of neutrality for a return to the source which once inspired them – the quest for social justice. The issue is not para-professionals, May 7th Cadre Schools, or new avenues to college but the rejection of formal, hierarchical institutions as the major means of supposedly solving human problems. The same trend of rejection exists in Western societies.

Who would claim success for formal Western bureaucracies in handling fundamental human crises such as venereal disease, drug addiction, violent crime, unsafe streets, lonely old age, etc.? Who does not know that prisons are failures which make professionals of amateur criminals? The experiments with half-way houses are but one of many signs that the isolation of so-called mentally ill into specialized institutions away from the community is no way to reintegrate them usefully in society. From the literature on the fiscal crisis of the state to the hopes for everything from a new federalism and revenue-sharing to community control and opposition to distant bureaucracies which cannot comprehend local needs, so much cries out for rethinking Mao's social explorations as at one with these, our own needs. No matter how innovative Mao was in these regards, the continuing identification of mainstream political science with quaint notions of human nature and the defeated project of the all-powerful, centralized nation state means that the stream of citizen's groups who visit China must, with no guidance from our experts, learn for themselves of China's innovations in these vital areas of social concern – from low-cost popular medicine and schooling in tune with community concerns, to officials who are people and treat others as people.

The rise to consciousness of crises of ecology and energy, of international dependency, blighted cities and state finance whose tax burden seems unbearable suddenly made the Maoist experiment seem relevant in industrial and industrializing societies. People with such concerns could readily see the wisdom of placing people before things, the quality of life before economic growth, the question of social cost before the commitment to industrialization at any cost.

Yet this rise of Mao to some positive prominence, facilitated perhaps by China's help to the national liberation struggle in Vietnam, may prove most misleading. The nastier truth is that social critiques must seem ethical to one's own group; and for most people outside of China this means a principled blindness to Mao's innovations, a seemingly principled dismissal of Mao. Before discovering that there is much to learn from him, Mao is damned on the grounds that he is a Communist or a murderer or a nationalist or an idealist or a Stalinist or a utopian or whatever one's devil is. All of which is to say that Mao's fundamental principle is painfully true, no-one can free us but we ourselves, surely not officials in state bureaucracies or foreign statesmen. For the most part it is inevitable that Mao's innovations will go unnoticed or condemned. Personal selfishness on behalf of one's state power structure is in charge.

To end blind worship of one's own state structure, people must be freed from visual distortions which prevent them from seeing their own political system with all its scars and flaws. Mao is most innovative in subverting this state ethic when he insists that if there are problems between the Han majority of China and China's minority peoples that the problem probably lies with the chauvinism of the Han, when he insists that China can and must learn even from enemy states, when he would not permit foreign visitors politely to praise China and ignore its endless problems and failings. He is most innovative when he risked the security of the state in breaking with the U.S.S.R., choosing instead the risks of international vulnerability in the face of hostile America and Russia for the possibility of creating a just socialist society in China, which would neither repeat the selfishness and inequalities of capitalism nor the costs and tragedies of the Soviet path. Although quite a nationalist and capable of ordinary selfish manoeuvring in international dealings, this slighting of state concerns won Mao great opposition at the centre of power. Yet it alone made possible Mao's social innovations. There is much to be learned about how difficult it is for us, patriotic citizens for the most part, to comprehend Mao's choice. Indeed, shocking though it should seem, social scientists call his opponents pragmatists and label Mao a fanatic for rejecting the Soviet shackles of its nuclear shield and attendant Stalinist strings (or chains).

Mao's innovations should help re-dedicate political and other social scientists to their original task. We should become less enthralled with our constitution, more open to the variety of the universe. Liberated (though an empathetic study of other areas such as China) from a belief that what is here is all that is possible, one is better able to understand what limits movement towards a just society here and everywhere. If so poor and weak a society as China's with its enormous problems could still achieve so much, then re-dedicating ourselves to our original promise may be less unrealistic than it often seems. Great achievements require great faith. Seeking to keep alive that hope by linking the end vision of a good society with the concrete dilemmas and demands of real people was Mao's major innovation. It appears and reappears in the idea of a rural revolution, of collectivization before technological breakthrough, of the multi-purpose Commune, of the Tachai model, of involving local people in education and medicine and economic planning. The innovation is not any of the fragile particular projects but the robust continuing quest to discover new practical modes to advance truly human goals.

Had Mao died at the close of the Cultural Revolution, he probably would have been apotheosized as the world's greatest revolutionary, the one who alone showed how to continue the revolution after winning state power. Actually that new and important project had barely begun. With the close of the Cultural Revolution, its gains had to be consolidated, its mistakes had to be rectified and, perhaps most important, what was learned in general about obstacles to a more egalitarian society had to serve as a starting point for a new thrust. In that learning Mao became something of a revolutionary ethno-methodologist.

That is, he began to wonder what in everyday life and in common sense made the ideals he held before people so difficult to grasp. Mao was like an insurrectionary Diogenes carrying, not a lantern, but a lighted match, looking, not for an honest person but for forces that would explode and advance egalitarian and communitarian goals. Why was it so difficult to find such explosive gases? Because China was still traditional and capitalist? As one Chinese analyst put it just prior to Mao's death: "What we have built is precisely this — a capitalist state without capitalists."[2]

From a complex of factors, a limited campaign was launched

[2] K'ang Li "On the capitalist classes of the socialist period," *Hsüeh-hsi yu p'i-p'an*, 1976, No. 7, p. 25.

against Confucianism. The goal was to subvert the remnants of the traditional culture which fettered the female and denigrated the young, which stressed harmony and compromise over struggle and quest, which insisted on the impossibility of leadership by dirty, manual workers, which put particular narrow bonds before true human concerns. Looking to the level of popular consciousness, it seemed that the inherited culture blocked further revolutionization.

Not only was the continuing daily cultural message counterrevolutionary but so was the experienced economic one. Mao pointed out that China had an unequal wage system and that people, in a situation of scarcity, naturally wanted to turn their earnings into the purchase of desired commodities. Hence people looked forward to jobs that paid better, family units that could pool earnings, desired seniority, positions and opportunities which promised more wages, more commodities. That is, whatever the Party preached about equality, the experience of daily life was a struggle to get more. Mao asked that means be found to check and restrict these tendencies. He claimed that it was this daily experience which gave natural allies and supporters to his opponents at the state centre, that virtually promised that one day a group could seize the levers of state power and win tremendous popular backing for changing from the egalitarian, communitarian course that Mao had set.

While no models came to the fore in his last years which dealt successfully with these crucial problems as Tachai had earlier with other matters, it is important to understand that Mao's innovations depended as always on creation by local citizens themselves. He did not invent solutions out of the air. He did, however, light the match. This is very different from a Leninist insistence on the unique role of the vanguard, the Party, the leading group, the leader as agencies of social revolution.

What Mao looked for, as did Marx, is what prevents a class for itself from coming into being, what keeps people from seeing in their lives a link to freedom for all. People were invited, even prodded, to struggle against experienced constraints. Whether transcendence follows from engaging in such conflict against limits is problematical. But what is central is not the vanguard but the willingness to engage continually in what may prove partial, endless, frustrating struggles, hoping for liberation, believing, as Mao's poem put it,

> Under this heaven nothing is difficult,
> If only there is the will to ascend.[3]

So much is Mao's stress on popular struggle and creativity that Maoism almost has no place in it for Mao, no place for the person with the prestige, position and power which Mao uniquely had to ignite such continual explosions. Thus the real test for his whole innovative approach comes only with his death when he can no longer intervene. Yet, he said,

> No matter who dies, it's nothing to be afraid of. Whose death would be a great loss? Haven't Marx, Engels, Lenin and Stalin all died? The revolution must still continue . . . Each person must be ready with successors. One must have three lines of successors.[4]

Mao had noted that on the issue of death the Soviets had taken umbrage at his endless dualisms. The Soviets insisted that death was the end of life. But Mao claimed that life and death were mutually transformable. Death made room for the new. It was a beginning. This meant more than "dust thou wast, dust thou will be," more than that dead matter became organic fertilizer for future life. It signified Mao's belief that anything could turn into its opposite, war into peace or oppressors into good people,[5] that eternal vigilance was the price of social progress. After all, even socialism could be reversed.

Death, however, was to be celebrated. "When someone dies, hold a celebration. Celebrate the victory of dialectics. Celebrate the extinction of the old."[6] Mao assures us that the process of change will continue, that one's heritage, however, is to assure that new revolutionary things will not die, or, if killed, will soon be replanted. The story is told how near the end Mao suggested to those around him that some had long wished him dead. Even with the attempts to imbue the new generation with a commitment to the endless quest, to make Maoist values the legitimat-

---

[3] Translated in Jerome Ch'en, Mao (Englewood Cliffs, N.J.: Prentice-Hall, 1969), p. 113. The poem is dated 1965.
[4] Wan-sui (1969), p. 504, dated 16 June, 1964.
[5] Wan-sui (1967), p. 126. Probably a 1959 document.
[6] Wan-sui (1969), p. 559, dated 18 August, 1964.

ing basis of politics, the question is asked whether Mao's innovations on succession were sufficient.

CONCLUSION

Mao Tse-tung's struggles with the great problems of the 20th century are not easily judged. The difficulty is not our ignorance of Mao's heroic matches with supposedly intractable forces. The factor clouding our vision is our own astigmatism. The Chinese idea, fulfilled in this volume, *kai kuan lun ting*, "when the coffin is covered, judgments are made," may be most misleading unless we can first gain perspective on our own moment in history, such that we abandon fashionable prejudices for true knowledge of where we fit into a dangerous future.

Situated in stable societies, the analyst wonders whether Mao relied too much on methods of chaos, turmoil and destabilization. But what if the next generation brings crises in dependent or developing societies related to great shifts in the international economy? And what if the relative economic self-reliance and minimal social inequalities which Mao's Jacob-like wrestling won for China saves China from the bloody civil strife which may come to bedevil these other more inegalitarian societies? In this not wholly improbable case, Mao will come to seem as one who provided a solid basis for holding together against extreme pressures of the kind which caused societies of more separated groups to unravel and come apart.

Thus in evaluating Mao's grappling with his century's dilemmas, can we be sure that we have a proper perspective on what are or will become our most painfully haunting nightmares? If there must of necessity be doubt, then perhaps the consensus which ranks Mao a titan of the century should lead us to pay heed to his definition of what most matters.

Mao's gift is greater than his living memory and social creations in China. This is not to diminish his monumental contribution to China's liberation from old oppressions, to its extraordinary fight to prevent the dynamism of change from reversing and rigidifying. Rather it is to remind us that as with all previous revolutionary surges, even Mao's will run its course. This is not the place to dilate upon the more conservative, vested interests which are so powerfully institutionalized in Chinese society that even the upheavals of the Great Proletarian Cultural Revolution could not budge them. Nor is this the place to develop a theory of the state to indicate that Mao's attack on bureaucratic selfishness hardly touches the causes, structures and felt necessities which create and legitimate massively concentrated power in a centralized state, such that ruling groups tied to the Chinese state can, like power-holders in other nation states, use control of the foreign policy apparatus (trade, aid, loans, diplomacy, military strategy, definition of enemies, access to secret information, etc.) to try to manipulate events to replicate the secrecy, anxieties and resource priorities which make their power unaccountable — yet seemingly an ultimate necessity — for the continuation of the state system which supposedly unites all citizens in their common patriotic quest. All we need to understand is that these forces, perhaps alone, certainly in combination, are sufficient to dry up the many life-giving oases needed to sustain long-distance travellers seeking to cross over the uncharted, shifting sands of revolutionary change. China's political future is still up for grabs.

Mao's legacy belongs to all those who share his values, all those who would join his caravan's long march. As Mao could be inspired by the struggles of Marx, as labourers in Shanghai could look to the moving ideals of the communards of Paris, so countless others around the world — including, of course, China — can and will, when they choose to, be moved by Mao.

In the advanced industrial societies of the West only a fragment of a faction of the young, those already disenchanted with the course of their country, already identify with Mao's quest. For most people, the sugar-coated bullets that Mao warned against seem sweeter than the joys of the permanent struggle for a promised just world that he preached. Indeed the risks of that struggle seem to most people far too dangerous.

What makes it finally impossible to judge Mao's innovations is our century's fear of risks. Hitler and Stalin, world war and depression always seem but a step away. And now the fear of nuclear holocaust. It is precisely on this last point that Mao's greatest innovation against the anxieties of our century is most apparent. Mao preferred the possibility of liberation against conceding to any risk no matter how hypothetically large.

Whereas most people in industrialized or industrializing

societies fear nuclear weapons, Mao insisted that the atom bomb was a paper tiger. This is the ultimate case where his optimism sounds crazy. Because the decisive question is evaluating Mao's untiring resistance to supposedly necessary statist imperatives, this, the ultimate one, the destruction of life itself, must be confronted head on. Mao in 1946 and after refused to concede to the supposed logic of the bomb.

> The consciousness of the people is the basic question. Not explosives nor oil fields nor atom bombs but the man who handles these . . . Its [the bomb's] great bursting over Hiroshima destroyed it. The people of the world have turned against it . . . In the end the bomb will not destroy the people. The people will destroy the bomb.[7]

Three decades later Mao's prediction that the bomb would not be used again remained accurate, the warnings of gloom and doom of the realists unfulfilled. Nonetheless, we assume that a precarious balance of terror continues; we cannot conceive that mere public opinion renders such a war impossible. And Mao continued on his seemingly crazy course. He opposed a treaty to stop the spread of nuclear weapons. He argued that such a treaty would freeze the bipolar arrangements of Russia and America, place all other peoples under the blackmail and protection of those two. Endless confrontation between the two giants, as in the Cuban missile crisis, hardly seemed a guarantee of peace.

Mao preferred, as did de Gaulle, the play of all parties to the paralysis and confrontation of such superpower hegemony. While political scientists usually like to show how multiple cleavages provide more stability than a fight between two parties, in this case, partaking in our century's fear of risks, we look aghast at Mao's seemingly mad insistence on just that proposition. Most analysts share with power-holders in the two superpowers a world view which cannot accept Mao's optimism and faith in people as rational. To do so one would have to judge as truly mad these powerholders in the superpowers who in basing their power on ultimate weapons they cannot use, and in refusing to destroy such weapons, help to encourage other nations to imitate their example and enhance their power by building yet more weapons. To find Mao rational, we would have to judge the

---

[7] Anna Louise Strong, The Chinese Conquer China (Garden City: Doubleday 1949), p. 44.

superpowers dangerously irrational in insisting on maintaining and using, at least for purposes of blackmail, this monstrous weaponry.

While our times prefer lesser evils and mistrust heroics, Mao insisted that wars of national liberation should not surrender to the superpower blackmail charge that little wars lead on to world war. Similarly state interests should not be permitted to obstruct the heroic struggles of all people everywhere in their everyday life for autonomy and community, equality and participation, conscious control of their destinies, true self-reliance. Mao's commitment, his faith and optimism made him the seemingly irrational opponent of the dominant ideology – nuclear rationality – which legitimates the greatest concentration of power in the fewest hands that this planet has ever seen.[8] His particular discoveries – e.g. the multi-purpose rural Commune, the Tachai model which prevents the growth of a separate class of power-holders – pale before his greatest innovation against the logic of our century: the liberation of people need never be sacrificed to the logic of state power. Mao contended that the latter, even when clothed in predictions of nuclear catastrophe, was always irrational, always a naked emperor, always to be exposed. As the prophets of old, Mao declared that – at least inside China – justice was to be done even should the world tremble. Nothing was more important than fulfilling the human project.

Mao's inheritance to future generations is therefore more than any one of his particular innovations, explorations or pioneering efforts, although all these contribute so much to the improvement of the quality of life of one quarter of the human race, the Chinese people. He moved on and up, from the war of Liberation, to economic growth, to self-reliance, to undermining bureaucratic power.

It is difficult not to be impressed at how Mao moved on to new issues and new problems. Neither age nor adversity kept him from trying anew. In fact, Mao's greatest innovative work did not occur until he was almost 70 years old. Had he lived longer he probably would have pioneered yet brighter trails on steeper mountains.

To learn from Mao, then, is not necessarily to copy him in any

[8] Franz Schurmann, The Logic of World Power (New York: Pantheon, 1974).

of his particulars. Rather it is to be willing to think afresh and confront humankind's ever-changing yet never-changing troubles and to do so with real faith in a better future. Mao's greatest contribution is the countering of the cynicism and pessimism of the century which insists that all our problems are intractable. Mao by the example of his struggle communicates the vigour of hope, the vitality of possibility, the vision of justice. Mao's message to the 20th century is elegantly simple: what should be can be.

SELECT BIBLIOGRAPHY

Baum, Richard, Prelude to Revolution: Mao, the Party, and the Peasant Question, 1962–66 (New York and London: Columbia University Press, 1975), 222 pp.

Ch'en, Jerome, Mao and the Chinese Revolution (London and New York: Oxford University Press, 1965), 419 pp.

Mao Papers: Anthology and Bibliography (London and New York: Oxford University Press, 1970), 221 pp.

Cohen, Arthur A., The Communism of Mao Tse-tung (Chicago and London: University of Chicago Press, 1964), 210 pp.

Elliott-Bateman, Michael, Defeat in the East: The Mark of Mao Tse-tung on War (London and New York: Oxford University Press, 1967), 270 pp.

Fitzgerald, C. P., Mao Tse-tung and China (London: Hodder and Stoughton, 1976), 176 pp.

Goodstadt, Leo, Mao Tse-tung: The Search For Plenty (London: Longman, 1972), 266 pp.

Han Suyin, The Morning Deluge: Mao Tse-tung and the Chinese Revolution, 1893–1953 (London: Jonathan Cape, 1972), 615 pp.

Wind in the Tower: Mao Tse-tung and the Chinese Revolution 1949–1975 (London: Jonathan Cape, 1976), 404 pp.

Hawkins, John N., Mao Tse-tung and Education: His Thoughts and Teachings (Hamden, Connecticut: Linnet Books, 1974), 260 pp.

Hsiung, James Chieh (ed.), The Logic of 'Maoism': Critiques and Explication (New York: Praeger, 1974), 227 pp.

Karnow, Stanley, Mao and China: From Revolution to Revolution (London: Macmillan, 1973), 592 pp.

Li Jui, The Early Revolutionary Activities of Comrade Mao Tse-tung. Translated by Anthony Sariti, and edited by James Hsiung, with a preface by Stuart R. Schram (White Plains: International Arts and Science Press, spring 1977).

Lifton, Robert J., Revolutionary Immortality (London: Weidenfeld and Nicholson, 1969), 178 pp.

MacFarquhar, Roderick, The Origins of the Cultural Revolution. 1. Contradictions Among the People, 1956–57 (London and New York: Oxford University Press, 1974), 439 pp.

Mao Tse-tung, *Selected Works*. 4 Vols. (Peking: Foreign Languages Press, 1961 to 1965).

Basic Tactics. Translated with an introduction by Stuart R. Schram. Foreword by Samuel B. Griffith (London: Pall Mall Press, 1966), 149 pp.

Payne, Robert, *Mao Tse-tung* (New York: Weybright and Talley, 1969 edit.), 343 pp.

Pye, Lucian, *The Man in the Leader* (New York: Basic Books, 1976), 346 pp.

Rice, Edward E., *Mao's Way* (Berkeley, Los Angeles and London: University of California Press, 1972), 596 pp.

Rue, John E., *Mao Tse-tung in Opposition, 1927–1935* (Stanford: Stanford University Press, 1966), 387 pp.

Schram, Stuart R., *Mao Tse-tung* (Harmondsworth: Penguin Books, 1967), 372 pp.

The Political Thought of Mao Tse-tung (Harmondsworth: Penguin Books, 1969). Revised and enlarged edition. 479 pp.

Quotations from Chairman Mao Tse-tung (New York: Praeger, 1967), 182 pp.

Mao Tse-tung Unrehearsed (Harmondsworth: Penguin Books, 1974), 352 pp.

Schwartz, Benjamin I., *Chinese Communism and the Rise of Mao* (Cambridge, Mass.: Harvard University Press, 1951), 258 pp.

Snow, Edgar, *Red Star Over China* (London: Victor Gollancz, 1968). First revised and enlarged edition. 543 pp.

Solomon, Richard H., *Mao's Revolution and the Chinese Political Culture* (Berkeley, Los Angeles and London: University of California Press, 1971), 604 pp.

Uhalley, Stephen Jr, *Mao Tse-tung: A Critical Biography* (New York: New Viewpoints, 1975), 233 pp.

CONTRIBUTORS

EDWARD FRIEDMAN teaches Chinese politics at the University of Wisconsin-Madison. He is the author of *Backward Toward Revolution* and is completing a new book on Einstein and Mao.

JOHN GITTINGS is Senior Lecturer in Chinese at the School of Languages, Polytechnic of Central London. He writes regularly for the *Guardian* and is the author of a recent study on Maoist foreign policy, *The World and China, 1922–72*.

JACQUES GUILLERMAZ was until recently the Head of the Research and Documentation Centre on Contemporary China at the École des Hautes Études en Sciences Sociales in Paris. He has served in French Embassies in China since 1937 and is the author of, most recently, *A History of the Chinese Communist Party (1921–1949)* and *The Chinese Communist Party in Power (1949–1976)*.

CHRISTOPHER HOWE is Reader in Economics in the Department of Economic and Political Studies at the School of Oriental and African Studies, London University, and, since October 1972, Head of the Contemporary China Institute. He is author of *Employment and Economic Growth in Urban China 1949–1957* and *Wage Patterns and Wage Policy in Modern China 1919–1972*.

MICHEL OKSENBERG teaches Chinese politics at the University of Michigan. His latest publication is *China in the Seventies: Problems, Policies and Prospects*.

ENRICA COLLOTTI PISCHEL is Associate Professor of the Modern History of Asia and Africa in the Faculty of Letters at the University of Bologna. Her books include *Origini Ideologiche della Rivoluzione Cinese* and a history of the Chinese Revolution.

STUART R. SCHRAM is Professor of Politics (with reference to China) at the School of Oriental and African Studies, London University. He was Head of the Contemporary China Institute from its establishment in 1968 until October 1972. His numerous books include *Mao Tse-tung*,

323

CONTRIBUTORS

The Political Thought of Mao Tse-tung and *Mao Tse-tung Unrehearsed*, and he edited *Authority, Participation and Cultural Change in China*.

BENJAMIN I. SCHWARZ is Leroy B. Williams Professor of History and Political Science and Associate Director of the East Asian Research Center at Harvard University. He is the author of *Chinese Communism and the Rise of Mao; In Search of Wealth and Power: Yen-Fu and the West; Communism and China, Ideology and Flux*, and numerous other works and articles.

FREDERIC WAKEMAN JR is Chairman of the Center for Chinese Studies at the University of California, Berkeley. His publications include *Strangers at the Gate: Social Disorder in South China, 1839–1861* and *History and Will: Philosophical Perspectives of the Thought of Mao Tse-tung*.

KENNETH R. WALKER is Professor of Economics (with special reference to China) and Head of the Department of Economic and Political Studies at the School of Oriental and African Studies, London University. He is the author of *Planning in Chinese Agriculture: Socialisation and the Private Sector, 1956–62*.

WANG GUNGWU is Professor of Far Eastern History and Director of the Research School of Pacific Studies at the Australian National University, and author of numerous articles on Chinese history and historiography. His latest book is *China and the World Since 1949: The Impact of Independence, Modernity and Revolution*.

DICK WILSON is Editor of *The China Quarterly*, former Editor of *Far Eastern Economic Review* and author of *A Quarter of Mankind, Asia Awakes* and *The Long March, 1935*.

INDEX

DATE			
DEC 1 '85			
MAR 1 4 '95			
DEC 08 '95			